HUME'S REFLECTION ON RELIGION

ARCHIVES INTERNATIONALES D'HISTOIRE DES IDÉES

INTERNATIONAL ARCHIVES OF THE HISTORY OF IDEAS

178

HUME'S REFLECTION ON RELIGION

by

MIGUEL A. BADÍA CABRERA

MIGUEL A. BADÍA CABRERA

Departamento de Filosofía
Universidad de Puerto Rico,
Río Piedras

HUME'S REFLECTION ON RELIGION

KLUWER ACADEMIC PUBLISHERS
DORDRECHT / BOSTON / LONDON

A C.I.P. Catalogue record for this book is available from the Library of Congress.

B
1499
. R45
B3313
2001

ISBN 0-7923-7024-4

Published by Kluwer Academic Publishers,
P.O. Box 17, 3300 AA Dordrecht, The Netherlands.

Sold and distributed in North, Central and South America
by Kluwer Academic Publishers,
101 Philip Drive, Norwell, MA 02061, U.S.A.

In all other countries, sold and distributed
by Kluwer Academic Publishers,
P.O. Box 322, 3300 AH Dordrecht, The Netherlands.

Printed on acid-free paper

Printed in the Netherlands.

To my wife, Marcela,
my son, David Miguel,
and my daughter, Luz Elena

TABLE OF CONTENTS

vii

PREFACE

The present work is a revised and enlarged English version of a book originally written in Spanish and published in late 1996, *La reflexión de David Hume en torno a la religión*. Since David Hume is arguably not only the most important philosopher who has ever written in the English language, but the most studied and influential, it is only natural that sooner than later I would feel the urgency to bring to the attention of a much wider public a work whose outlook is, I think, significantly different from that of other books which deal with the Scottish thinker's works on religion and natural theology. This desire was so strong as to allow me to overcome the all-too-natural fear that my wavering and uncertain command of English would make the few valuable insights the work might contain appear unclear, and my philosophical errors, even more astonishing.

This book is addressed not only to scholars who may be interested in modern philosophy in general or Hume's philosophy of religion in particular, but also to the more extensive compass of readers either intrigued or troubled by religion and the myriad of issues and problems it poses, which are, as it were, the prime matter for philosophical analysis and theorizing. In spite of its philosophical and linguistic limitations, for which I am entirely responsible, I fervently hope that this work may be found to contain something of that elusive truth after which Hume strove, and to which he remained constant to the end, particularly at a time when the price to be paid for the publication of controversial philosophical and religious views was considerably higher than that of becoming an easy target for universal ridicule.

The completion of this work has been made possible principally by a sabbatical leave that the University of Puerto Rico granted me for the year 1999. This leave gave me the necessary time to read and study the pertinent literature, as well as to write most of the English manuscript. It also allowed me to visit Edinburgh and spend most of July and August 1999 at the National Library of Scotland and the Edinburgh University Library. Although I have incorporated into the present work only a small part of my research at those libraries, if this book shows a greater appreciation of the immediate social and religious context of Hume's thought (particularly of Calvinistic theology and the Scottish Enlightenment) than its Spanish predecessor, it is in no small measure due to the books, articles, and manuscrits I was able to consult at the time. In this respect, I would like to thank Professor Peter Jones, Director of the Institute for Advanced Studies in the Humanities at the University of Edinburgh, who was very instrumental in making my visit to Edinburgh a reality, and generously put the facilities of the Institute at my disposal.

Many thoughts and lines of argument contained in this book date back to my doctoral dissertation, and some earlier versions of a number of chapters or sections of chapters have been published in different philosophy journals or anthologies. I list all of them in the bibliography under my name. But since my previous works on the subject have been revised and modified so many times in the light of new findings or to meet actual or possible criticism, I can say that they have been effectively superseded by the present writing.

The persons to whom I am philosophically indebted are almost innumerable. If I fail to mention all of them it is not for lack of gratitude but only due to space limitations. To the following scholars I owe most because their works have inspired and encouraged me in a more conscious manner to put together my peculiar interpretation of Hume's philosophy of religion. I must acknowledge my enduring admiration and gratitude to Páll S. Árdal, John C. A. Gaskin, Donald W. Livingston and Stanley Tweyman. Were it not for my great teachers at the New School for Social Research in New York, the late Aron Gurwitsch, Albert Hoftstadter and Hans Jonas, I would not have pursued the idea that Husserlian phenomenology might provide a fruitful approach to Hume's theoretical philosophy. And lastly I am greatly indebted to Norman Kemp Smith and Ernest Campbell Mossner, for there is no contemporary Hume scholar whose work has not been touched and improved by the truly awesome commentaries of the former and the monumental and vibrant intellectual biography of the latter.

For their criticism of the original manuscript submitted to the publisher, I wish also to thank the two anonymous referees. This book is, all in all, a less imperfect performance due to their comments and extremely valuable suggestions. In revising the manuscript, I have addressed all the particular points they raised and tried to answer their objections to the best of my abilities. If I have not followed all their general recommendations it is only because in order to do so I would have had to write an altogether different book which exceeded both my intentions and capacities.

Perhaps this is the right place to note that all references to Hume's works in this book will be made using the following abbreviations and from the following editions: DNR: *Dialogues Concerning Natural Religion*, 2d ed., ed. Norman Kemp Smith (New York: The Bobbs-Merrill Company, Inc., 1947; Indianapolis, 1981); E: *David Hume: Essays, Moral, Political and Literary*, rev. ed., ed. Eugene F. Miller (Indianapolis: Liberty Classics, 1987); EHU: *An Enquiry Concerning Human Understanding*, EPM: *An Enquiry Concerning the Principles of Morals*, in *Enquiries Concerning the Human Understanding and Concerning the Principles of Morals*, ed. L. A. Selby-Bigge, 3d ed. rev., P. H. Nidditch (Oxford: Clarendon Press, 1975); H: *The History of England, from the Invasion of Julius Caesar to the Revolution of 1688*, 6 vols. Based on the edition of 1778 (Indianapolis: Liberty Fund, Inc., 1983); L: *The Letters of David Hume*, ed. J. Y. T. Greig. 2 vols.

(Oxford: Clarendon Press, 1969); NHR: *The Natural History of Religion*, ed. H. E. Root. (Stanford, California: Stanford University Press, 1956); THN: *A Treatise of Human Nature*, ed. L. A. Selby-Bigge 2d ed. rev., P. H. Nidditch (Oxford: Clarendon Press, 1978); THN, A: *An Abstract of a Treatise of Human Nature*, in *A Treatise of Human Nature*, ed. L. A. Selby-Bigge. 2d ed. rev., ed. P. H. Nidditch (Oxford: Clarendon Press, 1978). References to these works are given within parentheses in the text and notes.

I wish to acknowledge and thank Professor Joel Donato Jiménez, Director of the Academic Computing Laboratory of the University of Puerto Rico (LabCad), at Río Piedras, whose technical assistance was essential for the preparation of the camera-ready manuscript of the book.

And finally, I would like to thank my wife, Marcela, my son, David Miguel, and my daughter, Luz Elena. Much of the strength I could muster to complete this project comes from their generous and constant love. Like my gratitude, my love for them is unbounded.

Departamento de Filosofía, Universidad de Puerto Rico
Río Piedras, Puerto Rico

INTRODUCTION

For most of my adult life, I have assiduously studied the thought of David Hume, the great eighteenth-century Scottish philosopher. My main goal has been to formulate an organic and comprehensive interpretation of Hume's broad, complex and profound investigation of religion. To my belief, these sustained efforts of elucidation and critical exposition have crystallized in the present work.

Perhaps the unique character of this book is that it approaches Hume's reflection on religion from the unitary perspective of his philosophical project. Throughout, the former is examined from the vantage point of Hume's main ontological, epistemological, and ethical principles. In Parts I and II I have sought to understand Hume's investigation of religion by taking into account the Enlightened ends, both moral and social, that Hume himself ascribes to his philosophical activity. And after tracing some of the deeper historical roots of Hume's scrutiny of religion, I have related his account about the origin, development, and most significant effects of religious beliefs to his own historical works, and conversely taken the former as the leading thread into the disclosure of a Humean philosophy of history that is unitary and consistent. In the final chapters of Part II, his still controversial and seemingly partial theses concerning the eminently irrational and feigned character of religious faith and its inevitable negative effect on morality are critically analyzed from the foundation offered by Hume's epistemological theory of belief and some basic tenets of his ethical philosophy.

Part III examines Hume's attack on the validity of the conclusions of rational theology: that is to say, his critique of the traditional proofs, such as the ontological argument, the appeal to testimony about miracles, and in particular, the argument from design. Finally, the last two chapters tackle the question: what and how much can human reason really establish about the existence and nature of God. On this capital issue, I argue that Hume's view is a kind of mitigated theism.

All in all, Parts II and III provide, I think, reasonable support for the most general and maybe up-hill claim of this study, which I have attempted to make intelligible and hopefully convincing in the last chapter: i.e. that although it does not arise from an instinct, and the empirical evidence does not sufficiently justify it, the belief in God, as an intelligent author of the universe, is nonetheless a natural and, in a non trivial sense, reasonable belief.

It almost goes without saying that this work, by virtue of being the result of a sustained effort of philosophical understanding, is also a very personal endeavor. But in the present case it is doubly so, for religion, I must confess, has been a potent and fateful presence in giving substance and delineating, for better or for worse, the whole texture of the inner and outward life of the person I have become. And I could have said the same thing about the effect of Hume's thought on my character and view of things. In a manner, I would like Hume to become for others what he has been for me since my early youth: the ideal interlocutor and most biting critic with whom I have ever conversed about some of the most pressing practical problems and interesting speculative questions that inevitably confront our fragile human nature, which Hume conceived as a reflective life existing within a world that is often quite hard and always annoyingly silent or, as he would say, enigmatic to our perennial quest. So my greatest hope is that this book may be of value to any person genuinely interested in those questions "of the utmost importance" which religion raises again and again. For Hume, at his best, neatly exemplifies the "Spirit of Impartiality," or critical empathy that is needed for their thorough and truthful philosophical clarification.

But, of course, the present book inserts itself within a long tradition of Hume scholarship. Thus I have also aimed at throwing light on at least a few of the central issues and problems of interpretation that are posed by Hume's diverse works on religion and rational theology, which have puzzled and divided generations of commentators and historians of philosophy. One such question regards the naturalness and the other, the rationality of religious beliefs. Concerning the first issue, the exemplary positions have been clearly drawn by the two most eminent contemporary scholars of Hume's philosophy of religion: John C. A. Gaskin[1] and Stanley Tweyman.[2] For the former, religious beliefs cannot be called natural in the same sense that, following Norman Kemp Smith,[3] the belief in necessary connection, the independent existence of sensible objects and the identity of the self, are said to be natural; for the latter, the belief in an intelligent author of the universe in particular, must be considered a natural belief, because it satisfies all the relevant criteria which hold for the other so-called natural beliefs. This has been an unsettled issue because Gaskin predominantly bases his interpretation on *The Natural History of Religion*, where Hume examines positive or historical religions, whereas Tweyman rests his case mainly on the *Dialogues Concerning Natural Religion*, where Hume princi-

---

[1] John C. A. Gaskin, especially in *Hume's Philosophy of Religion* (London: Macmillan Press, 1978), ch. 8, pp. 126–140.

[2] Stanley Tweyman, *Scepticism and Belief in Hume's Dialogues Concerning Natural Religion* (Dordretch: Martinus Nijhoff, 1986), ch. 8, pp. 97–156.

[3] Norman Kemp Smith, "The Naturalism of David Hume," *Mind* (1905) vol. 14, 149–173; and *The Philosophy of David Hume* (London: Macmillan, 1949), ch. 5, pp. 105–312; ch. 17, pp. 405–410; chap. 21, pp. 446–464; ch. 22, pp. 465–469.

pally discusses rational or natural theology. A main contribution of the present work to this discussion is that it shows in detail, particularly in Part II, that the case for the naturalness of religious beliefs not only can be successfully argued for the *Dialogues*, as I think Tweyman has done, but for the *Natural History* as well. It has not been easy to see that such is the case for various reasons.

First of all, concerning historical religions, Hume makes no appeal to an original universal religious instinct that would make religiosity a general and constitutive principle of human nature and to which the origin and development of religious beliefs, observances and institutions may be ascribed. What we do have instead are some tendencies of our imagination, elementary passions, and circumstances, more or less common to all human beings, which may account for the antiquity and wide extent of the belief in divinity, and for the diverse ways human beings conceive the gods. But in Hume's eyes, there is no "original instinct or primary impression of nature" (NHR, 21), and no innate idea of God that would attest to the primary character of religion in human existence.[4] However, without denying all of this, the main point in chapter 5 is precisely to show that hope and fear are not the sole source, nor complete explanation, of historical religion.[5]

Second, if religious belief, at least if we are dealing with historical religion, does not arise out of an instinct, and is inherently morally and socially harmful, then it seems that it can never have the same primary and necessary character that Hume ascribes to the so-called natural beliefs. About this subject I shall try to show in chapter 4, against the prevailing view, that belief in divinity is a genuine natural belief, and in the last chapter will try to explain the sense in which it is as primary and necessary as the other natural beliefs.

Third, it is clear that Hume's attitude towards historical religion was not exactly sympathetic. On the one hand, in the *Natural History* he judged its moral influence to be, at its worst, simply bad, for it leads to the extreme religious aberrations he called "superstition" and "enthusiasm," and, at its best, indifferent to morality and socially useless.[6] On the other hand, since the customary outcome of religious fanaticism is the spread of a great deal of distressing cruelty, Hume saw fit to say that, "generally speaking, the errors of religion are dangerous; those in philosophy only ridiculous" (THN, I, 271). But philosophy itself may become dangerous, and not only ridiculous, when it turns into an ideology that systematically exculpates the excesses of a ruthless popular faith. How can then philosophy (at least his), in

---

[4] In chapters 5 and 9 below, the sense in which Hume can be said to have denied that the idea of God is innate will be elucidated.

[5] In *The Philosophy of the Enlightenment* [trans. Fritz C. A. Koelln and James P. Pettergrove (Boston: Beacon Press, 1955)], Ernst Cassirer forcefully expresses this traditional reading of *Hume's Natural History of Religion*: "The affect of fear is the beginning of all religion, and all the various shapes and forms of religion are derived from, and are explicable in terms of, this emotion " (p. 107). "Appetites and passions are not only the source of the first religious ideas; they still are the roots of all religion . . . . It is the emotions of hope and fear which have led men to adopt beliefs and which support the continuance of faith" (p. 148).

[6] In chapter 8, section 4, we shall see that this in not quite the case in the *History of England.*

spite of this, oppose superstition, decisively correct its errors, and effectively prevent its terrible historical and social calamities? About the latter issue, I hope to show, in section 2 of chapter 2, that one of the greatest advantages of Hume's philosophy (that is, his investigation of human understanding), lies in its being a perpetual unmasker and check of superstition. With respect to the first point, in chapter 8, we shall hopefully see that the thesis that religion invariably has an adverse effect on morality is neither a corollary of his theoretical philosophy, nor of his moral philosophy, but instead a predictable consequence of certain questionable presuppositions which are historical in nature.

The preceding topic clearly shows why it is necessary to investigate sooner or later, in a book such as this, the relationship between *The Natural History of Religion* and Hume's historiographical works, such as his monumental *History of England* and some of his main essays. In chapters 3 and 6, I shall maintain, on the one hand, that the historical analysis of religion is a principal part of Hume's philosophical project, without which we would have no knowledge of the essence of religion, and on the other, that Hume's account of the origin and unfolding of religion allows us to disclose a unitary and essentially dialectical conception of history which is operative – at times tacitly, at others more explicitly – in all of his historical works. It is claimed, in essence, that the *Natural History* is more a metaphysical vision than a positive science of religion, and that the *History of England* is also, in Hume's sense, a "natural" history.

Moreover, in chapter 9, I shall try to make clear that Hume had few compelling reasons for establishing such a great abyss between "popular", or historical religion and "natural", or philosophical religion, since often (for Hume, in fact, most of the time) the "vulgar" or common person, and the "wise" person or philosopher, are one and the same person.

That sharp dichotomy brings into the fore the second question, or that concerning the rationality of religion. Does Hume provide a foundation for natural religion or rational theology, as he tries to do for the moral sciences? At the end of the *Enquiry Concerning Human Understanding*, he delimits the cognitive scope of the different disciplines that have some claim to knowledge. Of the moral studies, politics is the only one which Hume deems worthy of the title of science. Morals and criticism, or aesthetics, are grounded on taste and sentiment; they are saved from absolute subjectivity and relativity because they arise out of a set of primary and constant instincts, passions, and emotions virtually present throughout humankind. These are the generic endowment of a nature that even if not benevolent, in fact behaves as if it were so.

Can we say concerning natural religion that his analysis of human understanding finally brought about the considerable "improvements" that he hoped for in the Introduction to the *Treatise*? It is difficult to resist the temptation to simply answer: not at all. Hume seems to disavow forcefully the claim to knowledge of rational theology in one of his best known outbursts of eloquence:

> When we run over libraries, persuaded of these principles, what havoc must we make? If we take in our hand any volume; of divinity or school metaphysics,

for instance; let us ask, *Does it contain any abstract reasoning concerning quantity or number? No. Does it contain any experimental reasoning concerning matter of fact and existence?* No. Commit it then to the flames: For it can contain nothing but sophistry and illusion (EHU, 165).

Does this really imply that everything that has been known as rational theology is nothing but bad reasoning and Quixotic illusion? Or should we instead interpret this passage not as outrightly denying all validity to theology but as establishing the limits within which it could remain as a valid theoretical enterprise. In this case Hume might be requesting from the latter that it should attempt to establish its conclusion through experimental, not a priori, reasoning. Anyway, whether rational theology, even within this methodological limitation, can establish the truth of its principal claims continues to be an open and totally different question. We shall strive to answer this question in Part III.

Hume's expeditious rejection of the a priori way for demonstrating the existence of God will be dealt with in the first place; accordingly chapter 10 offers an analysis of his critique of the ontological argument and the principles upon which it rests, especially Hume's idea of "existence" and the concept of "necessary existence," which is of crucial importance also for the cosmological argument. After that, the critical exposition of Hume's analysis of the presumed factual or empirical foundations will follow. In chapter 11, we shall examine his critique of the attempt to justify the truth of religious faith by appealing to miracles, and in particular to human testimony about events that, being contrary to the usual course of nature, are accordingly taken as signs or empirical manifestations of a divine power; therein I have principally tried to establish that Hume's position is a tenable one if it is viewed as a tacit critique of Calvinistic theology, and also that with regard to the evidential value of miracles, his view is strikingly similar to Locke's. Finally, in chapters 12, 13 and 14 we shall study the preferred argument of rational theology during Hume's age, and to which he gives by far a more detailed and systematic treatment: to wit, the argument from design, which is but an early modern variety of the teleological proof. This particular reasoning is based on our experience of the order inherent in the universal course of natural events, and concludes that there exists a divine intelligence as the cause of that order.

There are various intriguing difficulties related to the preceding subject, but here I shall mainly dwell on the most enduring controversy. Tremendous problems await anyone who should strive to extract, out of Hume's quite diverse and mostly ambiguous verbal declarations in different works, a definite theoretical position about the possibility of establishing the existence of a first intelligent cause of the universe. In the *Treatise* he seems to adopt the famous argument from design:

The order of the universe proves an omnipotent mind; that is, a mind whose will is *constantly attended* with the obedience of every creature and being (THN, Appendix, 633).

Later, in the Introduction to the *Natural History,* he does not question the validity of that argument. However, at the end of the same book he takes a position which appears to be rather agnostic:

> The whole is a riddle, an ænigma, an inexplicable mystery. Doubt, uncertainty, suspence of judgment appear the only result of our most accurate scrutiny, concerning this subject (NHR, 76).

The conclusion of Section XI, "Of a particular providence and of a future state," to the *Enquiry Concerning Human Understanding* is quite akin to the position in the last passage. But it adds something of its own. We can interpret it as implying that the theistic, or "religious hypothesis" is afflicted by irreparable logical ills that instead of making it uncertain, deprive it of any cognitive meaning whatsoever. Concerning Hume's last statements on the subject, many commentators of the *Dialogues Concerning Natural Religion*, including Kemp Smith, have viewed this work as the systematic development of the negative position about our possibilities of having some kind of knowledge, distinct from faith, about divinity, in particular the God of Judeo-Christian tradition, and about the validity of the cognitive claims of rational theology or natural religion. In spite of this eminently negative view, a different interpretation is opened by Hume himself in the *Dialogues*, for Philo, the sceptical character in that work, contends that such a suspension of judgment "is scarcely possible" (DNR, 216–217). Whether such an impossibility is logical or rather psychological, is a matter to be investigated. Be that as it may, what is patent in Philo's assertion is an avowal that the discovery of order leads the mind – the scientific mind at least – almost with a force like that of sensation, to look for an intelligent cause of that order. Ultimately, and under the supposition that here Philo speaks for Hume (which is something that has to be justified as well), it seems that there is deep in our human nature an irresistible impulse akin to sensation that makes the reflective person, or "any one of good understanding" (NHR, 73) to view nature teleologically, i.e., as the product of intelligent design. Particularly at the end of chapter 13 and in chapter 14, I shall attempt to develop Philo's suggestion into an alternative general conclusion of Hume's philosophy of religion as a whole.

Yet if most beliefs of historical religions are frankly irrational, and natural religion cannot quite prove its most important conclusions, are we not forced in the end, to suppose that for Hume the only foundation for religious belief is faith? Let us suppose for the moment that one of Hume's main goals could be defined, as D. G. C. McNabb does inverting the Kantian formulation, as an "attempt to limit faith in order to make room for science."[7] Would that necessarily mean that faith is totally irrational? Or would there be some point of view – consistent with Hume's philosophical tenets – from which it would make sense to say that a religious as-

---

[7] D. G. C. MacNabb, *David Hume: His Theory of Knowledge and Morality,* 2nd ed. (Oxford: Basil Blackwell, 1966) p. 6.

sent is, even in the absence of a priori knowledge or insufficient empirical evidence, a reasonable alternative to scepticism or atheism? Or is it rather that the belief in an infinitely powerful, intelligent and good being is, after all, on an equal footing with the belief in immortality, which was for Hume – as he said a few days before his death, in a conversation with James Boswell – a most unreasonable fancy?[8] Because of its complex, comprehensive and central character, we shall deal with this problem in the last chapter, where the reasonable character of that belief will be elucidated.

In the light of all these and other problems of interpretation, we shall examine Hume's philosophizing about religion in close connection with his theory of knowledge and ontology. For it is my main presupposition that Hume's properly theoretical philosophy allows us to understand his reflection on religion, and conversely that the latter will also enable us to elucidate and determine the precise significance of some of his most important epistemological, ontological, ethical, and even historical doctrines. Accordingly we shall start in the next chapter with a comprehensive consideration of Hume's philosophical project. In so doing, it will be necessary to discuss a number of different approaches to Hume's theoretical philosophy, and dialogue for a while with some distinguished twentieth-century commentators of Hume's thought.[9] In this way I hope to achieve a sound understanding of Hume's philosophy of religion which may throw light on at least some of those unresolved questions, and allow us to make a just critical appraisal of his particular theories about religion and rational theology.

But before embarking on such a task, I should make explicit other significant presuppositions and methodological disclaimers. First, in investigating these problems, I have made an effort to keep at bay the temptation to speculate about the personal motives and intentions that may lie behind Hume's philosophical speculations concerning religion. I have done my best to follow this maxim even in chapter 2, which contains a brief and schematic historical background of Hume's critical analysis of religion. I do not intend to establish a genetic connection between such intentions and his actual philosophical doctrines. It is not arrogantly suggested that such task is illegitimate, or even unnecessary, methodologically speaking; yet, its interest is mainly biographical, and it almost always leads to uncertain results. The only exception to the preceding rule is mainly found in section 5 of chapter 11 and section 6 of chapter 13, and it concerns the utilization of well-established historical and biographical facts in order to clear up the meaning of some of Hume's key doctrines about religion that are expressed in texts which are almost universally acknowledged as very difficult to interpret, since they may reasonably be read either in a forthright, literal manner, or in an ironic, sarcastic fashion. On the whole, the

---

[8] *An Account of my Last Interview with David Hume*, Esq., from Kemp Smith's edition of Hume's *Dialogues Concerning Natural Religion*, 2d ed. (New York: The Bobbs-Merrill Co., 1947; Indianapolis, 1981), p. 77.

[9] In order to have a good idea of the many and different ways of comprehensively interpreting Hume's philosophy, see Nicholas Capaldi, "The Dogmatic Slumber of Hume's Scholarship," *Hume Studies* 18, no. 2 (November 1992): 117-135.

purposes and aims that will be logically connected with Hume's epistemological-ontological investigation and his theories about the religious will be derived principally from what he explicitly says about them in his philosophical works or from biographical materials, such as letters, that explicitly refer to those works.

Neither do I propose that the investigation of religious problems occupies a central or privileged place within the whole of Hume's philosophy, or that it provides, as it were, the leading thread, the pursuit of which may even give intelligibility to the development and theoretical results of his works on knowledge and being. Such enterprise would imply the issuing of a value judgment about the philosophy of Hume which we cannot, and do not, have to make at the beginning. At all events, the former would not precisely be a novel task. Charles Hendel, in one of the best overall twentieth-century commentaries on Hume's philosophy, has tried in a very laborious manner to trace the famous question of Book I of *A Treatise of Human Nature* – "Why a cause is always necessary?" – to the question "Why is it necessary to infer a cause for nature?"[10] The latter, according to Hendel, would have been motivated by Hume's questioning, very early in his youth, of the validity of the religious hypothesis that derives the existence of God from the experienced order of Nature:

> Hume was wrestling earnestly, as he tells us himself, with the arguments to confirm, in his own mind, the "common opinion" of the existence of a personal God.[11]

However, there is no single piece of unambiguous evidence that I know of which would establish with reasonable certainty that the religious was the driving force behind Hume's main theoretical works; in fact, almost the same biographical documents can and have been used to justify quite different estimates about the import and main general intentions of his philosophy.[12]

I must also make clear that this work is not an exemplar of a systematically historical treatment of all aspects of Hume's philosophy of religion, and should not be

---

[10] Charles Hendel, *Studies in the Philosophy of David Hume* (Princeton, N. J.: Princeton University Press, 1925), ch. 2, pp. 20–71.

[11] Ibid., p. 57. Hendel bases this conclusion especially on his analysis of a famous letter that Hume wrote at the age of twenty-three (and intended to send but most probably never actually sent) to an eminent physician, and in which he said that an important philosophical discovery had transported him into a "New Scene of Thought" (L, I, 12–16).

[12] Just to mention the most important and influential case, Norman Kemp Smith, using almost the same biographical materials as Hendel (especially that famous letter), adduces that Hume "was led to recognize that the judgments of moral approval and disapproval, indeed judgments of *value* of whatever type, are based not on rational insight or on evidence, but solely on feeling." [*The Philosophy of David Hume* (London: Macmillan, 1949), p. 12]. He asserts, in addition, that what then opened up to him "a new Scene of Thought," was the extrapolation of such a view to the purely theoretical domain, in order to give adequate solution to "chief problems" bequeathed to him by Locke and Berkeley (Ibid., p. 13).

taken to be so.[13] Nonetheless, a genuine effort has been made to provide an adequate, albeit brief, historical context to Hume's approach to religion, especially in chapter 2, and to his most important theses and arguments in all required places.

I should finally say that I harbor no exaggerated or conceited notions about the philosophical value of this book. Still, even if I were mistaken in most, if not all, of the particular theses defended in it, I would continue to believe that the considerable effort invested in its production had been justified. For, in spite of all its failures and limitations, it would still convey a somewhat different overview of Hume's philosophy of religion and new readings on some of its central issues which may stimulate others, more knowledgeable and capable than myself, to articulate a more adequate and encompassing interpretation of this subject of enduring interest.

---

[13] It has never crossed my mind to supersede works such as John C. Gaskin's seminal book, *Hume's Philosophy of Religion*, which in this respect, as in so many others, is simply admirable.

PART I

Hume's Scrutiny of Religion:
Its Theoretical Foundations, Historical Roots, and Ultimate Goals

CHAPTER 1

Hume's Philosophical Project
and his Reflection on Religion

1.1 THE "SCIENCE OF MAN" AS FIRST PHILOSOPHY: ITS NATURE AND
PROBLEMATICAL CHARACTER

A beacon to the present study is the conviction that the critical examination of the problems posed by religious faith, and the rational investigation of religious origins, representations, beliefs and practices are not mere isolated philosophical episodes but topics whose conceptual exploration is demanded by the peculiar kind of philosophizing Hume undertakes.

Yet even when it is animated by this sort of faith, such an investigation can still be approached with a narrow and dogmatic spirit, which stems from a generalized and deep-seated misconception about the general problematic and trend of Hume's theoretical philosophy. All too frequently the latter is reduced to epistemology, depriving all other problems which Hume tackles of any but incidental importance; in this fashion, a true understanding of the connection between the latter and his theory of knowledge is made difficult, if not impossible. From this perspective, Hume has been customarily seen through the eyes of Kant: he is the solitary sceptical thinker, whose main value resides exclusively in having developed with utmost consistency the gnoseological theses of Locke and Berkeley – producing almost a *reductio ad absurdum* of them – and thereby preparing the ground for the more mature and rationally tenable position of (to use J. Paton's memorable phrase) Kant's metaphysics of experience.[1] This widespread manner of interpreting Hume has been almost wholly discarded since the second half of the twentieth century, due to several important commentaries and studies, especially the writings of Norman Kemp Smith, Ernest Mossner's excellent biography of Hume, and more recently, the books of Páll S. Árdal and Donald W. Livingston.[2] Yet this

---

[1] J. Paton, *Kant's Metaphysic of Experience* 2 vols. (London: George Allen & Unwin and New York: The Humanities Press, 1936).

[2] Ernest Mossner, *The Life of David Hume* (London and Edinburgh, 1954); Páll S. Árdal, *Passion and Value in Hume's Treatise*, 2nd ed. (Edinburgh: Edinburgh University Press, 1989); Donald W. Livingston, *Hume's Philosophy of Common Life* (Chicago and London: University of Chicago Press, 1984).

view, after more than one hundred and fifty years of hermeneutic hegemony, continues still to exercise an effective influence on the majority, non specialist, reading public of Hume's philosophy, and even a silent, albeit attenuated, hold on many scholars who have consciously tried to emancipate themselves from it. Such is the force of habit, Hume might have said.

The main defect of this popular, purely epistemological and sceptical view is that it pays no heed to what Hume himself says. The *Treatise* is "an attempt to introduce the experimental method of reasoning into moral subjects," according to its subtitle. The first book, *Of the Understanding*, where the question "What can be known at all?" is investigated, is the logical foundation for the moral sciences, which are his main preoccupation. It was Hume's central conviction that a philosophy that estranges itself from the problems of human life is not worthy of that name. On the one hand, philosophy is an activity which naturally arises from life itself; since man is a reasonable being, "philosophical decisions are nothing but the reflections of common life, methodized and corrected" (EHU, 162).

Hume puts the emphasis on "common life": as a living creature within nature, man is also a social and active being. These three dimensions are vitally united in a natural way; for if action, work and social intercourse cannot be human without being reasonable, it is only because reason is primarily a guide for practical life. Thus Hume affirms that philosophy must remain human: "Indulge your passion for science, but let your science be human, and such as may have a direct reference to action and society" (EHU, 9)

Even if philosophy could not significantly extend the frontiers of our knowledge of reality, nonetheless "the genius of philosophy, if carefully cultivated by several, must gradually diffuse itself throughout the whole society, and bestow a similar correctness in every art and calling" (EHU, 10). The driving force behind Hume's spirit of endless enquiry is not a morbid desire for literary recognition, but as the preceding passage testifies, that particular form of social humanism typical of the Enlightenment.[3] Agreeably, his philosophy is but the science of man.

One may propose many different interpretations (perhaps all in some sense true) to the famous motto of Hume: "Be a philosopher; but admist all your philosophy, be still a man" (EHU, 9). For me, it seems to point to two things. First of all, it expresses his rejection of the philosophical paradigm represented by modern rationalism, where a complete order of things is deduced from the immanent resources of reason: the wildly speculative philosophical guessing and conjecturing that follows from the attempt at abandoning our human situation in order to assume the divine perspective. Second, it emphasizes that philosophy is not only a theoretical enterprise, but also a way of life, a way of taking decisions, and – true to his Socratic heritage (THN, Introduction, xvi) – an instrument for formulating and clarifying those most important ones: the moral decisions.

In sum, to reduce Hume's philosophy to epistemology is the best way to misrepresent Hume. It is also the best way to misunderstand Kant himself. From a neo-

---

[3] We shall examine Hume's peculiar type of enlightened humanism in section 2 of chapter 2.

Kantian predilection for the philosophy of science, one is led to overlook Kant's own estimate that practical reason is superior to theoretical reason, that the first *Critique* is done for the sake of the second. Thus one may disregard an outlook towards philosophy that is essentially shared by Hume and Kant. According to Kant, all the important questions of philosophy can be enclosed in the following: What is man? At the outset of the *Treatise* Hume says:

> There is no question of importance, whose decision is not compriz'd in the science of man; and there is none which can be decided with any certainty, before we become acquainted with that science (THN, Introduction, xx).

Certainly that remark serves to illustrate the great extent to which Hume was the heir to the critical temper of all modern philosophy that was inaugurated by Descartes and his methodical doubt. We should accept no doctrine or opinion as knowledge before we examine the principles and methods upon which that claim to knowledge is based. The Humean formulation has here, as in other places, very strong Lockean overtones. The knowledge of things, if it is certainty we strive for, should be preceded by reflecting on our means of knowing them; that is to say, one has first to provide an analysis of the cognitive powers of the human being in order to determine their effective possibilities and inherent limitations.

Still, even this small fragment seems to indicate that Hume's philosophy is done for much more than to answer the purely theoretical question, "What can be known at all?" It is the inescapable fact of having to live in a certain way and to entertain certain beliefs about ourselves and the way to live in the world that prompts such a question. What we are dealing with is not any belief whatsoever, but with those that make us what we are and support our being in the world. Hume's task is, in short, the elucidation of the meaning and investigation of the origin of our most universal, recalcitrant and in practice unavoidable beliefs, along with the modes of behavior to which these give rise, and also with the examination of the different ways in which men have tried to establish them, so that one may be really able to be certain about their truth and utility.

Hume's philosophy is the science of human nature. It is also the science of mind, and of the products of mind – those human dealings and activities in society (*common life*) being the most important. Perhaps his general attitude is germane to the moral philosophies of the Hellenistic period. Philosophy is ultimately undertaken in order to obtain the knowledge which will enable one to "live according to nature" and thus arrive at that *ataraxia*, or complete spiritual well-being and tranquillity that comes out of being in harmony with the universe. "We must submit to this fatigue [the exact scrutiny of the powers and capacity of the understanding], in order to live at ease ever after" (EHU, 12).

The question whose certainty is supremely important to us is the moral one, and the forms of knowledge whose certainty is to be analyzed, the sciences whose grounds are to be determined, are the moral ones.[4] These are for Hume: logic, morals (ethics), criticism (aesthetics), and politics. They are opposed to the natural or physical sciences, mathematics, and natural religion (rational theology). The somewhat paradoxical fact that Hume assumes that logic explains "the principles and operations of our reasoning faculty and the nature of our ideas," gives some plausibility to the following suggestion:

> 'Tis is evident, that all the sciences have a relation, greater or less, to human nature; and that, however wide any of them may seem to run from it, they still return back by one passage or another. Even *Mathematics*, *Natural Philosophy*, and *Natural Religion*, are in some measure dependent on the science of MAN; since they lie under the cognisance of men, and are judged of by their powers and faculties. (THN, xix).

This is not solely a declaration of the methodological priority of the science of man over all other sciences. It is also the expression of a cardinal presupposition, of a faith never shaken by any sceptical doubts: to wit, that our theoretical and practical activity is dependent to a great extent on principles and operations of a human nature that has an essentially permanent constitution, common to all human beings, with distinctive perceptions, propensities, passions, and emotions. As I shall hopefully show later on, this obtains even if one presupposes that the historical unfolding of humankind is progressive.[5] Human beings are like mirrors which reflect back to each other the same image (THN, 365). Out of the same mental structure of humankind there arise not only those cognitive activities that originate and set limits to scientific knowledge, but also those generic beliefs, emotions and corresponding habitual reactions necessary for our preservation and well-being. These provide the foundations not only for science, but for the other great institutions of culture: morality, art, the state, and religion itself. The science of man is the fundamental science; and the human nature Hume refers to must be factual and real, not the mere object of an a priori imagination. Therefore experience has to be the foundation upon which the science of man is to be erected. It is not strange that he conceived his task in a strict Newtonian way as an "Attempt to introduce the experimental method of reasoning into moral subjects." The "compleat system of the sciences" is the empirical science of human nature, which is the foundation of all the other sciences. Even Natural Religion, or the attempt to know something about God by the natural light of reason, falls under its scope. Thus the ideas, belief and practices (along with the historical institutions that perpetuate them) that this discipline aims to justify or validate are the subject-matter of Hume's critical scrutiny.

---

[4] The establishment of the moral sciences under a solid base is, according to John Passmore, the dominant theoretical intention of Hume's whole philosophy. See *Hume's Intentions*, (London: Gerald Duckworth & Co., 1968), p. 15.

[5] About this, see in particular chapter 6.

The Newtonian influence is indeed powerful. It operates in the treatment of a diversity of topics and is prominent in particular in his programmatic prohibition of the framing of hypothetical explanations of the ultimate causes of mental life:

And though we must endeavour to render all our principles as universal as possible, by tracing up our experiments to the utmost, and explaining all effects from the simplest and fewest causes, it is still certain we cannot go beyond experience; and any hypothesis, that pretends to discover the ultimate original qualities of human nature, ought at first to be rejected as presumptuous and chimerical (THN, xvii).

Those "ultimate causes" are the equivalent of the "occult qualities" that were banished from modern physical sciences and that should be eliminated if the moral sciences are to have, according to Hume, a scientific character, that is, if they are to rest "more on experience than on invention" (L, I,16). To the inspiration of Newton we should trace the use he makes of his "first principle" (according to which to every idea there corresponds an impression) as an instrument for solving the questions about the meaning of concepts by referring them to the experiences in which they arise. But the most obvious parallelism with Newton lies in his attempt – much attenuated and even ultimately abandoned, according to several interpreters – to decompose and reconstruct the world of human experience, out of ultimate mental entities, by recourse to general laws of association, quite similar in function to the laws of universal gravitation.[6]

Yet the application of Newtonian methodology to the critical task was not without its problems for Hume. It seems to lead his investigation to a kind of logical circle, which, I think, is at least one source of that complete scepticism that in the *Treatise* he is on the verge of adopting and that endangers the intelligibility of his own philosophy. The investigation that is to determine the validity of the claims to knowledge, including physical science, is compelled to use the very methods which are put into question. Some commentators, recognizing this difficulty, have nonetheless tried to justify Hume's approach. D. G. C. MacNabb is a typical case; he sees the circularity involved, but adduces that "to quell this unrest the Experimental Method is by itself powerless. It holds a mirror before the mind's eye, but does not reconcile us to what we see."[7] For his part, Hume seems, in gen-

---

[6] Nicholas Capaldi, *Hume the Newtonian Philosopher* (New York: Twayne, 1974), ch. 3 "Hume's Newtonian Program", pp. 45–70: "The principles of association are the great theory or the principle in terms of which Hume expected to explain all" (p. 67).

[7] D. G. C. MacNabb, *David Hume: His Theory of Knowledge and Morality*, 2nd ed., (Oxford: Basil Blackwell, 1966), p. 18. The talk about the need to "quell this unrest" seems a bit strange concerning logical matters. But it becomes more understandable when MacNabb tries to justify Hume's use of inductive generalization by the contention that no other methods are available, and that Hume has protected this conclusion by what he calls the "Method of Challenge," complementary to the "Experimental Method." According to him, Hume has challenged anybody who opposes him to show that other methods are available; since the opponent cannot produce such an instance, MacNabb thinks

eral, never to mistake or substitute a practical inevitability for a rational necessity (EHU, sec. iv, 38). On the other hand, Hume thought that not all subject-matters of inquiry are in need of, or admit, the same degree of certainty. Contrary to mathematics, inquiries into matters of fact and existence have neither intuitive nor demonstrative certainty; but they are not devoid of all certainty whatsoever. The physical and moral sciences rest on experience and observation; to them pertain *probable* certainty. In the *Abstract* of the *Treatise*, he views the goal of his epistemology as the establishment of the rules for the correct determination of what is probable.[8] And he calls the set of rules for determining the conditions under which to predicate the cause and effect relationship (Part III, Section XV of Book I of the *Treatise*), "all the logic I think proper to employ in my reasoning" (THN, 175).

Hume thus appears to have excised from the empirical sciences the need for absolute certainty. But can the same be done for the science of man, as it is the science that has to decide the certainty that pertains to all other sciences? Can it do this work without having a ground that is free from all uncertainty? If the investigation of thought – logic for Hume – states only facts about human nature which are established by the inductive method, then it is not easy to see how the same investigation can claim to be the fundamental science. If its own certainty is only probable, then the same type of argument that Hume uses against the methodical doubt of Descartes (which he calls "antecedent scepticism") could be directed again his own analysis of the human understanding: namely, that it leads to an infinite regress:

> It recommends an universal doubt, not only of all our former opinions and principles, but also of our very faculties; of whose veracity, say they, we must assure ourselves, by a chain of reasoning, deduced from some original principle, which cannot possibly be fallacious or deceitful. But neither is there any such original principle, which has a prerogative above others, that are self-evident and convincing: Or if there were, could we advance a step beyond it, but by the use of those very faculties, of which we are supposed to be already diffident. The Cartesian doubt, therefore, were it ever possible to be attained by any human creature (as it plainly is not) would be entirely incurable; and no reasoning

that Hume has rested his case confidently. Still, even MacNabb is led to recognize in the end, that this is not a demonstrative procedure, but a method of persuasion. One might retort that precisely there lies its inadequacy: arguments are refuted by arguments. Even if we were psychologically handicapped in answering Hume's challenge, it would not follow therefrom that there are no other alternative methods, or that the employment of the only available method does imply no logical circularity. Since it appeals to a factual incapacity in order to reply to a question of principle, MacNabb's defense fails.

[8] The celebrated *Monsieur Leibnitz* has observed it to be a defect in the common systems of logic, that they are very copious when they explain the operations of the understanding in the forming of demonstrations, but are too concise when they treat of probabilities, and those other measures of evidence on which life and action intirely depend, and which are our guides even in most of our philosophical speculations. In this censure, he comprehends *the essay on human understanding, le recherche de la verité*, and *l'art de penser*. The author of *the treatise of human nature* seems to have been sensible of this defect in these philosophers, and has endeavoured, as much as he can, to supply it (THN, A, 646–647).

could ever bring us to a state of assurance and conviction upon any subject (EHU, 149–50).

At the same time, one must emphasize that Hume does not criticize Descartes because he asserted the existence of self-evident truth, for this is something which Hume himself does not deny. What he opposed was the use Descartes made of the principle of the priority of our knowledge of mind over that of the external world. For him the whole program of the *Meditations* is an impossible task; there is no way to derive *more geometrico* from the axiomatic evidence of the *ego cogito*, its substantial character, the existence of God, and the objective reference of ideas to external reality, the last being guaranteed – as is well known – by God's veracity. Yet curiously enough, at the end of the *Enquiry Concerning Human Understanding*, Hume tries to rehabilitate the same Cartesian doubt that he consistently attacks in other places. In a passage in which Hume paraphrases the rules of Descartes' *Discourse on Method*, he shows not that it is impossible to begin with self-evident principles, but that the supreme certainty of the thinking ego cannot be put to do the epistemological job Descartes intended, even though it may be invaluable for the sort of investigation Hume himself undertakes.[9] In short, this shows no summary rejection of Descartes' method, but rather a mitigated, or conditional, adoption of it. Still, if the science of man for Hume has the same character that metaphysics had for Descartes, that is, the root of knowledge, or the ground of all sciences, then something more than mere probable certainty has to be available within its own realm. For in order to determine that probable certainty pertains to physics, one has to possess a paradigm case of perfect knowledge that has complete certainty, and in relation to which other cases may be judged. Since mathematics itself is dependent upon the science of man, and is judged in accordance with the mind's cognitive powers, it cannot fulfill that role. Thus if the science of man is to remain the supreme arbiter concerning the claims to knowledge of all other disciplines, the absolute instance of certain and perfect knowledge must be an inalienable property of mind itself.

It is somewhat paradoxical that, after all, it is the theory of ideas of Cartesian provenience that comes to Hume's rescue, providing him with the vantage point of absolute certainty that his epistemological investigation needs in order to start and reach its goals:

Every impression, external and internal, passions, affections, sensations, pains, and pleasures, are originally on the same footing; and that whatever other differ-

---

[9] It must, however, be confessed, that this species of scepticism, when more moderate, may be understood in a very reasonable sense, and is a necessary preparative to the study of philosophy, by preserving a proper impartiality in our judgments, and weaning our mind from all those prejudices, which we may have imbibed from education or rash opinion. To begin with clear and self-evident principles, to advance by timorous and sure steps, to review frequently our conclusions, and examine accurately all their consequences; though by these means we shall make both a slow and a short progress in our systems; are the only methods, by which we can ever hope to reach truth, and attain a proper stability and certainty in our determinations (EHU, 150).

ences we may observe among them, they appear, all of them, in their true colours, as impressions or perceptions. . . . For since all actions and sensations of the mind are known to us by consciousness, they must necessarily appear in every particular what they are, and be what they appear (THN, 190).

Since in themselves and as such "the perceptions of the mind are perfectly known" (THN, 366), "the intellectual world, though involved in infinite obscurities, is not perplexed with any such contradictions as those we have discovered in the natural. What is known concerning it, agrees with itself; and what is unknown, we must be contented to leave so" (THN, 232).

Even if Hume does not completely reject the Cartesian method and accepts the indubitable certainty of the *ego cogito*, he is not going to deny that the knowledge of the human mind is subject to limitations, even to impossibilities. These will inevitably appear whenever we attempt to go beyond what we consciously experience, as when we suppose the existence of a purely simple, immaterial and perfectly identical substance as an unknown substratum and ground of all our perceptions. With this *hypothesis non fingo* type of argument, he refutes again and again the reasonings of physicists, metaphysicians, and even mathematicians.[10]

At this point, it is Hume's consistency that should elicit our admiration, for he also applies this Newtonian argument in the realm of mental life, even if in the process it casts a doubt upon it. One ought not thrust aside, or ignore phenomena simply because they may contradict a hypothesis we antecedently have. Thus even when it is seen as contradicting our belief in the existence of a permanent identical self, Hume maintains that the self is but a bundle of perceptions. This is something to which experience, as he understands it, leads him. Perhaps the problem of accounting for personal identity is one *leit-motif* for the thorough scepticism in which he appears to land at the end of Book I of the *Treatise*. Another stimulating factor for this scepticism may have been – if Kemp Smith's influential interpretation is correct – his generalization of Francis Hutcheson's sentimentalism: in effect, feeling plays a dominant role not only in morals and criticism, but in natural science as well.[11] If the belief that every event must have a cause, rests solely on feeling (that is, habit or custom), we may also properly say that it is "not solely in poetry and music we must follow our taste and sentiment, but likewise in philosophy" (THN, 103).

No matter how useful in theory and practice scepticism may have been for Hume, inasmuch as he still had to provide a foundation for the moral sciences, he

---

[10] From this point of view at least, physical science is no less subjective than moral philosophy. It is true that, according to Hume, we can never know the essence of mind; however, neither can we apprehend the essence of material bodies, if when employing the word 'body', we refer to something more than a collection of sensible qualities.

[11] Thus supposes John Passmore in *Hume's Intentions*, p. 9. Yet I think that Kemp Smith's subjectivistic interpretation about the role of feeling in Hume's philosophy has been convincingly questioned by David Fate Norton in *David Hume: Common Sense Moralist and Sceptical Metaphysician* (Princeton, N. J.: Princeton University Press, 1982), and Páll S. Árdal in *Passion and Value*.

had to make sure that the former would not seriously compromise the theoretical integrity of his own first philosophy, i.e., the science of man. But how is it possible for Hume to avoid such a catastrophic outcome if his own philosophy is built out of antithetical elements? In short, the Cartesian axiom of the *cogito*, coupled with a Newtonian methodology sometimes led Hume even to deny rationality to his own epistemological enterprise. If experience is ultimately reduced to impressions and ideas, and these are "internal and perishing existences," mental and temporal events associatively organized, then we may ask if the common opinion that physical sciences gives knowledge about the external world is, at its best, seriously questioned, and, at its worst, is very difficult to differentiate from a bare prejudice. For, after all, does not Hume himself show us, especially in Part IV of Book I of the *Treatise*, that like the ghosts of superstition and the purely fictitious, or nominal entities of traditional metaphysics, science is equally an offspring of the human imagination? (THN, 267) When Hume follows this thick sceptical thread, not only the certainty of physics, but also that of mathematics seem to be thrown overboard:

> Our reason must be considered as a kind of cause, of which truth is the natural effect; but such a one as, by the irruption of other causes, and by the inconstancy of our mental powers, may frequently be prevented. By this means all knowledge degenerates into probability. . . . Now as none will maintain that our assurance in a long numeration exceeds probability, I may safely affirm, that there scarce is any proposition concerning numbers of which we can have a fuller security (THN, 180–181).

Many of Hume's difficulties at this point are due to a theory of belief with which he never quite appears to be completely satisfied, either because he could not formulate it with precision, or because he had some doubts concerning its theoretical adequacy. Again and again, Hume dwells on it in order to reformulate it or most likely to amend it.[12] But even on those occasions when he appears to view science as another product of the imagination, Hume nevertheless attempts to systematically distinguish science from those other products of the imagination which are erratic, arbitrary and irregular. He tries to show that it is in some sense more reasonable to stick to empirical science than to "false metaphysics," which is purely speculative, confused and obscure, and superstition, with which the former is frequently associated as a docile servant.[13]

In the last analysis, mathematics – at least in part – will step beyond sceptical doubt. From a theoretical point of view, the respective merits and demerits of mathematics and empirical science are inverse. It is true that the former discovers

---

[12] We shall analyze Hume's theory in chapter 7.

[13] The question whether Hume can in principle justify the distinction between reasonable belief and superstitious delusion, and even if to do this really is one of his dominant theoretical intentions, has been, and continues to be, the subject of a long and persevering controversy. Chapters 2, 7 and 14 contain my thoughts on this problem.

necessary connections between ideas; yet it has no existential significance (EHU, 25). On the other hand, physical and moral sciences, since they deal with matters of fact and existence, can never discover such necessary truths; but within certain limits, they nevertheless remain perfectly rational disciplines (EHU, 164–165). In so far as these sciences are back up, in the search for the causes and effects of things and events, by the experience of the constant conjunction of objects, the rules for making such inferences can be given; these provide the conditions, if not for absolute certainty, at least for a probable one. The physical and moral sciences cannot have complete immunity against error; both are ultimately human enterprises, and in every human activity error is at least a permanent possibility. What may be rational or irrational are the means and operations we may use in our attempt to avoid error.

Having this in mind, it appears somewhat strange that it is not the possibility of error, but its actuality that produces the famous argument of Part IV, Sect. I of Book I of the *Treatise*, "Of scepticism with regard to reason," which apparently ends up in the most extreme form of scepticism. From its domain not even mathematics can escape; in fact, it is not possible to exclude even the science of man. It is surprising that Hume had tried, even here, to transform a theoretical weakness that appears to be fatal into power. Thus he employs this total scepticism, which would leave absolutely unredeemed even the most insignificant doubt, as a tool to buttress theoretically his strongest pre-theoretical conviction, namely his naturalism – a kind of naturalism that may not be totally improper to denominate as providencialistic. In the end, as the following passage clearly illustrates, human nature comes to rescue us from that absolute perplexity towards which all our efforts in the search for truth seem destined:

> Should it here be asked me, whether I sincerely assent to this argument, which I seem to take such pains to inculcate, and whether I be really one of those sceptics who hold that all is uncertain, and that our judgment is not in *any* thing possessed of *any* measures of truth and falsehood; I should reply, that this question is entirely superfluous, and that neither I, nor any other person, was ever sincerely and constantly of that opinion. *Nature, by an absolute and uncontrollable necessity, has determined us to judge as well as to breathe and feel*; nor can we any more forbear viewing certain objects in a stronger and fuller light, upon account of their customary connexion with a present impression, than we can hinder ourselves from thinking, as long as we are awake, or seeing the surrounding bodies, when we turn our eyes towards them in broad sunshine. Whoever has taken the pains to refute the cavils of this *total* scepticism, has really disputed without an antagonist, and endeavoured by arguments to establish a faculty, which nature has antecedently implanted in the mind, and rendered unavoidable (THN, 183; italics added in the sentence beginning with the word 'Nature').

We simply cannot adequately consider here the question whether such an appeal to nature and instinct is more a reason for than against scepticism. At present, it is still difficult for me to see just how a factual impossibility (obviously supposing that such is what Hume has in mind in that passage) can refute the sceptical position. The sceptic might, nonetheless, be quite right in what he or she says, although unable to maintain his or her position in practice. In summary, Hume seems to contend that nature refutes the sceptic, for he or she cannot doubt in practice what he or she is able to question in theory.

Apart from that, it is certain that Hume thought that the moral as well as physical sciences rest on instinct. Against feeling and passion, against those general and permanent features of human nature, the philosophical doubts of the sceptic have no force at all. Life asserts its own rights; and, after all, is not reason itself nothing but a wonderful and unintelligible instinct in our soul? (THN, 179) Like the arguments of Berkeley, the cavils of the sceptic "admit of no answer and produce no conviction" (EHU, 155). These are but a *jeu d' esprit*, worthy of being practiced in so far as it may help us to appreciate the strict and narrow limits of our cognitive capacities.[14] As result, philosophers will strictly follow common sense.[15]

Anyhow, those beliefs rendered necessary by our being living organisms within nature, cannot be prevented. Furthermore, it is clear that we can explain their origin in human nature and even understand their role in human life. Now if religious faith were – as many suppose – a natural belief, then the same may be said to apply to it: namely, we would have to show that religious beliefs have the same basic, universal and inevitable character. In this case, the examination of its claim to truth would be much more urgent, for faith has traditionally presumed to possess the kind of knowledge which the passage just cited seems to declare impossible for us to attain.

On the whole, to what extent is Hume's naturalism theoretically convincing? Can it validly establish the priority of common (social and historical) life, and of natural instinct, so that our appeal to them may actually refute radical, or total scepticism? To my chagrin, I still cannot clearly see how this may be done by Hume. Perhaps an insuperable difficulty for Hume, is that the access to the world of daily experience, within which all of us readily assert that the use of reason is necessary and justified, appears to be impeded, and possibly voided, by two of his principal theoretical presuppositions: namely, the acceptance of Descartes' theory of ideas and the employment of a methodology inspired by Newton. The cardinal belief, "that blind and powerful instinct of nature" (EHU, 151) that leads us to suppose an external world independent of all perceptions, also comes under the critical scrutiny of his science of man, and has to be validated by it.

---

[14] In section 2 of chapter 2 we shall dwell not only on the negative, or restrictive functions of Hume's critique of religion, but especially on the positive, personal as well as social, benefits of the sort mitigated scepticism that Hume recommends.

[15] Thus Hume says that "those who have a propensity to philosophy . . . . will never be tempted to go beyond common life, so long as they consider the imperfection of those faculties which they employ, their narrow reach, and their inaccurate operations. While we cannot give a satisfactory reason, why we believe, after a thousand experiments, that a stone will fall, or fire burn; can we ever satisfy ourselves concerning any determination, which we may form, with regard to the origin of worlds, and the situation of nature, from, and to eternity?" (EHU, 162).

But can Hume somehow justify this "original instinct" and all the other natural beliefs? Páll S. Árdal has given one of the most original affirmative answers to this question in a by now classic study of Hume's moral philosophy. He argues not only that Hume's moral theory is based on the theory of the passions in Book II, but furthermore that the discussion of the virtues and vices in Book III clears up some important epistemological doctrines of Book I, in particular the doctrine about the so-called (since Kemp Smith) "natural beliefs."[16] He claims in particular that only by conceiving reason as a virtue one can justify the reasonability of the so-called natural beliefs. Here we are not dealing with demonstrative reason, but with reason "improperly so-called." Hume identifies this reason with the tendency to form natural beliefs which allow us to correct personal biases, to take up impartial points of view and to form general rules of reasoning and conduct. Árdal considers that reason in this latter sense is a virtue because the person who is guided by these beliefs works for his or her success in practice and is, in general, "loved" or esteemed because of it.[17] Sanity (in other words, reasonableness) consists in the habitual tendency to guide our thoughts and actions by the natural beliefs – such as the belief in the existence of the external world, causal efficacy, and the identity of the self, and even for Árdal, the rules of justice – is, according to him, a virtue for the following reason: "The tendency to have these beliefs is both a general quality of human nature and a characteristic that greatly helps us to secure our survival and effective agency."[18] Because of this, that predisposition is a virtue. In summary, the only justification for the natural beliefs, whose possession characterizes the sensible or reasonable person, is – Árdal seems to be saying – a pragmatical validation: those beliefs are useful for the individual and the society which acts according to them.[19]

Although I am basically in agreement with this analysis, and readily admits that Hume himself endorses those beliefs on pragmatic grounds in many places (especially in Sect. of Part IV of Book I of the *Treatise*, "On Modern Philosophy").

---

[16] Thus Árdal lays to rest, in the second edition of *Passion and Value*, an objection which is shared by a good number of the commentators of his book, a reservation that Nicholas Capaldi paradigmatically formulated in "Hume's Theory of the Passions," in *Hume, A Re-Evaluation*, ed. Donald Livingston and James King (New York, 1976), 175. Árdal is chastised for presumably having ignored the relation between Books I and II of the *Treatise*, and therefore for failing to consider the three books together, that is, in an unitary fashion.

[17] *Passion and Value*, x. Árdal clearly formulated his conception of reason as a virtue in "Some Implications of the Virtue of Reasonableness in Hume's *Treatise*," in *Hume, A Re-evaluation*, ed. Donald Livingston and James King, pp. 91–106.

[18] *Passion and Value*, p. xiii.

[19] Crucial passages of the *Treatise* and the *Enquiries* lend support to Árdal's claim, especially those sections in which Hume reflects on the nature of belief seemingly abandoning its previous characterization in terms of force and vivacity in favor of a consideration of belief as a *sui generis* sentiment which, among other things, is "the governing principle of all our actions." The most extensive exposition of this version of the theory of belief is found in the Appendix of the *Treatise*, 624–629. See below chapter 7.

I nonetheless think that Árdal should have omitted the employment of the term 'justification'. For not avoiding it, I fear that he plays into the hands of the Pyrrhonian sceptic and his irresolute doubts; for although an appeal to practice may be inescapable and even compatible with scepticism, it is not a rational or epistemic vindication against scepticism. In contradistinction to Árdal, I consider that the so-called natural beliefs neither admit of, nor require, any justification, not even a pragmatical one. We cannot help being guided by them for the simple fact that such is the manner in which our human nature is – according to Hume – originally constituted. I am not deprecating their usefulness, but only questioning the appeal to practice as their justification. One cannot deny, for example, that if one should challenge the Pyrrhonian to live out his or her doubts, he or she will be unable to meet that practical challenge. But the Pyrrhonian might still reply to us in a manner similar to Hume when he was arguing against the possibility of rationally justifying the principle that underlies all generalizations founded on experience:

> My practice, you say, refutes my doubts. But you mistake the purport of my question. As an agent, I am quite satisfied in the point; but as a philosopher, who has some share of curiosity, I will not say scepticism, I want to learn the foundation of this inference. (EHU, 38).

In sum, successful practice cannot validate the belief in the external world because successful as well as unsuccessful practice are undertaken under the tacit supposition of the validity of such a belief. The belief in the external word appears to possess, in some measure, the same character as those propositions which in the *Posterior Analytics* Aristotle called axioms, although in Aristotle we are dealing with ultimate indemonstrable principles of science (*epistéme*) whereas in Hume, with the foundations of all beliefs (*dóxa*).[20] It is certain that neither Aristotle nor Hume tried to offer a demonstration for such a belief. For Aristotle it is a sign of a mature mind to know which things are and which are not susceptible of being demonstrated.[21] For Hume this belief is the inevitable point of departure of all reasoning, but not something towards which we reason; it is simply "a point we must take for granted in all our reasonings."[22] Hume may as well have added that it something that we take for granted in all our actions. In spite of these reservations, Páll S. Árdal's interpretation of Hume's philosophy is not only encompassing and enlightening, but of incalculable value for all those persons who are passionately interested in connecting the different strands of Hume's philosophical thought.

Even if it were not possible to derive it from a more basic principle, can Hume still show us that our trust in the belief about the external world (both natural and historical) is not only inevitable as a matter of fact, but also in some sense defensible in principle, or reasonably justifiable? Only then we may assert that his appeal

---

[20] Aristotle, *Posterior Analytics*, I.10, 76^{b}12–23.

[21] Aristotle, *Nicomachean Ethics*, I.3 1094^b 23–28.

[22] THN, I, Part IV, Sect. II, p. 187.

to nature can be much more than psychologically persuasive. But this appeal becomes doubtful, if we begin with the presupposition that the immediate objects of awareness are not external things but our own mental states, or perceptions, and that out of these the whole world of experience is to be reconstructed. Here we are dealing with the world of the collective experience of humankind, which is the subject-matter of history, as well as with the natural world, the material universe that is studied by Newtonian science. This is the crux of what has been called the "psychologism" of Hume.

Of course, it is always possible to rehabilitate Hume's naturalism by outrightly denying the presupposition just mentioned. Donald W. Livingston has followed this path on the one hand, to oppose the psychologistic or phenomenalistic interpretation of Hume, and on the other, to show that Hume is not only a philosophical historian but a "historical philosopher." Thus he tries to establish – with reasonable success, I believe – that Hume's historical works (most of his *Essays*, *The History of England*, and *The Natural History of Religion*) are by no means extrinsic adherences to his speculative philosophy, but rather consistent corollaries of the gnoseological and ontological foundations established in the latter. With this thesis of Livingston one has to sympathize entirely:

> It is not just that there are traces of Hume's philosophical theories (moral, political, epistemological, etc.) scattered throughout *The History of England*. It is rather that some of Hume's deepest philosophical doctrines of knowledge and existence are structured by historical categories. . . . Historical thinking is now seen to be an integral part of his philosophical thought. . . . Hume's historical work may be viewed, in part, as the fulfillment of a demand inspired by his conception of philosophy.[23]

Now, for instance, the psychologistic interpretation would be wrong in supposing that impressions are internal, purely subjective mental states, that is, in conceiving experience as a private domain. For Livingston, on the contrary, "we are to think of perceptions as having internal and external dimensions," and thereby have to affirm that experience is from the beginning a public domain.[24] In short, if with perceptions Hume is referring to the world of public objects, then the psychologistic interpretation would be completely wrong, and thus the problem posed about the reasonableness of our belief in the external would simply dissolve itself.

This type of defense is, however, questionable, for its only strong support in the text itself is found in the Introduction to the *Treatise* and the essay "Of Essay Writing". In addition, Livingston almost entirely ignores many passages that are inconvenient for his interpretation, in particular from Parts III and IV of Book I of the *Treatise*, where Hume expressly takes for granted, as something which is "pretty obvious of itself" (THN, 67), the validity of the Cartesian point of depar-

---

[23] Donald W. Livingston, *Hume's Philosophy of Common Life*, p. 2.

[24] Ibid., p. 48.

ture.[25] In spite of this objection, I believe that the other part of Livingston's thesis, which is by far the chief one, remains untouched and sound, and hence should be incorporated to a unitary interpretation of Hume's philosophy. In conformity with that view, Livingston understands the principle according to which ideas refer to antecedent impressions, not only as a Newtonian maxim that demands the corroboration of our theories by empirical observation, but also as a proclamation that perceptions have to be seen in a "narrative context," and thus originally are historical entities. At all events, it is one thing to discover a genuine historical dimension in the foundations of Hume's philosophy, and another very different to assimilate it to a kind of historicism. But once Hume is transformed into a historicist, how can one be sure that such historicism does not, after all, share with psychologism the same features (for instance, the genetic fallacy) that makes the latter an easy prey for scepticism?

Notwithstanding the present influence of interpreters such as Kemp Smith, Árdal and Livingston, many commentators still continue to maintain that the greatest part of the puzzles and contradictions which Hume's discovers within the sciences he investigates, even within his own fundamental science, is due to a so-called deep psychological muddle. It is alleged that he simply confuses logic with psychology. There is, I believe, not much truth in this interpretation. But even if it were right, it cannot be assumed that Hume always confuses the logical and the psychological task, simply because sometimes he offers, as answers to the questions about the meaning of certain concepts and propositions, explanatory hypotheses about their psychogenesis, or in Locke's terminology, a "natural history" of our ideas. In sharp contrast to this outlook, we shall to exclude any sort of reductive interpretation, and shall analyze the pertinent cases one by one to see when, or whether, he was a victim to such a psychological confusion.

Against this psychologistic view, one should also remember that Hume thought that an investigation about the ways our concepts are derived from, and related, to sense experience gives us a clue to their meaning, and throws light on the effective possibilities and limitations of our cognitive endeavors. On the other hand, even if the reduction of the idea of substance – to mention just one instance – to a mere collection of sensible qualities appearing together, may perhaps be a defective and incomplete account of the true meaning of the word 'substance,' it is none the less true that its employment is quite defensible within the actual polemical context, as one more weapon of philosophical criticism by means of which Hume gives a fair indication of the actual, albeit sorely slight, evidence that rationalist philosophers can count on in order to justify the foundational concepts of their systems. For Hume, such philosophical constructions appear to be but fanciful suppositions arbitrarily drawn from what is really given to us with full evidence, that is, a succession of perceptions with constancy and coherence.

---

[25] Ibid., p. 35. There Livingston cites THN, xix and E, 569. For that reason, I think, Antony Flew, has few problems in disposing of Livingston's substantive contention in "Impressions and Experiences: Public or Private," *Hume Studies* 11, no. 2 (November 1985): 183–191.

Even less shall I attempt the more plausible although far from new endeavor of converting Hume into a logical positivist or contemporary analytical philosopher.[26] This is a more plausible interpretation, since, as we have seen, Hume indeed uses his peculiar analysis of concepts in order to attack traditional metaphysics. However, this can become another version of hermeneutic reductionism, particularly if one tries laboriously to cut off from Hume's philosophy everything that connects the answers to questions about the meaningfulness of concepts with the origin of these in entities that by now have been suppressed from the theories of philosophers of that tradition, such as "faculties and capacities of the mind," "mental acts," and above all "human nature."

Ultimately, we shall not impute Hume's theoretical failures, if there are some, to the inadequacies of his psychologism, because that would be, not only very questionable in itself, but in fact completely foreign to the way in which he conceived his own philosophical exercise. Instead of psychology, Hume was, in his own words, doing "true metaphysics": "And we must cultivate true metaphysics [the enquiry into the human understanding, its powers and capacity] with some care, in order to destroy the false and adulterate" (EHU, 12).

Hume is, I think, closer to the traditional metaphysics which he criticizes than to the later analytical philosophy to which he is taken to be a seminal thinker or forerunner. For that reason I also believe that there is much to say in favor of an admittedly speculative and metaphysical interpretation of Hume's predominant philosophical purposes. According to it, Hume's entire epistemological investigation is nothing but an instrument for establishing an ontology that would provide the moral sciences with a firm foundation. Well, yes – one may immediately reply to it – , but one that still would necessarily be a psychological ontology. Even in this case, such an enterprise would be quite different from empirical psychology,[27] and rather closer to the manner in which an eighteenth-century philosopher like Kant conceives his own philosophy, that is, as transcendental.

One may properly say that Hume's theoretical philosophy, as an analysis of the capacity of human knowledge, is a theoretical attempt to provide the basis for an ontology about the objects that we can know, that is, those entities to which we have a full and direct access. According to this view, for him, perceptions, or impressions and ideas are on the one hand, the "elements" out of which mental life is composed, and on the hand, the ultimate ingredients of anything which is real for us. Consequently he says in the *Abstract* that the associative links between ideas

---

[26] Two typical versions of this outlook are Farhang Zabeeh, *Hume: Precursor of Modern Empiricism* (The Hague: Martinus Nijhoff, 1960); and José García Roca, *Positivismo e Ilustración: La Filosofía de David Hume* (Valencia: Departamento de Historia de la Filosofía, Universidad de Valencia, 1981).

[27] What Gladys Bryson says, in general terms, about the key thinkers of the Scottish Enlightenment who made human nature their main theoretical concern, applies, in this sense, particularly well to Hume: namely, that "it was a philosophy of mind, and not a psychology, that they wanted, primarily, to construct, and it was such a philosophy that they did construct" [*Man and Society: The Scottish Inquiry of the Eighteenth Century* (Princeton, N. J. : Princeton University Press, p. 143)].

"are really *to us* the cement of the universe" (THN, A, 662). In addition, the present interpretation entirely agrees with the fact that relatively early in Book I of the *Treatise* (THN, 107–108), Hume had already bestowed "the title" of *reality* upon the perceptions which form the system of the senses and memory, and that of *realities* upon those that belong to the system of judgment (imagination guided by custom, or causation). In short, it seems as if all that is real to us, (i.e., any object that exists, existed or may exist for us), is anything that can inhabit one of those great collections or ensembles of impressions and ideas organized by the universal and regular principles of association. At the same time, one might say, employing the old Scholastic terminology, that for Hume sense perceptions are the *res verae*, for "they must necessarily appear in every particular what they are, and be what they appear" (THN, 190). This is confirmed by what he remarks about substance, the capital metaphysical category. If substance is defined as *"something which may exist by itself"* then, "all our perceptions. . . are therefore substances, as far as this definition explains a substance" (THN, 233). Moreover, even the old Parmenidean problem reappears within Hume's philosophy: namely, how to connect the world of truth (*alétheia*) with the world of opinion (*dóxa*). In Hume's case, the paradigm of truth is provided by the complete certainty of present perception; hence he says that "the perceptions of the mind are perfectly known" (THN, 366). The world of opinion – the one we instinctively believe to be in or inhabit – is the world of "common life," of nature and history, that the empirical sciences pretend to know but about which we have "rather conjectures" than certain "reasonings" (THN, 366); thus he says about our belief in that world, that "it is indeed difficult to resist, but which, like other instincts, may be fallacious and deceitful" (EHU, 159).

On the basis of this interpretation, I consider that Edmund Husserl's appraisal about the theoretical merit of Hume's philosophical project, is essentially correct:

> Hume's greatness (a greatness still unrecognized in this, its most important aspect) lies in the fact that . . . he was the first to grasp the universal *concrete problem* of transcendental philosophy. In the concreteness of purely egological internality, as he saw, everything Objective becomes intended to (and, in favorable cases, perceived), thanks to a subjective genesis. Hume was the first to see the necessity of investigating the Objective itself as a product of its genesis from that concreteness, in order to make the legitimate being-sense of everything that exists for us intelligible through its ultimate origins. Stated more precisely: The real world and the categories of reality, which are fundamental forms, become for him a problem in a new fashion. He was the first to *treat seriously the Cartesian focusing purely on what lies inside:* in that he began by freeing the soul radically from everything that gives it the significance of a reality in the world, and then presupposed the soul purely as a

field of "perceptions" ("impressions" and "ideas"), such as it is qua datum of a suitably purified internal experience.[28]

Yet at the same time Husserl was, I think, only partially right. I say "partially" because one cannot simply brush aside almost a century of Hume's scholarship, in particular that encouraged by the writings of Kemp Smith. In the end, there is, too, much truth in the naturalistic and historicistic interpretations that one should seriously endeavor to harmoniously include into a more adequate, complex and comprehensive outlook of Hume's philosophy. They may serve as a counterbalance to purely transcendental interpretations, such as Husserl's. Apart from this, Hume did not remained (if he ever was) strictly speaking in a "transcendental attitude"; the subject who exercises the philosophical reflection was not for Hume "pure consciousness," but a living human being, even though the self that can be disclosed by a posterior act of reflection may be but a "bundle of perceptions." On the other hand, it is necessary to exclude any reading of Hume that might transform it into a mere precursor of a quite later philosopher, such as Husserl. Notwithstanding all of this, one has to recognize that, on the whole, the elucidation of the fundamental modes of being of objects in their relation to us, or to use Husserl's words again, the explanation of the "legitimate being-sense of everything that exists for us," may remain a necessary and valid theoretical undertaking, and one that in some sense Hume himself set out to do.[29] But in his case it was done in order to provide the foundations of a naturalistic metaphysics geared to answer mostly practical concerns.

1.2 HUME'S FIRST PHILOSOPHY AND THE REFLECTION ON RELIGION

Although the preceding ontological and frankly speculative interpretation were misguided or far from adequate, and we were to continue to see Hume under the still more usual psychologistic, and purely sceptic, or even narrowly historicistic outlook, we would still be able say with reasonable confidence that in what pertains re-

---

[28] *Formal and Transcendental Logic*, trans. Dorion Cairns, (The Hague: Martinus Nijhoff, 1969), p. 256; *Formale und Transcendental Logik, Gesammelte Werke*, Husserliana, Band XVII, herausgegebene von Paul Janssen, (The Hague: Netherlands: Martinus Nijhoff, 1974), Sect. 100, p. 263.

[29] Even though I cannot justify it here, I think that a good portion of Hume's difficulties in establishing his main philosophical principles and theses might be more the effect of some of his ontological presupposition than of his alleged psychological reductionism. In other words, the former might be due to his conception that sense-impressions are the *res verae*, and his adherence to strict form of nominalism, according to which there exists only individual or particular objects, absolutely determined, qualitatively and quantitatively. This capital assumption is tersely formulated in the following passage:

> it is a principle generally received in philosophy, that every thing in nature is individual, and that it is utterly absurd to suppose a triangle really existent, which has no precise proportion of sides and angles (THN, 19).

ligious matters at least, he explicitly and lucidly distinguished the genetic from the logical question:

> As every enquiry, which regards religion, is of the utmost importance, there are two questions in particular, which challenge our attention, to wit, that concerning its foundation in reason, and that concerning its origin in human nature (NHR, 21).

The first, the critical scrutiny of the different ways, methods, considerations, evidences and arguments by means of which human beings have tried to establish and support their religious beliefs, is the topic to be discusses in the *Dialogues Concerning Natural Religion:* the second, the rational account of the ways and circumstances under which human beings come to entertain their diverse religious beliefs and to represent to themselves the object of their cult, is what *The Natural History of Religion* is about.

In Parts III and II of this book we shall study each of these questions, trying at the same time not to lose sight of Hume's main object of securing a base for the moral sciences. The attempt towards such a foundation was begun in the spirit of Newtonian science, but still not emancipated from the Cartesian emphasis on the priority of mind. However, the emphasis that his attempt laid upon the need to build a metaphysics or total science of human nature, helped to prepare the way, at least historically, for the opening of a new and different philosophical approach to the problems about human beings and reality. Hume drew attention to human nature, but not as predominantly rational – as it has been defined by modern rationalist philosophers and taken to be by the most leading exponents of natural religion. For him reason was not a strange destitute reality, a foreign ambassador from a higher realm, set apart from all the other functions of human nature, but on the contrary, one more function, coordinated – we might even say, biologically integrated – with all the rest. "Nature, by an absolute and uncontroulable necessity has determined us to judge as well as to breathe and feel" (THN, 183). Hume persistently appeals to nature, to a natural world were man is a living organism among others and reason is a vital principle whose operation serves natural needs and is subject to limitations of the same kind.

This metaphysics of nature comes through more clearly – although not exclusively – in his works on religion. In the *Dialogues* he offers two naturalistic theoretical alternatives to classical theism. In the *Natural History*, religions and religious representations of divinity are seen emerging, not only from certain elementary passions and determinate traits of the imagination, but also from the precarious situation of human life and activity that set those passions and imagination to work. Hume views the human being as an organism that, in order to keep on living, must satisfy particular basic needs within the realm of nature which he conceives, as it were, as the permanent horizon within which all the other human activities, beliefs, practices and institutions, social as well as historical, emerge.

All in all, and in the light of the preceding considerations, it becomes clear, I think, that the religious phenomenon in its diverse manifestations is a topic that has to be investigated by the kind of philosophizing Hume exemplifies. The analysis of human understanding is done to determine its actual cognitive possibilities. According to traditional religious thought, God is not only an object of *worship*, but also a being we in some sense *know*. Thus it is imperative for the science of man to determine the origins, as well as objective validity and real worth of the religious representations of the divine (especially of the theological idea of the God of Judeo-Christian tradition), and scrutinize the claims to knowledge of rational theology or natural religion. The latter (employing both a priori arguments and others drawn from the observation of a physico-biological Nature) claims to have knowledge of the existence and nature of God, and even derives from that presumed knowledge enormous practical consequences for human life, namely, ethical commandments which it holds as binding for all humankind:

> Even *Mathematics*, *Natural Philosophy*, and *Natural Religion*, are in some measure dependent on the science of MAN; since they lie under the cognisance of men, and are judged of by their powers and faculties. It is impossible to tell what changes and improvements we might make in these sciences were we thoroughly acquainted with the extent and force of human understanding, and could explain the nature of the ideas we employ, and of the operations we perform in our reasonings. And these improvements are the more to be hoped for in natural religion, as it is not content with instructing us in the nature of superior powers but carries its views further, to their disposition towards us, and our duties towards them (THN, Introduction, xv).

That the issues to be investigated in this book are – if focused from the theoretical foundations of Hume's philosophy – legitimate and important questions, is a claim that, I believe, the passage just quoted amply justifies. Since religion raises the problems of knowledge and morality, it is a topic which demands to be queried by that "true metaphysics" which in order to secure a solid ground for the moral sciences (social and historical), makes its start with a critical analysis of the faculty of human knowledge.

Now we go on to examine some of the deepest historical roots of Hume's investigation and critique of religion.

CHAPTER 2

Brief Historical Setting
of Hume's Investigation of Religion

2.1 THE RISE AND FALL OF NATURAL RELIGION

The claim that it is possible to gain exact and certain knowledge about some of the matters which the religious believer deems of supreme importance, solely through the employment of his or her rational capacities and without the need of any special revelation, has been customarily associated with the more or less equivalent terms of 'natural religion', 'rational theology', or 'philosophical theology'. It has seldom been pretended that human reason is able to know everything which the religious person believes to be important or necessary to know. Yet, whenever such a discipline has flourished (at least within Judeo-Christian tradition), it has usually presented itself as a set of truths about the existence and attributes of the Deity, moral government of the world, freedom of the will, and the immortality of the soul. This is particularly the case with the natural religion of the second half of the seventeenth and first half of the eighteenth century in England, which was in particular the object of Hume's critical scrutiny.

Up to this point there is a resemblance between modern natural religion and the innumerable typical attempts of Christian theology during the Middle Ages to harmonize faith and reason, and to some extent justify the latter by means of the former. Even though natural religion starts, especially in England, with the express purpose of reconciling Christian dogmas with the early scientific reason, or natural philosophy that was distinctive of the age, it is, however, also true that, almost immediately, it ceased to be a servant (if she ever was) of theology, and began to attack head on and reject her former master, to wit, Christian faith and revelation. The greatest figures of natural religion do not, as it were, try out any new arguments in order to establish their chief theses; instead, they mostly repeat the old demonstrations about the necessity of a divine existence and its essential attributes, and about our absolute obligation to obey its ethical decrees. Nonetheless, the assumptions under which they wield such arguments are different, the spirit that gives rise to them is frankly hostile to historical Christianity, and so the task to which they are destined is entirely opposed to Scholastic philosophy. One typical case is the different function which is assigned in each period to the ontological proof. Later on, in chapter 10, we shall deal at some length with this argument and Hume's criticism; now it will be useful to briefly compare St. Anselm, abp. of Canterbury (1033?–1109), paradigmatic medieval philosopher and inventor of the proof, and René Descartes (1596–1650), the most important inspirer of natural religion and, as it were, the resuscitator of the ontological argument in modern philosophy, with regard to the import that the proof has for each of them. Thereby we may perhaps be able to clearly display the distinctive character of the natural religion which Hume culminates, criticizes and brings to an end, both philosophically and historically.

The argument is the same in Saint Anselm and Descartes, even though their verbal formulations are different. However, the attitudes that animate both thinkers are quite opposite. Saint Anselm, in the *Proslogion*, carries out a meditation on the divine essence and an act of prayer and praise to God. His argument should not be seen merely as a logical exercise which is alien to the theological-religious attempt to unite himself with the object of worship, namely, God.[1] Anselm's proof is rather an ingredient of a faith that tries to comprehend the God who is already the recipient of love: "For I do not seek to understand so that I may believe; but I believe so that I may understand."[2]

Hence, the argument is exposed from the point of view of faith, that is, by someone who is previously convinced that God exists, and hopes that with the assistance of divine Grace, his intellect will be illuminated so that it may have a more direct and clearer view of the God he is searching with all his heart. For the faithful, God is but the apex of blessedness, or a happiness that can only be found in the enjoyment of His glorious presence. Likewise the argument is not presented as a piece of reasoning that may be sufficient by itself to convince someone who is not beforehand in possession of faith. On the contrary, Saint Anselm's point of departure is the situation "of one who is trying to raise his mind to contemplate God and seeking to understand what he believes."[3]

In summary, the ontological argument, instead of solely being a rational proof, is rather a profound and succinct meditation on the nature of the God that one loves, believes in and declares to be:

1. The most noble, and for religious consciousness indeed, the only possible object worthy of piety and worship: i.e., the most perfect Being that can be conceived, or "something-than-which-nothing-greater-can-be-thought."

2. The true Creator, of whose existence all that which is not Himself absolutely depends: the Being whose existence is not merely possible, but necessary. So necessary is the divine existence that it is not even possible that God may not exist.

---

[1] *St. Anselm's Proslogion, with a Reply on Behalf of the Fool, and The Author's Reply to Gaunilo,* trans. with an introduction. and philosophical comments by M. J. Charlesworth, (Oxford: Clarendon Press, 1968).

[2] Ibid., p. 115.

[3] Ibid., Preface, p. 103.

For his part, Descartes, in his *Meditations on First Philosophy*,[4] says that the questions about God's existence and immortality of the soul belong more to philosophy than to theology itself. Later on, he asserts that everything that can be known about God, we can procure it by simply examining our own mind and what it contains within itself. In sum, philosophy neither supervenes nor supplements theology, but simply displaces it.

Now, if everything that we can know about God can be known rationally (*"tout ce que se peut savoir de Dieu peut être montré par des raisons qu'el n'est pas besoin de chercher ailleurs que dans nous-mêmes"*),[5] then what need is there of faith? Is it not plainly the case that it becomes superfluous? Although that was not the conclusion drawn by Descartes himself (at least explicitly), this was done, however, by prominent philosophers who followed him, and who were in this matter very much influenced by him. Descartes, on the other hand, seems to have been sincere in his assent to traditional Christianity, and in pleading that his philosophy can conclusively dispel the doubts about the main tenets of faith; in this sense, he appears to have never discarded the Thomist doctrine he learned at the Jesuit College of La Flèche, i.e., that reason, does not oppose, but rather complements faith. In addition, he did never countenance the idea of erecting a religion of reason (he always emphaticallly presented himself as a philosopher, not as a theologian), and in the Dedication to the *Meditations* he even presents himself as fulfilling the duties of a Christian, and more narrowly Roman Catholic, philosopher by defending the dogmas of the Faith against all infidels. Still, it is much more probable that Descartes retained of Christianity what was, in his own eyes, made clearly and distinctly true by his philosophy instead of simply and prudently conforming the latter to the official religion.

But be that as it may, with Descartes the idea of constituting a natural religion, namely, a religion that – as Kant will say much later – operates "within the limits of reason alone" begins to take hold of modern mind. From this perspective, the ontological argument is not quite the product of faith striving to understand itself, but of reason's determination to free herself from the tutelage of traditional faith, or at least to get rid of everything in the latter which may be mere prejudice, error, superstition and impiety. In Descartes, the ontological argument is maintained as one unquestionable achievement of the critical analysis to which reason subjects faith; and in the end such a criticism will only retain as true all that and only that which reason can discover, comprehend and justify by itself. Descartes' meditation starts not from faith, as in Saint Anselm, but from doubt, which is but the methodological suspension of all beliefs that may have taken hold of our minds without our ex-

---

[4] René Descartes, *Meditations on First Philosophy*, "Dedication to the Most Wise and Illustrious The Dean and Doctors of the Sacred Faculty of Theology in Paris," in *The Philosophical Works of Descartes*, trans. Elizabeth Haldane and G. R. T. Ross, 2 vols. (Cambridge: Cambridge University Press, 1970), p. 133; *Oeuvres de Descartes*, ed. Charles Adam and Paul Tannery, 13 vols. (Paris: L. Cerf, 1897–1910) AT, IX, 4–5.

[5] Ibid., AT IX, 5; VII, 2.

plicit acquiescence, including the religious ones. In short, for Descartes it is more a case of understanding in order to believe than of believing in order to understand.

In general, the point of departure for modern philosophical reflection from Descartes on, is the thinking subjectivity; and this will not accept any principle whatsoever unless it first shows its undeniable evidence to the inquiring intellect. Yet all but a few traditional, or peculiarly Christian, beliefs will pass unscathed this critical test by reason. And even the one that succeeded, about the God that reason confidently presumes to demonstrate, i.e., the "Being of infinite or eminent perfection," appears to ordinary believers as no more than a pale and remote shadow, an inert and lifeless abstraction of the God that they really worship. Therefore Blaise Pascal (1623–1662), the great natural philosopher, mathematician and early follower of Cartesian philosophy, will defy its mentor, and entirely disallow the claim that reason can give us some knowledge of the God that reveals Himself through faith in Christ. Pascal will reinvindicate the primacy of faith, albeit in a extreme fideistic manner that makes one recall Tertullian (*Credo quia absurdum est,* or "I believe because it is absurd")[6] rather than Saint Anselm (*Fides quaerens intellectum,* or "Faith in Quest of Understanding").[7] In the same spirit, he will go on to say that the God of the philosophers is not the living God, or the God of Abraham, Isaac and Jacob. Reason is totally impotent to reveal us the living God, who is a God that hides Himself.[8] In spite of this intellectual darkness, we should not, according to Pascal, suspend judgment; for if we bet on God's existence and we lose, the lost will be insignificant; but if we win, the gain will be infinite. This rational wager gives us no certainty; it assumes, on the contrary, that there is none, that scepticism is right when it points out that the existence as much as the non-existence of God are matters whose truth or falsity cannot be validly demonstrated: "According to reason you cannot do either; according to reason you cannot leave either undone."[9] His famous wager, instead of being a new proof, should be viewed as a quest to show that it is not irrational to believe in God, even in absence of rational proof. Faith is, indeed, something that depends on the "heart," on a dark sentimental intuition rather than on the clear and distinct Cartesian intellectual intuition: "The heart has its own reasons which Reason does not know . . . This is Faith: God felt by the heart, not by reason."[10]

---

[6] Tertullian (165–220), the once celebrated apologist of Catholic faith and afterwards Montanist heretic, never exactly pronounced the above-sentence, which has historically been linked with his name. In the *De carne Christi;* V, 4, however, he expresses pretty much the same thing by asserting that it is credible that the Son of God was crucified because this is not possible, and that it is true that he resuscitated because this is impossible. See *Tertulliani Opera,* 2 vols. (Turnholti: Typography Brepols Editores, 1954), II, 881.

[7] Saint Anselm, *Proslogion,* Preface, p. 104.

[8] Blaise Pascal, *Pascal's Pensées,* with and English translation, brief notes and introduction, by H. F. Stewart (New York: Pantheon Books, 1950), sect. 247, "That God willed to hide himself," p. 133.

[9] Ibid., sect. 223, "Infinity – nothing," p. 119.

[10] Ibid., sect. 627, pp. 343 and 345.

Despite his impeccable scientific credentials and the tragic seriousness of his faith, Pascal was not heeded during his time. He was, like John the Baptist, another voice that cried out in the wilderness. Unfortunately, he addressed cultured persons who could pay no attention to him, for they were delighted with the continuous triumphs of the new mathematical science of nature in its efforts to know reality and transform the world. They were also full of optimism and confidence in the power of reason, the begetter of the scientific revolution, to contribute to the reform of society. Their great hope was that by establishing a succinct and reasonable creed to which all Christians in Europe could assent, philosophical enlightenment would solidify the basis and indispensable condition for any general improvement of society, in other words, that a rational or natural religion would help to reestablish permanently the peace that had been broken by the bloody wars between Catholics and Protestants. During the next century, Hume's critique of rational theology, will be mostly ignored, but in his case, in contrast to Pascal's, because he was generally perceived to be an infidel. Nevertheless, in his appraisal of the impotence of reason to account for the truth of the peculiar doctrines of the Christian faith, and further, in pointing out to the passionate or sentimental side of human nature as the foundation of the beliefs that fill our spirit and guide our lives, Hume, the man of little faith, coincides with the Pyrrhonian mysticism of Pascal, the man of tragic faith.[11]

In spite of Pascal's attempt to reivindicate historical Christianity, a great number of rationalist philosophers after Descartes continued to view traditional religious representations of the Deity as the products of unrestrained imagination, ignorance, superstition and fear. All these, they thought, transform the face of God into a coarsely anthropomorphic image, which frequently displays a minimum of humanity and an excess of capriciousness and cruelty. Not only these deformations are patent in beliefs that come from the remote past of humankind or are countenanced by barbarous people, but even in dogmas developed and consecrated by the most subtle and specious medieval and modern theology, Catholic as much as Protestant. As such aberrations, the doctrines of predestination and eternal damnation of most human beings are commonly referred to by the deists.

But natural religion, that is, the religious rationalism that was inaugurated by Descartes (who was himself orthodox with respect to the subordination of reason to faith), none the less began very soon to follow various heterodox paths, developing in three directions: pantheism, deism and, in some thinkers of the Enlightenment at the end of the eighteenth century, atheism. As a matter of fact, there were only few major differences to be found in the speculative and practical principles of the archetypal exponents of those tendencies. As we shall see in what immediately follows, the most substantive has to do with the manner of in which the relationship between God and nature, or the universe, is conceived.

Admittedly, any attempt to classify a philosopher so complex and profound as Baruch or Benedict Spinoza (1632–1677) is doomed to be equivocal and simplistic

---

[11] An interesting comparison of Pascal and Hume, is found José R. Maia Neto, "Hume and Pascal: Pyrrhonism vs. Nature," *Hume Studies* 17, no. 1 (April 1991): 41–49.

from the start; yet, in the confined context of the development of natural religion, it is not entirely inappropriate to consider him as the representative *par excellence* of pantheism, at least in so far as he asseverates that there exists only one infinite reality, God, which is identical with nature (*Deus sive natura*). It is well known that Spinoza coherently develops in a pantheistic direction Descartes' metaphysical presuppositions. The latter had admitted the existence of three kinds of substances: the finite thinking substance, or the self (the souls), the indefinite extended substance (the bodies), and the infinite thinking substance (God). Spinoza reduces them to one: God. If substance (*res*) is anything that does not need any other thing in order to exist, then God is, strictly speaking, the sole substance. In itself God has an infinite number of attributes of which human beings know only two: thought and extension.

In the *Theological-Political Treatise,* Spinoza indicates that natural religion (which he calls "universal religion") is the true religion, and consists in the simple rational acknowledgment of a handful of theoretical and practical truths about the Deity: his existence, omnipresence and supremacy; our need of worshipping Him exclusively through acts of love (*charitas*) and justice; the salvation of all those who obey him and the condemnation of those who don't, and his forgiveness for those who are sincerely penitent.[12]

There are, in spite of their innumerable similarities, two features that clearly differentiate English deism from Continental pantheism. First, although deism was influenced by Descartes and particularly by Spinoza, yet in contrast to the pantheism of Spinoza, English deistic thinkers, generally speaking, will deny the divine immanence. Second, the philosophical roots of English deism are indigenous. During Descartes' lifetime (1645), a book is published that anticipates some of the most famous deistic theses that were to be heatedly discussed at the end of the seventeenth and the beginning of eighteenth century, to wit, Herbert of Cherbury's, *The Religion of the Gentiles*.[13]

Concerning the first point, God, according to deism, has no other relationship with the world beyond his act of creating it and bestowing perfect order and harmony on all its operations. God certainly reveals himself in nature, for it is His work, but God is not nature. Deism, contrary to pantheism, stresses the absolute transcendence of the Deity with respect to the world. In this it coincides with traditional Christianity; but like pantheism, it maintains that God sufficiently and un-

---

[12] Benedict de Spinoza, *A Theological-Political Treatise and A Political Treatise,* trans. R. H. M. Elwes (New York: Dover Publications, Inc., 1951) ch. 4, "Of the divine law," pp. 55-68.

[13] Herbert of Cherbury, *De religione gentilium* (London: 1645). At any rate, such is the opinion of Sir Leslie Stephen, in a work whose first volume, in spite of its relative old age, continues to be the classic presentation, as it were, of the life, passion and death of deism in England: *History of English Thought in the Eighteenth Century*, 2 vols., 1876, 3rd ed. 1902 (New York and Burlingame: Harcourt, Brace and World, 1962), I, 70. According to Stephen, Cherbury in *Tractatus de Veritate*, a subsequent work, offers a list of rational precepts concerning the divine Being that is almost identical to Spinoza's. For a valuable study of Hume's relationship with deism, see J. O' Higgins, "Hume and the Deists," *The Journal of Theological Studies* 22 (1971): 479-501.

ambiguously reveals himself to human reason in the order exhibited by nature. Hence there is no need for any special revelation to be exclusively bestowed only on those who have faith in a supernaturally countersigned authority.

In the manner of Descartes, the English deists proclaimed the harmony between revelation and reason, but unlike him, they almost immediately began to repudiate the former in the name of the latter. Hence in a much open, albeit less subtle and scholarly, manner than Spinoza they pretended to cast out of traditional religion all supernatural dogmas, along with any external evidences or revelation that might entail mysteries, prophesies or miracles; at once they also declared that supplications and prayers are altogether vain and illusory. The titles of some of the most notorious deistic works give a very good inkling as to their general attitude of frank hostility to religion: Thomas Woolston (1666–1733), *Free Gifts to the Clergy, Six Discourses on the Miracles* [14]; Peter Annet (1693–1769), *The Resurrection of Jesus Examin'd by a Moral Philosopher* [15]; Conyers Middleton (1683–1750), *Free Enquiry into the Miraculous Powers.* [16]

On the whole, the deists drew the consequence that Descartes apparently was not willing to deduce, namely, that faith and supernatural revelation are redundant, and that reason suffices for the fulfillment of all of our religious and ethical obligations. Hume himself, while analyzing in the *History of England* the political doctrines of the deists, takes the dogmatical and absolute rejection of faith and divine revelation as the distinctive feature of that group:

> The second [group of opponents of King Charles I] were the deists, who had no other object than political liberty, who denied entirely the truth of revelation, and insinuated, that all the various sects, so heated against each other, were alike founded in folly and in error (H, VI, 59). [17]

But to come back to the second point, the deists, in general, did not derive these conclusions, which were contrary to traditional faith, precisely from Cartesian rationalist premises. Curiously enough, they were not altogether inconsistent developments of John Locke's empiricist philosophy, who in this aspect, even influenced Hume himself. For this reason, it may be worthwhile to indicate how Locke

---

[14] Thomas Woolston, *Free Gifts to the Clergy, Six Discourses on the Miracles* (London, 1727–1730).

[15] Peter Annet, *The Resurrection of Jesus Examin'd by a Moral Philosopher* (London, 1740).

[16] Conyers Middleton, *Free Enquiry into the Miraculous Powers* (London, 1748).

[17] Hume's estimate about the nature of deism is reasserted in his description of king Charles II inconstancy of character, who in his moments of physical vigor and mental acuteness exhibited such "a contempt and disregard to all religion," that then "he might more properly be denominated a deist than a catholic" (H, VI, 185).

is linked to arguably the two most important figures of English deism: John Toland (1670–1722)[18] and Matthew Tindal (1657?–1733).[19]

In spite of their many differences, the philosophers and theologians who defended traditional orthodoxy and the deists, had in common a rationalistic basis. It was this starting point that made the controversy possible in the first place. However real and bitter their particular disagreements may have been, still the differences between them were – as Hume himself appears to suggest at the end of the *Dialogues* (DNR, 217–216) – more of degree than of species. This shared philosophical ancestry is easier to appreciate in the archetypal representatives of orthodoxy and deism, respectively: John Locke and John Toland. According to the first, *"Reason must be our last judge and guide in everything."*[20] For the second, *"Reason* is the only Foundation of all Certitude."[21]

It may reasonably be objected that it is improper to present Locke as an exemplar of orthodoxy, not only because of his rationalistic attitude towards religious truth, but also because of the well-establish fact of his alliance to heterodox views, such as Socianism and Arianism. In a general sense, and from a strictly historical perspective, one can concede the validity of that objection. However, from the present, and certainly narrow, perspective offered by the complete rejection of faith and revelation that, as we have just seen, Hume took to be the kernel of deism, one can justifiably consider Locke to be a sincere believer in, and defender of, the established faith, even though he might have questioned a handful of its theological dogmas. In fact, Hume appears to consider this to be the case with respect to Locke. So he casually remarks in the *Natural History of Religion:* "I maintain, that Newton, Locke, Clarke, &c. being *Arians* or *Socinians*, were very sincere in the creed they professed: And I always oppose this argument to some libertines, who will needs have it, that it was impossible but that these philosophers must have been hypocrites" (NHR, 64).

So the orthodox Locke, unlike Pascal, does not seem to believe that there is any absurdity in the idea of a reasonable Christian religion.[22] Reason, in effect, is capable by itself of knowing some of the central truths about God and our duties to-

---

[18] John Toland, *Christianity not Mysterious*, (London: 1696); Reprint of the 1st ed. (New York & London: Garland Publishing Co., 1978).

[19] Matthew Tindal, *Christianity as Old as the Creation: Or, The Gospel, A Republication of the Religion of Nature* (London, 1730); Reprint of the first ed. (New York & London: Garland Publishing Co., 1978).

[20] John Locke, *An Essay Concerning Human Understanding*, ed. A. C. Frazer, 2 vols. (New York: Dover, 1959), II, Part IV, ch. 18, "Of Faith and Reason, and of their Distinct Provinces," pp. 438–439. In the preceding section, Locke had said the same even more unambiguously: "he who governs his assent right, and places it as he should, who, in any case or matter whatsoever, believes or disbelieves according as reason directs him" (ch. 17, pp. 414–415).

[21] John Toland, *Christianity not Mysterious*, reprint of the 1st ed. published in 1696 (New York and London: Garland Publishing, Inc., 1978), ch. 1, p. 6.

[22] Of course, this is made manifest by the title of his book. See John Locke, *The Reasonableness of Christianity, as Delivered in Scriptures* (London: 1695).

wards Him, and is in perfect harmony with the Christian revelation. On the one hand, the sober observation of nature proves the truth of Christendom,[23] and on the other hand, revelation does not contradict the principles of natural religion.[24] But no matter how orthodox Locke may have been, his rationalism is plain enough, since it is reason that has to determine in any case which doctrines and principles are to be considered as genuinely revealed by God: "Whatever God hath revealed is certainly true . . . but whether it be a divine revelation or no, reason must judge."[25] Still, revelation retains a necessary and primordial character, for according to the orthodox, reason cannot by itself disclose everything that is necessary for us in order to reach the holiness and righteousness on which our salvation depends; and no one can achieve it without the providential assistance and special revelation that Christian faith offers to human beings:

> God, out of the infiniteness of his mercy, has dealt with man, as a compassionate and tender Father. He gave him reason, and with it a law: that could not be otherwise than what reason should dictate; unless we should think, that a reasonable creature should have an unreasonable law. But, considering the frailty of man, apt to run into corruption and misery, he promised a Deliverer, whom in his good time he sent; and then declared to all mankind, that whoever would believe him to be the Saviour promised, and take him now raised from the dead, and constituted the Lord and Judge of all men, to be their King and Ruler, should be saved. This is a plain, intelligible proposition.[26]

In the *Discourse Concerning the Unchangeable Obligations of Natural Religion,* Samuel Clarke, chief defender of orthodoxy and admirer of Locke and Newton, formulates in an exemplary manner this conviction which is shared by all the opponents of deism:

> To remedy all these Disorders, and conquer all these Corruptions; there was plainly wanting some extraordinary and supernatural *Assistance*; which was above the reach of bare Reason and Philosophy to procure, and yet without

---

[23] John Locke, *An Essay Concerning Human Understanding*, II, Part IV, cap. X, "Of our Knowledge of the Existence of God", pp. 307–324.

[24] Ibid., ch. 17, pp. 412–414.

[25] Ibid., ch. 17, p. 425; see also, p. 424.

[26] John Locke, *The Reasonableness of Christianity, as Delivered in Scriptures,* in *The Works of John Locke,* 10 vols. (London: Thomas Tegg; W. Sharppe and son; G. Offor; J Evans and Co.: also R. Griffin and Co, Glasgow; and J. Cummins, Dublin, 1823; Reprinted by Scientia Verlag Aalen, Germany, 1963) VII, sec. 252. p. 157. See also sections 234–246 (pp. 134–151) where Locke numbers the reasons that made divine revelation indispensable for us.

which the Philosophers themselves were sensible there could never be any truly Great and Good Men.[27]

About the relationship between reason and faith, Locke's position approaches that of Saint Thomas Aquinas. In spite of Locke's consistent critique of Scholasticism, he takes over the threefold division of things that are contrary to reason, those that are according to it, and those that are above it.[28] The latter – the type of truths that deism attempts to get rid of – are the truths of faith: those things "that are *above reason*, when revealed, *are the proper matter of faith.*"[29]

For the deist Toland, on the other side, Christianity is so much reasonable that is not in the least mysterious. Although it is definitely the most perfect and true religion, the revelation it offers is just the means of communicating that truth to us, and not the reason why we should assent to it: "Not the bare Authority of him that speaks, but the clear Conception I form of what he says, is the *Ground of my Perswasion.*"[30] In this way, we dispense with the authority of the Church Fathers, general councils, and even Scripture interpreted literally or according to some "spurious Philosophy" that only systematically expounds long held sectarian prejudices. Natural religion, implanted at the beginning by the Creator in the hearts and minds of human beings, suffices for knowing and worshipping God. Revelation is at best a redundant complement, for reason is autonomous and capable by itself of disclosing the truth essential for our blessedness and well-being. One should even reject any presumed revelation if and when it depicts the Deity as behaving in a cruel, capricious or irrational manner, and issuing commands that demand from us a conduct of the same blameworthy nature; for it can be proved that "the Doctrines of the *New Testament* [are] perspicuous, possible, and most worthy of God, as well as all calculated for the highest Benefits of Man."[31] The subtitle of *Christianity not Mysterious* reveals clearly, and even militantly, both the common rationalism and

[27] Samuel Clarke, *A Discourse Concerning the Unchangeable Obligations of Natural Religion, and the Truth and Certainty of the Christian Revelation, Being Eight Sermons Preach'd at the Cathedral-Church of St. Paul, in the Year 1705, at the Lecture Founded by the Honourable Robert Boyle Esq.* (London, 1706), p. 239–240.

[28] Saint Thomas Aquinas, The *Summa Contra Gentiles*, trans. the English Dominican Fathers, 2 vols. (Burns, Oates & Washbourne, 1924), I, chs. 3–8, pp. 8–15.

[29] John Locke, *An Essay Concerning Human Understanding*, II, Part IV, ch. 18, p. 423. Locke (Ibid., p. 416) distinguishes reason from faith in the following terms:

Reason, . . . I take to be the discovery of the certainty or probability of such propositions or truths, which the mind arrives at by deduction made from such ideas, which has got by the use made of its natural faculties; viz. by sensation and reflection.

Faith, on the other side, is the assent to any proposition, not thus made out by the deductions of reason, but upon the credit of the proposer, as coming from God, in some extraordinary way of communication. This way of discovering truths to men, we call *revelation*.

[30] John Toland, *Christianity not Mysterious*, ch. 2, p. 38.

[31] Ibid., "The Conclusion", p. 174.

the core of the dispute with the philosophers who defended orthodox faith, such as Locke, Clarke, and perhaps even Newton himself.[32] Toland's work is "A Treatise shewing, That there is nothing in the Gospel Contrary to Reason, not Above it, And that no Christian Doctrine can be properly call'd A Mystery."

Despite his sharp hostility to supernaturalistic interpretations, Toland's deism will not in the end bring about a radical rupture with traditional Christianity. And in several cases his position is almost indiscernible from Locke's. A case in point is his judgment about the miracles and prophesies attributed to Jesus Christ. Locke takes miracles and prophesies to be guaranties of the divine character of the authority that reveals the doctrine whose truth the miracle or prophesy in question confirms: "It is to be considered, that divine revelation receives testimony from no other miracles, but such as are wrought to witness his mission from God who delivers the revelation."[33] Like Locke, Toland believes to be impossible that such putative facts could count as evidence for unintelligible or immoral doctrines. His express assent to traditional faith goes so far as to admit that the prophesies of Jesus are reasonable credentials of the divine nature of revelation, and therefore confirmation of the truth of his teachings: "to leave no room for doubt, he proves his Authority and Gospel by such Works and Miracles as the stiff-necked Jews themselves could not deny to be Divine."[34] What is then the core of his disagreement with Locke on this issue? Whereas for the Locke miracles confirm the authority of the person who proclaims doctrines which "are above reason," for Toland, on the other side, even though miracles serve as confirmation of true doctrines, these are not in principle unintelligible to us:

---

[32] Richard S. Westfall has plausibly argued in favor of the old thesis according to which Newton really was a deist; see his "Isaac Newton's *Theologiae Gentilis Origines Philosophicae,*" in *The Secular Mind: Essays Presented to Franklin L. Baumer,* ed. Warren Waggar (New York: Holmes & Meier Publishers, Inc., 1982), p. 15. In my opinion, James E. Force decisively refutes that interpretation in "Samuel Clarke's Four Categories of Deism, Isaac Newton, and the Bible," in *Scepticism and the History of Philosophy,* ed. Richard H. Popkin (Dordrecht: Kluwer Academic Publishers, 1996), pp. 53–74.

[33] John Locke, *A Discourse of Miracles,* in *The Works of John Locke,* IX, p. 257; see also *An Essay Concerning Human Understanding,* II, Part IV, ch. 19, pp. 439–440, and *The Reasonableness of Christianity,* sec. 237, p. 135:

> The evidence of our Saviour's mission from heaven is so great, in the multitude of miracles he did before all sorts of people, that what he delivered cannot but be received as the oracles of God, and unquestionable verity. For the miracles he did were so ordered by the divine providence and wisdom, that they never could be denied by any of the enemies or opposers of Christianity.

Locke's position is in this, again, apparently identical to that of Saint Thomas, who in the *Summa contra Gentiles,* I, ch. 9, p. 16 , says:

> In a special way may the opponent of this kind of truth [of faith] be convinced by the authority of Scripture confirmed by God with miracles: since we believe not what is above human reason save God has revealed it.

[34] John Toland, *Christianity not Mysterious,* ch. 3, p. 47.

Now to what purpose serv'd all these Miracles, all these Appeals, if no Regard was to be had of Mens Understandings? if the Doctrines of Christ were incomprehensible? or were we oblig'd to believe reveal'd Nonsense?[35]

Toland distances himself from most later deists by not classifying miracles as mysteries or events contrary to natural laws. Why is this so? There are at least two possible explanations that are not necessarily incompatible with each other: Toland might have not paid special attention to miracles, and hence rather focused his analysis on the doctrines themselves; or he might have not taken such presumed facts as miracles, but only as extraordinary occurrences. Even though Toland's stance is not completely exempted from ambiguity, I think that the text itself gives greater probability to the second interpretation: "miracles are produc'd according to the Laws of Nature, tho above its ordinary Operations, which are therefore supernaturally assisted."[36]

It appears therefore that Toland assented to the essentially historical character of miracles, at the least those of the New Testament, which was something that succeeding deists immediately questioned. The problem concerning the veracity of Holy Writ, considered simply as a historical text, is of some interest to us. Hume, himself a historian, will take this as the starting point of a very polemical argument of his own according to which it is not possible for any human testimony to establish the occurrence of a miracle that is presented as confirming the truth of a particular religion.[37]

The rejection of faith and traditional revelation is equally, if not more, pronounced in Matthew Tindal, the author of the most notorious book of English deism, *Christianity as Old as the Creation:*

FAITH consider'd in itself can neither be a Virtue, or a Vice; because Men can no otherwise believe than as Things appear to them: Nay, can there be an Higher Affront to God than to suppose, he requires Men to judge otherwise than the Faculties he has given them enable to them to do? Or what can be more absurd than to image, that God will shew his Favour to one for believing what he could not but believe; and his Displeasure to another for not believing what he could not believe.[38]

Tindal, just like Toland, considers that natural religion differs from revealed religion only in the manner in which we get to know it, but not in its contents, which is the same. With him, though, the Cartesian influence is dominant. Whereas we derive natural religion from innate ideas in ourselves, we obtain the revealed

---

[35] Ibid., p. 49.

[36] Ibid., ch. 4, pp. 156–157.

[37] See below, chapter 11.

[38] Matthew Tindal, *Christianity as Old as the Creation*, ch. 5, pp. 51–52.

kind from the external testimony represented by the life and doctrine of Jesus.[39]
The rebuff of revelation on Tindal's part shows a frankness that almost lacks decorum. Hence Tindal scoffs at the above-quoted passage of Clarke's *Discourse*, and even appears to enjoy himself immensely in presenting Clarke as an atheist who is ignorant of the fact. According to Tindal, it is contrary to God's infinite goodness to assert that He requires from human beings, as a condition for achieving perfect virtue and beatitude, a revelation for which human reason is effectively blind. Tindal ironically suggests that had this been the case, then one should have said, plainly and simply, that God is unjust, at least in so far as such a doctrine appears to imply "not only to be in vain, but a Crime in them [human beings], to endeavour to change that State [of universal Degeneracy and Corruption], in which, God, of his infinite Wisdom and Goodness, thought fit to place them."[40]

In regard to miracles, the distance that separates Tindal from Toland is greater than that which separates the latter from Locke. Even though Toland gives only an episodic and oblique consideration to this matter – leaving us to discern his position as a tacit corollary, without directly formulating it – , one may, however, reasonably affirm that he did not view miracles as events contrary to the regular course of nature.[41] And in this, Tindal appears to agree with Toland. Yet Tindal, with more self-assurance but much less philosophical penetration, goes farther than Toland by insinuating about most miracles that fall under his glance that they are but useful fabrications, or "pious Frauds" perpetrated by religious leaders for hastening the growth of their faith. In such a fashion he says that "the first Propagators" of any religion based on tradition, not on reason, deceive themselves as much as they deceive other people.[42] Moreover, and in contradistinction to Locke and even Toland himself, Tindal supposes that prophesies and miracles are completely unnecessary to confirm, or increase our confidence in, the certainty of the doctrines of true religion. Likewise he argues against Clarke, who in this only follows Locke:

And if the whole of Religion consists in the Honour of God, and the Good of Man . . . nothing can more effectually strike at the Certainty of all Religion,

---

[39] Ibid., ch. 1, p. 3.

[40] Ibid., ch. 14, p. 375, see also pp. 374–375, 389–390.

[41] Tindal asks, in a rhetorical manner, whether there are not "Examples in Scripture, which, taken in their literal Sense, seem to make God break in upon the common Course of Nature," and he immediately responds that "there must be some Mistake" in this sort of story (Ibid., ch. 13, p. 266); a bit farther, he almost leaves no room for any misunderstandings: "there are several Mistakes crept into the Old Testament; where there's scarce a Chapter, which gives any historical Account of Matters" (Ibid., 267). And in page 337, he intimates his denial of the supernatural character of miracles with comparable clearness but less caution. "ANOTHER difficulty in understanding both the Old and New Testament, is, that most Things, tho' owing to second Causes, are referr'd immediately to God."

[42] Ibid. ch. 13, p. 243. Hence, according to Tindal, "as you will find in Church-History, had afforded a Number of Miracles for the *Orthodox*, and as many Judgments on the *Heterodox*: And if there be Miracles on both Sides, ours to be sure are divine, and yours diabolical." (Ibid., ch. 11, p. 159). See also ch. 11, pp. 156–157; ch. 13, pp. 243, 326–327.

than the supposing, that Mankind cou'd not be certain, that whatever evidently tended to promote the Honour of God, and the Practice of Righteousness, was the Will of God, 'till they were convinc'd of it by undeniable Miracles.[43]

Yet if the Doctrines themselves, from their internal Excellency, do not give us a certain Proof of the Will of God, no traditional Miracles can do it; because one Probability added to another will not amount to Certainty.[44]

But as the subtitle of the book indicates, Tindal's main intention is to put the emphasis on a doctrine which complements the one Toland emphasizes: Christianity, that is, "the Gospel" is but a "Republication of the Religion of Nature." In such a defiant manner, Tindal formulates the typical deistic conception of a natural religion, not supernaturally revealed, which is as universal and permanent as is the reason that all human beings share; in it lies the truth of the Christian religion, whose task is simply to reiterate or "republish" the religion known to humankind since its beginnings.

But how does it come to pass that the history of at least the last fifteen hundred years of Christianity (not to say of all religions) is filled with so much violent fanaticism and so many shuddering and cruel images of the gods, and hence it is so difficult to detect even the blurred vestiges of that original and rational worship? Tindal's reply to this obvious objection is the one that will be given by all deism, and it consists in a servile, that is, uncritical and unsubstantiated, attachment to a secular version of a decadent view of human history, which conceives it as a fall from a state of initial perfection or purity, or as a degeneration from another sort of golden age. The difference between the orthodox and the deistic understanding of history is, again, of degree, not of substance, and it concerns the causes to which each group attributes the decline. Whereas the orthodox pointed, as was to be expected, to an ancestral act of disobedience to God, the deists on the other hand, had recourse to a no less subversive theory: to wit, the gradual corruption of the religion of nature must have been the work of the cunning artifice, fraud and deception of priestly castes and ecclesiastical hierarchies. The clergy foster tremendous fears in the mind of superstitious worshippers in order to secure their continued ascendancy over them and their own advantage, while at the same time deform the face of the Deity, making it unrecognizable by converting it into a terrible, arbitrary and despotic power:

Thus you see, how Fraud and Force are unavoidable, when 'tis believ'd Things, having no Foundation in Nature or Reason, are Necessary Parts of Religion; and Ecclesiastical History contains a continued Scene of Villany, for the Support of such Notions: And that the more good Sense, Piety, and Virtue any Man was

[43] Ibid., ch. 14, p. 372.

[44] Ibid., p. 374. See ch. 12, pp. 200, 204, where Tindal asserts that all doctrines inconsistent with the dictates of reason, "tho' they plead endless Miracles, must be look'd upon as diabolical Impostures."

endow'd with, the more, if he did not come into those Notions, was he hated and persecuted as a most dangerous Enemy.[45]

The more Superstition the People have, the earlier they may be impos'd on by designing Ecclesiasticks; and the less Religion the Clergy have, the more unanimous they will be in carrying on their common Interest; and when the Clergy are without Religion, and the People abound in Superstition, the Church, you may be sure, is in a flourishing Condition; but in great Danger, when Men place their Religion in Morality.[46]

Although Hume will share with the deists the conviction that the lost of personal and civil liberty is one major calamity commonly brought about by the superstition fostered by priests and ministers, yet he certainly will not explain the origins of such an illness in the same manner. On the other hand, he will question the decadent outlook on .history held by both deists and their Christian antagonists.[47]

The last development of natural religion is atheism, which is but the culmination of the naturalism subscribed both by pantheism and deism. Its most important representative is Paul Henri Thiri, Baron d'Holbach (1723–1789), who was one of the principal collaborators of the French Encyclopedia. Hume became a friend of Holbach while in Paris as Undersecretary of the British Embassy (1763–1766), and expressed "the sincere and inviolable attachment to him."[48] But the genuine sympathy that Hume had for the person of Baron d'Holbach in any way extended to his philosophical tenets.

The most important, thorough and philosophically developed statement of d' Holbach's naturalistic atheism is found in *The System of Nature*.[49] Pantheism rejects the traditional God and identifies God with nature; deism retains the creative and transcendent character of the traditional God; yet it discards mysteries, miracles, in short the supernatural, and looks for God exclusively in the intelligible order of nature. What atheism does is simply to close the circle: it expels God in order to

---

[45] Ibid., ch. 11, p. 164; see ch. 12, p. 192.

[46] Ibid., p. 169. It is easier for Tindal to speak more freely against Catholicism; however, what he says next (Ibid. p. 171) applies equally to all traditional ecclesiastical orders:

> The Popish Priests are so far from giving the People any just Idea of God, that they represent him as an arbitrary and tyrannical Being, imposing, on the highest Pain, the Practice of ridiculous Ceremonies, and the Belief in absurd Doctrines; as a fantastical Being, angry without Cause, and pleas'd without Reason; as a vain-glorious Being, fond of having his Ministers and Favourites, that is, themselves, live in Pomp, Splendor, and Luxury, to the Miserable Oppressions of the People.

Against religious leaders, Catholics as well as Protestants, he energetically expresses himself in ch. 13, pp. 312–315.

[47] Hopefully, this will be made clear specially in chapters 4, 5 and 6.

[48] L, II (Letter 485: To Jean-Baptiste-Antoine Suard), 275.

[49] Paul Henri Thiri, Baron d'Holbach, *Le système de la nature, ou des Lois du monde physique et du monde moral* (Paris, 1770).

embrace nature alone and its immanent laws. Ernest Mossner is quite right in suggesting that Hume may have felt an aversion for the dogmatical character and a priori nature of the atheism typical of d' Holbach and his inner circle of dinning guests at his home on Rue Royale.[50] Still, I think that Hume's misgivings about any atheism, such as Holbach's, do not precisely spring, as Mossner supposes, from Hume's presumed agnosticism.[51]

In the third part of this book, while analyzing the *Dialogues Concerning Natural Religion*, we shall consider the manner in which Hume critically examines, through the dialectical clash between the main characters of the piece, these three theoretical alternatives in which natural religion branches out, and ultimately rejects them. At the moment it will be enough to indicate, generally speaking, that the most important historical contribution of natural religion was practical rather than theoretical. Positively, natural religion, and deism in particular, expressed and fostered a spirit of intellectual autonomy. By diffusing it throughout society it hoped to influence public opinion, and thus combat and help overthrow outdated, excessively intolerant and oppressive doctrines and institutions that effectively obstructed the social improvement of the modern European nations and kingdoms. In other words, philosophical critique presented itself as a weapon against superstition. Since Hume culminates and brings to a close this culturally significant philosophical frame of mind, one may naturally ask the question: Does he continue to endorse, and even discharge, this civil office of natural religion? Quite apart from his trenchant criticism of the cognitive claims of rational theology, does Hume still share the conviction that true philosophy, in addition to its theoretical pleasures, also has an indispensable practical efficacy and social utility? Or does he rather give up that Enlightened optimism as just one more fantasy of a rationalism which loses sight of those brute facts of human nature that not only set narrow constraints to our efforts to know reality, but also to our utopian projects for a thorough reconstruction of human society.

Finally, and notwithstanding its almost Pascalian assessment of the overwhelming power of the passions and acutely critical awareness of the confined force of human understanding, can Hume's philosophy somehow become a worthy adversary of superstition? This is the question to be investigated in the section that follows.

---

[50] Ernest Mossner, *The Life of David Hume*, pp. 483–488.

[51] As I hope to be able to show in chapter 13, Hume's main objections to atheism can be gathered from criticisms made by various characters, especially in Parts VIII–IX of the *Dialogues Concerning Natural Religion,* to various naturalistic accounts of the order of the universe.

2.2 THE "MODEST" ENLIGHTENED AIMS OF HUME'S CRITIQUE OF RELIGION

David Hume is rightly considered to be "one of the most outstanding figures of the eighteenth-century Enlightenment."[52] Can we also justifiably say that he shared the Enlightened optimism about the power of philosophy to effectively influence society, educate and emancipate human beings from the obstinate dominion that superstition – or any kind of obscurantist, alienating and oppressive belief – exerts over their minds, and so contribute to their genuine progress. It has been generally taken for granted that he did. The most emphatic formulation of this outlook is offered by Peter Gay in his very important and influential book on the Enlightenment: "David Hume proclaimed philosophy the supreme, indeed the only, cure for superstition."[53]

This usual way of interpreting Hume's doctrine about the precise nature of the relationship between philosophy and superstition has been contradicted by James Dye in a lively and thought provoking article.[54] Overall this challenge is successful in so far as it shows that there are no good grounds for supposing that Hume had ever held the view that philosophy can eradicate superstition from human existence. What is problematic in this pessimistic thesis is that it falls into a position as extreme as the one it rejects, by foisting to Hume an almost complete scepticism, which is quite alien to the way in which he conceived the nature of philosophical investigation and its final aims.

Hume's reputation as one of the most important philosophers of the eighteenth century would not decrease, even if he had consistently maintained that philosophy is impotent against superstition. But if one ascribes such a doctrine to him, it would be extremely difficult, however, to continue viewing him as a major representative of the Enlightenment. The great difficulty in accepting this consequence is one of the reasons that have led me to delineate in what follows a middle-ground interpretation of Hume's aims, that is, a "modest," albeit still Enlightened, optimism. Such an interpretation, even though it has affinities with the pessimistic view, it sharply differs from it by recognizing a much greater efficacy to philosophy, as being a perpetual check to superstition, and a more extended social influence, and in doing this it better reproduces, I think, Hume's own opinion.

It is universally agreed upon that, for Hume, philosophy is our best weapon against superstition.[55] Yet, according to the negative view, it can never effectively

---

[52] José García Roca, *Positivismo e Ilustración: La Filosofía de David Hume*, p. 20. The English translation of that passage is mine.

[53] Peter Gay, *The Enlightenment: An Interpretation*, 2 vols. (New York: Alfred A. Knopf, 1975), I. p. 129.

[54] James Dye, "Hume on Curing Superstition," *Hume Studies*, 12, no. 2, (November 1986): 122–140.

[55] Perhaps forced by a too-compromising text, Dye has to admit that, according to Hume, philosophy can indirectly attack superstition, being in fact "the best weapon with which to oppose superstition" (Ibid., p. 122). He further admits that Hume held that his philosophy can counteract the false philosophy behind which superstition hides itself. Dye adds, however, that one thing is to unmask superstition

defeat it. But why? Where does precisely this incurable impotence of philosophy against superstition stems from? Philosophical critique would be incapable of changing the general climate of opinion in any given society because it can only influence that handful of men and women who due to "an accident of personal temperament" are philosophically predisposed.[56] According to Dye, Hume subscribes to a secular version of the Presbyterian doctrine of predestination: Philosophy and superstition are, in reality, "permanent alternative responses to human curiosity about the causes of events, which individuals choose on the basis of sentiment rather than reason. . . . Those who heed the call of philosophy are precisely those who are predispositionally foreordained to do so."[57]

What I find most objectionable in this thesis about Hume's presumably radical pessimism, is, in general, its connection with an interpretation of his thought that places a greater emphasis on the theoretical results of his grandiose philosophical project than on the its basic intentions: the ethical, political and even religious ends that animate it. Hence, the conclusions at the end of Book I of the *Treatise* are exaggerated, and are made equivalent to a radical scepticism that would finally even undermine the intelligibility of Hume's own philosophy. If this is so, then of course the "rational credentials" of philosophy "seem no more valid than those of superstition."[58] It is still granted that Hume recommends the former over the latter, but only due to practical, mainly psychological, considerations, for, after all, philosophy is not, theoretically speaking, superior to superstition. It is rather that philosophy is an amusing activity that does not greatly disrupt the natural course of our inclinations, and thus maintains us in a state of ease and tranquillity. What justifies philosophy, according to this interpretation, is not the idea of progress but an Epicurean ideal.

Yet, this *ataraxia*, which is conceived in narrowly hedonistic terms, neither is the only, nor the principal advantage of philosophy over superstition. For Hume openly contradicts this in another passage of the same text of the *Treatise*, where he also plainly points to a typically Enlightened goal. Although it is true that if he did not do philosophy, he "should be a loser in point of pleasure," (THN, 271) it nonetheless true that he exercises such an activity with the hope "of contributing to the instruction of mankind" (THN, 271). In addition, when Hume is interpreted in such a pessimistic and radically sceptical fashion one loses sight of the fact that he

---

and another quite different to vanish it. That philosophy has no such power, he attempts to establish by means of a somewhat questionable reinterpretation of passages from essays that Hume wrote during the period after the publication of the *Treatise* and before that of the *Natural History*, such as "Of Superstition and Enthusiasm" (E, 73–79) and "The Sceptic" (E, 159–180). In these works, the explicit sense of Hume's words appears to suggest that philosophy has a more efficacious role: thus, for instance, in the essay "Of Superstition and Enthusiasm," whose principal aim is to analyze the effect of these on civil liberty (whether they foment or hamper it), Hume asserts that "nothing but philosophy is able to conquer these unaccountable terrors" of superstition (E, 75).

[56] James Dye, "Hume on Curing Superstition," p. 126.

[57] Ibid., p. 137.

[58] Ibid., p. 124.

did not only rejected all kinds of dogmatism, religious as well as secular,[59] but also what he denominated Pyrrhonian or excessive scepticism.[60] That is why he bestows the name of mitigated scepticism on his own dominant philosophical position.

If one bears all of this close in mind, then one should rather say that with respect to the potentialities of philosophy for educating the human spirit and becoming a causative factor of eminently progressive historical transformations, Hume's consistent attitude is neither of excessive optimism nor of radical pessimism. In spite of all these qualifications, does not the pessimist outlook still appear to be closer to the truth? For, after all, the roots of superstition lie very deep in the permanent and universal spiritual framework of human nature and in circumstances which unavoidably confront all human life. Indeed, in this respect Hume shows himself to be more the outspoken critic than the archetypal figure of the Enlightenment. Still, this does not make him a pessimist either, for – as we shall see in chapter 6 – he likewise attacked *The Natural History of Religion* what has been commonly called the "Golden Age" or "Paradisiacal" view of history, as a sort of fall or process of continuous degeneration of human nature, while holding a conception of history as one of slow but not altogether straightforward progress. But that philosophy is, according to Hume, powerless to definitively overthrow superstition from the dominion it has over the minds of most persons and so prevent the many evils its brings into their lives, shows that he was no unqualified optimist either. All of this also shows that Hume rejected the Enlightened idea according to which the prodigious dissemination of knowledge promoted by the philosophic spirit, and its methodical application through the agency of empirical sciences to political and social problems, would progressively and inevitably lead to the perfectibility of humankind. Additional evidence that appears to corroborate this "modest," or cautious and conditioned, endorsement of Enligthment's aims is Hume's last conversation with Adam Smith,[61] as the latter relates in a letter to

---

[59] In "Of the Original Contract" Hume rhetorically asks whether to talk of philosophers who have embraced a party is a contradiction in terms. (E, 469). On the other hand, Hume believes that this *"Spirit of Impartiality"* is what motivates his philosophy and at the same time what the latter encourages; on the other hand, it is what has guided him in the composition of *The History of England*. See E. C. Mossner, *The Life of David Hume*, 2 ed., p. 637, textual supplement from p. 485, n. 3.

[60] Most probably, Hume misinterprets the nature of the actual or historical phenomenon that Pyrrhonian scepticism really was, as Ezequiel de Olaso asserted in *Escepticismo e Ilustración* (Valencia, Venezuela: Universidad de Carabobo, 1981). Yet even if it were the case that the conception which Hume disseminates were "untenable" (p. 21), or that "his interpretation of Pyrrhonism is false," this would in no way affect the substance of our claim, namely, that Hume rejected the scepticism to which he gave the epithet of Pyrrhonian.

[61] "Letter from Adam Smith to William Strahan," supplement to Kemp Smith's edition of Hume's *Dialogues Concerning Natural Religion*, pp. 243–248.

William Strahan, and a letter to Anne-Robert-Jacques Turgot, the famous philosopher of progress and physiocrat economist.[62]

What factors account for the historical stubbornness of superstition as well as for the incapacity of philosophical critique to vanish it? In general, such opposed systems of attitudes, beliefs and practices stem from the permanent propensity of the mind to search for the causes of phenomena. They are, according the pessimistic view forcefully asserted by Dye, permanent alternative potentialities of the mind that are actualized by different individuals not on the basis of a deliberate rational choice, but out of the particular innate disposition of each individual's temperament. Due to it, it is not possible to eradicate superstition from the minds of those which are congenitally afflicted by it.[63]

There are, I think, no good reasons to attribute to Hume that gloomy assessment. Let us grant that philosophy cannot uproot superstition; yet this does not imply that, according to Hume, it is basically ineffective against it, or able to conquer entirely the terrors only in those who are in no need of it, since they are already predisposed to philosophize and devoid by their peculiar temperament of those hopes and fears upon which superstition feeds itself. Given the natural or innate inequality of mental endowments that such almost Platonic reading of Hume seems to suggest, and if we take into account the ubiquity of the conditions that engender superstition, what truly appears as an almost miraculous event is that superstition had not long since emerged as the indisputable victor. The inborn inequality of human beings that this interpretation implies is difficult to reconcile with Hume's emphatic declarations in his political writings about the natural equality of men. In "Of Polygamy and Divorces" he talks about the natural equality of mankind" (E, 185); meanwhile in "Of the Social Contract" he attenuates his expression a bit in order to refer to "the equality, or something approaching equality, which we find in all the individuals of that species." (E, 468). But even here, it is not character, but education the factor to which he assigns the individual differences: "how nearly equal all men are in their bodily force, and even in their mental powers and faculties, till cultivated by education" (E, 467–468).

Although philosophy and superstition may be permanent alternative responses to human curiosity concerning the causes of events, they are not the answers given only or mainly by different types of individuals. The purely superstitious person or the "mere philosopher" are more ideal types than empirical realities. Amidst his philosophy, as Hume would say, the philosopher is still a man, and as such also prone to feel "the incessant hopes and fears, which actuate the human mind" (NHR, 27). The control of superstition over the person is, like philosophy's, intermittent:

---

[62] L, II, 179–181. With respect to the thesis about the inevitability of the progress brought about by the diffusion of knowledge, Hume comments: "You see, I give you freely my Views of things, in which I wish earnestly to be refuted: The contrary Opinion is much more consolatory, and is an Incitement to every Virtue and laudable" (L, II, 181).

[63] "Whoever is truly of a superstitious bent of mind has his heart permanently hardened against philosophy so that every reason marshaled against his course of life makes it that so much meritorious – *credo quia absurdum est.* James Dye, "Hume on Curing Superstition," p. 124.

its "empire" over the mind is "wavering and uncertain" (NHR, 62), and "it acts only by intervals on the temper" (DNR, 222). For the most part we are both the philosopher and the superstitious. Their persistent struggle primarily occurs within the mind of each of us, and not so much or exclusively between individuals of opposite turns of mind. Reasonableness and folly rather seem to partake more of the nature of alternating moods connected in a periodic movement, in a way similar to the oscillation, or "the flux and reflux of polytheism and theism" (NHR, 45–48) that perpetually takes place in the mind of the religionist. Each of us is susceptible to assume both attitudes, but the degree to which anyone may be prone to either may vary markedly from one person to another, thus making one person more readily identifiable than another as either superstitious or reasonable. And indeed innate temperament may account for those wide differences.

Nevertheless, philosophy and superstition appear to be, generally speaking, more the products of art – that is, of habit and education – than of inborn talent. On the one hand, superstition, Hume says, "arises naturally and easily from the popular opinions of mankind" (THN, 271), whereas on the other hand, he also remarks, that "more than half of those opinions, that prevails among mankind to be owing to education" (THN, 117). Moreover, in the essay "The Sceptic" Hume points out that character itself is not something which is entirely fixed by nature, for it can be improved by "the prodigious effects of education" (E, 170). Even if it is true that in "Of Superstition and Enthusiasm," Hume derives the superstitious beliefs from a certain kind of weak character, yet in *The Natural History of Religion*, the superstitious beliefs themselves are the determining factors in the formation of moral character(NHR, 51–53). In summary, if most superstitious attitudes and beliefs are, for Hume, the products of education, then one cannot see why superstition must necessarily be incorrigible by philosophy.

However, even if it is not education, after all, the factor which may lead us to excel in either practice and become either professional philosophers or priests, temperament *per se* does not have to extinguish, except in rare or pathological cases, those other capacities in us which may incline us to appreciate and even exercise the opposite activity. No matter how strong the dose or regimen of philosophy or superstition, no one is totally immunized against either condition.

Under this modified version, or moderate optimism, it still does not follow that philosophy can ever definitively cure superstition. But it does not follow either that philosophy is totally innocuous. Indeed, it can do very little against the natural terrors or the fears *antecedent* to superstition, "the anxious concern for the events of life" (NHR, 27); the conditions which provoke them are omnipresent and unavoidable. But perhaps it can do something against "the artificial terrors," as Hume calls them, or fears *consequent* to superstition, which man directs to "his imaginary enemies, the daemons of his fancy, who haunt him with superstitious terrors, and blast every enjoyment of life" (DNR, 195). In Part II of the *Treatise* Hume declares that reason, that is causal reasoning, can extinguish a desire, or a fear, or a hope by showing us that these are "founded on false suppositions" (THN, 416), or in other words, by showing us that the object we wish or expect does not really exist. Philosophy could then perhaps alleviate the fears of those "imaginary enemies" in the same manner, that is, by showing that the superstitious object we fear or hope for does not really exist. This must happen, for "the moment we perceive the false-ness of a supposition . . . our passions yield to our reason without any opposition" (THN, 415).

Superstition will yield to our reason, although not without opposition and for-ever, because it is precisely education – the constant repetition of creeds and rituals – , and not so much the individual temper, that is responsible for its penetrating and obstinate influence (NHR, 60). Hume even predicts the easy victory of philo-sophical education at the end of Book I of the *Treatise*. Since superstition is founded on principles " which are changeable, weak, and irregular . . . neither un-avoidable to mankind, nor necessary," and since these are opposed to custom and reasoning, hence they "may easily be subverted by a due contrast and opposition" (THN, 225–226). Hume might have moderated this optimism later in *The Natural History of Religion*, but he never wholly abandoned it. This is clearly shown in the introduction to the essay "Of Suicide," a work that Hume wrote more or less during the same period and intended to publish along with the *Natural History*, but was forced to suppress at the last moment:

> One considerable advantage that arises from Philosophy, consists in the sovereign antidote which it affords to superstition and false religion. All other remedies against that pestilent distemper are vain, or at least uncertain. . . . But when sound Philosophy has once gained possession of the mind, superstition is effectually excluded; and one may safely affirm, that her triumph over this en-emy is more compleat than over most of the vices and imperfections incident to human nature. Love or anger, ambition or avarice, have their root in the temper and affections, which the soundest reason is scarce ever able fully to correct. But superstition being founded on false opinion, must immediately vanish when true philosophy has inspired juster sentiments of superior powers. The contest is here more equal between the distemper and the medicine, and nothing can hinder the latter from proving effectual, but its being false and sophisticated (E, 577–579).

Truth is the only thing that philosophy can oppose to superstition and to any kind of oppressive belief, and if truth cannot set us free, then there is no other thing that will be able to do it. Such seems to be Hume's final verdict in this passage. It is, in addition, the textual evidence that supports the thesis of Peter Gay which was mentioned at the beginning of this chapter. Moreover, this is not the only text that militates against the pessimistic view of philosophy's social influence: in Volume II of the *History of England*, which must have been written after the essay "Of Suicide," Hume forcefully expresses, even employing the same medical metaphor, his firm conviction about the civilizing role that philosophy performs and should never relinquish:

> The view of human manners, in all their variety of appearances, is both prof-itable and agreeable; and if the aspect in some periods seems horrid and de-

formed, we may thence learn to cherish with the greater anxiety that *science and civility*, which has so close a connexion with virtue and humanity, and which, as it is *a sovereign antidote against superstition*, is also the most effectual remedy against vice and disorders of every kind (H, II, 518–519; italics added).

Once one gives serious regard to these emphatic texts, then one can clearly see the need to at least substantially modify the contention about the alleged impotence of philosophy against superstition.

For all those reasons I propose a more positive view: in brief, that in addition to its modest capacity to oppose the "false philosophy" which serves as "a shelter to superstition" (EHU, 16), philosophy can act as a perpetual check to those excesses in thought and deed which the superstitious passions may lead us to commit. These, like all "the blind motions of the affections" when not guided by the understanding, can "incapacitate men for society" (T, 493). The strongest condemnation that philosophy can address particularly against religious superstition is not that it falls into theoretical and moral errors, but that by nurturing intolerance, enmity, cruelty and violence towards others it utterly harms our humanity. And when human beings "mutually discharge on each other that sacred zeal and rancour, the most furious and implacable of all human passions" (NHR, 49), militant sects may produce as well the greatest social and historical turmoils. But superstition may also cloud our vision; by reducing men and women to passivity and submission, it obliterates their capacity to think by themselves, which is what the Enlightenment thinkers, with unanimous voice, exhort us to do. Simply put, superstition enslaves the whole human being.

That is why Hume forcefully stresses the positive attitudes and feelings that he thought his philosophy could nurture and disseminate, and which seem to be, more or less, the opposite of the evils of superstition just mentioned. His mitigated scepticism aims at making us aware of our own ignorance and fallibility, and so stimulates modesty and caution in all our determinations, which in turn may lead us to have more indulgence to the opinions and more respect for the persons of our antagonists (EHU, 161–162). The bigot is the typical antithesis of this human ideal of moderation, generosity and reasonableness; yet that aberrant type is, as Hume himself reiterates in the *History of England*, more the outcome of ignorance and the vicissitudes of personal experience than of innate temperament. Thus, by contrast, he brings to the forefront the virtues that his mitigated scepticism seeks to spread in his portrayal of the personality of Queen Mary Tudor (*Bloody Mary*):

Naturally of a sour and obstinate temper, and irritated by contradiction and misfortunes, she possessed all the qualities fitted to compose a bigot; and her extreme ignorance rendered her utterly incapable of doubt in her own belief, or of indulgence to the opinions of others. (H, III, 407).

"To live at ease ever after" (EHU, 12): This goal of his investigation of human understanding may well point to an Epicurean aim, although it may also be a way of calling to our attention the social values that sustain and at the same time are encouraged by philosophical investigation and dialogue. Hume seems to suggest that philosophy can teach all persons something about the way to live with each other, and that to that extent it can contribute to the development of their humanity and their real progress.

It is true that in the *Enquiry Concerning Human Understanding* Hume's claims about the beneficial effects of his practice on society are quite modest. One has to recognize too that he presents his philosophy as an opponent of "false philosophy" rather than as a vanquisher of superstition. Nonetheless, when he recommends his philosophy as the means to overthrow the false one, he does not seem to limit his recommendation only to those persons who are destined by temperament to heed his call. Hume, on the contrary, makes his philosophical exhortation with an unrestricted claim of universality, seemingly appealing to our human nature, and perhaps manifesting still, in a mitigated manner, the not-totally extinguished hopes of the Enlightenment:

> Accurate and just reasoning is the only *catholic* remedy fitted for *all* persons and *all* dispositions (EHU, 12, italics added)

But by and large, philosophy cannot, and even less inevitably, overthrow historical forces, such as superstition and religious fanaticism, that stand in the way of the material progress and spiritual and moral development of human beings. At best, it can only restrain them again and again.

PART II

The Origin, Development and Historical Effects of Religious Beliefs

CHAPTER 3

The Nature of Hume's Investigation of Religion

Is *The Natural History of Religion* an empirical hypothesis that seeks to account for the rise and diversity of historical religions? Or is it rather a second-order task, a philosophical reflection on the religious life of humanity, attempting to assess its ultimate significance for a human existence viewed within the framework of the whole of reality or Nature? Because this work is, so to speak, at the crossroads between philosophy and what we now call science, it seems to lend support to both possibilities of interpretation. Hume was writing at a time when neither discipline was sharply distinguished;[1] he is, perhaps, doing both things; and the question is, which of the two constitutes the substantive theoretical task of the *Natural History*.

But if it is the case that these points of view are not really contradictory, then why should we embark on a controversy that seems to be only one of emphasis? After all, Hume, speaking through Philo at the end of the *Dialogues Concerning Natural Religion*, has emphatically remarked that there is no possible way to solve a dispute if it is exclusively one of degrees (DNR, 227–228). Certainly, almost always this would be enough to abandon such a quarrel. The overall appraisal of the theoretical value of Hume's investigation into the history of religion will be quite diverse depending on which of these two trends one judges to be the dominant one, i.e., that of the positive scientist or that of the speculative philosopher.

Those who hail Hume for his pioneering work in opening new fields for the objective and rigorous approach of empirical science do so in a strange way. Very much aware of the manifest inadequacy of most of Hume's specific theories, and viewing the *Natural History* through methodological canons of a latter-day scientific research into society and history, they easily assume a sympathetic but patronizing attitude towards his work. Thus *The Natural History of Religion* is typically seen as "an entertaining exercise an arm-chair anthropology from secondary sources".[2]

---

[1] See e.g., John Passmore, *Hume's Intentions*, p. 9.

[2] D. C. G. MacNabb, "David Hume," *Encyclopedia of Philosophy*, ed. Paul Edwards, IV (New York and London: Macmillan, Inc., 1967), 89.

But to those to whom the contemplation of the flights of the philosophical imagination does not give vertigo, it is precisely its speculative audacity that constitutes the virtue of Hume's work on the religious, and not a vice or mistake due to a kind of methodological misbehavior. For them, Hume's interest in the *totality* of human experience, that comes forth very strongly in the *Natural History*, even transforms him into a precursor of the universal outlook typical of the philosophies of religion of German Idealism.[3]

Both dimensions are present in the *Natural History*; nonetheless it is the empirical aspect that has received all the attention, almost totally eclipsing the speculative one. Yet, even if a speculative or metaphysical theory is not developed in that book, its possibility is to a limited extent adumbrated by Hume's broad historical vision of religion. Furthermore it is the second interpretation which is, philosophically speaking, not only more interesting, but even perhaps more consistent with the ultimate foundations of his philosophy, as he defined these in the *Treatise*. In what immediately follows I shall try to justify this contention.

In *The Natural History of Religion* Hume set out to determine the real origins and essential characteristics of religion and religious representations of the divine such as they appear in the world. On the one hand, he deals with religion as we come to know it through experience, i.e., through direct acquaintance or through the testimony of others, both contemporaries and predecessors. In this broad sense, the term 'experience' encompasses in principle the whole history of the human species; thus it is the religious life of humankind, as it unfolds and continues to unfold itself in the course of time into an immense, rich and complex multiplicity of distinct and particular forms, the phenomenon whose genesis and development Hume has to grasp conceptually.

Hume's real interest lies not in the in-depth examination of the enormous and disconcerting multitude of variegated religious manifestations for what they have that is unique or peculiar, He does not bother to make a complete catalogue of them; he does not care to trace a relatively exact chronological sequence in which each and every form of the religious life would find its temporal position, and much less does he proceeds to assign determinate causes for the emergence and development of particular cases as such. He does indeed assign causes for them, but only in so far as they are viewed as individual instances or types of a very general nature.

Hume is concerned with the history of religion: yet one cannot say that *The Natural History of Religion* is an historiographical enterprise in the sense that his own *History of England* undoubtedly is. In the former work he manifested a candid trust in the fidelity of his sources – an impressive and heterogeneous collection of ancient and modern, pagan and Christian, testimony – from which he gathers the historical facts. One is left with the impression that he has not quite critically questioned the status of his sources as providers of true accounts of real happenings. In

---

[3] Roberto Torretti, *Hume y la religión*, Ediciones Revista Atenea, Separata del Núm. 395 de la Revista Atenea (Santiago de Chile: Editorial Universitaria, S. A.), pp. 29–30.

dealing with religious history, Hume seems to have taken for granted that the relevant facts are well attested to and well-known, and that the real task before him consists, not in offering an imaginative interpretation of the mass of details of the religious phenomena, but rather in framing the most comprehensive pattern of interpretation possible by means of which their genesis and overall dynamics of development would be intelligibly presented. It is not quite the case that Hume is blind to the richness, vitality and complexity of religion; his book is heavily sprinkled with a large collection of examples of religious beliefs, practices, institutions, and especially aberrations, taken from the most diverse epochs and places; in fact, most of the literary beauty and delight of the book derives from the sprightly and lively manner in which these are intercalated with his main arguments.[4]

Yet Hume's basic intention is not to immerse himself in the description of the multiplicity of religious phenomena; his aim is to reduce the multiplicity to unity, and also to arrest the permanent features and necessary stages in their temporal flux. Thus he defines the task of explaining the origin of religion in human nature as one of determining "what those principles are which give rise to the original belief, and what those accidents and causes are, which direct its operation" (NHR, Introduction, 21). In other words, *The Natural History of Religion* exhibits one of the overriding motives of Hume's philosophical inquiry – the Newtonian ambition to frame universal laws which may be able to explain the greatest possible number of facts by reducing them to their simplest and fewest causes. Accordingly this work is a *natural* history not only because it is a modern exemplar of an old literary genre, that is, the "natural history" of manifold human manners and cultural institutions,[5] but primarily because it is the culmination of Hume's "attempt to introduce the experimental method of reasoning into moral subjects".[6] It is an integral part of the general science of human nature, the constitution of which he began in his early youth in the *Treatise*, where he tried to give that science its philosophical foundations.

Furthermore, the natural character of this work refers to the fact that it is a search for natural, not for supernatural, causes of the events in question; Hume purports not to go beyond human experience; his theories shall not make use of occult or un-perceivable entities, and the search for universal explanations shall be

---

[4] However, the actual selection of his examples does not quite make Hume a model of methodological scrupulosity; on the contrary, is here that we have a clear manifestation of his personal biases against popular religions; almost all of his examples are intended to do one job: to show how bad and harmful religion has been and still is. We shall dwell on this subject in chapter 8.

[5] There is an abundant bibliography on the genre of "natural history". The following works throw much light on the subject: Gladys Bryson, *Man and Society: The Scottish Inquiry of the Eighteenth Century*, especially pp. 87–92, 105–113; Ernst Cassirer, *The Philosophy of the Enlightenment*, chs. 2 and 4, and Robert Nisbet, *Social Change and History: Aspect of the Western Theory of Development* (New York and London: Oxford University Press, 1969), ch. 4, pp. 139–158. With respect to its bearing on Hume's *Natural History of Religion*, see Peter Harrison, *'Religion' and the Religions in the English Enlightenment* (Cambridge: Cambridge University Press, 1990), especially ch. 5, pp. 157–172.

[6] This was the subtitle of the *Treatise of Human Nature*.

satisfied with the most general principle which would still be possible to subject to some empirical confirmation.[7] One may speculate that it is precisely for this requirement that Hume rejects as artificial and unfounded the traditional dichotomy between profane and sacred history; all the phenomena that are laid under observation are on the same footing; there is no reason for giving a higher or privileged status, an exemption from a critical and unprejudiced scrutiny, to any specific religion or faith over all the others. His Newtonian outlook indeed makes Hume one of the pioneers of the empirical science of religion; in other words, the *Natural History* gave impetus to the comparative studies of religions of an anthropological, psychological, or sociological kind that began in the nineteenth century and that since have grown both in quantity and depth.

Finally, the term 'natural' also means that Hume looked for the solution of his problem at hand to the same human nature, the foundation of all the sciences, whose analysis he made the main topic of the *Treatise* and the *Enquiries*, and in which he finds the clue for the solution of the problems posed by epistemology and ethics. Hume's insight consists: first, in considering human nature as a whole, as much more than purely rational; second, in maintaining that our theoretical and practical activity is dependent upon principles and operations of a human nature which manifests a permanent spiritual structure, virtually present and common to all men, and which includes distinctive perceptions, passions, instinctive dispositions, and emotions.[8] That insight, if it is such, can be interpreted as being no more than the product of an empirical generalization. I believe, though, that it rather seems to partake more of the nature of a metaphysical postulate, or at least to be a postulate of a philosophical, not an empirical, anthropology. At any rate, it is something that no experience can conclusively validate, but which was certainly that presupposition under which it is possible, as Hume says in the *Enquiry Concerning Human Understanding*, not only to study the history of religion, but to study history as such:

> It is universally acknowledged, that there is a great uniformity among the actions of men, in all nations and ages, and that human nature remains still the same, in its principles and operations. . . . Mankind are so much the same, in all times and places, that history informs us of nothing new or strange in this particular. Its chief use is only to discover the constant and universal principles of human nature, by shewing men in all varieties of circumstances and situations, and furnishing us with materials, from which we may form our

---

[7] See especially THN, Introduction, xx–xxiii; and EHU, Sect. I, 14–15. Nicholas Capaldi has stressed with clarity and intelligence Hume's faithfulness to this Newtonian program in *David Hume: The Newtonian Philosopher*, chap. 3, pp. 49–70.

[8] This general outlook on this matter owes a great debt to the seminal studies of Norman Kemp Smith. See in particular, his "concluding comments" about human nature in *The Philosophy of David Hume*, pp. 526–566). I have made clear in chapter 1 in what my way of understanding Hume's naturalism differs from Kemp Smith's. I also find that the cited works of Páll S. Árdal throw much light on this issue.

observations, and become acquainted with the regular springs of human action and behaviour (EHU, 83).[9]

That is why even the *History of England*, and not only the *Natural History of Religion*, is ultimately a natural history. It is also this constant spiritual activity of one and the same human nature, omnipresent in each and every one of the cultural products of humankind, which perhaps even justifies the claim that the *Natural History* has some affinities with the more speculative theories of the great German idealist philosophers who tried to comprehend the necessity and variety of the process of development of the different religions by connecting them with the active unity of the human spirit.[10] In addition, if one loses sight of this metaphysical principle, not only is the philosophical value of the *Natural History* severely depreciated, but even the intelligibility of Hume's methodological approach to religion will become suspect.

Let us not forget that Hume's genetic account of religion, that is, his conviction that the investigation into the origin of religious beliefs throws light into the permanent constitution of religion in general, follows from prominent doctrines of the *Treatise* and the *Enquiry Concerning Human Understanding*. According to these works, the investigation into the genesis of our concepts in sense-experience is the condition for apprehending their true meaning and, many times, the only way to determine whether our words are truly meaningful or just mere sounds:

When we entertain, therefore, any suspicion, that a philosophical term is employed without any meaning or idea (as is but too frequent), we need but enquire, *from what impression is that supposed idea derived?* And if it be impossible to assign any, this will serve to confirm our suspicion. By bringing ideas into so clear a light, we may reasonably hope to remove all dispute, which may arise, concerning their nature and reality (EHU, 22).

Antony Flew has strongly criticized this theory of meaning, saying that it is guilty of what he calls the *genetic fallacy*. For him, a theory such as Hume's contains the seed of a very prevalent danger:

It is the danger of being misled to argue that because Y originated from X therefore Y must really be X: that 'ultimately', 'essentially', or 'in the last analysis' oaks just are acorns, and men are nothing but apes. In philosophy the general temptation takes the particular form of wanting to equate the sum of all possible evidence for a proposition with its meaning. Part of the price of this move is the conclusion that any proposition must be meaningless which cannot in principle be conclusively verified.[11]

---

[9] This passage is important for other reasons as well; these will be made manifest in chapter 6.

[10] See Roberto Torretti, *Hume y la religión*, p. 29.

[11] Antony Flew, Hume's *Philosophy of Belief*, (London: Routledge and Kegan Paul, 1961), p. 132.

Whether Hume was guilty or not, in the formulation of his general theory of meaning, of committing the genetic fallacy, is something I just simply cannot discuss here.[12] But interestingly enough, a quite similar objection is made, in a totally different context, against any genetic account, such as Hume' that might at the same time pretend to obtain some knowledge about the nature of religion. Basically, what Rudolf Otto says in what follows about mysticism can be extended to cover religion in general:

> No mere inquiry into the genesis of a thing can throw any light upon its essential nature, and it is hence immaterial to us how mysticism historically arose.[13]

We can see here a sound methodological warning against all sorts of facile reductionism that, without much ado, simply explain away, for instance, the nature of cultural products and institutions by dissolving them into their temporal antecedents, without at the same time carefully analyzing and exhaustively describing those features that the thing in question displays. In defense of Hume we have to say that it seems *prima facie* implausible to suggest, especially concerning human spiritual phenomena, that the process of their historical generation can disclose nothing about their essence. This is to take almost a strict Platonic view of the matter, as if the whole task were that of just faithfully reproducing – also in the realm of the products of man's spiritual activity – what is contained in eternal and totally determined essences, the objects of an intellectual intuition (*Wesenschau*).[14]

Hume's apparent conviction that the search of its origin may help us in making transparent the nature of religion derives much of its impulse from his metaphysics, that is, from his naturalism. The latter seems to share much of the Pre-Socratic assumption that the beginnings of things are not simply left behind, something that once was, but is no more; on the contrary, what things originally were, that is what they really are, and what they continue to be and will always be: that nature which manifests and unfolds itself in time through a multiplicity of appearances. Is this Pre-Socratic metaphysical ancestry a merely poetical or imaginary attribution, or is it really founded on the letter and spirit of Hume's philosophy? Key doctrines which he expounds in different places of the *Natural History* decidedly support the second alternative.

---

[12] Nicholas Capaldi aptly defends Hume against this type of reproach in *David Hume: The Newtonian Philosopher*, pp. 47–48

[13] Rudolf Otto, *The Idea of the Holy*, trans. John Harvey (Oxford: Oxford University Press, 1923), pp. 21–22.

[14] Hume is no Hegel, in the sense that we cannot look in his philosophy for a clear distinction between the "abstract" and the "concrete" universal. We say of the "abstract" universal (as it is the case with mathematical concepts and ideas) that it is timeless, changeless, and given all at once as totally determined; of the "concrete" – for instance, historical phenomena or what Hegel calls "objective spirit" – we can say that its essence is not given all at once, but that it only fully discloses itself in and through the process of his own self-becoming.

This presupposition underlies, for example, his account of the "flux and reflux of polytheism and theism."[15] Not only did monotheism arise out of polytheism, but there is a natural tendency in the actual development of monotheism forms to gradually transform or revert themselves into their opposite. Hume is thus to conceive of the historical genesis of the diverse forms of religion as a process of continuous alternation of two "ideal types": polytheism and monotheism. In turn what brings about this historical oscillation is the perpetual struggle in the mind of persons of two opposite propensities of imagination,[16] of a cyclical movement that will last as long as human nature remains the same.

In fact, and as we shall see in chapter 6, the enduring power of the irrational element in *all* historical, or "popular" religions is explained along the same lines. Superstitious practices and rituals, absurd, barbarous, and impious conceptions of divinity are not merely nor mainly the convenient invention of priests in order to bring men into passive submission, and safeguard their own well-being. They have indeed a necessity of their own, a necessity that lies within human nature:

> the artifices of men aggravate our natural infirmities and follies of this kind, but never originally beget them. Their root strikes deeper into the mind, and springs from the essential and universal properties of human nature. (NHR, 73).[17]

And even the comparative study of monotheism and polytheism which Hume undertakes in the *Natural History* is grounded upon that tacit metaphysical principle. It is precisely the uniformity and constancy of human nature that manifests and unfolds itself in the historical process which makes all religion commensurable.[18]

Thus also in religion what is basic is what is original, and what is original is what is abiding in it.[19]

In the following chapters we shall examine the characteristic features of that which is for Hume the permanent nature of religion.

[15] *The Natural History of Religion*, Sect. VII, pp. 47–48.

[16] Ibid., p. 48.

[17] In the *History of England* Hume, more than once, establishes the same point. Hence he interprets the celibacy of the Catholic clergy: "though this practice is usually adscribed to the policy of the court of Rome . . . yet this institution was much forwarded by the principles of superstition inherent in human nature" (H, III, 365).

[18] For these reasons, I think it is clear that Hume does not question the deistic "tpresupposition that there is a human nature which is everywhere the same" (Ernest Cassirer, *The Philosophy of the Enlightenment*, p. 178). We shall hopefully be able to see in the following chapters that such a presupposition is instead one of the few theses he shares with the deists.

[19] Even though I agree with Peter Harrison that for Hume there is "no 'hidden' nature of religion that can be discovered by historical investigation" (*'Religion' and the Religions in the English Enlightenment*," p. 169), I hope to show in the next three chapters that this permanent essence of religion is what makes its historical investigation possible.

CHAPTER 4

The Conception of the Phenomenon to be Investigated

4.1 THE PERMANENT ESSENCE OF RELIGION

The attempt to provide an adequate and precise comprehension of Hume's theory concerning the origin of religion cannot lose sight of what he took the basic feature of all religion to be. The same applies to any just critical appraisal of his theory.

Curiously enough, Hume did not offer in the *Natural History* an strict definition of the phenomenon whose genetic explanation he undertakes. There are reasons which may lead us to think that such move is not a mere casual omission; first of all, it appears to be consistent with the nominalistic position he expounds in Section VII, Part I of Book I of the *Treatise*. To formulate a general definition that would state clearly and exhaustively those features, and only those features, that are universally present in religion as such, that would enable one, when confronted with a particular candidate, to unequivocally say that such is a genuine case of religion or not, was perhaps for Hume impossible as well as unnecessary. Particular instances of what we usually call religion may share many common features among themselves; one instance may resemble another in one feature while differing from a third case, which happens to agree with the second instance in another feature, and so forth; yet there might not be a factor or set of factors common to them all. If that were the case with respect to the things designated by the word 'religion', then the effort to arrive at a truly universal definition of religion would be a sort of logical aberration, or misunderstanding.[1]

---

[1] This thesis has been defended, under what one may call Wittgensteinean presuppositions, in many places and very ably by William P. Alston. See in particular *Religious Belief and Philosophical Thought*, (New York: Harcourt, Brace & World, 1963), pp. 1–15; and "Religion," *Encyclopedia of Philosophy*, ed. Paul Edwards, VII (New York and London: Macmillan, Inc., 1967), 140–145. I don't share Alston's thesis, but since Hume's explanation does not depend on the truth of Alston's claim, I feel relieved of the duty of refuting it in this place. On the other hand, one should note that in his famous account of those universal concepts which are arrived at through a distinction of reason (*distinctio rationis*), Hume anticipates the fundamental idea of the Wittgensteinean doctrine upon which Alston bases his own, that is, the theory of "family resemblances." See THN, Book I, Part. I, ch. 7, pp. 24–25. In chapter 10, I shall try to elucidate the relevance of this theory for Hume's critique of the ontological argument.

Be that as it may, Hume seems to hold the following twofold conviction: First, that there is, among the astoundingly heterogeneous characteristics of the religious phenomenon, a quite generalized one which constitutes the most basic source out of which all other features have arisen. Second, that it is simply because there is a permanent nature of religion that the investigation into the genesis and rise of this primordial feature will throw some light on the nature of religion in general. We have examined the second presupposition in the preceding chapter; now we shall analyze the first.

Even though none of the following is a trait common to all religions, yet it is difficult to find an instance of a historical religion which does not partake of various, or at least one of these characteristics. William P. Alston has given the name of "religion-making characteristics" to those features. These are: the belief in supernatural beings or agents, conceived in many different ways; different rituals, ceremonies, practices; feelings, emotions and attitudes; objects, held to be sacred, which occasion both those rituals and feelings; furthermore, general beliefs about the nature or reality and the place and duties of human beings within that world; various kinds of human organizations and institutions; plus all the manifold functions that all the preceding factors may perform for the individual and the religious community.[2]

But which among the staggering variety of features exhibited by historical religions is really the basic and original one, namely, the one that will take us to us the innermost core of religion? Feeling, ritual and belief are in most cases mutually connected in religion. Yet the beginnings of the religious life, and the dynamics of its peculiar development, are only given when human beings begin to entertain a peculiar kind of belief about the sources of becoming in the universe: the belief that "invisible, intelligent power," or gods intervene in the production or regulation of those events in nature and human life that have sovereign practical importance. "The only point of theology, in which we shall find the consent of mankind *almost* universal, is that there is invisible, intelligent power in the world" (NHR, 32; italics added). One has to remark, incidentally, that here Hume is using the term 'theology' to refer, not so much to rational or philosophical theology, but – as he remarks in what immediately follows the above quotation – to "popular systems of theology," or historical religions; in this specific case points to typical beliefs about the nature of the divine in two very general kinds of historical religion – the monotheism of Hebrew-Christian tradition and the anthropomorphic polytheism of Greece and Rome. In this section Hume's main interest is to show how very different the ideas of divinity are in each, notwithstanding their agreeing in being conceived as invisible, intelligent powers. The title of the section is telling: *Deities not considered as creators or formers of the world.*

But to return to the main issue, that Hume conceived the belief in invisible, intelligent power to disclose something of the essential nature of religion is confirmed by what he says in the Introduction to the *Natural History*. There he defines

---

[2] William P. Alston, *Religious Belief and Philosophical Thought*, p. 3.

the task concerning religion as one of investigating "its origin in human nature" (NHR, 21): then, after remarking that the belief in invisible power has not been truly universal, he ends up by reducing the task of explaining the origin of religion in human nature to one of determining the general causes or principles out of which the "original belief" rises and the particular circumstances that condition their operation (NHR, 21). In conclusion, to determine the origin of religion is, reciprocally, to establish how our ideas of God and the gods arise.

In chapter 5 we shall see that the genetic account of the idea of God in the *Natural History* follows from some of the most prominent doctrines of the *Treatise* and the *Enquiry Concerning Human Understanding;* in fact, the first is but a more detailed and complete version of the explanation about the origin and meaning of the idea of God that Hume summarily sketches in these two works. In this section, we shall analyze that belief which Hume takes as the permanent essence of religion; in the next section, I will hopefully explain why Hume denies that religious belief has an instinctive character, along with the significance of such a denial and the implications that follow from it. Now we shall focus our attention on the following question:

Why does Hume confer this central place on belief – specifically the belief in invisible, intelligent power – in his theory of religion. To be quite honest, what I offer as answers to this question are hypotheses suggested and based on the deep connection between this theory and Hume's epistemology. In any case, these are not an exhaustive list of motives, and even less of personal ones, about which I will not speculate.

Hume's mitigated scepticism, instead of throwing any doubts, rather reaffirms again and again the well-established and close interrelationship that in daily life exists between beliefs, feelings and human actions. Obviously, most actions we habitually perform are founded upon beliefs (most of them tacit, but for that matter no less effective ones). For instance, if we buy a bottle of apple juice instead of a certain soda beverage, even when we do not as much like the taste of the apple juice, it is probably because we attribute a greater nutritive value to it. On the other hand, beliefs may influence the way we feel about things. If we believe, and not merely conceive, that cigarette smoking causes pulmonary cancer, that may lead us to abandon such habit; even if it does not succeed in doing this, it will certainly affect our attitude and feelings towards that practice, which is, more often than not, its only effect. Conversely, it frequently occurs that such as we feel towards something, thus we tend to believe and act with regard to it. If something or someone is disagreeable to us, we may be more inclined to think ill or badly of it, or of him or her. And it is even more common to find that the continuous performance of an action or set of actions may consolidate or psychologically strengthen in us those beliefs and feelings associated with that action or set of actions. Pascal particularly comes to mind for having unashamedly indicated how the habitual practice of religious ritual may give rise, or at least fortify, the belief in the creed tied up with those ceremonies.[3]

But Hume does not only stress the factual interdependence between these three factors; he goes on to establish in the *Treatise* an intimate theoretical connection between belief on the one hand and feeling and action on the other. At least according to one of the most complete and general renderings of his theory, the mental activity that belief consists in is assimilated to a determinate, irreducible type of feeling that anyone can introspectively can find in himself or herself, but which stands outside any proper definition. The clearest and most emphatic asseveration of this theory occurs in the *Appendix* to the *Treatise* (THN, 664–629). There he says that:

> [B]elief consists merely in a certain feeling or sentiment; in something that depends not on the will, but must arise from certain determinate causes and principles of which we are not masters (THN, 624; c.f., THN, 625 and *passim*). . . . and this different feeling I endeavour to explain by calling it a superior *force*, or *vivacity*, or *solidity*, or *firmness*, or *steadiness*. This variety of terms, which may seem so unphilosophical, is intended only to express that act of the mind, which renders realities more present to us than fictions, causes them to weigh more in the thought, and gives them a superior influence on the passions and imagination (THN, 629).[4]

It is noteworthy that in his last definition of belief in the Appendix, Hume confers that title only on those ideas which are foundations of human practice, or which issue into action; in other words, belief is not only ultimately defined in terms of feeling, but also in terms of the role it has and the purposes it serves in human life:[5]

---

[3] This well-known passage is found after his famous Wager:

You would fain reach faith, but you know not the way? You would cure yourself of unbelief, and you ask for a remedy? Take a lesson from those who have been bound like you, and who now stake all they possess. These are they who know the road you would follow, who are cured of a disease of which you would be cured. Follow the way by which they began, that is by making believe that they believed, by taking holy water, by hearing mass, etc. This will quite naturally bring you to believe, and will calm you . . . will stupify you (*Pascal's Pensées*, p. 121).

[4] In chapter 7 we shall examine in detail Hume's theory of belief and its relationship with his account of religious faith.

[5] Here Hume seems to have anticipated José Ortega y Gasset's formulation of the distinction between ideas and beliefs ("ideas y creencias"): "Las ideas se tienen, en las creencias se está". Loosely translated this means: One has ideas, but on beliefs one stands. Ortega y Gasset makes this distinction in an ontological context; that is, in terms of the existential relevance each may have for the self's meaning-constitution and organization of its lived through or spiritual "circumstance" ("circunstancia"), or specific ways of being in the world. What Ortega calls *circunstancia*, comes quite close to Edmund Husserl's *Lebenswelt* (life world). See e.g., *Ideas y creencias*, in Vol. 5, *Obras Completas*, (Madrid: Revista de Occidente, 1940), p. 379.

it is something *felt* by the mind, which distinguishes the ideas of the judgment from the fictions of the imagination. It gives them more force and influence; makes them appear of greater importance; infixes them in the mind; *and renders them the governing principles of all our actions* (THN, 629; italics added with the exception of the word 'felt').

Yet belief remains paramount; for that which gives its human character to human conduct of life is not feeling by itself, nor action alone, but these in so far as they come to be connected with determinate beliefs, which are offered as motives, reasons, purposes, or ends for them. It is thus quite natural that belief should have been considered by Hume the central feature of the religious life of humankind.

To a large extent the *Treatise* is a philosophical analysis and critique of what Kemp Smith has called the "natural beliefs," namely, those generic beliefs upon which not only our search for knowledge is based, but the whole guidance of human life in the world, such as our belief in causal connection between events, in the permanence and independent existence of the external world, and in the identity of the self. And Hume extends the same type of analysis and critique to religious beliefs. Why? Simply because these are taken by many to possess the same primordial and necessary character for human existence that the so-called "natural beliefs" have.[6] In the last analysis, perhaps it is because Hume wanted to probe whether religion really is such a primary and necessary constituent of human existence that he made the belief in intelligent, invisible power the main characteristic of religion. For if this is its core, then – as we shall see in the next section – at least the universality of religion is immediately compromised.[7] But there might as well be other reasons for this move.

In doing so, Hume is, I think, merely appealing to the usage and understanding of the term 'religion' shared almost universally by his age (the Enlightenment): i.e., that religion implied some sort of belief in a God or gods, from which all its other characteristics, like ritual worship, peculiar feelings, rules of conduct, moral injunctions, etc., naturally followed. Such a vision naturally grows out of the religious experience of Western man, drawing its sustenance from two basic sources: the

---

[6] See especially Norman Kemp Smith, *The Philosophy of David Hume*, chap. 5, pp. 443–459, and chap. 6. pp. 465–496. Kemp Smith's posture has been subsequently reformulated and defended by Barry Stroud, in *Hume* (London: Routledge and Kegan Paul, 1977). Páll S. Árdal makes a comparable emphasis on the natural beliefs, although in a more complex manner than that of the preceding authors.

[7] It is curious that Hume, who sees religion as a natural product of our humanity, should have questioned what many contemporary sociological or anthropological conventionalistic approaches to religion take for granted. A case in point is Wilfred Cantwell Smith. Although he suggests that the very notion 'religion' is an Enlightenment concept, or a construct of Western imagination, he still upholds the universal character of the phenomenon to which that presumably conventional concept refers:

In every human community on earth today, there exists something that we, as sophisticated observers, may term religion, or a religion. And we are able to see it in each case as the latest development in a continuous tradition that goes back, we can now affirm, for at least one hundred thousand years. Man is everywhere and has always been what we today call 'religious' [*The Meaning and End of Religion* (New York: Harper and Row, 1978), p. 18].

Graeco-Roman world and the Hebrew-Christian tradition. From this point in time, this conception appears as it really is: i.e., a pretty parochial view. With the prodigious growth of anthropological and historical knowledge, there is no need of enshrining the Western modes of religiosity into an absolute paradigm, having so to deny the title of "religious" to many primitive, Asian, African, or Pre-Columbian-American forms, simply because they might happen to be non-personalistic or even non-theistic types. The great paradox is that in spite of our more refined knowledge, most of us still share in our unguarded or inattentive moments (that is, most of the time) more or less the same historically biased understanding of religion of Hume and his contemporaries.

In Hume's case, the emphasis in the belief in a god or gods is one reason why his theory captures well the dynamics of sacramental and prophetic forms of religion which are geared towards the invocation and propitiation of divine forces believed to be subjected to some sort of control through quaint quasi magical procedures or other devises, but is so inadequate to account, even within the theistic model of faith, for those other sacramental and mystical contemplative forms in which the positive belief-content is minimal, and more importantly, the divine is sought for itself (in order to identify with, and enjoy it), and not so much, or at least not mainly, for the benefits it can bring, or the calamities it can prevent from coming, to the devotees. Later – especially in chapters 5, 7, and 8 – we shall deal with the self-interested character of what was for Hume the typical religious worship.

But now it is necessary to justify this express identification of the terms 'invisible, intelligent power in the world' with 'God' or 'gods'. This usage is unobjectionable so long as we keep the following points in mind. In the first place, our main departure from common usage is in not making the possession of any moral quality a necessary condition for calling any thing a god; a divine being may either be good or bad, or indifferent to good and evil;[8] what the term must rather imply is that the beings in question are thought of as being productive or efficacious forces superior to human beings.

Second, the term 'invisible' presupposes not only that these causes are literally un-seen, not an object of direct sense perception, but that these divine causes are not-totally transparent to human understanding, or mysterious. In order to better grasp the meaning of 'invisible' applied to gods, we shall contrast Hume's approach to that of Rudolf Otto. Many may be inclined to think that compared to Otto's memorable phenomenological analysis of the object of religious experience, i.e., the "numinous," Hume's account of the origin of religion is quite prosaic and near-

---

[8] See DNR, Part XI, 212: Philo's rebuttal of Cleanthes' attempt to empirically prove the moral goodness of the Deity seems to indirectly confirms this point:

> There may *four* hypotheses be framed concerning the first causes of the universe: *that* they are endowed with perfect goodness; *that* they have perfect malice; *that* they are opposite, and have both goodness and malice; *that* they have neither goodness nor malice. Mixed phenomena can never prove the two former unmixed principles; and the uniformity and steadiness of general laws seem to oppose the third. The fourth, therefore, seems by far the most probable.

sighted. According to Otto, any naturalistic or "animistic" account, such as Hume's, is unfaithful to the phenomenon involved since it fails to take notice that representations of "spirits," or "souls," or invisible powers, are "rather one and all early modes of 'rationalizing' a preceding experience to which they are subsidiary."[9] And what this original religious experience discloses is something essentially mysterious, wholly other, which fills us with awe and fascination. Yet Hume seems not to have been altogether unaware of these features which Otto so superbly describes. Perhaps lacking an adequate language in which to express his conceptual insights, at first sight it seems as if Hume, instead of apprehending, rather ignored the genuine religious phenomenon. But that is not the case. On the contrary, he is really pointing to the same phenomena. Thus he says about these powers, that they are "secret and unknown causes" (NHR, 29). They are originally conceived in a "confused and general manner" (NHR, 29), and hence afterwards the imagination "must labor to form some particular and distinct idea of them" (NHR, 29). Furthermore, Hume, just like Otto, asserts that it is the exceptional, the great, the unfamiliar in human experience that first directs the human mind to sketch its first ideas of divine powers. And these extraordinary events are viewed by the religious person as the effects, embodiments, or manifestations of the divine, but not as the divine itself. At the same time, as H. J. Paton has remarked, even Otto's theory is not entirely free from difficulties and perhaps contradictions.[10] On the one hand, he seems to maintain – in contradistinction to Hume – that we have in religious experience a direct encounter with divinity, and on the other, that this reality is grasped in events which are viewed as "signs" of it.[11] All this seem to justify Paton's reproach: "It is not easy to see how a 'direct encounter' can take place by means of signs, or how awareness by means of signs can be properly described as feeling."[12]

We may, on the whole, recapitulate the differences and likenesses between Hume's and Otto's approaches in this manner: We see God, in Saint Paul's famous phrase, as "through a glass, darkly," not only because the object of our worship cannot be entirely grasped by reason, but also because we do not apprehend it directly in experience. To both these two propositions, Hume would have given, I think, his "sound philosophical assent." Otto does say yes to the first, and tries, with debatable success, to invalidate the second. In short, Hume will emphatically and consequently deny what Otto takes for granted: that there is something like a religious experience or immediate awareness of divine attributes. We shall see later, in chapter 5, that the consciousness that we have of the divine is mediate, and about the ideas of the gods, that we form them by means of a complex act of reflection on, and projection of, the attributes of our own nature.

---

[9] Rudolf Otto, *The Idea of the Holy*, p. 26.

[10] H. J. Paton, *The Modern Predicament* (London: George Allen & Unwin Ltd. and New York: The Humanities Press, 1955), pp. 142–144.

[11] See chapter 8, pp. 163–164, for Hume's position about this possibility of a direct encounter with the Deity through the medium of "external signs."

[12] H. J. Paton, *The Modern Predicament*, p. 144.

Third, the word 'intelligent' applied to God suggests that for Hume this idea implies – however superior and different from humans the divine object may be conceived – at least a modicum of anthropomorphism. God or gods are conceived as somehow similar to us; we attribute to divinity some sort of psychical life, at least intellect; and truly our most diverse capacities, activities, feelings, purposes, and all other attributes, physical as much as mental, in a vague as well as specific manner, have been liberally bestowed to the gods throughout the history of humankind.

In synthesis, under these limiting conditions, the terms 'God', 'gods' and Hume's 'invisible, intelligent power' can be freely interchanged.

We could even use 'supernatural beings or agencies' for 'gods'. But the term 'supernatural' could easily produce much confusion, for it may easily suggest that there exists a sort of ontological schism between the divine and the world, if considered synonymous with 'transcendent' or 'ultra-mundane'. In this sense, the term can be applied to the God of Hebrew-Christian tradition, but not to the Greek and Roman gods. But if this term is used not so much to signify an ontological priority of the "invisible, intelligent power" in question, but rather to point to the specific mode of its causative activity, it could still be kept in use. The term 'supernatural being' should then be pointing to entities that, besides possessing all the attributes we have just mentioned above, produce their effects in the world in a way similar to our own, to wit, by means of "intelligent," purposive, or intentional causation. By contrast, a natural cause, even when still unknown to us, is supposed to behave and act according to general laws of a mechanical type; and these laws are derived, not from any sort of plans or purposes which the agency in question may have, but from the nature of its inmost constitution and structure. At least this seems to be Hume's understanding of the matter. For instance, when explaining the origin of polytheism Hume makes it clear that extraordinary phenomena like floods, droughts, earthquakes – whose causes are unknown to man – are viewed by humans as the works of gods if attributed to the activity of some invisible, intelligent being. These unknown causes, which awaken in human beings the first ideas of the divine, would be considered natural, and not supernatural, if or when human beings come to be cognizant of the fact that:

> these causes are nothing but the particular fabric and structure of the minute parts of their own bodies and of external objects; and that, by a regular and constant machinery, all the events are produced, about which they are so much concerned (NHR, 29).[13]

But when one goes over the many different functions that this general outlook of religion fulfills for Hume, then one begins to understand with greater clearness

---

[13] It is difficult to say whether Hume ever subscribed such a strong mechanism. Against that opinion (and even against mechanism as a theoretically viable natural philosophy) and in favor of a moderate scepticism counts the panegyric to Newton, which is found at the end of his *History of England* (H, VI, 542). See below chapter 13, section 4.

why he attaches such a great importance to the belief in a God or gods. So, and with all its obvious limitations, this conception is still sufficiently broad to cover both historical ("popular" religions) and philosophical theology ("natural" religion); hence both fideistic and rational approaches to divinity fall under the compass of his investigation. Incidentally, it is the centrality of belief in invisible, intelligent power that also enables Hume to retain the name 'religion' for the mitigated theism to which he seems to give his "sound philosophical assent" at the end of the *Dialogues Concerning Natural Religion*.[14]

In addition, this outlook opens the way for a genuine comparative study of religion. Amidst their vast heterogeneity, it makes commensurable the principal modes of religiosity known to Hume. It also justifies on the one hand, the investigation of the actual connections and similarities between those religious forms, and on the other, the search for the factors which may make their origin intelligible to us as well as for the laws of their historical transformation.

But even much more significant than all the rest is that of all historical characteristics of religion, the belief in invisible, intelligent power is, indisputably, the factor most amenable to rational criticism. Even if it may not be the most manifest of Hume's theoretical purposes in the *Natural History*, it is nonetheless true that this work also attempts – although by way of implication covered by a good ideal of sarcastic irony – to invalidate, or at least to seriously weaken, the claims of the "zealots", that is, of those who look into the history of religion for support or confirmation of the presumed truth and original moral purity of their own religion. Allowing for certain freedom of expression, Hume seems to be saying something like this: How can you "religionists" dare to say that history offers unequivocal proof of the truth of your particular faith? The way divinity has been conceived of are numberless, and the ways of worshipping it, even greater. Yet basically the same few natural principles and causes suffice to explain the origin of all these; and from this standpoint there is no compelling reason to say that history confers on any specific religion any privileged status; all of them are – in spite of their diversity – on an equal footing, being derived from the same factors in our human nature. An unprejudiced rational enquiry into all these religions finds no exceptional superiority in any of them over the rest, either in terms of rationality or morality. They are products of our human nature, and, as such, all historical religions reflect something of our goodness, strength and wisdom, but also a great deal of our cruelty, weakness and folly:

> Every by-stander will easily judge (but unfortunately the bystanders are few) that, if nothing were requisite to establish any popular system, but exposing the absurdities of other systems, every voter of every superstition could give a sufficient reason for his blind and bigotted attachment to the principles in which he has been educated (NHR, 57).

---

[14] This possibility first occurred to me while reading what Kemp Smith says about "true theism" in the Introduction to his edition of Hume's *Dialogues*. See also *The Philosophy of David Hume*, pp. 25–44.

It may be the case that one religion provides a truer or purer revelation or representation of divinity than the rest. But the criterion or standard by which to determine this primacy cannot be derived from the mere genetic study of religion as such; if we do really possess such standard, we must have obtained it from other source, and must afterwards have surreptitiously imported it into the consideration of the history of religions.

Yet, generally speaking and taking into consideration all of these possible factors, Hume looked at religion from the standpoint of the belief in a God or gods because the close focus on this aspect made it easier for him to challenge a substantive contention: that religion is a primary and necessary part of human existence in the absence of which life would not be human at all, or at least that it is an indispensable factor for practice, since it satisfies elemental human needs. This major claim can be understood in many ways, and can be defended accordingly. However, in the *Natural History* Hume questioned a quite specific formulation of it: that religion is not only natural to man, but that it is, as well as other basic activities of human life, the product of a fundamental instinct. Now we go on to the critical examination of the argument by means of which Hume denies an instinctive character to religion.

4.2 THE NATURAL ALTHOUGH NOT INSTINCTIVE CHARACTER OF RELIGION

A conspicuous thesis of Hume's *Natural History of Religion* is that belief in God or gods, i.e. in "invisible, intelligent power," does not rise out of an original instinct. If this contention is examined under the light of what Hume says about other contents of mental life to which in the *Treatise of Human Nature* and the *Enquiries Concerning the Human Understanding and Concerning the Principles of Morals*, he bestows the title of instincts, then much of what he affirms to that effect in the *Natural History* becomes less puzzling and more understandable. Furthermore, this analysis may even throw some light on the twentieth-century discussion about the presumed "natural" character of the belief in the divine. On the one hand, interpreters of Hume's philosophy who deny that religious beliefs are on the same footing with beliefs in causal efficacy, in the continuous and independent existence of perceptible objects, or in personal identity sustain their case precisely by emphasizing those passages of the *Natural History* in which Hume denies to religious beliefs an instinctive character.[15] On the other hand, those other commentators who affirm the opposite view, more or less disregard the *Natural History*, and direct their attention mainly to the *Dialogues Concerning Natural Religion*, and attempt

---

[15] To my mind, the most prominent exponent of this current of interpretation is John Gaskin, especially in *Hume's Philosophy of Religion*. See in particular ch. 8, pp. 126–140. Peter Jones, in his very enligthening work, *Hume's Sentiments, Their Ciceronian and French Context* (Edinburgh: Edinburgh University Press, 1984), defends a similar view: "In due course, Hume tries to establish that religious beliefs are not natural, in any significant sense" (p. 60).

to demonstrate that the belief in an intelligent cause of the universe satisfy all the conditions that in his mainly epistemological works Hume assign to what since Norman Kemp Smith onwards have been denominated "natural beliefs."[16] A tacit presupposition shared by interpreters on both sides of this question is the identification of 'instinctive' and 'natural'. For that reason those who include the religious among the natural beliefs labor under no small inconvenience. Generally speaking, I think that the latter are fundamentally right, but only if one abandons such identification of instinctive and natural.[17]

In what follows I propose a reading of the relevant passages of the *Natural History* from which it follows that, although not instinctual in Hume's sense, the religious beliefs (and here we mean those of "popular" or historical religion), yet at least their common principle may be natural in the sense used by those immersed in the aforementioned hermeneutical dispute.

Sharply, succinctly, and very early in the *Natural History* Hume deploys his main arguments against the existence of such *sui generis* religious instinct. He does not dwell here on the trait that first comes to mind when one considers the term 'instinct': that is, the innate or inborn origin of the actions and capacities customarily attributed to the operations of instincts. Hume rather directs his attention to the traits that the activities and dispositions themselves must possess or display in order to be called instinctive or the outcome of instinctive impulses or drives. These are: universality, uniformity in the manner of operation irreducibility to more basic factors. And since religious beliefs do not quite fulfill any of these conditions, one can say, therefore, that religion "springs not from an original instinct or primary impression of nature" (NHR, 21).

Concerning universality, Hume remarks that there has been, and still are, entire communities without religion. It:

---

[16] Norman Kemp Smith, "The Naturalism of David Hume," *Mind* [(1905) vol. 14, 149–173]; and *The Philosophy of David Hume*, ch. 5, pp. 105–312; ch. 17, pp. 405–410; chap. 21, pp. 446–464; ch. 22, pp. 465–469). A paradigmatic case of the opposite trend is Stanley Tweyman's, *Scepticism and Belief in Hume's Dialogues Concerning Natural Religion*, which is the most thorough and lucid commentary on the *Dialogues* since Kemp Smith's. See especially ch. 8, pp. 97–156: "The position I will defend is that the belief in an intelligent designer of the world satisfies all the criteria of a natural belief and, therefore, must be regarded as being such a belief" (p. 136). D. W. Livingston, in his truly admirable book, *Hume's Philosophy of Common Life*, approaches a somewhat similar view: "The propensity to philosophical theism, though more variable by custom than the propensity to believe that our perceptions are of continuously and independently existing objects, is, nevertheless, a universal propensity of human nature" (p. 131).

[17] See, for example, J. C. A. Gaskin, *Hume's Philosophy of Religion*, p. 126: "The expressions 'original instinct', 'natural instinct', and 'natural belief' are all used. The first two are Hume's. The third is his commentators'. The sense is the same in each case." Stanley Tweyman, in *Scepticism and Belief in Hume's Dialogues*, more or less seems to agree: "the unavoidability and universality of a given natural belief can be made manifest by showing the influence of instinct (Nature) . . ." (p. 17); ". . . only in so far as the belief is instinctive or natural is it action-guiding and essential to our well-being" (p. 19).

has been very generally diffused over the human race, in all places and in all ages; but it has neither perhaps been so universal as to admit of no exception.... Some nations have been discovered, who entertained no sentiments of Religion, if travellers and historians may be credited"[18] (NHR, 21).

If religious beliefs were the effect of a specific instinct, the same uniformity operation that we observe to have occurred in the effects of others so-called instincts. But whereas any instinct, like "self-love, affection between the sexes, love of progeny, gratitude, resentment . . . has always a precise determine object, which it inflexibly pursues," religious belief, on the contrary, "has not been uniform in the ideas, which it has suggested . . . no two nations, and scarce any two men, have ever agreed precisely in the same sentiments" (NHR, 21).

Hume uses the term 'original' not only to point to the innate character of instincts, but also to emphasize that this notion is ultimate. It is primitive in the sense of being unanalyzable, or not reducible to simpler notions. It is precisely this lack of strict universality and regularity what made patent to Hume that the predisposition to belief in God, or gods cannot be due to the operation of an instinct, at least if this is conceived as an original and simple cause; thus such a belief must instead arise out of the conjunction of different factors.

In order to arrive at this conclusion, Hume is relying on two of the "Rules by which to judge of causes and effects," enumerated in Section XV, Part III, Book I of the *Treatise*. According to Rule 4, "the same cause always produce the same effect, and the same effect never arises but from the same cause" (THN, 173); and Rule 6 says that "the difference in the effects of two resembling objects must proceed from that particular in which they differ" (THN, 174).

Religious beliefs do not always occur, and when they do, these beliefs are by no means identical. And if we exclude from consideration the possibility of innumerable different instincts, operating for each and every different theistic belief, then Hume's contention that the cause of religious beliefs must not be original or primary, but a secondary or compound one, in other words, a plurality of causes, appears reasonable enough. Accordingly he says that:

The first religious principles must be secondary; such as may easily be perverted by various accidents and causes, and whose operation too, in some cases, may,

---

[18] Long before Hume, but in order to deny the innate character of the idea of God, Locke affirmed: "Besides the atheists taken notice of amongst the ancients, hath not navigation discovered, in these latter ages, whole nations, at the bay of Soldania, in Brazil, in Boranday, and in the Caribbee islands, &c., amongst whom there was to be found no notion of a God, no religion?" (*An Essay Concerning Human Understanding*, Book I, ch. 3, pp. 96–97). Hume follows Locke in denying an actual innate idea of God, and in the manner in which he accounts for the origin of that idea, which is very similar to that offered in Book II, ch. 23, pp. 418–419, of the *Essay*. See below chapter 9, pp. 182–183, where the question whether Hume thought the idea of God was innate is discussed. Hume, however, strongly criticizes Locke's doctrine of innate ideas (EHU, 22ff; *Abstract to the Treatise*, 648); on the other hand, he does not deny that religion may be natural although the idea of a God may not be innate in Locke's sense.

by an extraordinary concurrence of circumstances, be altogether prevented (NHR, 21).

In reaching that conclusion Hume is simply following a maxim which is but a conjunction of Rules 4 and 6:

For as like causes always produce like effects, when in any instance we find our expectation to be disappointed, we must conclude that this irregularity proceeds from some difference in the causes (THN, 174).

From all of this one can infer by no means that religion is not natural. One can justly deduce, however, that it is not an original, but rather a derivative factor. Still, religion is a natural outcome of the typical character of certain primary human desires and passions (the anxious concern for our well-being and "the incessant hopes and fears, which actuate the human mind"), a particular situation of humans in the universe precariously striving to survive and in utter ignorance about the causes upon which their happiness as well as misery depend, and the peculiar constitution of imagination that leads them to form suitable representations of those causes as personal powers, which are either benevolent or hostile.[19]

Religion is secondary in the sense of being in turn explained precisely by the conjunction of those more primitive factors. But it is natural. Whereas in the *Natural History* Hume seems to suggest that belief in invisible, intelligent power is not, strictly speaking, universal, he also recognizes there that the predisposition to form such religious representations – "the propensity to believe in invisible, intelligent power" – is "a general attendant of human nature" (NHR, 75). In essence, Hume is now granting to it the claim of universality which he seemed to deny it at the beginning. In fact, he gives the epithet of "universal" to that propensity.[20]

The case of religion is in some sense similar to that of justice, concerning which the question about whether it is natural or not also arises. Since justice arises out human conventions (THN, 489, and *passim*), and the sentiment of justice in not derived from any instinct, many philosophers have denied that justice is natural. But for Hume the question is a dispute of words which only arises due to

---

[19] See NHR, Sections 1–2, 26–32.

[20] I have to admit that the passage of the *Natural History* alluded to is quite ambiguous. Gaskin (*Hume's Philosophy of Religion*, p. 137) plausibly derives from it an interpretation opposite to mine's: "In the *Natural History of Religion* he comes close to speaking of a belief in god as a natural belief but he shies off it: 'The universal propensity to believe in invisible, intelligent power, if not an original instinct, is at least a general attendant of human nature' (N.H.R., 75)". Yet Gaskin does not quote what immediately follows that clause, which if taken in a straightforward fashion and not as an ironical aside, seems to concede an innate character to that universal propensity, such that it "may be considered as a kind of mark or stamp, which the divine workman has set upon his work" (NHR, 75). On the whole, I think that Tweyman is right against those who share Gaskin's opinion, when he argues for Hume's recognition, even in the *Natural History*, of the universality of that belief. See *Scepticism and Belief in Hume's Dialogues*, pp. 136–138.

the ambiguity of the word 'natural'. In a broad sense justice is natural because it is the outcome of the operation of several constitutive principles of human nature:

> If self-love, if benevolence be natural to man; if reason and forethought be also natural; then may the same epithet be applied to justice (EPM, 307; c.f. THN, 483–484, 526).

This reference to justice has indirectly brought forward another constitutive ingredient of the Humean notion of instinct: that is, the absence of premeditation or "forethought" in the instinctual actions, which is the main reason why Hume calls it a "mechanical power" (EHU, 108). Furthermore, it is this quality which leads us to believe that instincts are innate or "original properties," as Hume sometimes refers to them. So perhaps it will be instructive for us to dwell briefly on Hume's notion of instinct. In Section IX (Of the reason of animals) of the *Enquiry Concerning Human Understanding* he characterizes instinct along the traditional lines by contrasting instinctual capacities with those which are the product of habit or custom; the first sort are innate, the second are learned from observation, or acquired in the course of experience. Yet Hume himself blurs this distinction by asserting at the end that experimental reasoning itself is an instinct or the effect of one:

> But though animals learn many parts of their knowledge from observation, there are also many parts of it, which they derive from the original hand of nature; which much exceed the share of capacity they possess on ordinary occasions; and in which they improve, little or nothing, by the longest practice and experience. These we denominate Instincts, and are so apt to admire as something very extraordinary, and inexplicable by all the disquisitions of human understanding . . . the experimental reasoning itself, which we possess in common with beasts, and on which the whole conduct of life depends, is nothing but a species of instinct or mechanical power, that acts in us unknown to ourselves; and in its chief operations, is not directed by any such relations or comparisons of ideas, as are the proper objects of our intellectual faculties (EHU, 128; c.f., THN, 176–179, especially 179).

What is new in all of this is the suggestion that instincts fulfill valuable and essential functions for the survival, furtherance and conservation of living or organic beings. We should keep this in mind if we want to know why Hume denied the existence of a religious instinct.

Indeed Hume will assign a place to instincts within his inventory of the contents of human experience, that is, within his original classification of perceptions as impressions and ideas. In the *Natural History* he uses interchangeably the terms 'original instincts' and 'primary impressions'. This might have led one to expect that he should have placed instincts alongside original impressions only. But he also introduces instinctive propensities into the realm of secondary impressions, i.e., impressions of reflection. This should not surprise us, for in the *Enquiry*

Concerning Human Understanding he had already said that all impressions are original or innate (EHU, 22f.).

In fact, the expansion and modification of his original scheme is more significant in what pertains to impressions of sensation. In Book I of the *Treatise*, alongside the usual sensible qualities, Hume only recognizes bodily pains and pleasures as members of that group; but in Book II he adds to the general appetite for pleasure and aversion to pain, a considerable number of "instincts originally implanted in our natures, such as benevolence and resentment, the love of life, and kindness to children" (THN, 417). In other words, there are springs or "actuating principles of the mind," in addition to pain and pleasure as such. When analyzing direct passions like grief and joy, hope and fear, desire and aversion, he says that these urges can arise, not only by reflecting on the pleasure or pain that a given object might afford us, but "from a natural impulse or instinct, which is perfectly unaccountable. Of this kind is the desire of punishment to our enemies, and of happiness to our friends, hunger, lust, and a few bodily appetites" (THN, 439).

It should be stressed that among instincts there are bodily as well as mental desires. All these are original as against other desires and passions which are reflective or secondary. And one should further note that in Appendix II to the *Enquiry Concerning the Principles of Morals*, Hume makes 'secondary' synonymous with 'interested'. What is the difference between original and secondary or interested desires? The first "produce good [i.e., pleasure] and evil [i.e., pain], and proceed not from them" (THN, 439).

Reflective passions are interested because their object is not simply desired for itself; on the contrary, we rather seek its possession because we reflect or think about the pleasure its possession or use may bring to us. We primarily seek to increase our happiness, which is the end in itself, and secondarily look after the object in so far we believe it to be a means to increase our pleasure. It is otherwise with original instincts; we seek possession of the object not because we deliberately view it as a means to augment our well-being, but simply because we feel an immediate inclination or impulse towards it. Since the gratification of these impulses produces pleasure and their frustration pain, we may, afterwards, pursue these objects in an interested manner, to wit, with our own happiness in view. However, the objects of such instinctive appetites and desires are pursued even when we do not know whether their possession will produce such a pleasure, and, what is more important, even when we know that our search for them is against our best interest, leading in the long run to more pain that pleasure, as sometimes happens with the desire for food, with sexual attraction, or with the urge for revenge:

> In all these cases, there is a passion, which points immediately to the object, and constitutes it our good or happiness; as there are other secondary passions, which afterwards arise, and pursue it as a part of our happiness, when once it is constituted such by our original affections (EPM, Appendix II, Of Self-love, 301).

One must note, on the one hand, the striking similarity of this terminology with that which Hume employs in the Introduction to *The Natural History of Religion*, and on the other hand, that religion is also, in this other sense of 'secondary', a predominantly interested activity. For according to Hume, the original and ever-present motive of religion is self-interest. Gods are the constant objects of our hopes and fears; yet we only experience hope and fear before such things as can probably bring us either pleasure or pain, happiness or misery (THN, 439).

Hume likewise acknowledges that instincts are at work in the field of secondary impressions, the most conspicuous case being that of pride and humility, the reflective passions *par excellence*. For convenience I will only refer to the first of these passions. Pride has in common with instincts like self-love, gratitude, vengeance, love of kind, etc., that it is inflexibly oriented towards a precise, determined object, in this case the self. We only feel pride for, and before, such things and persons which are related to us; pride make us cast an eye upon ourselves:

> the peculiar object of pride and humility is determined by an original and natural instinct, and that it is absolutely impossible, from the primary constitution of the mind, that these passions should ever look beyond self, or that individual person, of whose actions and sentiments each of us is intimately conscious THN, 286).

Another tendency of pride that Hume also takes to be an original property is that it is a pleasant sensation, that it always produces pleasure in us (THN, 286).

It is noteworthy that for Hume these impulses or tendencies are not only natural, but original properties of pride. A natural property, as Hume defines it here, is one that is constant and steady in its operation; thus to say that the self-oriented tendency of pride is natural is to say that a uniform correlation has been observed between pride and the idea of the self. But in the case of pride we want to say something more: i.e., that this correlation "proceeds form an original quality or primary instinct"(THN, 280). Original qualities have two characteristics: they "as are most inseparable from the soul, and can be resolved into no other" (THN, 280). The first characteristic implies that these are properties (in this case instincts) that we possess because our mental life is what it is; they are derived from "the primary constitution of our mind," and thus are essential characteristics upon whose removal our mental life would not be what it is. In the case of pride, this self-oriented tendency – in conjunction with the tendency to produce pleasure – constitutes the very essence of pride; that is upon its removal, there is no longer pride. The second characteristic is irreducibility: an original property is a primitive factor.

It seems obvious that an original quality is *ipso facto* a natural one. But a property may be natural without being original, and we should not say, according to Hume, of such a quality that it is the outcome of an instinct unless it is both natural and original. Hume gives the following example. Pride has many causes, since innumerable objects are capable of arousing pride in us; among these Hume mentions power, riches, beauty and personal merit, or virtue. Hume acknowledges that the causes of pride are natural, because throughout human history the same type of objects, with slight variation, give rise to pride (THN, 281). Yet he denies that what leads us to pursue each one of those objects is a different instinct: "it is utterly impossible they should each of them be adapted to these passions by a particular provision, and primary constitution of nature" (THN, 218). Hume applies here Ockham's razor: if this were the case, then we would have a prodigious number of instincts, which would keep multiplying themselves so long as art would continue creating objects capable of arousing pride; it is, on the other hand, much more simpler to suppose that "there are some one or more circumstances common to them all, on which their efficacy depends" (THN, 281–282).

And with pride we are brought back to religion. Neither can the origin of religion nor that of pride be accounted for by reference to a particular, irreducible, *sui generis* instinct. Since the objects and situations that can elicit a religious response are innumerable, there would follow, as with pride, a prodigious multiplication of instincts. But in spite of this, the predisposition to believe in gods may be natural enough. All the different objects and situations that humans encounter may be adapted to the production of the religious belief by virtue "of some one or more circumstances common to them all," in this particular case the anxious preoccupation with our well-being, or the hopes and fears before the unknown causes of the events upon which the latter depends. These common features may trigger or set in motion, not a special and unique impulse or urge, but some general mental principles and capacities of the imagination which may not only be operative in the case of religious beliefs, but which may also be at work in the genesis of other and quite different types of beliefs. The way Hume summarized his task at the end of the Introduction to the *Natural History* is quite compatible with the preceding interpretation:

> What those *principles* are, *which give rise* to the original belief, and what those *accidents* and *causes* are, *which direct its operation*, is the subject of our present enquiry (NHR, 21; italics added).

Furthermore, if we keep in mind what he has said in the case of pride, one may convincingly argue that the propensity to believe in invisible, intelligent power is also due to a natural property precisely because it is a "general attendant of human nature."

Notwithstanding all of this, pride presupposes (if not in its causes at least in its effects) the activity of an original impulse, something which he absolutely denies with respect to religion. Whereas religious belief "has not been uniform, in the ideas it has suggested" (NHR, 21), in the case of pride "nature . . . has assigned a certain idea, viz. that of self, which it never fails to produce" (THN, 287): in short, whereas the object of pride is one – the self – , the objects of religion worship are many. In other words, the belief in invisible, intelligent power has given rise and continues to give rise to an enormous multitude of ideas of divinity. And, as we have already seen, this heterogeneity is not in keeping with the manner that – according to Hume's conception – instincts normally operate, that is to say, unless we were willing to advance the totally preposterous suggestion that each one of the deities worshipped is the object of a different instinct.

In spite of what has just been said, perhaps the most crucial reason that Hume ultimately had for denying an instinctual origin to historical religion was his deep conviction that it fulfills no basic human need, and that its removal from human life (even if it were not possible to accomplish it), would not be fatal but beneficial; at any rate it would not surely follow that upon its removal "human nature must immediately perish and go to ruin" (THN, 225), as he supposes the case would be if it we were deprived of the other natural beliefs.

We should keep in mind that one of the main purposes of the study of religions which Hume undertakes in *The Natural History of Religion* is to show that religion almost invariably has morally negative effects and instills in its votaries undesirable, even cruel and capricious, character traits.[21] And in the *Dialogues Concerning Natural Religion*, where his principal inquest concerns the validity of the cognitive claims of theism, he remains, I believe, in the few pages devoted to the real relationship between religion and morality, similarly adamant in this conviction.[22] Even when religious practices are not immoral, they still disturb the person's commitment to morality:

> But even though superstition or enthusiasm should not put itself in direct opposition to morality; the very diverting of the attention, the raising up a new and frivolous species of merit, the preposterous distribution which it makes of praise and blame, must have the most pernicious consequences, and weaken extremely men's attachment to the natural motives of justice and humanity (DNR, 222).

It is not by accident that the only religion to which he confers the title of "true" is of the philosophical kind, which rests the belief in God on the observation of order in the world, and from which no practical consequences can legitimately ensue. By calling this true theism, he at once reduces most others, that is to say historical religions or "religion as it commonly has been found in the world" (DNR, 223) to the level of superstitious worship or frantic enthusiasm.[23] Indeed he will endeavor

---

[21] This is particularly manifest in Sections IX–XV, pp. 48–73. Thus he suitably titles Section XIV: "Bad influence of popular religion on morality." Contrary appraisals of the theoretical worth of Hume's ethical depreciation of religion are given by Gaskin in Hume's Philosophy of Religion, ch. 9, "The Causes and Corruptions of Religion," pp. 143–158; and J. B. Stewart, *The Moral and Political Philosophy of David Hume* (New York and London: Columbia University Press, 1963), Preface, vi–vii, and ch. 10, pp. 256–287.

[22] On this point I agree with Gaskin, *Hume's Philosophy of Religion*, p. 153. Yet this thesis presupposes that on this matter it is Philo, and not Cleanthes, who voices Hume's opinion. And this is a debatable point.

[23] Gaskin forcefully points to this feature in *Hume's Philosophy of Religion*, pp. 146–149. Perhaps religion is, even for Hume, much more that fanatical rage and laborious idolatry, and in order to adequately defend what Gaskin attacks, i.e., the "practical inevitability" of the belief in god, one would

to show in the *Natural History* that pure or speculative rationality has quite a meager role to play in the process of the actual genesis of those religious beliefs which are very much alive and efficacious.

In the end this the greater "inconvenience" (in the sense of Philo, the sceptic of Hume's *Dialogues*) that besets our own position; in other words, we are almost compelled to land in the somewhat strange conclusion that it is the philosophical, and not the "popular" religion which appears better to deserve the epithet of "natural," since it is the logical development of a natural propensity of human understanding in its search for the causes of events. This propensity is one of those permanent, irresistible and universal principles of the imagination (THN, 225) that Hume had already analyzed in the *Treatise*:

> Nothing is more curiously enquired after by the mind of man than the causes of every phenomenon; nor are we content with knowing the immediate causes, but push on our enquiries till we arrive at the original and ultimate principle (THN, I, 266).

Yet the idea of an intelligent creator of the world typical of "philosophical" religion and the heterogeneous and quaint ideas of the divine found in historical religions are both "natural" products of human imagination, even though we may properly call the first conception sound and reasonable and the latter representations weak and merely whimsical. We should bear in mind that, in Section IV, Of Modern Philosophy, Part III, of Book I of the *Treatise*, when distinguishing between the necessary and avoidable principles of imagination, Hume had said that a person "who concludes somebody to be near him, when he hears an articulate voice in the dark, reasons justly and naturally," whereas "one who is tormented he knows not why, with the apprehension of spectres in the dark, may perhaps be said to reason, and to reason naturally too: but then it must be in the same sense that a malady is said to be natural; as arising from natural causes, though it be contrary to health, the most agreeable and most natural situation of man" (THN, 225–226). In the same sense, at the end of the *Natural History*, and after concluding that the propensity to form the ideas of the gods is "universal," or a "general attendant of human nature" (NHR, 74), Hume asserts that those who are endowed "with good understanding" (NHR, 74) from the "visible works of nature. . . infer its supreme Creator," whereas the more common ways by which people represent to themselves the divine are "but sick men's dreams," or "the playsome whimsies of monkies in human shape" (NHR, 75).

As we shall see later in chapters 5 and 9, a cardinal objective of the *Natural History* is to show that the belief in God founded in the disinterested contemplation

---

have to show that historical religion *always* is something else than mere superstition or enthusiasm. I think that a straightforward, non ironical, reading of the "General Corollary" of the *Natural History* lends support to this interpretation. Although Tweyman has effectively disposed of the objections to the universality claim, due to the fact that he predominantly deals with the *Dialogues* in his book, he has not addressed in full Gaskin's questioning of the presumed "practical inevitability" of that belief.

of the order of nature plays a negligible part in the actual origins and unfolding of historical religion (NHR, 24). In short, the distance between a theoretically disinterested philosophical religion and a pragmatically self-interested historical religion appears to be too immense so as to justify my contention that the principle common to both – the recognition of the operation of invisible, intelligent power in the world – is a natural belief.

Still, I consider that this thesis is essentially correct and a consequence of the previous analyses. But to argue at length in its favor would go beyond the scope of this chapter, and, after all, we shall address this problem again in chapters 9 and 14. I should say at least now that, in my opinion, Hume had no compelling reason for not recognizing, even in the *Natural History*, that in the origins of religious beliefs there is also operative the natural as well as rational demand that he mentions in the *Treatise*. Hume is entirely right, though, when he emphasizes that the gods principally fulfill other and very different needs.[24] But this is not incompatible with the acknowledgment of the existence of a permanent speculative feature in historical religion, even if it is usually immersed in, obscured and corrupted by, the over-abundant vital functions which religions preeminently discharge for their votaries.[25]

Finally, if it were true that in the *Dialogues* Hume places the belief in an intelligent Author of the Universe alongside the other natural beliefs, then the rift between his two main works on religion would be closed, and my admittedly speculative contention would be provided with a solid ground.

At any rate, what seems reasonably clear to me at the moment is that Hume's reflections on instincts and what he says at the conclusion of the *Natural History*, pave the way – provided that we do not readily identify 'instinctive' and 'natural' – for the recognition that the common core of all religions, namely the belief in invisible, intelligent power, is, according to Hume, a genuine natural belief. We shall return to this subject in chapter 14, immediately after the analysis of Hume's treatment of that belief in the *Dialogues*. Then I will hopefully present a more founded, and so less tentative, conclusion.

---

[24] In chapters 5 and 9 we shall see that Hume attacks the deistic account of religious origins in terms of pure rationality.

[25] On this issue, too, my opinion is different from Gaskin's. According to him, "true religion, *if any could be found, would be an inconspicuous personal thing* which would enforce morality" (*Hume's Philosophy of Religion*, p. 170; italics added). At the end of chapter 8 below I give the reasons for my discrepancy with Gaskin; these take very much into account the peculiar socially beneficial role that Hume unequivocally assigns to religion in the *History of England*.

CHAPTER 5

The Origin of Religion:
Critical Exposition of Hume's Theory

> ... l' idée d' une puissance souveraine est l' idée
> de la souveraine divinité, & l' idée d' une
> puissance subalterne est l' idée d' une divinité
> inférieure ...
> Malebranche[1]

As a means for achieving an adequate understanding of Hume's genetic theory of religion I will establish a connection between the argument of the *Natural History of Religion* and related arguments and doctrines expounded earlier in Book I of the *Treatise* and the *Enquiry Concerning Human Understanding.* I hope to show that his works on knowledge provide not only the philosophical foundations for the genetic account of the *Natural History,* but even the substantial anticipation of that theory. In addition, Hume's general conception of our mental capacities and limitations may give some clue as to why he came to formulate precisely such a type of explanation about the origins of the idea of God or gods.

Hume's policy is to look at human nature as it is, not as it should be. He is, accordingly, in *The Natural History of Religion* supremely concerned with the "living God," or rather the living gods. Thus the representations of divinity whose rise and development Hume attempts to make intelligible are "those tremendous images" that "predominate in all religions" (DNR, 225), the true objects of awe, prayer, veneration, and surrender: that is, the vivid ideas of the gods which are effective moving forces in the life of individuals and entire historical communities. On the other hand, the Deity or the God of the philosophers, that distillate of rational speculation or "pure" theism – a Being of infinite perfection, creator and preserver of the Universe – receives a very cursory treatment in the *Natural History.* The English orthodox divines and the deists of the second half of the seventeenth

---

[1] Nicolas Malebranche, *De la recherche de la vérité,* in *Œuvres Complètes de Malebranche,* Vol. III, ed. Geneviève Rodis-Lewis (Paris: Librairie Philosophique J. Vrin, 1963), Book VI, Part II, Ch. 3., p. 309.

and the first half of the eighteenth century agree to bestow upon this highly abstract conception the name 'God.'[2] It is noteworthy that Hume's references to the philosophical God are really calculated blows at one tacit presupposition of the whole controversy, which in the *Natural History* he systematically repudiates: the Paradisiacal or Golden Age paradigm of history:

> [I]t must appear *impossible*, that theism could, from reasoning, have been the primary religion of human race, and have afterwards, by its corruption, given birth to polytheism and to all the various superstitions of the heathen world (NHR, 26; italics added).[3]

Hume, by contrast, appeals to a different view of history in the manner typical of the Enlightenment.[4] He sees universal history as a slow, and not altogether straightforward, process of development from elemental, imperfect beginnings to a more complex and less imperfect future. His outlook may be rudimentary and even somewhat equivocal, but he sufficiently formulated a conception of historical progress.[5]

Viewed under such an assumption, the facts of history seem, according to Hume, to disprove both the deists and the divines. So long as we can rely on indisputable evidence, we can find no traces in the rude beginnings of humankind of that universal religion of nature. Our history is one of progress; thus if there is also a "natural progress of thought from inferior to superior" (NHR, 26), the idea the Deity or of God of "pure" theism can only be a very late cultural product. And the

[2] Sir Leslie Stephen, *History of English Thought in the Eighteenth Century*, 2 vols., 1876, 3rd ed. 1902 (New York and Burlingame: Harcourt, Brace and World, 1962) I, 2, 62–76. The first volume is a classic and sound summary of the deistic controversy.

[3] The preceding assertion is immediately directed against the typical deistic conception of an original religion of nature, which is as universal and permanent as is the reason which all men share. But with slight modifications, these remarks can he brandished against the divines; after all, we might as well suppose that Adam, at the beginning, was in full possession of the same exalted conception of divinity. In other words, Hume also cuts through the doctrine of the fall and subsequent corruption of human nature. Hume might well have in mind Herbert of Cherbury, *De religione gentilium* (London: 1645), one early attempt at such a conception of a natural religion. And maybe his own religious tradition may also have inclined Hume to think of Calvin himself, who asserts that the "seeds of religion" are found in an original notion of God, which at the beginning all humans clearly conceived, and in a knowledge of God as a perfect Creator, which is awakened by our experience of the visible universe. See John Calvin, *Institutes of the Christian Religion*, 2 vols., ed. John T. McNeill, trans. and indexed Ford Lewis Battles (Philadelphia: The Westminster Press, 1960), I, Book I (Of the Knowledge of God the Creator), chapters 1–5.

[4] See chapter 2, section 2 above.

[5] I say 'equivocal' because Hume's conception of the historical process is, oddly enough, a peculiar combination of a progressive or forward looking and a regressive or cyclical view. This clearly comes forth in Section 8 of the *Natural History*, "Flux and reflux of Polytheism and Theism," pp. 46–48. See in particular chapter 6 below.

historical forms of monotheism the world has known suggest to us rather that this belief arose out of reasons very different from those which the deists suppose: not from reasoning, but out of feeling. The case of the orthodox is, however, not much stronger. The same impartial examination of history does not give a greater plausibility to the supposition that belief in a perfect Creator was the product of a special and direct revelation given to humankind in a specific time and place, and transmitted to us, more or less faithfully, by tradition. Hume, on the other hand, traces this and all beliefs in divine beings or deities to causes and principles which he derives from the nature of our human constitution, appealing to the same laws by which the origin of other ideas, beliefs, or human opinions are explained. Which are these principles?

In order to explain the actual origins and unfolding of religion and religious representations of divinity, Hume points to certain primary passions, some characteristic operations of the human imagination, and an original situation of man precariously striving to survive within a world of scarcity. In an open challenge to the deists, he affirms that human beings did not first come to conceive of that idea prompted by the basic need of satisfying a purely intellectual curiosity about the causes of the order and frame of a Universe. Religion, in other words, does not have a rational origin.[6] On the contrary:

> the first ideas of religion arose not from a contemplation of the works of nature, but from a concern with regard to the events of life, and from the incessant hopes and fears, which actuate the human mind (NHR, 27).

Hume only provides one compelling argument that is, however, grounded on anthropological considerations for which he simply provides no empirical evidence. Living in rudimentary societies, in great ignorance of and in constant war with an inhospitable environment which customarily inflicted on them great and innumerable adversities, and full of pressing practical needs, human beings were completely deprived of the peace and leisure, without which it was "impossible" that their speculative curiosity could be awakened by the regular face of nature.[7]

But if the deist is wrong in suggesting an original love of wonder, the orthodox is no less mistaken when he strives to point to a *sui generis* religious sentiment as the real source of religious ideas. This has been, I think, reasonably established in the preceding chapter. Under the supposition that human history is one of development, and that human nature exhibits a permanent structure, which is constant in its manner of operation, Hume goes on to infer that the passions strong enough to pro-

---

[6] About this, see Terence Penelhum's insightful remarks in *God and Skepticism: A Study in Skepticism and Fideism* (Dordrecht: D. Reidel Co., 1983), pp. 133–135, and in *Hume* (London and Basingstoke: The Macmillan Press Ltd., 1975), pp. 171–172.

[7] See in particular NHR, 24–25. In chapter 9, section 1 below this thesis about the allegedly non-speculative origins of religion will be critically analyzed.

duce in primitive man the first surmises of divinity had to be hope and fear, that is, those emotions most closely connected with his supreme preoccupation, the securing of his survival and well-being in a world where he was in constant danger of losing both. Passions such as the concern for happiness, the dread of future misery, the terror of death, and the desire for revenge lie at the basis of religious beliefs:

> Agitated by hopes and fears of this nature, especially the latter, men scrutinize, with a trembling curiosity, the course of future causes, and examine the various and contrary events of human life (NHR, 28).

Hope and fear are nourished by an uncertain and unstable vital circumstance where human beings are ignorant of the causes upon which their well-being depend. And these passions in turn put the third factor to work, namely, imagination:

> We hang in perpetual suspence between life and death, health and sickness, plenty and want; which are distributed amongst the human species by secret and unknown causes, whose operation is oft unexpected, and always unaccountable. These *unknown causes*, then, become the constant object of our hope and fear; and while the passions are kept in perpetual alarm by an anxious expectation of the events, the imagination is equally employed in forming ideas of those powers, on which we have so entire a dependance (NHR, 28–29).

Hume's language here seems to suggest that he was aware of the fact that a "feeling of dependence" is at the basis of religion. It would be preposterous for us to try to derive, out of Hume's few remarks, Friedrich Schleiermacher's metaphysical interpretation of religion as a feeling of dependence on the Infinite: "True religion is sense and taste for the Infinite."[8] In Hume's case, that "entire dependance" may only amount to an anxious awareness of man's many limitations, a vivid realization that he is subject to much infirmity by virtue of being a living organism whose very life is determined by natural circumstances and by a natural environment.

Despite this, Hume at any rate did grasp the specific initial phenomenon upon which Schleiermacher grounds his doctrine about this characteristic aspect of religious experience.[9] In other words, Hume's "natural" feeling of dependence might be the first obscure adumbration of what after successive progressive stages finally

---

[8] Friedrich Schleiermacher, *On Religion: Addresses in Response to its Cultured Critics*, trans. Terrence N. Tree (Richmond: John Knox Press, 1969), p. 82.

[9] Wittgenstein has also put forward this sentiment as a basis for religious consciousness in *Wittgenstein's Notebooks 1912–1916*, ed. G. E. M. Anscombe, R. Rhees and G, H. von Wright (Oxford: Basil Blackwell, 1961), p. 74[e]: "The word is *given* me, i.e. my will enters into the world completely from outside as into something already there. . . .That is why we have a feeling of being dependent on an alien will. However this may be, at any rate, we are in a certain sense dependent, and what we are dependent on we can call God" (8. 7. 16).

transforms itself into the specifically religious feeling of dependence, and which Schleiermacher, using a philosophical language very different from Hume's, characterizes as pious feeling, an immediate consciousness or "revelation of the Infinite in the finite, God being seen in it and it in God."[10] Hume could say that such hopes and fears, or such a natural feeling of dependence connected with the origin of religious representations are the result of the operation of the world upon us. Schleiermacher, on the other hand, affirms that "your feeling is piety in so far as it is the result of the operation of God in you by means of the operation of the world upon you".[11] After all, piety, or religious feeling, was not, for Schleiermacher, an affection among others, or a *sui generis* sentiment qualitatively different from all the rest. The feeling of dependence is rather a modality of being sensibly affected by either the natural or the human world that can accompany any particular feeling whatsoever; in short, it is the peculiarly religious, and more basic, dimension of human sensibility:

> This is the peculiar sphere which I would assign to religion – the whole of it, and nothing more. . . . This series is not made up either of perceptions or of objects of perceptions, either of works or operations or of different spheres of operation, but purely of sensations and the influence of all that lives and moves around, which accompanies them and conditions them. These feelings are exclusively the elements of religion and none are excluded. There is no sensation that is not pious . . . "[12]

Hume's historical perspective is by no means incompatible with the possibility of a progressive purification of that feeling. Schleiermacher, like Hume, considered that the idea of a universal natural religion is but a fiction; for him, the real religion is historical religion, and all of these historical forms are more or less inadequate representations of an Infinite God that we can not rationally apprehend. Indeed, the romantic Scheleiermacher is not, like Rudolf Otto, hostile to historical considerations in the examination of the essence of religion. And, in fact, my attempt to establish at this point a an unsuspected connection between Hume's and Schleiermacher's account gains plausibility from Otto's own critique of

---

[10] *On Religion: Addresses in Response to its Cultured Critics*, p. 79.

[11] Ibid., p. 82.

[12] Ibid. In the same fashion, Schleiermacher asserted later that the feeling of religious, or absolute dependence is not about any particular dependence the self may have with respect to any finite thing within the world; on the contrary, "absolute dependence is the fundamental relation which must include all others in itself" [*The Christian Faith*, 2 vols., ed. H. R. Macintosh and J. S. Stewart (New York and Evanston: Harper and Row, 1963), Vol. I, Introduction, p. 17]. The feeling of dependence is, in fact, "the God-consciousness in the self-consciousness" (Ibid.), an awareness of the divine which may be, as it were, lighted on, and mediated by, the consciousness of our finite existence within the world that sensibly affects us and that we actively counter-affect; in this sense God is but "the *Whence* of our receptive and active existence, as implied in this self-consciousness" (Ibid., p. 16).

Schleiermacher's theory. For Otto, one of the defects of Schleiermacher's interpretation of the feeling of dependence is that it does not distinguish the "religious" from the "natural" dependence. Thus he says that the latter's "mistake" is to reduce such a distinction to the difference between the "absolute" and "relative" dependence, and therefore to transform it into a mere "difference of degree, and not of intrinsic quality."[13] And finally if, despite Otto, the difference between these two sentiments is only one of degree, then the phenomenon that Hume describes might contain the germs of what may eventually develop into an absolute feeling of dependence in Schleiermacher's sense.

But what Hume says about the birth of religion not only invites us to compare his account with later and seemingly very different theories, but also evokes the remembrance of considerably earlier explanations with which his own appears to have a great resemblance.

The great number of quotations from classical authors indicates that, in framing his theory, Hume may have been much influenced by their own speculations about religion. One of the earliest philosophical theories was that of Xenophanes:

Ethiopians imagine their gods as black and snub-nosed, Thracians as blue-eyed and red-haired (Fr. 16)

But if oxen and horses or lions had hands, or could draw and fashion works as men do, horses would draw the gods shaped like horses and lions like lions, making the bodies of the gods resemble their own forms (Fr. 15).

Men suppose that gods are brought to birth, and have clothes and voice and shape like their own (Fr. 14).[14]

And Hume explains the origin of the first ideas of the gods or deities in a way somewhat reminiscent of Xenophanes; these first conceptions are the natural products of our imaginative faculties, viz., of a tendency of sympathetic projection. Imagination ascribes to, or hypostatizes into, those unknown powers upon which human life is utterly dependent, attributes which human beings experience in themselves.

No wonder, then, that mankind, being placed in such an absolute ignorance of causes, and being at the same time so anxious concerning their future fortune, should immediately acknowledge a dependence on invisible powers, possessed of sentiment and intelligence. . . . Nor is it long before we ascribe to them

---

[13] Rudolf Otto, *The Idea of the Holy*, p. 9.

[14] Xenophanes' fragments are given in translation by W. K. C. Guthrie in *History of Greek Philosophy* 3 vols. (Cambridge: Cambridge University Press, 1969), I, 5, 371. Cited in S. G. Kirk and J. E. Raven, *The Presocratic Philosophers: A Critical History with a Selection of Texts* (Cambridge: Cambridge University Press, 1957, 1976) , pp. 168–169.

thought and reason and passion, and sometimes even the limbs and figures of men, in order to bring them nearer to a resemblance with ourselves (NHR, 30).

Briefly put, Hume traces the many historical images of divinity to the propensity of human beings "to conceive all beings like themselves, and to transfer to every object, those qualities with which they are familiarly acquainted, and of which they are intimately conscious" (NHR, 30). Hume readily emphasizes that this tendency to transfer emotions, passions, and other qualities which the subject experiences in itself to other objects is not a feature peculiar only to religion. It is, on the contrary, a very general mental disposition which is activated in quite different contexts – i.e., poetical allegory, and even in philosophy, where such fancies as the horror of a vacuum, sympathies and antipathies attributed to matter, are also products of the same universal tendency of the imagination (NHR, 29–30)

Thus if the origins of religion are not rational, and if human beings invariably see themselves reflected in all those things that are extremely important for bringing about their happiness or misery, then Hume's thesis that the original religion of humankind is idolatrous polytheism appears plausible enough. And this is a blow against both deists and Christian divines. This theory, he believes, receives additional evidence from the fact that "barbarous" nations are still polytheists, and even in civilized nations common people also remain polytheists at heart. And, of course, the gods worshiped by such people, i.e., by most people during all ages, are conceived in a frankly anthropomorphic manner:

They suppose their deities, however potent and invisible, to be nothing but a species of human creatures, perhaps raised from among mankind, and retaining all human passions and appetites, together with corporeal limbs and organs (NHR, 30–31).[15]

If polytheism was the first religion of human beings, and "has prevailed, and still prevails, among the greatest part of uninstructed mankind" (NHR, 31), then Hume task is to show how monotheism arose out of polytheism. Since the same human nature is involved here too, as one might expect, his account about the beginnings of monotheism does not differ in kind from that of polytheism. What is different is the direction the imagination takes in forging its imaginings of the divine, images, which in spite of the language with which they are associated, remain as "tremendous" as in the beginning. The movement goes from polytheism to monolatry (henotheism), and from monolatry to monotheism. From "the crowd of

---

[15] See also NHR, 45, 67, 73, and 75. Hume would have completely approved the following remarks of Ludwig Feuerbach: "The divine being is nothing else than the human being, or rather, the human nature purified, freed from the limits of the individual man, made objective – i.e., contemplated and revered as another, a distinct being. All the attributes of the divine nature are, therefore, attributes of the human nature." Ludwig Feuerbach, *The Essence of Christianity*, trans. George Elliot (New York: Harper, 1957), p. 14.

local deities," one gains ascendancy over the rest on the hearts and minds of the worshippers, and after a long process of excessive exaltation of its merits, this favorite deity ends up being the only worshipped god. What probably happens, according to Hume, is that in order not to awaken the anger or jealousy of his preferred deity, the frightened idolater begins to lavish upon it higher and higher praises at the expense of all other deities. Overwhelmed with such flatteries, this god is raised so much higher than the other divinities in the imagination of the worshiper that the idolater eventually denies that they exist at all. And this indefinite conferring and augmenting of praises and eulogies can stop only when infinite goodness, power, intelligence, that is, when infinite perfection, becomes the property of that deity (NHR, 41–45). Thus monotheism is not the result of a miraculous illumination of human minds, nor the natural resting point of the disinterested contemplation of the universe by reason. It is rather the logical outcome of the adulation, hypocrisy and self-deceit which are nurtured by our natural hopes and fears.

At this point I shall not pass judgment upon the truth, or even verisimilitude, of Hume's theory, especially his hypothesis about the origins of monotheism, but will rather examine the doctrines of the *Treatise* and the *Enquiry* that support and implicitly anticipate them.

The critical outlook of Hume's philosophy naturally fosters a close interconnection between the psycho-genetic and the logical task. Hume's cardinal presupposition is that in order to determine the true nature or meaning of our concepts, and their objective reference, we have to examine their true origin, i.e., we have to go to the activities and contents of the human knowing subject, and find out the experiences in which those concepts are originally constituted. We have to keep in mind that the horizon of the *Natural History* is that of common life, as it is demanded by its historical orientation. Therefore an exact terminological correspondence between these two types of works cannot be expected. At any rate, the following cardinal principle that Hume establishes in the *Treatise* has to be applicable to the idea of God:

'Tis impossible to reason justly, without understanding perfectly the idea concerning which we reason; and 'tis impossible perfectly to understand any idea, without tracing it up to its origin, and examining that primary impression, from which it arises (THN, 74–75; cf. EHU, 21–22).

In this particular case we have to look for the impressions from which the idea of God is derived if a precise signification is to be ascribed to that term. Hume's First Principle that all our ideas – at least all simple ideas – are derived from impressions voids the possibility of deriving our notion of divinity from a purely intellectual intuition. This idea cannot, therefore, be innate, like the imprint that the

Divine Artisan left on His work.[16] The Cartesian explanation is unintelligible to Hume; our sole source of knowledge is sense intuition; there lies the origin of all our ideas, which are copies or representations of sensations, "either outward or inward" (EHU, 22), or impressions of sensation and reflection, as he says in the *Treatise*.[17]

Hume in fact points out in the *Treatise* itself – although in an incidental way, without unfolding its implications – that the idea of God is not an innate one, but that it arises out of sense impressions. This comment is made in a polemical context, in Part III, Section XIV, "Of the idea of necessary connexion." His immediate concern here is to refute the Cartesian explanation – more exactly Malebranche's development of a theory of Cartesian inspiration – about the origin of the idea of "force," "power," or "necessary connexion." Matter or extension is, according to Malebranche, inert or inactive; from the clear and distinct idea of extension we cannot deduce that it possesses the power to communicate motion. But motion exists; thus there must be a power capable of producing it. If it is not located in bodies, it must reside in the Deity or God Himself. According to Malebranche no body can be said to be the cause of the movement of any other body, but only the occasion for God to exert his own power.[18] And this applies to all cases of causal efficacy: to thought as well as to matter. An act of willing is as much the cause of the movement of our hands as the thought of a beautiful person is the cause of our amorous desire. Neither of them is a proper cause. Creatures do not act. The occasionalism of Malebranche is complete; the Deity is the only and sole cause of all modifications in the universe, material and mental alike. To affirm that Malebranche's occasionalism had a great influence in the development of Hume's conception of causality, would be an understatement. Verily, Hume's mention of this theory (and very few philosophers he does cite by section and chapter) is, more than a critique, an open acknowledgment of his debt to Malebranche.

Be that as it may, Hume implies that the hypothesis about the origin of causal efficacy in a first and constantly operating and sole cause, or God, is consistent only under the supposition of innate ideas. If the latter is denied, then the former is left without an adequate foundation:

> We have establish'd as a principle that all our ideas are deriv'd from impressions, or some precedent *perceptions*, 'tis impossible we can have any idea of

---

[16] The predisposition to form such beliefs may, nonetheless, be instinctive; see Section XV, "General Corollary," (NHR, 75).

[17] "Reflection" is a problematical conception; yet Hume's talk in the *Treatise* of "impressions of reflection" seems an attempt to interpret the former under the paradigm of sensation, i.e., in THN, 157–158 he even appears to identify consciousness with sensation.

[18] Nicolas Malebranche, *De la recherche de la vérité*, Book VI, Part II, Ch. 3., pp. 309–320.

power and efficacy unless some instances can be produced wherein the power *is perceiv'd* to exert itself. (THN, 160).[19]

But that is precisely what can never be shown. On the one hand, that a cause, or productive principle is always necessary for everything that begins to exist may be true, but is beyond the possibility of being rationally demonstrated.[20] On the other hand, experience does not teach us that there is a necessary connection between two events, because we directly perceive a power or energy by which the first event as cause necessarily gives rise to the second as effect. What we do perceive, according to Hume, is that any events causally related are constantly conjoined – i.e., that one constantly follows the other. It is because the Cartesians implicitly acknowledge this, that when hard pressed, they ultimately resort to the "supreme spirit or deity." But this is for Hume an arbitrary supposition. Even if we grant the possibility of its being true, it can, however, never be known to be true, since it lies beyond the sphere of human experience, that is, assuming straightforwardly that the difference between the Divine mind and the human is infinite.[21] If we are talking about the human mind, then it is clear to Hume that the connection between ideas, being exact copies of impressions, is as unintelligible as that which exists between objects.

Against Hume's objection, the Cartesian might insist that he has a clear idea of God from which he discovers that He is the "only active being in the universe," the Infinite Will, ultimate producer of all that happens in the world. The argument by means of which Hume tries to disprove the Cartesian thesis is interesting because it offers the first hints as to the actual mechanism of the genesis of the idea of God or the Deity. Either the Cartesians have a clear and distinct idea of God or they do not; and if they have it, they must have gotten it from somewhere; either it is innate or not innate. Since under his premises Hume has to discard the theory of innate ideas,

---

[19] C.f., THN, 157, he says that "reason alone cannot give rise to any original idea."

[20] THN, I, Sec. III, "Why a cause is always necessary," 79–82.

[21] In Part IV of the *Dialogues*, Philo appears to mischievously deny that we can have any idea of the God of the philosophers, or a being of infinite perfection. For if all impressions are particular and totally determined existences, then it is nonsense – at least according to Hume's theory of perceptions – to say that we could have an experience of divine attributes: "Our ideas reach no farther than our experience: We have no experience of divine attributes and operations: I need not conclude my syllogism: You can draw the inference yourself" (DNR, 142–143). In the *Natural History* Hume emphasizes the same point. In Sections XI and XII he says that the traditional or mythological polytheism, however false, is more reasonable than the monotheism of scholastic theology: "The former is often more reasonable, as consisting only of a multitude of stories, which however groundless, imply no express contradiction." (NHR, 65). He will even suggest that the idea of God, as a being of infinite perfection, is unintelligible, i.e., an absurd or impossible concept: "Thus they [the idolaters] proceed; till at last they arrive at infinity itself, beyond which there is no farther progress: And it is well, if, in striving to get farther, and to represent a magnificent simplicity, they run not into inexplicable mystery, and *destroy the intelligent nature of their deity*, on which alone any *rational* worship or adoration can be founded" (NHR, 43; italics added).

then this idea has to be derived from experience, and if this is the case, the Cartesian hypothesis of the sole and constant Laborer is doomed:

> *For if every idea be deriv'd from some impression, the idea of a deity proceeds from the same origin*; and if no impression, either of sensation or reflection, implies any force or efficacy, 'tis equally impossible to discover or even imagine any such principle in the deity (THN, 160, italics added; see also *Abstract* of the THN, 656, p. 100, below).

Moreover, in Part IV, Sect. V., p. 248, Hume again emphasizes that we do not have an idea of God as cause, since it is impossible for us to form any idea of God which does not arise from sensible impressions, and between these no essential tie can ever be apprehended. Thus we are brought into the following dilemma: Either nothing can be the cause of any other thing unless the idea of the one implies that of the other, or constant conjunction between two objects is a necessary and sufficient condition for declaring them to be causally connected.[22] Analyzing the first part of this dilemma, Hume once again reaffirms what he said about the idea of the Deity on page 160:

> We in reality affirm, that there is no such thing in the universe as a cause or productive principle, not even the deity himself since our idea of the Supreme Being is derived from particular impressions, none of which contain *any* efficacy, nor seem to have *any* connexion with another existence. As to what may be said, that the connexion betwixt the idea of an infinitely powerful being, and that of any effect, which he wills, is necessary and unavoidable; I answer, that *we have no idea of a being endowed with any power, much less of one endow'd with infinite power* (THN, 248, italics added).

Although the tone of this argumentation seems to be emphatically critical of some of the claims of traditional theology, it has to be remarked, also emphatically, that the strict denial that God is the first and supreme cause of all movement and generation does not follow from it, as was all too readily deduced by some of

---

[22] In a famous letter to his friend Gilbert Elliot of Minto (March 10, 1751), Hume clearly upholds the second clause of this dilemma:

> You ask me, If the idea of Cause & Effect is nothing but Vicinity, (you shoud have said constant Vicinity, or regular Conjunction), I woud gladly know *whence is that farther Idea of Causation against which you argue?* This Question is pertinent; but I hope I have answer'd it. We feel, after the constant Conjunction, an easy Transition from one Idea to the other, or a Connexion in the Imagination. And as it is usual for us to transfer our own Feelings to the Objects on which they are dependent, we attach the internal Sentiment to the external Objects. If no single Instances of Cause & Effect appear to have any Connexion, but only repeated similar ones, you will find yourself oblig'd to have Recourse to this Theory (L, 1 Lt. 72, 155).

Hume's contemporaries.[23] The only thing he denies is that we have a distinct idea of causal efficacy, if by this we understand something like a metaphysical necessity. Since we cannot deduce it as a constitutive property from the essence of any known definite object, either internal or external, we can even less legitimately infer it to be a predicate of the divine nature.

But what is worthy of special attention is the manner in which Hume arrives at this conclusion. Hume refers to the idea of God as that of an "infinitely powerful being"; and he also says that we should not look for any a priori knowledge of this idea, but that its origin must be sought in experience; in other words, in "particular impressions," in the primary contents of the human mind or consciousness.

Yet, what are precisely those particular impressions in which the idea of God originates? Certainly the impulse that leads us to attribute an efficacy, a force, or power, or necessity to objects and ultimately to God has proved itself fallacious. But it might be no less true that this impulse may give an important clue for answering our former question. What I suggest is that perhaps those impressions and operations of the understanding that lead us to postulate a productive principle in the objects of our experience, quite beyond what this experience can legitimately guarantee, are also the same mental contents and imaginative tendencies involved in the genesis of the idea of God. That is to say, perhaps the idea of "necessary connexion" between events and the idea of God have the same or a common origin in human nature or human consciousness. For that reason, before asking about the origin, that is, the impressions out of which the idea of God arises, we shall stop for a while to reflect on Hume's account of the origins of the idea of "necessary connexion." The latter may throw some light on the genesis of the idea of God, at least, in so far as we conceive God as a cause.

Neither reason nor experience can ever show that "necessary connexion" holds between the objects themselves. Abstract reasoning only discloses that "the power by which one object produces another, is never discoverable merely from their idea" (THN, 69). And that power by which one object must always necessarily give rise to another escapes the most careful empirical inspection, which only discloses in the objects the uniform conjunction but never their "necessary connexion." This idea is derived from experience, to be sure; yet it is found, not in the perceived object, but in the percipient subject. In other words, it is derived not from an impression of sensation, but from an impression of reflection. Custom or habit produces

---

[23] Some of Hume's opponents, or the adversaries of Hume's friends, published in 1745, a pamphlet full of out-of-context quotations by means of which the accusations of heresy, deism, scepticism, and atheism were substantiated. The defamatory campaign was successful and Hume was denied the chair of Professor of Moral Philosophy at the University of Edinburgh. Hume belatedly answered those charges in an interesting pamphlet: *A Letter from a Gentleman to his Friend in Edinburgh*, ed. E. C. Mossner and J. V. Price (Edinburgh: Edinburgh University Press, 1967). It is noteworthy that in it Hume even attempted to show himself as a defender of orthodoxy; to what extent this is true is, due to the circumstances in which he wrote this little work, very difficult to determine. See below, note 26.

similar types of objects, a strong feeling of expectancy for the second, when confronted with the first object. This determination lies not in the objects; it is rather a feeling of compulsion or determination which arises in the mind that surveys them: "we ... feel a determination of the mind to pass from one object to its usual attendant" (THN, 165). Or according to the version of the *Enquiry* :

> This connexion, therefore, which we *feel* in the mind, this customary transition of the imagination from one object to its usual attendant, is the sentiment or impression, from which we form the idea of power or necessary connexion (EHU, 75).

Thus when we believe and say that this "power" resides in sensible objects or in God, what we really do is to transfer into them a quality of the mind; we inevitably follow a powerful instinct or disposition of the imagination which makes us transform our own feeling of expectancy, the subjective compulsion to associate a present impression with the idea of its usual attendant, into an objective necessity in things themselves. For Hume the case of "necessary connexion" is but the most striking instance of a natural tendency of the imagination, also operative in many other instances, to attribute to other objects qualities that reflection discovers only in ourselves:

> the mind has a great propensity to spread itself on external objects, and to conjoin with them any internal impressions which they occasion, and which always make their appearance at the same time that these objects discover themselves to the senses (THN, 167).[24]

---

[24] My treatment of Hume's account of "necessary connexion" has been very cursory since I have only tried to establish a connection between it and Hume's explanation of the origin of the idea of God. I have passed over many of the serious difficulties that it raises. We shall briefly dwell on two of these. For instance, when analyzing the last quotation, John Passmore, in his important commentary, *Hume's Intentions*, pp. 77–78, affirms that Hume's explanation can be held only under certain presuppositions that he in no way justifies. "It is not enough to say that there is first of all the impression C, then the impression of necessity N, then a vivid idea of E, because, for one thing, there would then be a simple sequence of perceptions and no way of apprehending, or supposing, a connexion between C and E, and for another thing, Hume wants to explain the origin of N. This he can only do by assuming the persistence of the mind which can be affected by the occurrence, on quite distinct occasions, of a C followed by an E. And when he goes on to describe the mind's propensity to 'spread itself on external objects and to conjoint with them any internal impressions which they occasion', he assumes that we can distinguish three things – 'external' objects, 'internal' impressions, and a mind to which this externality and internality are relative, and which can confuse one with the other".

But the controversy that presents the most serious difficulties of interpretation is that centering around the question whether Hume's account is circular or not. I shall mention a few typical postures. Passmore again takes the attack against Hume: "Hume sets out to explain what it means to say that 'C is necessarily connected with E.' His explanation runs as follows: 'A person P necessarily thinks of E when he encounters C. But the real point of difficulty in the explicandum lies in the word 'necessarily,' which Hume's analysis simply repeats. If the explanation simply means: 'A person P always thinks of

We attribute to God the same "power" that we believe to belong to the perceived objects, but which is only a subjective quality, a feeling of determination. In doing this, we are just following this tendency of the imagination to its ultimate consequences. Even the highly abstract conception of God which Hume examines in this section of the *Treatise* seems to be the product of the generalization of the propensity of the mind "to spread itself on external objects"; after all the idea of God as Supreme cause, the "power" *par excellence*, is that of a Will from which everything that happens in the world follows as an effect. And it is the same principle which is involved, not only in attributing to God the "power" we erroneously believe according to Hume to manifest itself in our acts of volition, but in ascribing to Him any

---

E when he encounters C,' then presumably the explicandum means: 'C is always conjoined with E.' Then there is no impression of 'necessary connexion'; this is either a meaningless impression with no idea attached to it or else a synonym for constant conjunction. If, on the other hand, 'necessarily' (in the assertion, 'P necessarily thinks of E when he encounters C') means 'something more than' constant conjunction, the problem of explaining in what this 'something more' consists will still remain with us" (*Hume's Intentions*, p. 76).

Alfred N. Whitehead in *Process and Reality* (New York: Macmillan, 1929), p. 196, asserts, in a similar vein, that Hume's explanation implies an infinite regress.

In the often quoted, *The Philosophy of David Hume*, Norman Kemp Smith, on the other hand, seems to be saying the same thing as Passmore: "Now, clearly 'determination' is here more or less synonymous with causation"; but he stops short of accusing Hume of circularity. He adduces that Hume was not defining causation "in a strict logical sense," but only offering an ostensive definition of it (pp. 400–403).

A less hesitant defense of Hume against the charges of circularity and infinite regress is that of D. G. C. MacNabb in *David Hume: His Theory of Knowledge and Morality*, 2nd ed. (pp. 114–115): "Hume is not saying that the necessary connexion between flame and heat consists in a necessary connexion between our impression of flame and our idea of heat, and that necessary connexion consists in a necessary connexion between the thought of an impression of flame, and the thought of an idea of heat, and so on. That would indeed be a vicious infinite regress. He makes clear that each time we say 'necessary connexion,' we express a new feeling of determination. The necessary connexion between flame and heat is the feeling attending the transition from the impression of flame to the idea of heat. The necessary connexion between the impression of flame and the idea of heat is the new feeling attending the transition from the thought of an impression of flame to that of an idea of heat. The two feelings are separate entities, and the two necessary connexions are two distinct necessary connexions. The former is not identified with the latter, nor even defined in terms of it. The necessary connexion between the flame and the heat is defined in terms of the feeling attending our thoughts about them. The necessary connexion between our thoughts about them is something different, and is defined in terms of the feeling attending our thoughts about those thoughts." Long before, John Laird had defended Hume against these charges in a similar way in *Hume's Philosophy of Human Nature* (London: Methuen, 1932), pp. 94–95, 128. More recently, Nicholas Capaldi has assumed Hume's defense along the same lines in *David Hume, The Newtonian Philosopher*, pp. 95–129. A sympathetic treatment of Hume's account is given by Tom. L. Beauchamp and Alexander Rosenberg in *Hume's Theory of Causation* (New York and Oxford: Oxford University Press, 1981), pp. 3–32. They assert that Hume's text contains two theories of causation and two resultant definitions of "cause" and argue scrupulously against a purely regularity theory of causation, which is the more prevalent way of interpreting Hume's account.

other faculty or state of which we are aware in ourselves, like intelligence, goodness, and even certain passions. The difference between God and other causes and effects is that the Supreme power is, in the language of the *Natural History*, "an unknown cause," or using the terminology of the *Treatise*, "an object that does not discover itself to the senses." On the whole, the supposition that the origin of the idea of God lies in the same disposition of the imagination that gives rise to the idea of "necessary connexion" or "power" is quite compatible with, and makes understandable the very broad definition of divinity which Hume gives in the *Natural History* as "invisible, intelligent *power*."

The statements made by Hume in Section VII of the *Enquiry* are also compatible with our supposition. Here he analyzes again the origin of the idea of "necessary connexion" and criticizes Malebranche's occasionalism. But he does not only say on this occasion, as in the *Treatise*, that the idea of a Deity is derived from "particular impressions." He significantly adds that: "we have no idea of the Supreme Being but what we learn from reflection on our faculties" (EHU, 72). What Hume is doing is just repeating his sketchy explanation of that idea, expounded earlier in Section II of the *Enquiry*, whose title is "Of the origin of ideas":

> The idea of God, as meaning an infinitely intelligent, wise, and good Being, arises from reflecting on the operations of our own mind, and augmenting, without limit, those qualities of goodness and wisdom (EHU, 19).

Essentially the same account is anticipated in the *Abstract* :

> *What idea have we of energy or power even in the Supreme Being?* All our idea of a Deity (according to those who deny innate ideas) is nothing but a composition of those ideas, which we acquire from reflecting on the operations of our own minds (THN, A, 656).

The natural impulse by which the imagination reflects into perceived objects the determination that only exists in the percipient mind is basically the same tendency which leads the mind to reflect on the Supreme cause its own volitive, intellectual, and even sensitive and emotive operations. But for this propensity of the imagination to operate, it is first necessary for the mind to become aware of its own mental states or "impressions of reflection." Thus reflection or self-consciousness is a condition of possibility for the genesis of the idea of God. Hume is not saying that the subject is consciously attributing his or her own states and dispositions to the deity, because what happens is exactly the opposite. The believer is not aware of this process of sympathetic projection. In saying that the idea of God arises from reflection, Hume only commits himself to the weaker thesis that self-consciousness is a necessary, but by no means an exclusive condition. Furthermore, the other conditions, that is, the anticipatory urge that emerges from our experience of the constant conjunction between similar events, or the feeling of "easy transition" between a perceived or remembered object and the thought of its usual attendant, and the projective tendency of imagination, or the "propensity of the mind to spread itself on external objects," and in this particular case to objectify that subjective necessity, or compulsion to precipitate the usual union – are habitual, and as such mechanical or automatic dispositions: In this instance too, custom "may operate in such an insensible manner as never to be taken notice of, and may even in some measure be unknown to us" (THN, 103; see also T, 104, and EHU, 28–29). For this reason, Hume might have given the nod to Ludwig Feuerbach's famous dictum:

> But when religion – consciousness of God – is designated as the self-consciousness of man, this is not to be understood as affirming that the religious man is directly aware of this identity for, on the contrary, ignorance of it is fundamental to the peculiar nature of religion.[25]

On the whole, religion was also for Hume, in more than one sense, a process of alienation.

But the main point is that the idea of God and the idea of "necessary connexion" spring from the same principles of human nature. In both cases this operation of the imagination gives rise to "illusions," to the supposition of a power or energy in the cause by which the effect must always necessarily follow. And the imagination goes beyond what is given in sense experience not only by supposing an ultimate cause for every event, but also in the "most usual conjunctions of cause and effect," because the necessary connection between the objects of daily experience can never be apprehended:

> This deficiency in our ideas is not, indeed, perceiv'd in common life, nor are we sensible, that in the most usual conjunctions of cause and effect we are as ignorant of the ultimate principle which binds them together, as in the most unusual and extraordinary. *But this proceeds merely from an illusion of the imagination; and the question is, how far we ought to yield to these illusions* (THN, 267; italics added).

For that reason, and also because it is impossible to rationally justify the presupposition which underlies all inferences concerning cause and effect (that is, that future experience must be similar to the past), Hume assigns all causal reasoning to an act of belief rather than of knowledge: he even calls it "an implicite Faith."[26]

If we take all of this into consideration, it seems fair to conclude that the account of the *Natural History* about the origin of the idea of God is virtually con-

---

[25] Ludwig Feuerbach, *The Essence of Christianity*, p. 13.

[26] *A Letter from a Gentleman to his Friend in Edinburgh*, p. 21: "And can one do a more essential Service to Piety, than by showing them [heretics and deists, etc.] that this boasted Reason of theirs, so far from accounting for the greatest Mysteries of the Trinity and Incarnation, is not able fully to satisfy itself with regard to its own Operations, and *must in some Measure fall into a kind of implicite Faith, even in the most obvious and familiar Principles?"* (italics added)

tained in the *Treatise* and the *Enquiry*. However, there remains a main difference between the *Natural History* and the *Treatise*. In the latter, Hume also takes into consideration the philosophical idea of God, or better, the philosophical extrapolation of the Hebrew-Christian tradition. And the most interesting divergence of the *Treatise* is that Hume seems to recognize here the operation of a passion or affection which sets the imagination in motion – an innate curiosity, or an original love of wonder that he completely disregarded in the *Natural History* as a factor in the origin of "vulgar" or historical religions:

> Nothing is more curiously enquir'd after by the mind of man than the cause of every phenomenon: nor are we content with knowing the immediate causes, but push on our enquiries, till we arrive at the original and ultimate principle (THN, 266).

Even if another moving force of imagination has been incidentally recognized, the ideas of the "living God" and the God of the philosophers and theologians arise, nonetheless, out of the same operations of imagination that produce the idea of causation – this, I think, the *Natural History* and the *Treatise* have in common. The *Enquiry*, on the other hand, goes beyond the *Treatise* since it even anticipates in its broad outlines Hume's theory about the historical origins of religion given in the *Natural History*. There he dwells on the circumstances, passions, and motives which are involved in the framing of the popular conceptions of divinity.

The common person naturally believes he or she perceives the necessary connection between the objects of daily experience, investing them with a "power" or "force." It is only in those situations where the cause escapes detection or observation – especially when the effect is uncommon or extraordinary – that this same person goes on to suppose that the cause lies in an invisible, intelligent power. Thus Hume says in Section VII, Part I, of the *Enquiry Concerning Human Understanding* that:

> It is only on the discovery of extraordinary phaenomena such as earthquakes, pestilence, and prodigies of any kind, that they find themselves at a loss to assign a proper cause, and to explain the manner in which the effect is produced by it. It is usual for men, in such difficulties, to have recourse to some invisible intelligent principle as the immediate cause of that event which surprises them, and, which, they think, cannot be accounted for from the common powers of nature (EHU, 69).

It is, on the contrary, an opposite perplexity that leads the person of a reflective mind, the philosopher, from the observation of the regular course of events, to suppose the existence of God as the intelligent mind, which is the cause of such universal order. And it is even a more acute observation that guides a Cartesian philosopher, like Malebranche, not only to an ultimate cause, but to an "immediate and sole cause of every event" (EHU, 70–71), since he is well aware that the power and efficacy do not belong to any creature. In any case, the actual mechanism of imaginative projection is everywhere essentially the same; common persons reflect into the Divine cause any states and emotions that they may experience in themselves; the pious man, goodness; the theologian or philosopher, infinite wisdom and power; and the Cartesian philosopher, the efficacy that he may outwardly deny, but that he no less acknowledges or believes to be present in the volitive act. A sceptic like Hume knows that this power or necessary connexion is to be found in no object (THN, A, 656); but he also knows that it is scarcely possible to believe this power not to be present in them; it is "as unavoidable as to feel the passion of love, when we receive benefits; or hatred, when we meet with injuries" (EHU, 46). Precisely because of this impossibility of suspending judgment, I think that those who view Hume, not as a subjectivist, but as a realist about causal efficacy or objective necessity are right. And if the belief in God arises out of the same universal propensity to believe in causal powers, then one should seriously entertain the possibility that Hume may be also a realist of sorts concerning God's existence. In this sense, God might perhaps be the object of an analogous "implicite Faith," or natural belief. This is the thesis for which chapters 13 and 14 in particular hopefully will provide reasonable support.

Be that as it may, what at the moment clearly stands out is that the *Natural History* is – always taking into account Hume's specific presupposition about the historical process – a plausible and natural development of the doctrines of the *Enquiry* just briefly examined; that is, his contention in the *Natural History*, that it is under the pressure of common daily life and the preoccupation for survival that the imagination is led to cast the first ideas of the gods, seems to follow directly from the remarks of Section VII, Part I of the *Enquiry*. In addition, the account of the *Natural History* is not only foreshadowed in the *Treatise* and the *Enquiry*, but is also given a foundation in these works. The latter contain, as it were, the static and the former, the dynamic consideration of the same phenomena. In short, the *Natural History* describes and illustrates the real succession, namely, the actual historical process in which certain universal and constant principles of human nature unfold; but those principles and operations have been already explained and dissected by the *Treatise* and the *Enquiry*.

In brief, the ultimate account of the origin of the idea of God lies in Hume's analysis of the "extent and force of human understanding" (THN, xv). Given the capacity for self-consciousness or reflection on our own internal states, and given also the tendency of the mind to "spread itself on external objects," it is not strange that a historical consideration of religious representations of divinity should disclose that the mind, operating under the pressure of passions such as hope and fear, first conceives ideas of powerful but limited beings, with human passions and appetites, limbs and organs (NHR, 24), i.e., that idolatrous polytheism is the first religion of humankind.

Before leaving the present subject, it will be useful to add a few comments on topics that are directly or indirectly connected with it, but hitherto only summarily touched upon.

How essential or dispensable is the influence of Hume's theory about the capacities and limitations of the human mind, that is his scepticism, in the actual framing of his genetic account given in *The Natural History of Religion?* To what extent is it possible to maintain that such a theory determines him to view religion from a standpoint which thrusts into the limelight certain aspects (most of them dismal) of this human phenomenon while it at once obscures or disregards other more intractable although no less undeniable features of religion?

It is not easy to give a general answer to these questions. However, in the next chapters I shall attempt to point out to what degree some important theses of Hume's reflection on religion can be attributed to the a presumed influence of his epistemological theory. In fact, we have already begun this task in the present chapter by establishing a relationship between his account of the origins of historical conceptions of divinity with prominent doctrines of the *Treatise* and the *Enquiry Concerning Human Understanding*. I concede, though, that I have side-stepped several serious difficulties, of which I will address only two:

In the first place, "reflection" is a necessary condition for the idea of God to arise. Yet I have merely establish that this is the case, and have still to provide a more careful and penetrating examination of this concept. And the latter is needed in order to ascertain whether Hume's explanation of the idea of God truly rests on an intelligible and solid foundation. It is difficult to say whether Hume provides a satisfactory theoretical explanation of how we are capable of becoming conscious of the operations of our own minds. I think that there are signs in the *Treatise* and the *Enquiry* that Hume indeed was aware of the problematical character of such an act. Even though it is true that he takes over the Lockean distinction of sensation-reflection as the source of experience, he modifies it by transforming it into the dichotomy of "impressions of sensation and reflection." The latter, along with the principles of synthesis, or the links which are the products of the force of mental attraction that association of ideas is (resemblance, contiguity and causation), seems to be the kind of mechanism that has been particularly designed to account for consciousness, as much as for all other acts of mental connection by means of which the real world, in so far as it is known by – or exists for – us, is constituted. We have dealt with this aspect of Hume's philosophy already in the first chapter.

For certain, the sceptical conclusion of Book I of the *Treatise*, in addition to his explicit perplexity before the problems posed by personal identity, provides us with strong evidence that Hume's confidence in association as a kind of panacea for explaining mental life slackened; and thus he finally confesses that association is not sufficient in order to make intelligible some basic acts of that same life. Among these we find reflection, or the consciousness that the thinking self has of its own states, which is supremely important, since it is such an activity that even makes the investigation into the extension and limits of human understanding possible:

> I am sensible that my account is very defective. . . . Most philosophers seem inclined to think, that personal identity *arises* from consciousness, and consciousness is nothing but a reflected thought or perception. The present philosophy, therefore, has so far a promising aspect. But all my hopes vanish when I come to explain the principles that unite our successive perceptions in our

thought or consciousness. I cannot discover any theory which gives me satisfaction on this head (THN, Appendix, 635–636).[27]

Even though the *Enquiry Concerning Human Understanding* does not discover any new theoretical alternative for solving that question, it testifies to the fact that Hume finally abandoned both the associative mechanism, at least as an explanation of self-consciousness, and the presumption that one has to account for it by means of a more fundamental principle. With respect to the dissatisfaction or non-fulfillment of his theoretical aspirations, Hume appears to follow the maxim which in the very Introduction to the *Treatise* he proposes that holds for all the desires of life: once we become aware of the impossibility of their being satisfied, they immediately cease (THN, xvii). The absence of mention in the *Enquiry* of topics such as the distinction between impressions of sensation and reflection, the difference between ideas of the memory and imagination and the problem of personal identity, are cumulative evidence in favor of it. To corroborate the second part of this thesis, we may point to the fact that in the only place where Hume examines the problem of the certainty that pertains to the consciousness that the mind has of its own operations and contents, he confers on reflection a kind of axiomatic character that from afar makes one recall Descartes, when he transforms the *ego cogito* (I think) into a first principle of his first philosophy: "For it is so evident of itself that it is I who doubts, who understands, and who desires, that there is no reason here to add anything to explain it."[28] But closer to home, it makes one think of Hume himself, when in Section IV of Book I of the *Treatise* he bestows on the belief in the continuous and independent existence of sensible objects the same rank: accordingly he upholds that it is not something to which we reason, but something that we take for granted whenever we reason (THN, 187). Likewise in the *Enquiry* Hume seems to say that reflection or self-consciousness is in itself more evident, primary and indubitable that any explanation one may invent in order to account for it, and that precisely for that reason it is immune, in theory as well as in practice, from the inveterate doubts of the most radical scepticism; for self-consciousness is the condition that makes possible not only the search for truth, and the doubts whether it is possible to achieve it, but also even that investigation that probes those powers and capacities which the mind employs when it sets out to know the truth:

[27] This declaration is even stronger than the sceptical conclusion of Book I of the *Treatise*. See the whole section, in particular THN, 265, where in spite of his suggestion that our belief in causes and effects, the continued existence of perceived objects – even any consciousness of objects, of ourselves as much as of others, that goes beyond actual or present perception – has no rational justification, and we assent to it only because imagination bestows a greater vivacity on certain conscious data or ideas. But even in this section Hume appears to cling, if not to sufficient reasons which might validate our common beliefs, at least to a causal-associative explanation that presumably accounts for the manner in which we form them. This is also questioned, I think, in the Appendix. to the *Treatise*.

[28] René Descartes, *Meditations on First Philosophy*, Meditation II, Adam-Tannery, IX, 22; Haldane-Ross, I, 153.

Nor can there remain any suspicion, that this science is uncertain and chimerical; unless we should entertain such a scepticism as is entirely subversive of all speculation, and even action. *It cannot be doubted*, that the mind is endowed with several powers and faculties, that these powers are distinct from each other, *that what is really distinct to the immediate perception may be distinguished by reflection*; and consequently, that there is a truth and falsehood in all propositions on this subject, and a truth and falsehood, which lie not beyond the compass of human understanding (EHU, 13–14; italics added).

The second question is the following: It is clear that in the *Treatise* and the *Enquiry Concerning Human Understanding* Hume denies that we have a distinct idea of God as an infinitely powerful being. And as we have just seen, in the *Natural History* he appears to insinuate the same thing. This idea rises out of a reflection on our own faculties, that is, from "particular impressions" in which no "power" or causal efficacy can ever be discovered. If this is truly the case, should Hume have rather said what he never explicitly asserted: namely, that the term 'God' (the god of the philosophers, of course) is without meaning, or that the idea of God is a fiction? Since this question is logically independent of the explanation we have just examined, about the genesis of the idea of God, and it has however to do with its objective validity, I shall postpone answering it until we have analyzed the *Dialogues Concerning Natural Religion*, where Hume deals with this matter extensively.

Now we shall take a glance at Hume's account of the evolution of historical religion and how it elucidates his conception of the historical process in general.

CHAPTER 6

Religion and History

Does Hume present in *The Natural History of Religion* a unitary and coherent conception of history? Under the supposition that such is the case, is it the same or at least consistent with the vision of history that can be extracted from the *History of England* and some of his principal historical essays? These are the questions I shall attempt to answer in what follows. Let us begin with the *Natural History*.

In this work, Hume not only offers an explanation of the actual origins of religion, but also tries to find an orderly pattern of development in the process out of which the multiple and heterogeneous forms of religious life of humankind have emerged. He is not principally interested in the particular religious events as such, but rather in the laws according to which these arise and develop. Hume understands those forms of life as involving a process in which each type of religion follows in some measure necessarily from the preceding types; and his main purpose is to apprehend the principles that permit us to understand the historical origination and development of religions as an ordered sequence of events.

At least in the *Natural History*, the Humean outlook on history is not totally exempted from a certain ambiguity because it seems to be made up of two divergent views about the sort of intelligible pattern that human events configure through the course of time. With some difficulty, Hume brings them together, seemingly never abandoning either. There is, first, a progressive view, according to which historical events, i.e., ideas, institutions, develop from the more rudimentary to the less rudimentary, from the less to the more civilized. This is the dominant tendency in Hume's thought, and in this regard he stands as an important representative of the Enlightenment. Yet another view is latent in his thought, according to which the course of history is cyclical: basically the same constellation of events recurs again and again; in other words, historical phenomena reproduce a fundamental pattern of orderly sequence that repeats itself in its essentials. Although in the *Natural History*, this second view is in certain contexts of preeminent importance, from a general perspective and in comparison to the first it has a secondary role. By holding it, even if in a hesitant manner, Hume distances himself from the philosophers of history of the Enlightenment.

It is probable that Hume derived this second outlook from the historians of Ancient Greece and Rome, particularly Thucydides. In accordance with this, one could interpret his assertion in another writing that the first page of Thucydides is "the commencement of real history."[1] A beautiful passage of the *History of the Peloponnesian Wars* illustrates the cyclical or reiterative pattern:

> But if he who desires to have before his eyes a true picture of the events which have happened, and of the like events which may be expected to happen hereafter in the order of human things, shall pronounce what I have written to be useful, then, I shall be satisfied. My history is an everlasting possession, not a prize composition which is heard and forgotten (*History*, I, 22).[2]

This conception of history is also perfectly consonant with his insistence on the view that human nature is permanent and his confessed Newtonian methodology, which aspires to frame universal explanations for phenomena.

The first conception, according to which in history the more developed arises out of the less developed, is used at the beginning of the *Natural History* to establish the temporal priority of polytheism over monotheism. If religion arises out of the non-rational elements of human nature, then idolatrous polytheism had to be the first religion of humankind, and monotheism must have emerged out of it. In what follows, this progressive outlook of Hume finds a clear expression:

> It seems certain, that, *according to the natural progress of human thought*, the ignorant multitude must first entertain some groveling and familiar notion of superior powers, before they stretch their conception to that perfect Being, who bestowed order on the whole frame of nature. *We may as reasonably imagine, that men inhabited palaces before huts and cottages, or studied geometry before agriculture; as assert that the Deity appeared to them a pure spirit, omniscient, omnipotent, and omnipresent*, before he was apprehended to be a powerful, though limited being, with human passions and appetites, limbs and organs. *The mind rises gradually, from inferior to superior:* By abstracting from what is imperfect, it forms an idea of perfection: And slowly distinguishing the nobler parts of its own frame from the grosser, it learns to transfer only the former, much elevated and refined, to its divinity (NHR, 24; italics added).

---

[1] "Of the Populousness of Ancient Nations," (E, 422).

[2] Thucydides, *History of the Peloponnesian Wars*, trans. by Benjamin Jowett, in *The Greek Historians*, ed. R. B. Godolphin (2 vols.; New York: Random House, 1942), I, 576. That Thucydides' influence was powerful, is testified by a letter which Hume wrote during the beginning of the composition of the *History of England*; in it, he not only says that his own history is "very concise, after the manner of the Ancients," but even ends it by transcribing a telling part of the above quoted passage of Thucydides: κτῆμα εἰς ἀεί" ["an everlasting possession"] (L, I, letter 79, 170–171). See also, L, I, letter 94, 193.

Still, quite early in the *Natural History* this linear view recedes into the background and the cyclical one takes center stage. The latter view is employed to account for a notable and puzzling feature of religious life: the prominent role and the tremendous enduring power of the irrational element in all historical ("popular") forms of religion – both ancient and modern. Hume will, almost in a jubilant spirit, point to paradoxes and inconsistencies, to the perseverance of superstitious and foolish customs and beliefs even in quite late and sophisticated forms of monotheism. The whole of the *Natural History* is prodigally sprinkled with many such instances, but the following are sufficient to illustrate the phenomenon in question:

Who can express the perfections of the Almighty? say the Mahometans. Even the noblest of his works, if compared to him, are but dust and rubbish. How much more must human conception fall short of his infinite perfections? His smile and favour renders men for ever happy; and to obtain it for your children, the best method is to cut off from them, while infants, a little bit of skin, about half the breadth of a farthing. Take two bits of cloth, say the *Roman catholics*, about an inch or an inch and a half square, join them by the corners with two strings or pieces of tape about sixteen inches long, throw this over your head, and make one of the bits of cloth lie upon your breast, and the other upon your back, keeping them next your skin: There is not a better secret for recommending yourself to that infinite Being, who exists from eternity to eternity (NHR, 46).

These, and many other such facts are taken, by Hume, to be a sort of cumulative evidence in favor of the thesis that religion is not only irrational in its origins but is always irrational. One of the most prominent among such facts is what Hume calls the "flux and reflux of polytheism and [mono]theism." Not only did monotheism arise out of polytheism, but there is even a natural tendency in the actual development of monotheistic forms of religion to gradually transform into their opposite. Hume is thus led to conceive of the historical genesis of the diverse forms of religion as a process of continuous alternation of two "ideal types": religious monotheism and idolatrous polytheism.

In the last three chapters we have seen already that Hume rejects the traditional *ad hoc* explanations for the actuality of these phenomena: they are neither a manifestation of humankind's blindness and corruption – resulting presumably from being deprived of divine Grace – nor the fabrications of hypocritical and unscrupulous leaders, ministers, or priests, who by strange rituals and truculent superstitions, subjugate the majority of the people. Now we shall only dwell on the reasons he gives for the recalcitrance of superstition in historical religion and for the continuous cyclical transformation of polytheism into monotheism and vice versa.

Absurd and barbarous practices (present, according to Hume, everywhere and always in religious history), the conspicuous vestiges of polytheism in monotheistic religions and the tendency of these to regress into polytheism are not simply due to an unfortunate folly, nor to the malevolence of the many or of a few, nor to pure chance. Their ubiquitous and reiterative occurrence makes patent its inevitable character, and is a sign of an essential necessity, of a necessity that has its roots in what we are, in what lies deep in human nature. If the latter has a uniform and permanent constitution, it is not strange that in paramount phenomena of human life there should be a certain type of reiterative pattern.[3] The mind exhibits in its operation constant dispositions and propensities, which however trivial they may seem to the rational thinker, are essential for the constitution of the world in which we believe to be, the world of human experience, both cognitive and practical. But sometimes these emotive and imaginative propensities, due to an intrinsic dynamics, tend to oppose each other in a kind of perennial and irresolvable conflict. Already in the *Treatise*, Book I, Part IV, Sect. IV, "Of modern philosophy," Hume had shown that the tendency of the imagination which makes us place our trust in causal inference can clash with our immediate propensity to believe in the distinct and continuous existence of sensible objects. And this is one, perhaps not the most important, instance of immanent tensions or almost dialectical oppositions of this type.[4]

In the case of the "flux and reflux of polytheism and [mono]theism," the opposition is between two tendencies of the imagination: the disposition to believe in invisible and intelligent power and the equally strong propensity to confer a solid assent to sensible objects only.[5] The first propensity, left to itself, will stop only after the believer attributes absolute unity and perfection to God, transforming Him into an infinite Being, totally other and different from nature. In such a manner, the devout also confers to his or her deity the indisputable capacity of exercising that absolute power for the benefit of those who are its votaries, which explains why, for Hume, monotheism in not necessarily morally superior nor less idolatrous than polytheism. The other tendency leads us, first, to make God resemble ourselves more and more, and later to introduce intermediaries of a lesser rank between Him and ourselves. In the course of time, these intermediary deities

---

[3] In this I think that the great scholar of the philosophy of history, R. G. Collingwood, is wrong in his interpretation of Hume's philosophy of history. See *The Idea of History* (Oxford and New York: Oxford University Press, 1946), pp. 71–85. There, he typically says that: "History never repeated itself, but human nature remained eternally the same (p. 82). Yet it is significant that he does not mention even once the *Natural History of Religion*, where this cyclical conception is, I believe, operative.

[4] THN, 231; c.f., 266. Likewise, the inclination to attribute identity to perceived objects contradicts their undeniable interruption (THN, 205); and the desire to discover the principle by which causes necessarily produce their effects clashes with the consciousness that such necessity does not lie in the objects, but rather in the mind that perceives them (THN, 266–267). Even the modern "philosophical system" (the representative theory of consciousness, *à la* Locke), which ascribes the interruption or discontinuousness to the perceptions and the continuity and independence to the objects that they presumably represent, is no more that a desperate and fictitious expedient, which is forged in order to solve, or at least alleviate, the conflict between the principles of reason and imagination, principles to which the mind alternatively assent, even though they are mutually opposed (THN, 211–216).

[5] "The only existences, of which we are certain, are perceptions, which, being immediately present to us by consciousness, command our strongest assent, and are the first foundation of all our conclusions" (THN, 212).

become the only true objects of worship, for no matter how emphatic the "declamations of the religionists" may be, their belief in such an infinite God in the background is, ultimately and from the very beginning, only nominal, not genuine. Very soon this propensity to represent the deity in our own image ends up by imputing it not only our virtues, but all sort of vices which are also ours; thus, our superstitious hopes and fears again activate the contrary disposition to augment the degrees of perfection of the deity, re-initiating a new cycle.

The perpetual tension in the mind of human beings between these two dispositions is what brings about the historical alternation between monotheism and polytheism, a circular movement that will last as long as human nature remains the same:

> The feeble apprehensions of men cannot be satisfied with conceiving their deity as a pure spirit and perfect intelligence; and yet their natural terrors keep them from imputing to him the least shadow of limitation and imperfection. They fluctuate between these opposite sentiments. The same infirmity still drags them downwards, from an omnipotent and spiritual deity, to a limited and corporeal one, and from a corporeal and limited deity to a statue or visible representation. The same endeavour at elevation still pushes them upwards, from the statue or material image to the invisible power; and from the invisible power to an infinitely perfect deity, the creator and sovereign of the universe (NHR, 48).

Hume sees what is obviously there to see. Quite often priests have profited from the fears and the tendencies of the imagination that produce this flux and reflux, and they have encouraged superstitious rituals and capricious conceptions of God. And thus they have brought men and women to their knees before their deities, bringing them into a passive and voluntary submission. Nonetheless, even though Hume admits that this usually occurs, his explanation of the ubiquity of the phenomenon is more profound than the conspiratorial theories of the English deists and the philosophers of the Enlightenment. When accounting for the oscillation between the monotheistic and the polytheistic forms, as well as for the diverse idolatrous cults that this oscillation gives rise to, Hume, as it were, does not ascribe the incidence of the malady to the perversity or convenience of the physicians, but to an innate inclination on our part to contract the disease:

> Thus it may be allowed, that the artifices of men aggravate our natural infirmities and follies of this kind, but never originally beget them. Their root strikes deeper into the mind, and springs from the essential and universal properties of human nature (NHR, 73).

To recapitulate, it seems that in the *Natural History*, we are left with an ambiguous conception of history that is made up of two diverse views of that process. These are difficult to reconcile, but Hume needs them both in order to explain the historical development of religion. One may ask also: Whence in the last analysis do they come from? In answering this question one must not lose sight that Hume historical studies are not extrinsic additions to his philosophy;[6] on the contrary, these investigations were latent in the attempt of the *Treatise* "to introduce the experimental method of reasoning into moral subjects". When he affirms that one of his objectives is to discover the constant principles of human understanding through well-made "experiments," he is not exclusively, nor mainly, referring to an introspective activity, which here he seems almost to reject (for a premeditated reflection would alter or interfere with the operations of those mental principles); what he proposes instead is the careful observation of human behavior in the affairs of common life (THN, xxii–xxiii). With this in mind, I propose that Hume's ambiguous outlook, or more precisely, dual and antagonistic conception of history appears to arise out of two conflicting tendencies of his own philosophy.

The genuinely historical dimension of Hume's philosophy ultimately derives from his empirical approach to the problem of knowledge. To know the meaning and cognitive validity of our concepts one has to disclose their origin in experience. Hume inherits from Locke this empirical outlook, which the latter calls, the "historical plain method".[7] We can only determine the effective possibilities and limitations of our cognitive faculties in so far as we can explain the nature of our ideas (THN, Introduction, xix; EHU, 6), or in the words of Locke, by a "natural history" of our ideas. Hume's empirical approach is originally historical at least for two reasons: On the one hand, if the nature of our ideas cannot be really separated from their genesis in experience, this means that they are historical entities; and if this is true of human ideas, then it has to be even truer of the products of ideas, namely, of "moral subjects": all moral, political, artistic and, in general, cultural institutions.[8] One should remember that Hume supposes that this holds not only for the moral sciences, but even for subjects such as mathematics, natural philosophy and natural religion, which deal with objects which are independent of our will, because those disciplines likewise depend on the capacities and limitations of the human mind (THN, xix). And on the other hand, in the same manner that we determine the meaning and validity of our concepts, by referring them to past experience, we may disclose the true nature of those products of human activity, by studying their historical origin and development. This is precisely what Hume was already doing in the *Natural History of Religion*. The progressive theory of history seems mainly to stem from this emphasis on experience. However, even if Hume's

---

[6] While composing *The History of England*, Hume said, in a letter to the Abbé Le Blanc: "The philosophical Spirit, which I have so much indulg'd in all my Writings, finds here ample Materials to work upon" (L, I, letter 94, 193).

[7] John Locke, *An Essay Concerning Human Understanding*, Introduction, p. 27.

[8] This is the germ of truth that R. G. Collingwood's commentary on Hume contains: This germ has grown into an encompassing and coherent view in Donald W. Livingston, *Hume's Philosophy of Common Life*. Yet Livingston is right when he questions Collingwood's interpretation, and attempts to demonstrate, in opposition to it, that the fundamental categories of Hume's speculative philosophy are intrinsically historical; See, in particular, the following chapters 1, pp. 44–59; 4, pp. 91–111, and, 5, pp. 112–149.

general attitude is not antihistorical, one may still object that his conception did not completely crystallize into a genuinely historical consciousness because it was limited by other factors.

It is well known that Hume attacked the logical legitimacy of the traditional notion of substance, thereby emphasizing the features of process, change, and flux, as intrinsic to the nature of all perceptual things and, in particular, of the human mind itself. Thus he refers to the latter, as "nothing but a bundle or collection of different perceptions, which succeed each other with an inconceivable rapidity, and are in a perpetual flux and movement" (THN, 252). Yet I think that Hume remained chained to a vestigial substantialistic belief, although certainly not in an immutable stuff. I say 'belief,' for Hume appears to have taken more seriously than some of his commentators the sceptical consequences of his philosophy; it is due to his scepticism that he emphatically asserts the central role of Nature as it operates in and through all of us. Nature, as it were, gives us a hand at the point where pure reason fails us, so that we may effectively, by means of ineradicable, instinctive, and fundamental beliefs, be able to find our way, live and act in the world. In very different contexts, Hume alludes to constant and uniform principles of a human nature that is universal and permanent as well as the authentic protagonist of history:

> It is universally acknowledged, that there is a great uniformity among the actions of men, in all nations and ages, and that human nature remains still the same, in its principles and operations. . . . Mankind are so much the same, in all times and places, that history informs us of nothing new or strange in this particular. Its chief use is only to discover the constant and universal principles of human nature, by shewing men in all varieties of circumstances and situations, and furnishing us with materials, from which we may form our observations, and become acquainted with the regular springs of human action and behaviour (EHU, 83).

Just as Hume does not hold the uniformity of nature as the conclusion of an empirical observation, he does not assert the uniformity and constancy of our human nature as the result of an inductive generalization. It appears, on the contrary, to partake more of the character of an a priori presupposition that is incorporated into our way of visualizing and relating the historical events, and which is, as such, what also ultimately makes the study of history itself possible. For if the reflective consideration of the life of human beings, in "different circumstances and situations," may reveal something to us about the "regular springs of human action and behaviour," one has to suppose that from what other people say and do, we can obtain some knowledge about their interiority or the springs ("motives or reasons") that made them the sort of people they in fact are, i.e., about their ideas, intentions, character, opinions, feelings and desires. This presupposition holds not only for the direct observation of the actual behavior of other people, but for those occasions in which our spatial and temporal remoteness from the events prevents us from being witnesses, and we get a mediate knowledge of those facts through the oral or written testimony of third persons, such as Hume himself gathered the facts he analyzed in the *Natural History* from the stories of "travelers and historians" (NHR, 21). In sum, that it must be possible for us – when we read the narration of a historian – as much as for the latter – when she or he examines the records, documents and even artifacts of the period with which her or his narrative deals – , to have access to the mind of other human beings through the testimony of third persons. When Hume was dealing in the *Treatise* with the doctrine of sympathy, he said that we gain such knowledge by the observation of the "external signs" of human behavior.[9]

But to which presuppositions Hume appeals in order to justify our belief in the reality of this intersubjective communication, both of the present with the present and of the present with the past? He points precisely to the same human nature that he mentions in that presumably "antihistorical" passage of the *Enquiry*.[10] We are dealing here with the nature of the human mind, and in particular, with a complementary aspect of his theory of the self which seems to be in a sort of dialectical opposition with its plurality and impermanence. If one overemphasizes this Heraclitean feature, one may thereby overlook that Hume also stresses the organic unity of the mind and that in order to account for something which is of extreme importance for any type of historical comprehension, that is, for explaining how is it possible for different persons to communicate to each other both their passions and ideas, he likens the self to a mirror (THN, 365).[11]

It remains an open question whether Hume's attempt to causally explain, employing the mechanism of the association of ideas, phenomena such as interpersonal understanding and sympathy with others was successful or not. I will only emphasize now that if the minds of other people, be they contemporaries or predecessors, were not similar to our own, then these phenomena such as interpersonal communication, sympathy, and especially, historical understanding, would be entirely unaccountable. For as we have seen, according to Hume, neither the passions, nor the ideas, nor the intentions of others are directly apprehended; they have to be inferred from what they do or say. And this is only possible because there is a specific similarity between our minds and those of others' – in sum, because in this, too, we share in the same human nature.[12]

In spite of all this, one may object that what the passage of the *Enquiry* more clearly shows is something else; i.e., that here Hume's professed Newtonian

---

[9] THN, 317–318, 477. In order that a book of history may "instruct" us, we have to suppose exactly the same as Demea, the defender of religious orthodoxy in the *Dialogues Concerning Natural Religion*, who says that we have to suppose, when reading any book, that the written text allows the reader to penetrate into the mind of its author and gain access to his or her intentions and ideas, in such a fashion that we, who read, "become him, in a manner, for the instant" (DNR, 155).

[10] See Donald W. Livingston, *Hume's Philosophy of Common Life*, pp. 210–215, for a summary and refutation of this type of antihistorical interpretation of Hume.

[11] With respect to its unity, Hume compares the self to a republic or political state (commonwealth), for "the true idea of the human mind, is to consider it as a *system* of different perceptions or different existences" (THN, 261; italics added).

[12] The minds of all men are similar in their feelings and operations; nor can any one be actuated by any affection of which all others are not in some degree susceptible (THN, 575–576).

methodology, as applied to his peculiar naturalism, interferes with his historical interests. As this capital passage suggests, it is not the historical happenings per se, but the general and unchanging laws that govern the relations between such happenings, which is the subject matter of his investigation into history. His conception of history remained, to a great extent, tied to a sort of naturalism that views historical. events as expressions of immutable or at least regular laws. In short, Hume, who most forcefully attacked the pretension of converting empirical science into an entirely deductive system, comparable to mathematics, could not, at least in his general reflections about history (although not in the concrete exercise of the historiographical activity) totally free himself from this deductive ideal.[13] Since human nature is constant and uniform, if this vision had been pushed to its limits, then eternity would have absorbed temporality, and true change, denied, and the possibility of conceiving history as a creative process, abolished: in the end, history would have been in a literal sense "the eternal return of the same," to use Nietzsche's well-known formula.

Yet in general, Hume never conceives of the historical process in this manner, nor is the cyclical the dominant, much less, the exclusive view of the *Natural History*. Had this been the case, Hume would have explained the development of religion in non-historical terms, at least if we refer by 'historical' to those changes in which intrinsically novel entities are gestated out of the past. Nevertheless, that outlook is complemented by, and subordinated to, another, according to which history is not only a process of continuous transformation through successive oppositions and conflicts, but a creative process, specifically of change in the direction of human improvement from dark beginnings to a more luminous future, from ignorance to science, from rusticity to civilization.

Furthermore, Hume's phrase, "that history informs us of nothing new," should neither be interpreted as denying genuine novelty and change, nor as supposing that the same constellations of events occur all the time, or that events that are extraordinary or different from those to which we are accustomed to, have never or will never occur.[14] Due to the context in which this declaration is emitted (with an emphasis on the universality of human nature as the genuine agent of history and also as the factor that permits us to understand it and study it in a systematic fashion), I

---

[13] Thus, when considering physical theories, such as the law of the conservation of motion, he says that: "Geometry assists us in the application of this law . . . but still the discovery of the law itself is owing merely to experience, and all the abstract reasonings in the world could never lead us one step towards the knowledge of it" (EHU, 31).

[14] Otherwise, Hume would have not been able to affirm at once, as he does in the essay "Of Some Remarkable Customs," the maxim of the uniformity and constancy of nature and the occurrence of extraordinary and unpredictable historical happenings:

Irregular and extraordinary appearances are frequently discovered in the moral, as well as in the physical world. The former, perhaps, we can better account for, after they happen, from springs and principles, of which every one has, within himself, or from observation, the strongest assurance and conviction: But it is often fully as impossible for human prudence, before-hand, to foresee and foretell them (E, 366).

believe that the purpose of this supposedly "antihistorical" phrase of the *Enquiry*, is instead to stress that history does not register events that are absolutely or specifically different from those that we can make objects of empirical observation: in sum, that history is, like poetry, the kingdom of the archetypal or universal, or – such as Aristotle says when he opposes poetry to history – the realm of the verisimilar. If this were not the case, its study would be useless to us. For if – as Hume emphasizes in the essay "Of the Study of History" and says in other places – history "instructs" us and not merely entertains us (E, 563) or, in the last analysis, if we do indeed learn something from the past that we may put to use immediately or in the future, then not only with respect to natural events but also with reference to human affairs, the past has to be somehow similar to the future.

Why is it necessary to presuppose this typical resemblance between the past and the future? Otherwise historical happenings would not be relatable; in other words, the succession of human events is susceptible of being woven into a historical narrative because those incidents, circumstances and subjects can be viewed under a typical or specific aspect, and not as exclusively singular facts. For that reason he says in the *History of England*, when commenting on the rhetorical excesses of both English parties, that "however *singular* these events may appear, there is really nothing *altogether* new in any period of modern history" (H, VI, 533; italics added). That is also why Hume groups the various historical religions in two types: polytheism and monotheism.

On the other hand, Hume certainly believed that his own historical narrative is – like Thucydides' – an "everlasting possession" because in instructing us about the non-straightforward and uncertain character of the historical progress of humankind, it can contribute to the improvement of our understanding, that is, to our genuine progress. But if this progressive feature is stressed, then one may object that Hume's theory precisely leaves the most peculiarly historical element of human events unexplained, i.e., the creativity that is given in the process of opposition and mutual dependence of the past and the present, or the intrinsic novelty of historical products, which *prima facie* at least, seems to distinguish them from the reiterative character of the productions of nature. In general, one may reject my hypothesis on the grounds that, even though Hume emphasizes that human nature is the subject of history, perhaps he did not see that it is also transformed by that process; in other words, that the most prominent creation of human history is the manner in which human nature modifies itself through the products of its own activity: in short, that the human being is the subject as well as the object of its own history.

Even though this objection is credible – for Hume verily puts an enormous and perhaps excessive emphasis on the invariability of our nature –, it is not, however, correct. For, as we shall see in sections 2 and 3, in his actual way of explaining the emergence of things as diverse as historical events, technical, artistic and scientific advances, economic and cultural institutions, manners and customs of diverse communities, and even the peculiarities of national temperament, in the *History of England* and some of his most prominent historical, political and moral essays, Hume shows us that, historically speaking, the human being is the builder of its own humanity. One can properly talk about a "natural progress of human thought" inasmuch as are the products of mind the principal causes of the fundamental changes of human life or history, in particular of those "advances" and "inventions" on which the intellectual and moral improvement as well as its decadence, the attaining and preserving of civilization as well as the regress into barbarism, depends.

On the whole, I think that the preceding considerations justify our tentative judgment according to which the *Natural History of Religion* instead of exhibiting an unresolved opposition of two diverse visions of history, or merely the juxtaposition of two opposing views – a cyclical and a progressive –, rather attests to a unitary conception of history. Ultimately, perhaps Hume is unclearly adumbrating the dialectical nature of the historical process. In human history there is conservation as well as creation; progress and continuity are inevitably intertwined. The present stage is something new only by virtue of being the outcome of the preceding ones; the present one at once stands in opposition to them and preserves them, and overcomes them in order to give rise to new oppositions. In brief, that instead of leaving us with two disparate views, Hume formulates a more complex theory in which they are – instead of contraries – complementary aspects of an essentially coherent conception of the historical development.

I will now try to show that the *History of England* and some of Hume's most important historical essays, viewed from the perspective obtained from the *Natural History of Religion*, provide some additional evidence in its favor.

6.2 THE CONCEPTION OF HISTORY IN THE HISTORY OF ENGLAND

In all his works, Hume rejects the theory of the golden age or the inevitable decadence of the historical development. But in the *History of England*, this rebuke is overwhelming and it manifests itself in its very first page. Here, in a single stroke, Hume eliminates the remote past, the pre-Romans as well as the post-Roman Saxon origins of England, from the field of facts that he will make the subject of his narrative and reflective consideration:

> THE CURIOSITY, entertained by all civilized nations, of enquiring into the exploits and adventures of their ancestors, commonly excites a regret that the history of remote ages should always be so much involved in obscurity, uncertainty, and contradiction. Ingenious men, possessed of leisure, are apt to push their researches beyond the period, in which literary monuments are framed or preserved; without reflecting, that the history of past events is immediately lost or disfigured, when intrusted to memory and oral tradition, and that the adventures of barbarous nations, even if they were recorded, could afford little or no entertainment to men born in a more cultivated age. The convulsions of a civilized state usually compose the most instructive and most interesting part of its history; but the sudden, violent, and unprepared revolutions, incident to Barbarians, are so much guided by caprice, and terminate so often in cruelty that they disgust us by the uniformity of their appearance; and it is rather fortunate for letters that they are buried in silence and oblivion (H, I, 3-4).

Why does Hume exclude the Britons and the Anglo-Saxon barbarians from his history? Although it is true that Hume, to a certain extent, believed that the recorded evidence available to him would not have permitted him to construct a trustworthy and true story about the period between the fall of the Roman Empire and the Higher Middle Ages, this is not the principal reason. I think that Donald W. Livingston is right when he asserts that such an exclusion has its origin in Hume's historical presuppositions: from the vantage point of his progressive theory, the history of the barbarians "is not worth telling."[15] Yet one has to reject the particular reason he offers to explain why the progressive idea of history demands the exclusion of the barbarians, because it is totally at odds with prominent tenets which we have seen that Hume defends in the *Natural History of Religion*. According to Livingston, Hume is asserting that the barbarians suffer from a species of spiritual subdevelopment that prevents us from entering into their mind, and that accordingly does not permit us to adequately understand the meaning of their actions, such as these have been preserved in written testimony and can be inferred by the artifacts and tools they have bequeathed us:

> They are excluded because, in not being civilized, they lack fully developed rational interiors, and so it is impossible for the historian to carry out his proper task of working through, in his own mind, the rationale behind their actions.[16]

This interpretation is radically discordant with Hume's explanations about how the first representations of the divine arise in the hypothetical first human communities. When he refers to the primitive mind, to the circumstances of a hostile natural environment, to the hopes and fears that afflicts it, and to the anthropomorphic propensities of its imagination, in brief, to all that which leads it to form the first "tremendous images" (DNR, 225) of the gods, it is quite revealing that again and again Hume should employ the plural of the first person of the personal pronoun. Thus when he talks about "such barbarians," he says, for example, that *"we* hang in perpetual suspence between life and death," and *"our* hope and fear" lead us to form the figures of the gods, and immediately *"we* ascribe to them thought and reason and passion, and sometimes even the limbs and figures of men, in order to bring them nearer to a resemblance with *ourselves"* (NHR, 28–30; italics added). I think this is enough to refute Livingston's hypothesis. But moreover, that long passage of the *History of England*, which Livingston also quotes, does not really support his interpretation. Even though the history of the civilized nations may teach us more, from this admission it does not follow that the history of the barbarian peoples may not teach us anything. What the latter cannot afford the civilized or en-

---

[15] Donald W. Livingston, *Hume's Philosophy of Common Life*, p. 236; See, in general, the section of chapter 8 titled "Barbarians and the Idea of History," pp. 235–246.

[16] Ibid., pp. 241. Livingston even goes to say that "Hume conceives of the behavior of savages and, to a lesser extent, of barbarians also as virtually a natural process. Such people can no more be said to have a history than can bees or moths" (Ibid.).

lightened person is "entertainment." In addition to moral repulsion, the uniform appearance of the ruthless, unsettling routine exercise of violence and cruelty of the barbarians will provoke disgust in him or her, in much the same fashion as the contemplation of a work of art or literature that manifests a servile subjection to an aesthetic canon will displease him or her.[17] The complete fidelity to a set of precepts will turn the appearance of an artistic work completely uniform, that is, monotonous, and this in turn will produce disgust or boredom in the spectator: "To check the sallies of the imagination, and to reduce every expression to geometrical truth and exactness, would be the most contrary to the laws of criticism; because it would produce a work, which, by universal experience, has been found the most insipid and disagreeable" ("Of the Standard of Taste," E, 231).[18] Furthermore, Livingston's tone of seeming belittlement is quite distant from the sympathy that Hume abundantly expresses in the *Natural History* for our remote ancestors.

Without abandoning the thesis according to which the exclusion of the British barbarians is due to the progressive idea of history, I still find more adequate the traditional thesis that relates such a removal to Hume's polemical rejection of the ideological outlook of most English historians, who sought to find, or even reconstruct, the original constitution that presumably lied in the remote feudal past of England. Such historians tried either to justify the royal pretensions or "prerogatives" of the *Tories* (by appealing to a divine cession of power), or to validate the demands of the Whigs (by appealing to a pact or a popular cession of authority) in favor of the "rights and privileges" of the Parliament. This attitude is but another version of the golden age idea of history, or the conception of history as a fall or corruption from a glorious past.[19] Hume, however, does not adhere to the official interpretation of British history as a member of any of the two political parties in dispute, but he rather enlists (as he says in a famous letter) in "the party of humanity," in order to assume an objective and impartial point of view, which may retain what is true and avoid the errors and excesses of both ways of narrating English history.[20]

---

[17] In this habitual infliction of inhumane and senseless suffering, too, we are quite far from having left behind the barbaric ethos.

[18] The following words of Cleanthes, in Part III of the *Dialogues Concerning Natural Religion*, is completely consonant with it: "Some beauties in writing we may meet with, which seem contrary to rules, and which gain the affections, and animate the imagination, in opposition to all the precepts of criticism, and to the authority of the established masters of art" (DNR, 155).

[19] John B. Stewart, *The Moral and Political Philosophy of David Hume* (pp. 319–320), formulates this thesis in a paradigmatic fashion. Even though it has not led Donald W. Livingston to correct his judgment about the supposed mental subdevelopment of savages, he is also aware that Hume expressed such a programmatic intention at the time he was composing the *History of England*, and Livingston cites pertinent passages in support of that thesis. See D. W. Livingston, *Hume's Philosophy of Common Life*, pp. 249–262.

[20] *Letter to Andrew Millar of 26 August 1765*, quoted by E. C. Mossner, *The Life of David Hume*, p. 634. See also, L, I, 179 y 185: "I have the impudence to pretend that I am of no party, and have no bias" (L, I, 185). In the essay, "Of the Coalition of Parties," Hume expresses with vigor and clarity his

In short, although the barbarians and the circumstances of their life still can teach us much about ourselves, and even about what religion continues to be today, it seems as if it is relatively little that we can extract from their rudimentary forms of government in order to understand the complex structure of later political constitutions. Thus the reason one should look for both "pure theism" and the "original constitution" at the end and not at the beginning, is the same: because there has to be "a natural progress of thought . . . from inferior to superior" (NHR, 24). In both cases, to suppose the contrary would be as reasonable for Hume as imagining "that men inhabited palaces before huts and cottages, or studied geometry before agriculture" (NHR, 24). The following passage of the *History of England* corroborates this thesis:

> Above all, a civilized nation, like the English, who have happily established the most perfect and most accurate system of liberty that was ever found compatible with government, ought to be cautious in appealing to the practice of their ancestors, or regarding the maxims of uncultivated ages as certain rules for their present conduct. An acquaintance with the ancient periods of their government is chiefly useful by instructing them to cherish their present constitution, from a comparison or contrast with the condition of those distant times. And it is also curious, by shewing them the remote, and commonly faint and disfigured originals of the most finished and most noble institutions, and by instructing them in the great mixture of accident, which commonly concurs with a small ingredient of wisdom and foresight, in erecting the complicated fabric of the most perfect government (H, II, 525).

Moreover, even in the *History of England* the typical aspect of opposition and reiteration of the historical process, the "flux and reflux," is also present: "The English constitution, like all others, has been in a state of continual fluctuation" (H, IV, Appendix 3, note 1, 355). At least from the conclusion of the Middle Ages, in particular from the reign of Henry VII onwards, Hume's narrative begins to depict a sort of cyclical alternation between the royal power and those diverse popular elements that will form an ever increasingly stronger assembly or parliament.

> The constitution of the English government, ever since the invasion of this island by the Saxons, may boast of this preeminence, that in no age the will of the monarch was ever entirely absolute and uncontrouled: But in other respects *the balance of power has extremely shifted* among the several orders of the

---

purpose of mediating in the "historical disputes" between the parties "by proving that each of them was justified by plausible topics; that there were on both sides wise men, who meant well to their country; and that the past animosity between the factions had no better foundation than narrow prejudice or interested passion" (E, 478–479). In a similar passage of the *History of England*, V, 93–95, Hume summarizes the historical arguments of the partisans of the King and the parliament in a style reminiscent both of the antithetical arguments of Sextus Empiricus and the antagonistic discourses of Thucydides. "Of the Coalition of Parties" was first published in 1758 and that volume the *History* in 1757, the same year in which *The Natural History of Religion* appeared.

state; and this fabric has experienced the same mutability, that has attended all human institutions (H, II, 524; italics added).

It is within this "flux and reflux" between those political poles, in this species of dialectical progress, that little by little the British nation will evolve and become civilized.

Furthermore, the typology "superstition" (exemplified by the Catholic and the Anglican churches) and "enthusiasm" (represented by the Protestant churches, in particular, Puritanism), which he describes in the *History of England*, is – viewed from the vantage point of universal history – almost identical to that of polytheism and monotheism which dominates the *Natural History of Religion*. This notable coincidence occurs not by mere chance, but is rather a consequence of the movement of periodic oscillation that characterizes the course of history in general:

> Such circumstances, though minute, it may not be improper to transmit to posterity; that those, who are curious of tracing the history of the human mind, may remark, how far its several singularities coincide in different ages (H, V, 240).

In like manner one should emphasize that the "successive alterations" of the British constitution instructs us about the peculiarly historical character of all cultural products. When the "continual fluctuation" of political systems is viewed within the wider context of universal history, or of the "general revolutions of society" (H, II, 519), we may apprehend the real nature of historical progress, no less than its dialectical and precarious character, and also begin to catch a glimpse on the identity of the true protagonist of history. Even though the ups and downs of political constitutions, military victories and defeats, along with the physical poverty and desolation that they produce, and all those crucial events and changes (which contain, as we have seen, a great dosage of "accident" and very little "wisdom"), constitute the greater part of Hume's narrative, they are, nonetheless, like the secondary characters of the historical account.[21] Undoubtedly, they all are important, but rather as supporters or obstacles of another and more "general" process: that is, of a polar movement "of depression, as well as of exaltation," (H, II, 519) in which the great but unsteady outlines of the improvement of the spiritual nature of humankind are delineated. The more profound history, in which the history of England inserts itself and which makes it intelligible in the last analysis, is the history of the progress or improvements of the human mind (H, II, 519), in particular, as such advancement manifests itself in the most noble creations of the human spirit – i.e., the arts and sciences:

---

[21] In the following passage Hume reaffirms and argues in favor of this thesis: "But even trivial circumstances, which show the manners of the age, are often more instructive, as well as entertaining, than the great transactions of wars and negotiations, which are nearly similar in all periods and in all countries of the world" (H, IV, 44).

The rise, progress, perfection, and decline of art and science, are curious objects of contemplation, and intimately connected with a narration of civil transactions. The events of no particular period can be fully accounted for, but by considering the degrees of advancement, which men have reached in those particulars (H, II, 519).

The leading thread of universal history is the same we have already seen at work in the history of religion, the transition from ignorance to learning, and its *télos* is the improvement of our nature. From the kingdom of necessity, the human race moves to the sphere of freedom that it constructs for itself. We go – as Hume himself has said in the *Natural History of Religion* – from "so entire a dependance," in which that "barbarous, necessitous animal" (NHR, 24), such as human beings are in the beginnings of primitive communal life, to – as he also says in the *History of England* – "the most perfect and most accurate system of liberty that was ever found compatible with government," which the modern British constitution makes possible. Hence political history is secondary; political institutions (including the juridical, military, and economic ones) are the means for fostering the liberty without which the arts and sciences cannot arise and develop.[22]

Thus it is fitting that Hume should dedicate the most brilliant paragraph of the last pages of the *History of England* to the author of *Principia Mathematica*: "In Newton this island may boast of having produced the greatest and rarest genius that ever arose for the ornament and instruction of the species" (H, VI, 542). Hume's tribute is not only a testimony of his personal admiration for the man, but also a corollary of his conception of historical progress.

And even for the progress that takes place in universal history, it obtains the same as for the history of particular political systems: that is, there is the same "continual fluctuation," or flux and reflux that manifests itself in religious history, and in this instance also between the poles of learning and ignorance, civilization and barbarism. From the summit of the era of Augustus, when "almost all improvements of the human mind had reached nearly to their state of perfection" (H, II, 519), we descend to the chasm represented by the period of William the Conqueror. Out of this "point of depression," human affairs begin their return to a new "point of exaltation": and "from that aera, the sun of science, beginning to re-ascend, threw out many gleams of light, which preceded the full morning, when letters were revived in the fifteenth century" (H, II, 519). Likewise, the process of universal history not only is not straight, but much less is inevitable, for it is subject to innumerable events that are fortuitous and unpredictable, and that can either arrest it or accelerate it. Among the latter, Hume mentions the accidental finding of a copy of Justinian's *Pandects* in the town of Amalfi: to the diffusion of the juridical and political principles contained in that code, he attributes a good portion of the

---

[22] Hume develops this thesis in the essay "Of the Rise and Progress of the Arts and Sciences," (E, 111–137). See in particular, pp. 115–119.

notable political and cultural development enjoyed by European nations in the second half of the Middle Ages (H, 520–21).

On the basis of all these considerations, I believe that one has reasonably established that there is a unitary vision of history in the *History of England*, which is essentially identical with the one Hume formulates in the *Natural History of Religion*. Now we go on to examine some of his principal historical essays.

6.3 THE CONCEPTION OF HISTORY IN HIS ESSAYS

In "Of the Populousness of Ancient Nations," Hume not only maintains that peculiar progressive theory, but also suggests an explication for the prevalence of the belief in the inevitable fall of human history. This view seems to be a product of an illusion of the imagination, which is generic in nature and which depends very little on the character of the individual; it is rather analogous to those distortions which occurs in the perception of the shape and size of sensible objects due to their spatial proximity or remoteness from us. Likewise, it is owing to the temporal remoteness of past events that we are oblivious to their pains and inconveniences. Thus they appear to be better than the present ones, which we cannot so easily ignore, because of the force and liveliness with which they impose themselves to the mind. Hence it follows that:

> The humour of blaming the present, and admiring the past, is strongly rooted in human nature, and has an influence even on persons endued with the profoundest judgment and most extensive learning (E, 464).

In Book I of the *Treatise*, Hume makes clear that on the basis of the careful observation of the constant conjunction between events of the same type and the causal inferences that we found upon it, reason proceeds to form general rules about the size and other real qualities of objects with which we correct sensible appearances; and this is what in turn enable us to make perceptual judgments of universal validity. In Book III, he also shows us that in practical life, when judging about moral actions and characters, the same faculty, that is, "reason . . . called so in an improper sense," forms other general rules with which we modify our personal prejudices and limited sympathy that may lead us to overappreciate those persons which are near to us; in such a fashion we are able to assume a moral point of view, which is impartial and disinterested.[23] In a similar manner, reason also corrects our historical judgment with respect to the past and counterbalances the natural illusion that inclines us to believe that the past was better than the present, and better than it actually was ("Todo tiempo pasado fue mejor").

---

[23] For this interpretation of reason as a virtue, see Páll S. Árdal, "Some Implications of the Virtue of Reasonableness in Hume's Treatise," in *Hume, A Re-Evaluation*, ed. Donald Livingston and James King,, pp.. 91–106.

The essay "Of the Study of History" is consonant with the preceding thesis. On the one hand, Hume supposes that the historical perspective is not essentially different from the ordinary reflection on empirical matters of fact, and on the other hand, he asserts that the former only expands it, because past history is nothing else but the experience of the human race:

> And indeed, if we consider the shortness of human life, and our limited knowledge, even of what passes in our own time, we must be sensible that we should be for ever children in understanding, were it not for this invention, which extends our experience to all past ages, and to the most distant nations; making them contribute as much to our improvement in wisdom, as if they had actually lain under our observation (E, 566–567).

Moreover, Hume asserts that the study of history – the reflection on collective experience – enables us to evaluate human actions and characters from an unbiased moral perspective, and to emit correct and fair judgments. On the one hand, these judgments are not mediated by any personal or selfish interest that may cloud our appraisal, as frequently happens in the social interchange with our contemporaries. On the other hand, we make them with sufficient interest in the historical events and persons that are the subjects of our study, so that our moral praise and reproach of them may be objective and impartial: "History keeps in a just medium betwixt these extremes [of self-interest and indifference], and places the objects in their true point of view" (E, 568).

In sum, *Of the Study of History* clearly reveals that Hume's historical perspective is made possible by, and is in essence indistinguishable from, his empirical outlook on persons and events, and that it strives for the same goal, for "truth . . . is the basis of history" (E, 564).[24] It also shows that history is advantageous not only because it entertains us, "as it amuses the fancy," and may help us to better the circumstances in which we live, but primarily because "it improves the understanding, and . . . strengthens virtue" (E, 563). To that extent history is, among all the sciences, the one that may have really fulfilled Hume's juvenile ambition – which he expressed in the concluding chapter of Book I of the *Treatise* – "of contributing to the instruction of mankind" (THN, 271).

But if history is useful improving our understanding and character as well as for properly meeting the challenges of the future, must not the future be like the past? And if this is so, does it not presuppose a cyclical, instead of progressive, vision of the historical process? Certainly not.

This similarity does not entail identity; for neither with respect to any causes nor any effects, be they natural or moral, the present or future event has to be an exact replica or repetition of the past. On the one hand, since what is contrary to any matter of fact is always distinctly conceived and thus possible, there is no way to

---

[24] In a letter to the Earl of Hardwicke, while referring to the volume on the House of Stuart of his *History of England*, Hume asserts: "I have always sought Truth, I am sure without Interest, and I hope, without Partiality" (L, I, Lt. no. 248,, 461).

exclude the possibility that the future may be radically different from the past. On the other hand, impressions do not come back or repeat themselves.[25]

In general, although "Of the Study of History," places, as it should, a controlling emphasis on the enduring and universal human value of such a discipline, it attests to the same historical outlook that we have seen operative in the *Natural History of Religion*. Once again, we do not have an irresolvable opposition of two diverse views of history, but rather the picking out of two strands that are inexorably interwoven in the historical unfolding of humankind: permanence and change, continuity and progress.

In addition, one must emphasize that Hume's moral and political essays provide a basis ample enough to reasonably answer the objection that Hume's view of history is too static, allowing for too little transformation of human beings themselves and for no novelty. Although one may multiply the instances almost indefinitely, I only will point to three notable examples that show that Hume certainly conceives of history as a creative process of and by humankind itself:

1. Unlike Montesquieu, Hume – although he does not ignore them – gives no decisive importance to "physical" causes in explaining the emergence and differences in structure and degree of development in cultural products, political and economic systems of diverse nations or epochs. Thus a phenomenon, which seems purely biological, such as the increase in population-density of a social group, becomes intelligible when we also analyzed its "moral" causes: the products of human "abilities" and "invention," that is, of the mind. Hume mention some of these: the forms of government and work, with the plentifulness and indigence they generate for the members of the state or nation. These human creations, when they operate on the mind as "motives or reasons" (E, 198), fix the persons, through habit, in a certain common way of life, which cause them to be, mentally speaking, the sort of persons they effectively are: hence, "poverty and hard labour debase the minds of the common people, and render them unfit for any science and ingenious profession" (E, 198). In "Of the Populousness of Ancient Nations," the detailed analysis of these moral causes is a crucial ingredient in his refutation of the thesis prevalent during the Eighteenth century according to which the city-states of Classical Antiquity must have had, in the aggregate, a greater population than the modern nations of Europe.

In general, what the study of history reveals to us is that the formation, fixation, and alteration of the character of human beings depend more on the operation of moral causes, such as the laws and particular forms of government, than on the influence of physical causes, such as the air and climate.[26]

---

[25] Precisely because of it, Hume is forced to admit that it is impossible to distinguish memories from the fictions of imagination, "it being impossible to recall the past impressions, in order to compare them with our present ideas, and see whether their arrangement be exactly similar" (THN, 85).

[26] Thus, for example, Hume says in "Of National Characters," that "the CHINESE have the greatest uniformity of character imaginable: though the air and climate, in different parts of those vast dominions, admit of very considerable variations" (E, 204).

2. Similarly, in "Of the Rise and Progress of the Arts and Sciences," the principal factor for the sustained flourishing of these is neither any climatic advantage, nor the genetic superiority of a peoples such as the Greek, in antiquity, or the British, in modern age, over the neighboring peoples; it is rather the civil liberty that their respective constitutions fomented. This political freedom, or the protection that general laws give the common people against the oppression and the despotic and arbitrary exercise of power by kings, magistrates, or any other rulers, is like the fertile soil in which the authentically creative genius of the arts and sciences can germinate:

> From law arises security: From security curiosity: And from curiosity knowledge. The latter steps of this progress may be more accidental; but the former are altogether necessary. A republic without laws can never have any duration (E, 118).

It is noteworthy that Hume should explain in a progressive manner the rise of religion as well as that of the arts and sciences. Nonetheless, in any case is his adherence to a progressive theory unconditional. On the one hand, progress is not necessarily linear or indefinite, for the apogee of the arts in a nation or state also marks the moment of its inexorable decadence (E, 134–135).[27] On the other hand, the unraveling of the process in the direction of improvement is far from being inevitable: Hume admit that its later stages are "accidental." In both these particulars Hume distances himself from the optimism that is typical of the Enlightenment.

3. Hume also reveals how moral causes form, or rather uniform, the typical character of the members of various human groups independently and in spite of the tremendous differences that may obtain in the personality or peculiar temperament of the individuals that compose those collections. In the essay "Of National Characters," Hume mentions those other human inventions that are the professions of the soldier and the priest in order to illustrate how the different types of customs foment the development of the eminently positive moral qualities of the first and the overwhelmingly negative traits of the latter: the character of the priest "is, in most points, opposite to that of a soldier; as is the way of life, from which it is derived" (E, 199).

In that essay Hume is only anticipating, in passing and in a lengthy footnote, a phenomenon that he will analyze in detail in the *Natural History of Religion*, particularly in Section 14: that is, the negative effect of religion on morality. We will critically examine this issue in chapter 8. Now I only wish to remark that the contention that religious beliefs (and principally so the monotheistic ones) instead of

---

[27] This historical thesis, which here and in "Of the Populousness of Ancient Nations" Hume defends conditionally or *ad hominen* (e.g., against those who assert the greater population of Ancient cities), is essentially identical to that which he later exposes, more categorically, in the *History of England* (H, II, 219–223).

forming, rather deform the character of their votaries, unequivocally illustrates that Hume was keenly aware that some of the historical products of human beings modify their nature and tend to produce and reproduce a certain human type.

Moreover, between the character of the person and the religious belief there is also a species of "flux and reflux," or a relation of reciprocal determination: a certain type of religious belief tends to form a weak or a strong character and a certain type of weak or strong character is predisposed to form a certain type of religious belief. Hence, in the *Natural History of Religion*, Hume stresses that monotheism weakens the character of the devout person, and encourages its submission and debasement together with "the monkish virtues of mortification, penance, humility, and passive suffering," whereas polytheism strengthens the moral fiber, and exalts, among other virtues, "activity, spirit, courage, magnanimity, love of liberty" (NHR, 52). Yet, in the essay "Of Superstition and Enthusiasm," he shows exactly the opposite; instead of deriving the character from the beliefs, now he draws the beliefs themselves out of the different types of character. In such a fashion, the religious beliefs classified under the general type "superstition" are the natural offspring of – among other factors – weak temperaments, i.e., those which are particularly predisposed to feel fear and melancholy, whereas the faiths that are instances of "enthusiasm" are spontaneously born out of strong characters, which are more susceptible to feel hope, pride, and presumption (E, 74). This account agrees with the *Natural History*. In addition to ignorance and the "entire dependance" that human beings have about the unknown causes of their well-being and misery, and the propensity of the imagination to represent those powers by analogy with themselves, we find among the operative factors in the origin of religion the lasting hopes and fears that afflict the human mind, in other words, the anxiety which expresses its uncertainty and almost exclusive preoccupation with those events on which its own life, or as Heidegger might have said, its being in the world depends (NHR, 27).

In sum, I think that all these examples drawn from Hume's historical essays, no less than the brief comparative analysis of the *History of England*, have the cumulative effect of making convincing the opinion according to which the conception of history that is transparent in the *Natural History of Religion*, even though he formulates it with an attenuated optimism, is typically modern: progressive, creative, and even dialectical, at least in the modest and reasonable sense of expressly acknowledging that historical events are in a perpetual oscillation, that is, dynamically connected in opposition and reciprocal causal interaction, or within an order in which mutual determination, "the flux and reflux," prevails.

CHAPTER 7

Belief and Faith

7.1 THE PROBLEM

In previous chapters our attention has been almost exclusively directed to the general mechanism, to the causes by which all the different ideas of divinity are generated. But this is only part of the story. The religious person not only conceives his or her god in a certain manner, namely, entertains a definite idea of his deity, but, what is more important, she or he believes that such a being exists. And, furthermore, upon such a belief he or she founds other beliefs, for instance, belief in immortality and eschatology, moral rules whose truth or falsity and/or validity is taken to be a direct consequence of the existence, character, attributes, and behavior towards us of the god or gods in question. To a much greater extent than natural religion, historical religion, "is not content with instructing us in the nature of superior powers, but carries its views farther, to their disposition towards us, and our duties towards them" (THN, xix).

The question to probe is: how does religious belief, or faith, differ from belief in ordinary matters of fact and existence? To elucidate this matter, an examination of Hume's complex doctrine of "belief," as expounded in the *Treatise of Human Nature* and the *Enquiry Concerning Human Understanding*, is called for. We have seen that Hume reduces the beliefs of all historical religions, almost without distinction, to mere superstition or enthusiasm. I hope that the analysis which follows may help us to understand why Hume threw traditional religious faith out the universe of rational discourse. Yet, although we will not entirely lose sight of the problem about the reasonableness and validity of faith, an answer to the preceding question is, in the last analysis, sought after as a means for tackling a problem that is more phenomenological than epistemological, and which arises out of Hume's own startling observations in the *Natural History of Religion* as to the nature of religious faith: Is it possible for the religious person to make a genuine or sincere act of assent to the presumed truths of his or her religion? In other words, can religious faith approach the degree of conviction that is typical of common-sense belief (i.e., about the existence of the diverse facts and objects of ordinary experience), which is for Hume the paradigm of real assent? If it cannot, should it then be constructed as half-belief or a forced and self-imposed conviction, as some of Hume's statements in the *Natural History* seem to imply? At the end we may perhaps see that the elucidation of the second question will help us to solve the first one.

One must acknowledge that an immediate and not entirely unjustified reaction to this way of looking at religious belief may be to dismiss it as improper, unfaithful to the relevant facts, and even as outright absurd. That Hume, nonetheless, did not take at face value the expressed and repeated confessions of faith of religious people, seems to be well-established fact. In this chapter I shall try to show that such assessment of religious faith stems from his doctrine of "belief." But this should not be taken to imply that there may not be other reasons as well, i.e., historical or biographical, which might have inclined Hume to assume such a somber outlook on religious faith. For instance, one may still affirm the essential correctness of an hypothesis that Norman Kemp Smith[1] formulated long ago. According to him, in the forging of his theories about religion, Hume was influenced – more than is generally acknowledged – by that religion he grew up in and knew best – a stern form of Calvinism, which put special stress on the infinite attributes of God, predestination, and the eternal damnation of all but a few. It was also a fundamental tenet of this religion that salvation depends absolutely on divine grace, and that faith is even a result of grace or the inscrutable decrees of God's will. It is not surprising then, that Hume again and again accused religion of leading men and women to a life of simulation and hypocrisy in the sense that it demands of them – as a condition for evading eternal condemnation – an assent to those tenets of religion which, like the preceding are, for Hume, not only utterly unintelligible but also patently merciless.

In short, religious belief is not a genuine and natural acquiescence; it is instead, in a literal sense, a "profession" of faith (DNR, 221–225), that is, a violent exercise of self-deceit. Rather than being a sincere and spontaneous assent, faith is but a deliberate and forced persuasion that places the religious devotees in an equally "artificial" way of life. This is so since its merit exclusively resides in the declamation of doctrines whose absurdity and inhumanity make them in fact repugnant to our intelligence and moral sense, and also in hiding from others as well as from themselves that inner conflict: "The heart secretly detests such measures of cruel and implacable vengeance; but the judgment dares not but pronounce them perfect and adorable" (NHR, 67).

It seems that Hume went on to generalize this estimate – probably biographically conditioned – and to make it a characteristic of all religion, at least of religion as "it appears in the world":

We may observe, that, notwithstanding the dogmatical, imperious style of all superstition, the conviction of the religionists, in all ages, is more affected than

---

[1] Introduction to the *Dialogues Concerning Natural Religion*, pp. 1–8; c.f. Ernest C. Mossner, *The Life of David Hume*, pp. 20–34.

real, and scarcely ever approaches, in any degree, to that solid belief and persuasion, which governs us in the common affairs of life (NHR, 60).

And this abysmal assessment of Hume is far from being a late opinion, for the preceding passage is entirely consistent with judgments that he makes in passing in his first work, the *Treatise*; so he says that immortality cannot properly be an object of genuine belief (THN, 114–115). What we have before our eyes is, on the contrary, a general and constant assessment that remains unaltered throughout all his philosophical writings, and which also makes its appearance, either in an open or thinly veiled manner, in different places of *The History of England*. The following declaration is exceptional only because Hume's manner of expression is more transparent and less circumspect than usual:

The religious hypocrisy . . . is of a peculiar nature; and being generally unknown to the person himself, though more dangerous, it implies less falsehood than any other species of insincerity (H, VI, 142).

Religion is not, indeed, the same as secular belief. But why should it be for that matter something less than sincere persuasion? Why should the belief in the existence of some things for which we cannot give sufficient empirical evidence, or in something totally different from what we have habitually experienced, be interpreted merely as a form of self-deceit or self-delusion, and in some cases, even as outright hypocrisy?

For my part it seems that to take at face value the "declamations of the religionists" is not only a more sensible but a more empirical approach; thus we shall suppose from the start that genuine religious conviction, even if less noticeable, is as much a fact as prudent, hypocritical confessions of faith are, and that the leap of faith, with all its fear and trembling, is something more than a rare occurrence in human life. Accordingly, we shall examine Hume's theory of belief to see if this theory is one of the reasons for his seeming failure to grasp some fundamental features of the essence and vital dynamics of religious faith.

Now we go on to examine his general theory of belief.

7.2   ORDINARY BELIEF ABOUT MATTERS OF FACT

In a plain and naive manner I said at the beginning that the religious person does not only have an idea of God, but that he or she also believes that God exists, as if conceiving of something and conceiving it to be existent were two different things. Believing and conceiving certainly are not identical, because many things can be conceived without being believed; on the other hand, to believe is not to add the idea of existence to our original conception. The idea of existence is not a different or distinct idea from the idea of any object. "Whatever we conceive, we conceive to be existent. Any idea we please to form is the idea of a being; and the idea of a being is any idea we please to form" (THN, 67).

Hume would agree in that it is impossible to think of God without thinking of him as existent; what he will contend, against the defenders of the ontological argument,[2] is that this holds for everything, and not only for the idea of God:

Thus, when we affirm, that God is existent, we simply form the idea of such a being, as he is represented to us . . . . When I think of God, when I think of him as existent, and when I believe him to be existent, my idea of him neither encreases nor diminishes (THN, 94).

Hume's difficult task is to account for the origin and meaning of this straightforward, immediate, attribution of reality that seems to pertain to those mental operations we group under the name of 'beliefs'. Since in believing X and conceiving X, the idea of X remains the same, in other words, since the difference lies not in what is conceived, since the idea of existence is not a distinct idea that is added in the case of belief to our original idea, then, Hume concludes, the difference "must lie in the manner in which we conceive it" (THN, 95). But the only variation that an idea can admit of, without changing its contents ("the parts and composition of the idea"), that is, without being transformed into another, is by increasing or decreasing the degree of strength or vivacity with which it imposes on the mind: "So that as belief does nothing but vary the manner, in which we conceive any object, it can only bestow on our ideas an additional force and vivacity" (THN, 96).

It is this lively manner which constitutes for us the characteristic reality attributed to sense-experience and the trust we have that memory refers to actual happenings of past experience.[3] And this lively manner of conception or vivacity Hume resolutely calls belief or assent:

Thus it appears, that the *belief* or *assent*, which always attends the memory and senses, is nothing but the vivacity of those perceptions they present; and that this alone distinguishes them from the imagination. To believe is in this case to feel an immediate impression of the senses, or a repetition of that impression in the memory. (THN, 86).[4]

---

[2] We will not examine here the implications that such conception of existence has for the critique of the ontological argument. See below chapter 10.

[3] "Those very sensations are for them ("the generality of Mankind") the true objects" (THN, 202). Hume also distinguishes ideas of the memory from ideas of the imagination in the same way. He readily admits or supposes with the rest of humankind that memories preserve the order of our original experiences or impressions; yet, since it is impossible to recall the past impressions – these being "perishing existences" – in order to compare them with the present ideas, the only mark by which we can sort out memories from fictions is also here their force and vivacity; ideas of the memory are stronger, ideas of the imagination fainter and more obscure" (THN, 85).

[4] Hume's mode of expression is somewhat careless; impressions – he had said in the preceding page – cannot be recalled; but his meaning seems clear, the assent we give to memory images is due to the liveliness they have in common with impressions.

Hume characterizes belief in the preceding passage – and also in the Appendix to the *Treatise* – as a certain feeling, as something *felt* by the mind. He says that "those faculties [memory and imagination] are only distinguished by the different *feeling* of the ideas they present" (THN, THN, Appendix, 628). But the nature of this feeling is nothing distinct from the ideas themselves, it consists in their force and vivacity: "the ideas of memory are more *strong* and *lively* than those of the fancy" (THN, Appendix, 629).[5]

If belief or assent reduces itself to vivacity, then the ideas we believe are those which approach impressions in force an liveliness. Accordingly, in order to explain how we come to repose belief in certain ideas – and especially in ideas of those things whose existence is causally inferred – what we have to do is to point out and analyze the process by which these come to be enlivened. In the *Treatise* Hume will in essence account for the origins of belief in terms of the working of the mechanism of association of ideas. Ideas acquire the additional force that transforms them into beliefs from the impressions (or ideas of the memory) with which they are usually associated: "*when any impression becomes present to us, it not only transports the mind to such ideas as are related to it, but likewise communicates to them a share of its force and vivacity*" (THN, 98).

Once admitted that the operation of this principle is constant and universal in human nature, Hume's official, or at least most emphatic, definition of belief follows:

An opinion, therefore, or belief may be most accurately defin'd, A LIVELY IDEA RELATED TO OR ASSOCIATED WITH A PRESENT IMPRESSION (THN, 96).

Hume recognizes three general principles by which imagination associates ideas: resemblance, contiguity and causation. But the most important in conditioning belief is causation. Cause and effect is the only relation that carries the mind beyond the impressions of senses and memory: we infer the existence of either a cause of effect that is not immediately given to perception. Now since in causal reasoning the existence of one object is inferred from that of others, and since the mind cannot carry its inferences *ad infinitum* if it is going to end in a conclusion about matters of fact and existence – as different from an imaginary chain of argument – , then some impression of memory or the senses must be present in order to serve as a foundation that removes all doubt and uncertainty from the inference. Although experience cannot prove either that everything must have a cause or that a specific ob-

---

[5] Yet in other passages, even if reaffirming that this feeling is not distinct from the idea, the peculiar way Hume describes it makes it very difficult not to view this feeling as something different and separate from the idea; for instance: "It is only annex'd to it [the idea or conception] after the same manner that will and desire are annex'd to particular conceptions of good and pleasure" (THN, Appendix, 625).

ject must necessarily produce another, it certainly conditions the production of that habit out of which the causal inference arises and the inferred idea comes to be believed.

What experience teaches here is only that two species of objects have been regularly related by contiguity and succession. And from this past regularity, or the observed constant conjunction of these objects in the past, their ideas spontaneously, without reasoning, acquire a similar union in the imagination, from which in turn arises the custom of passing to the idea of the one whenever an object of the other sort presents itself to the memory or senses. Custom effects the transition from the present impression to the inferred idea; the impression customarily associated with that idea imparts or communicates to it a degree of its own force and vivacity; and the belief or assent we repose on the inference precisely consists in the vivacity that is infused through custom to the idea in question:

> Now, as we call every thing CUSTOM which proceeds from a past repetition, without any new reasoning or conclusion, we may establish it as a certain truth, that all the belief, which follows upon any present impression, is derived solely from that origin. (THN, ̍102).

Custom produces in us a felt, invincible need to mentally pass – a compelled albeit "easy" transition – from the present impression to the enlivened idea; and from this feeling of immediate and expeditious passage from the one to the other, the belief in the necessary connexion between the impression and the idea arises.

The ambiguity with which Hume refers, in his account of belief as a process of enlivening, sometimes to the constant conjunction between impressions, at other times to the constant conjunction between objects, and still occasionally to that which holds between impressions *of* objects is perhaps a fair indication that this account of the genesis or particular beliefs, as the enlivening of distinct and specific ideas, presupposes the operation or another sort of belief – the generalized belief in the distinct, continuous and independent existence of sensible objects.[6] In Part IV, Sections I, II, and III of Book I the *Treatise* he will also attempt, as in the case of belief in causal connexion, to explain the origin of this general belief in terms of association of ideas. But Hume, I think, has by then come to recognize explicitly that these are two irreducible foundations which establish the general underlying framework within which all our behavior – cognitive, practical and moral – arises and is performed. These two beliefs, along with the conviction in the identity of the conscious self, are instinctive: primary, ineradicable, and universal, for they stem from the original constitution of our human nature. When Hume said that "Nature, by an absolute and uncontroulable necessity has determin'd us to judge as well as

---

[6] He calls this belief a "natural instinct or prepossession" (EHU, p. 151). In this I but subscribe in general one of the classic (and still sound) theses of Norman Kemp Smith, the most important Hume scholar of the twentieth century. From it he derives a measured critique Hume's account of the idea of necessary connection (*The Philosophy of David Hume*, pp. 65–83).

to breathe and feel," he was seemingly not referring to any particular belief which one might or might not come to hold in the course of one's life, but precisely to those universal beliefs.

Now if we turn again to Hume's more restricted account of belief in terms of liveliness of conception produced by a related impression, there surfaces a difficulty that Hume himself acknowledges (THN, 107), and whose satisfactory solution appears to be demanded if the difference between reasonable belief and irrational belief, or superstition is to be maintained with consistency. On the one hand, Hume explicitly asserts – perhaps to emphasize that we ought to give our assent only to those propositions that arise out of the observation of the invariable and universal conjunction of objects in experience – that "belief arises only from causation, and that we can draw no inference from one object to another, except they be connected by this relation" (THN, 107). On the other hand, if such were case, then neither resemblance nor contiguity should be capable of generating belief. But of course this is something that does not happen. Hume's general answer seems to be that the effective operation of the relations of resemblance and contiguity depends on another "Kind of implicit Faith," that is, on the tacit belief in the existence of their respective objects.[7] Yet, while examining particular instances, he concedes the main point. Since resemblance and contiguity connect ideas with impressions, they in some degree enliven those ideas: in short, these relations produce only a weaker and inconstant belief, but by no means causality alone leads to belief.[8]

---

[7] Hume endeavors to show, that the enlivening power of resemblance and contiguity, instead of being an exception, is a "proof" or confirmation that belief issues from causation, as well as evidence that belief is a lively idea related to a present impression. He does admit that these relations have such power. For instance, a picture of my friend enlivens the idea of her as well as on the way home those objects and places closer to it more strongly evoke the idea or my house (THN, 99–100). Hume seems to say that these two relations produce that effect not entirely by themselves, but only precisely by strengthening ideas which I already believe through the operation of causal connection between my present impressions and my memories, i.e., the beliefs in my friend and my house are firmly established in my memory. In the first case, the idea of my friend comes to mind only because I already believe the present portrait to be a portrait of him or her, which of course "supposes, that we believe our friend to have once existed" (EHU, 54). And the same holds for contiguity. The idea of my house is enlivened because past experience has constantly shown me that going my way and passing by these objects I eventually reach my house. It may be objected in this case it is contiguity that produces the vivid conception of my house. But Hume would retort that something more than mere contiguity is involved. Even though I may be able to evoke ideas of other things which are close to my house, these cannot enliven that idea as can those other contiguous objects that I presently perceive (EHU, 52). In this case it is the idea of my house, and not of any other neighboring thing, that vigorously comes to mind precisely because it is the one that has habitually been connected with the now present objects in our past experience.

[8] Be that as it may, unassisted by causation, resemblance and contiguity have a "very feeble and uncertain influence" (THN, 109) in occasioning belief. Hume offers some examples – most of them coming from the sphere of religion – which show that when we voluntarily and capriciously annex an imaginary resemblance and contiguity to this or that other object, the process or enlivening is weak and inconstant (THN, 109–110). At the end what Hume will contend is strictly that resemblance and contiguity, when united to an idea which is by custom associated to a present impression, reinforce belief

Whatever the case may be with respect to resemblance and contiguity, Hume probably continued to view belief in its strict sense, not as the product of any sort of association, nor of any kind of custom, but as that manner of conceiving an idea which arises from "custom, or if you will, the relation of cause and effect" (THN, 108), or a custom which is derived from the constant conjunction in perception of similar kinds of objects.[9] By using the term 'belief' in this sense, Hume is implying that only ideas which are vouched for by an invariable experience are worthy of our assent. Kemp Smith seems to be right when he says that ultimately "experience" and not custom, is "king," and thus, such an experience comes in the end to have for Hume a "normative" sense.[10] In accordance with this, Hume distinguished between "good" and "bad" customs, or means of endowing ideas with strength. The first sort operates through universal conjunctions of objects, that is, "experience." The second kind works through the constant repetition of ideas which are provided by the many teachers one encounters in the course of life, namely, "education." Acknowledging that "more than half" of the opinions cherished by humankind are the product of hearsay or education, he remarks that "philosophers [that is, the "wise" in contrast to the "vulgar"] do not recognize it." And he gives the following reasons for this disavowal of an attitude that, by the way, he seems to share with the "philosophers":

> But as education is an artificial and not a natural cause and as its maxims are frequently contrary to reason, and even to themselves in different times and places, it is never upon that account recogniz'd by philosophers; tho' in reality it be built almost on the same foundation of custom and repetition as our reasonings from causes and effects (THN, 117).

In which sense is education artificial? The propositions that we are led to believe on the authority of educators establish the connexion between objects that, no matter how strongly united they may be in the mind of educators, all-too-commonly have no natural connexion with anything which exists in fact and reality. Sometimes the maxims of one teacher are contradicted by another authority; frequently these maxims are absurd or incoherent propositions, and in this sense it is said that they contrary to reason. In all this Hume seems to be implying that since education rests "on almost the same foundation" as belief in causality, i.e.,

---

whereas when causality is unsupported by resemblance and contiguity the belief is weakened (THN, 113).

[9] In the Appendix to the *Treatise*, Hume on several occasions refers to belief as a feeling which makes "firmer and more solid" some ideas (p. 624); yet this feeling is quite different from "poetical enthusiasm, "being annexed only to serious conviction" (p.631). Of the former he says that *"the vigour of conception,* which fictions receive from poetry and eloquence, is *a circumstance merely accidental,* of which every idea is equally susceptible"; and that *"such fictions are connected with nothing that is real"* (p. 631; italics added).

[10] Kemp Smith, *The Philosophy of David Hume*, pp. 382–388.

custom, it should always be trusted only when checked against and supplemented by experience. And only thereby can custom be "the great guide of life" (*Abstract*, THN, A, 16; EHU, 44–45).

In the end it is a rational criterion *par excellence*, consistency, which prevails.[11] Why? It is true that should stick to custom in this second sense because only through causal inferences linked to the impressions of memory and senses can we, out of discontinuous and fleeting perceptions, gain access to the stable, uniform, and coherent world demanded by our practical and moral action. Belief in this regulative sense make us advance into the real world through the construction of a system of causally interrelated perceptions that supplement and complete the direct but limited view of the world that its immediate perceptions provide to the self. All that is compatible with these beliefs comes to receive the assent of reality. And since belief can be properly defined as a "a lively idea [causally] related to a present impression", it is not by chance that this system is twofold. The first is the system of the memory and the senses:

> Of these impressions or ideas of the memory we form a kind of system, comprehending whatever we remember to have been present, either to our internal perception or senses; and every particular of that system, joined to the present impressions, we are pleased to call a *reality*. (THN, 108).

And the second is that of the "judgment":

> But the mind stops not here. For finding, that with this system of perceptions there is another connected by custom, or, if you will, by the relation of cause or effect, it proceeds to the consideration of their ideas; and as it feels that it is in a manner necessarily determined to view these particular ideas, and that the custom or relation, by which it is determined, admits not of the least change, it forms them into a new system, which it likewise dignifies with the title of *realities*. . . . It is this latter principle which peoples the world, and brings us acquainted with such existences as, by their removal in time and place, lie beyond the reach of the senses and memory. By means of it I paint the universe in my imagination, and fix my attention on any part of it I please (THN, 108).

Through belief the imagination extends custom and reasoning beyond actual perception in order, as it were, to install itself in the real world. Yet this world is not an external archetype, one and stable, of which internal perceptions would be transitory and approximate representations. The world of "reality" and "realities"

---

[11] Of course, this is not an assertion in keeping with a completely sceptical reading of Hume's philosophy, and it is not even forcefully emphasized by Kemp Smith himself, who paradigmatically opposes such an interpretation. But it has been exemplarily maintained by other notable interpreters sympathetic to Kemp Smith's general outlook, such as John Passmore, *Hume's Intentions*, pp. 100–102; and D. G. C. MacNabb, *David Hume: His Theory of Knowledge and Morality*, pp. 79–80, 96–100.

still remains a sort of home that imagination sets up for itself with the "bricks" furnished by its own perceptions. Although I certainly express this conclusion in an somewhat excessive metaphorical manner, yet it think it contains a literal truth; that is, Hume's theory of belief stands at the crossroads between his epistemology and his ontology. Belief, as a product of the universal and permanent operations of imagination, is the means of access for an understanding of the meaning of what is real for us. It is because of this, I think, that Hume describes belief as:

> that act of the mind, which renders realities, *or what is taken for such*, more present to us than fictions, causes them to weigh more in the thought, and gives them a superior influence on the passions and imagination (EHU, 49; italics added).

Hume is seemingly saying to us that it is not the case that at first there is world and afterwards we come to form beliefs about it. What happens is exactly the opposite: the activities of the mind involved in our beliefs construct, or as he himself says, "form" the real world which is their object or to which they refer. I think that passages such as the following provide strong evidence for the present interpretation:

> All these and everything else, which I believe are nothing but ideas, tho' by their force and settled order, arising from custom and the relation of cause and effect, they distinguish themselves from the other ideas, which are merely the offspring of the imagination (THN, I, 108).[12]

Hume calls this world of belief the system of judgment as if to imply that these beliefs, although incapable of being justified by abstract reason, really are the genuinely reasonable ones. However, even belief in the causal sense "stands almost on the same foundation" as education and other purely fortuitous processes of enlivening ideas. And since understanding issues in such beliefs, and since philosophical tradition has equated understanding with the faculty of judgment, several interpreters, following Kemp Smith, have maintained that what Hume is really saying is that when making causal inferences, understanding does not – in a purely logical sense – judge at all. And this interpretation commonly finds support in passages like the following:

---

[12] My view has affinity with Annette Baier's. See "Hume, David (1711–1776)," in *The Encyclopedia of Ethics*, ed. Lawrence C. Becker and Charlotte B. Becker. *The Encyclopedia of Ethics*, 2 vols. (New York: Garland Publishing Co., 1992), I, pp. 565–577. "Our moral projections add to our other more 'cognitive' projections. Hume is no more a non-realist about moral virtues than he is about causal necessity, or about the identity over time of physical objects and even of ourselves as persons" (p. 569).

Thus, all probable reasoning is nothing but a species of sensation. . . . Objects have no discoverable connexion together; nor is it from any other principle but custom operating upon the imagination, that we can draw any inference from the appearance of one to the existence of another (THN, 103).

I think, however, that this passage is also consistent with an interpretation that may not lead us to say that understanding does not judge rationally when it expresses beliefs founded on causal inferences. Accordingly one may rather say that it judges according to a principle which really is, like sensation, a "first foundation of all our conclusions," and therefore, incapable of being justified by other more basic and general principles (THN, 212). Although they are not, strictly speaking, conclusions of a deductive reasoning, the foundations of our beliefs about all that is and can be real for us, are, for Hume (as Cleanthes says in the *Dialogues* about the design argument), "irregular arguments" that, despite this feature, irresistibly lead us to assent in the same manner that some literary works, even if do not follow or deviate from accepted standards, do procure our "universal" approbation (DNR, 155).

What is clear at this point, even if one totally rejects the preceding interpretation, is that Hume effectively eliminates the distinction between imagination and understanding. In the last analysis understanding is reduced to imagination; or more exactly, the distinction subsists but only in order to mark the difference between the genus and species: 'understanding' is but the name for that function of the imagination which operates according to principles that are "permanent, irresistible and universal," in contrast to those other principles "that are weak, changeable, irregular," and – what is of supreme importance – "not even useful for the conduct of life" (THN, 225; see also THN, Appendix, 628–629, and EHU, 47–50).

In summary, sensible beliefs (the products of understanding and its probable reasonings) not only have a primary character, vigor and vivacity comparable to sensation, order, systematic coherence and universal assent, but also an undeniable and incalculable practical relevance. And this last feature is at least as important as all the rest. Genuine beliefs are those that have pragmatic value: By influencing the passions, which are the prime movers of human behavior, they effectively become "the governing principle of all our actions" (THN, Appendix, 629 and c.f., EHU, 50). If it were not because Hume never confounds truth with usefulness, and even less attempts to justify the former by means of the latter, we could have given the name of 'utilitarian doxism' to this theory.[13] Once again, reason is the slave of the passions, and knowledge is but an instrument for the pursuit of the practical and moral life. If understanding is to be preferred, it is ultimately because the beliefs that it generates upon the foundation of experience (the "systems" of "reality" and

---

[13] This eminently pragmatic element of Hume's theory of belief has been stressed with great care and good judgment by Páll S. Árdal, in *Passion and Value in Hume's Treatise*. See in particular the extensive "Introduction to the Second Edition," pp. ix–xxxiv.

"realities") are more reliable for regulating human activity than those fantasies and vagaries of enthusiasm and superstition. This directly leads us to Hume's examination of faith.

7.3 RELIGIOUS FAITH

The following passage strikingly depicts Hume's very poor opinion of the sincerity and reasonableness of religious faith:

> Men dare not avow, even to their own hearts, the doubts which they entertain on such subjects: They make a merit of implicit faith; and disguise to themselves their real infidelity, by the strongest asseverations and most positive bigotry. But nature is too hard for all their endeavours, and suffers not the obscure, glimmering light, afforded in those shadowy regions, to equal the strong impressions, made by common sense and by experience. The usual course of men's conduct belies their words, and shows, that *their assent in these matters is some unaccountable operation of the mind between disbelief and conviction, but approaching much nearer to the former than to the latter* (NHR, 60 italics added).

With respect to most of the aspects we have examined in the preceding section, religious faith seems to oppose ordinary belief in matters of fact and existence: weak, inconstant, confused and obscure, improbable and even contrary to experience, possibly absurd, and finally worthless for practice. However, in the light of his theory of belief, Hume's suggestion that religious faith is not a genuine belief but a form of self-deceit, appears not to stem from his broader conception of belief as a more vivid conception. If that were the case, his suggestion would be disproved by easily observable facts, for with the possible exception of the political arena, there is no other sphere of human life where interested parties seem to assent with so much vigor to the objects of their particular devotion. When contrasting belief to faith he rather tended to employ the term 'belief' in its strict and normative sense, in order to refer to that attitude that arises from custom and the relation of cause and effect, and which he seems to have equated with reasonable or justifiable conviction. And he appears to be saying two things: first, that the feeling of assent produced by ideas backed up by experience is the prototype of our assent to what we take for real things, and this is, after all, qualitatively or specifically different, and not merely quantitatively distinct (i.e., because it has greater degree of force and vivacity) from the inconstant and short-lived flashes of sudden illumination which are the outcome of the religious emotions. And second, that religious faith shows a systematic disrespect for the last arbiter of truth concerning matters of fact and existence, viz. experience. And here 'experience' is understood in the sense of the systems of *reality* and *realities.*

Hume assumes that faith, when this term denotes the beliefs of historical religions, is derived almost exclusively from what he denominates as "education." It is, generally speaking, principally the result of early and continuing indoctrination which is hardly ever corroborated by, or confronted with, the teachings of experience. Although Hume was not oblivious to the intense conviction that frequently attends those opinions, he nonetheless held that this is due to "artificial" or irregular means of enlivening ideas. What is at work here is not the experienced customary transition from effects to causes but the constant repetition of ideas, i.e., accidental resemblances and contiguities arbitrarily connected with circumstances and situations we already believe by virtue of their being part and parcel of our *system of realities*. For instance, if it were not for the effects of contiguity some religious beliefs would gradually vanish; that is, if they were they not constantly repeated, they would simply fade away:

> It has been remark'd among the Mahometans as well as Christians, that those *pilgrims*. Who have seen MECCA or the HOLY LAND are ever after more faithful and zealous believers, than those who have not had that advantage. A man, whose memory presents him with a lively image of the *Red-Sea*, and the *Desert*, and *Jerusalem*, and *Galilee*, can never doubt of any miraculous events, which are related either by *Moses or the Evangelists*. The lively idea of the places passes by an easy transition to the facts, which are supposed to have been related to them by contiguity and encreases the belief by encreasing the vivacity of the conception. The remembrance of these fields and rivers has the same influence on the vulgar as a new argument; and from the same causes (THN, 110–111).

Hume's observations on immortality are by way of instances that illustrate how the presence or absence of resemblance is responsible for the credulity or incredulity we place in certain ideas. Immortality cannot really be a proper object of belief. Even those who most emphatically proclaim it, do not truly believe in it. Their complete indifference towards immortality, as it manifests itself in their habitual dealings in common life, amounts to a *de facto* incredulity. In this Hume is stressing the pragmatic dimension of his theory, and appears to suggest that genuine beliefs should work like premises from which actions, or better, habitual dispositions to act in a certain way, may be derived as efficacious conclusions. Now since between the conduct of typical believers and the presumed belief in an after-life there is no such kind of connection, the pragmatic sterility of the latter patently discloses the absence of real conviction in the former. It is noteworthy that Hume does not indeed attribute this almost non-existent credulity to the practical fruitlessness, but in turn explain this phenomenon by appealing to a more elemental factor. It is the absence of resemblance with common life that weakens or makes this belief fade away in us:

> I rather choose to ascribe this incredulity to the faint idea we form of our future condition, derived from its want of resemblance to the present life, indeed the want of resemblance in this case so entirely destroys belief that except those few, who upon cool reflexion on the importance of the subject, have taken care

by repeated meditation to imprint in their minds the arguments for a future state, there scarce are any, who believe the immortality of the soul with a true and establish'd judgment, such as is derived from the testimony of travellers and historians (THN, 114-115).

Even those who excel in the daily practice of repeating to themselves the doctrines from which the truth of immortality (along with its tremendous consequences) follow, only succeed in conferring upon it a forced and weak conviction, which is even much inferior to the trust we place in human testimony. From this it also appears to follow as a corollary that we would not believe in the testimony of "travellers and historians" whenever they reported to us the occurrence of events totally different from daily life or common experience. It is clear, however, that such is not the case; and this is due to the operation of a new principle that explains why the belief of humankind in fantastic tales is so widespread, namely, the fascination for the marvelous. He stressed that factor particularly in Section X of *An Enquiry Concerning Human Understanding*, "Of Miracles." It is, in short, the lack of resemblance what almost entirely destroys a belief that, as he will suggest in the *Essay on Immortality*, is not supported by observable facts, since no constant conjunction vouches for it, and that otherwise runs counter to the usual course of events.[14]

But resemblance also has other striking effects. We have already seen that in the *Natural History* Hume maintains that it is only because the devotees of the God of monotheistic religions bring him to a closer similarity with themselves that they can sustain and reinforce a belief in a Spiritual Being of Infinite Perfection, along with other beliefs associated with it. But Hume had already formulated that doctrine in the *Treatise*, and he repeats it *verbatim* in the *Enquiry Concerning Human Understanding*:

The ceremonies of the *Roman Catholic* religion may be considered as experiments of the same nature. The devotees of that strange superstition usually plead in excuse of the mummeries, with which they are upbraided, that they feel the good effect of those external motions, and postures and actions, in enlivening their devotion and quickening their fervour, which otherwise wou'd decay away, if directed entirely to distant and immaterial objects. We shadow out the objects of our faith, say they, in sensible types and images, and render them more present to us by the immediate presence of these types, than 'tis possible for us to do, merely by an intellectual view and contemplation. Sensible objects have always a greater influence on the fancy than any other; and

---

[14] E, 590–598. "The physical arguments from the analogy of nature are strong for the mortality of the soul: and these are really the only philosophical arguments, which ought to be admitted with regard to this question, or indeed any question of fact" (E, 596).

this influence they readily convey to those ideas, to which they are related, and which they resemble (THN, 99–100).

It is this tendency to anthropomorphism that is responsible for the constant reversion of monotheism into polytheism.[15] Yet Hume seems to be suggesting here something else. It is only because such a resemblance is effected or fabricated, that is, because God is conceived in a clearly natural manner that a belief in Him is possible at all. To be somehow believed, an idea has to be conceived in a lively manner that excludes from consideration all other possible alternatives.[16] When the belief is concerning some matter of fact and existence, the repeated experience of the constant conjunction of similar impressions (i.e. of two species of objects) is – as the final clause of the quoted passage from the *Treatise* suggests – what enlivens and fixes in the mind the idea of some particular event, and make us disregard all others which have never or almost never occurred in the past. Thus, for instance, when we see a flame, it is the idea of heat that becomes enlivened because of its usual union with impressions that resemble the flame we now perceive; in such a way, even though it is not inconceivable that the flame will make us cold, it is the idea that it will make us warm if we approach it that comes to be enlivened and fixed in our minds, i.e., actually believed, due to its customary association or constant conjunction in our past experience with impressions similar to the present one.

Concerning what Hume calls "relations of ideas" (for the most part, analytic propositions) the solution is even easier. We believe, for instance, the proposition 'Two plus two equals four' because the contrary proposition, being self-contradictory, is, Hume says, inconceivable, and is thus necessarily excluded as an alternative. Our original "relation of ideas" is strongly enlivened and fixed in our mind since:

the person, who assents, not only conceives the ideas according to the proposition, but is necessarily determin'd to conceive them in that particular manner, either immediately or by the interposition of other ideas. Whatever is absurd is unintelligible; nor is it possible for the imagination to conceive anything contrary to a demonstration (THN, 95).

[15] As we have seen in chapter 6 above, in the "flux and reflux of polytheism and theism," there is an opposition between the disposition to believe in invisible, intelligent power, and the propensity which we are now examining, which makes us bestow a solid assent primarily on sensible objects and secondarily on ideas causally connected or similar to them.

[16] This aspect of Hume's theory has been perspicuously stressed by D. G. C. MacNabb, *David Hume: His Theory of Knowledge and Morality*, pp. 73–74. I am very much indebted to his enlightening and plain analysis for opening my eyes to the relevance of this feature for understanding Hume's account of faith.

To believe is, at least, to have a lively idea; on the other hand, what is absurd cannot be conceived by the imagination. Thus it seems to follow that we cannot really believe what is known to be unintelligible, Yet we sometimes give our assent to absurd and contradictory notions. What happens in this case is that the obscurity of some ideas hides their unintelligibility. But since ideas are copied from impressions (at least simple ones) and all impressions are strong and clear, this malady can be remedied, these ideas can be brought to a "so clear a light" by examining the impressions from which they are derived (EHU, 22).

Hume seems to imply that some ideas of divinity, in particular the conception of an infinite, simple and spiritual Deity, are as obscure and logically absurd as those "refined and spiritual" conceptions of the mathematicians which he summarily dismissed after placing them under the same "so clear a light" (THN, 72). Neither the one nor the other can properly be objects of belief. And it is precisely for this reason that anthropomorphism – which is but one effect of resemblance – is called forth to gradually alter "such refined ideas" (NHR, 47) of divinity as are proclaimed by the official creeds, and in this fashion it enables the religionist to give some degree of assent to the existence of his or her deity. The emphasis on this feature also appears to be one of the reasons behind Hume's unconvincing account of the origin of monotheism in terms of adulation and hypocrisy:

> the assent of the vulgar is, in this case [belief in a Being of absolute Perfection], merely verbal, . . . they are incapable of conceiving those sublime qualities, which they seemingly attribute to the deity. Their real idea of him, notwithstanding their pompous language, is still as poor and frivolous as ever. (NHR, p 45: italics added) . . . . Thus it may safely be affirmed that popular religions are really, in the conception of their more vulgar votaries, a species of daimonism (NHR, 67).

The inconceivability and therefore, incredibility, of some tenets of historical manifestations of monotheism might explain Hume's suggestion to the effect that the ancient Graeco-Roman religion was as sincerely held as Christianity, and even more believable than the latter:

> Upon the whole, the greatest and most observable differences between a *traditional, mythological* religion, and a *systematical, scholastic* one are two: The former is often more reasonable, as consisting only of a multitude of stories, which, however groundless, imply no express absurdity and demonstrative contradiction; and sits also so easy and light on men's minds, that, though it may be as universally received, it happily makes no such deep impression on the affections and understanding (NHR, 65).

The steadfastness in imagination of such traditional stories and the conviction bestowed upon them by ancient idolaters is explained by the same principles which give "an easy reception in the imagination" to the tales of poets; in fact, he even talks, while referring to ancient polytheism, of a "poetical religion" (NHR, 61).

Hume is not suggesting, of course, that the attitude of the idolater is poetical in the sense of feigned, or because the assent of reality is tacitly withdrawn from the deities. Far from it, the term 'poetical' rather refers to what is true or genuine in such an act of assent, and which it shares with the convictions of common-sense; both types of beliefs are natural in the sense of being spontaneous, easy and un-premeditated. And thus they are quite unlike the assent given to ultra mundane dogmas, which is "artificial" in the sense of forced and deliberate. It is precisely for its lack of similarity with common experience that much labor and premeditation is needed on the part of the mind in order to acquiesce somehow on such beliefs. In sum, polytheistic beliefs sit almost as "easy and light" on the mind as the opinions of common-sense, and thereby derives the sincerity with which they are held.

On the other hand, all historical or "popular" religions always have a powerful influence on the will and passions. But ancient anthropomorphism, in addition to the permanent enlivening power of repetitive action, or ritual, and strong passions, has a greater resemblance with the world of daily life, or common experience. Hume has already said in the *Treatise*, Part I, Section X, "Of the influence of belief," that "even when ideas have no manner of influence on the will and passions, "truth" and "reality" [i.e., their likeness to the objects of common life] are still requisite, in order to make them entertaining to the imagination" (THN, 121); so we should not be surprised by his assertion in the *Natural History* that traditional polytheistic beliefs not only maintained a durable hold on the imagination of their votaries, but even continue to exercise it in the minds monotheistic believers who are really only nominally so. Since in chapter 6 we have already examined the phenomenon of the "flux and reflux of polytheism and theism," now it will be sufficient to point out that such a thesis is not only prefigured in the *Treatise* and the *Enquiry Concerning Human Understanding*, but also that Hume had already maintained it in an essay which was published before *The Natural History of Religion*, that is, "The Sceptic." In it Hume declares that the official monotheistic dogma is unintelligible as well as incredible for the common devotee, and that he or she can sincerely assent to such that creed only because his or her devotion is directed, not to that infinite God, but to a limited, frankly anthropomorphic deity:

> [A]n abstract, invisible object, like that which *natural* religion alone presents to us, cannot long actuate the mind, or be of any moment in life. To render the passion of continuance, we must find some method of affecting the senses and imagination, and must embrace some *historical*, as well as *philosophical* account of the divinity. Popular superstitions and observances are even found to be of use in this particular (E. 167).[17]

---

[17] This essay was published in the second edition of his *Essays, Moral and Political*, in 1748; *The Natural History of Religion* was published in 1758.

In *The History of England,* Hume will offer many particular instances which show how by means of the repetitive activity of liturgy or ritual, which is customarily associated with sensible images, devotees succeed in hiding to themselves their own real incredulity about dogmas that they cannot comprehend at all; for this reason, the authorities of the Church of England had to reintroduce some of the previously reviled "pious ceremonies" of the Catholic Church:

> [Archbishop] Laud and his associates, by reviving a few primitive institutions of this nature, corrected the error of the first reformers, and presented to the affrighted and astonished mind, some sensible, exterior observances, which might occupy it during its religious exercises, and abate the violence of its disappointed efforts. The thought, no longer bent on that divine and mysterious essence, so superior to the narrow capacities of mankind, was able, by means of the new model of devotion, to relax itself in the contemplation of pictures, postures, vestments, buildings; and all the fine arts, which minister to religion, thereby received additional encouragement (H, V, 459).

Resemblance, as we have already seen more than once, fortifies belief and bestows conviction upon things which otherwise would not be believed at all. And resemblance also produces excessive or over-beliefs in other things which ought to be believed only on the strength of experience and by way of a careful causal reasoning; in other words, resemblance is responsible for the all-too-common phenomenon of human credulity, or a too easy faith in the testimony of others. One should take into account this factor, for otherwise the following passage would appear to contradict, rather than corroborate, his contention that religious assent is forced and contrived because its ideas have no parallel in customary experience, and so receive from the latter no share of its force and vivacity:

> we . . . have a remarkable propensity to believe whatever is reported, even concerning apparitions, enchantments, and prodigies, however contrary to daily experience and observation (THN, 120).

Here an additional propensity enters into operation – the fascination for the marvelous. At least in the *Treatise,* Hume attempted to account for this universal inclination by an appeal to the associative principle of resemblance. According to him, human testimony can be taken to be a sort of effect of past happenings; but it is also a representation or mental "image" of them. The ideas associated with an oral or written report resemble it; they are like copies of the previously perceived event:

> Other effects only point out their causes in an oblique manner; but the testimony of men does it directly, and is to be considered as an image as well as an effect (THN, 113).

Testimony from other people, viewed as a description of events, is not only associated in the narrator with a mental image of the original impression, but also produces in the hearer or reader a mental representation of the reported incident which in turn is added to, and reinforces, the relation of causality that is already supposed to hold between the narration and the fact. And thus we usually come to bestow on human testimony a much greater trust than it really deserves. Although in the *Enquiry Concerning Human Understanding* Hume remains silent about to the likely causes of our fascination with the marvelous, he nonetheless points to this predisposition as the cause of the excessive and almost inevitable assent that we give to testimony about miracles:

> [W]hen anything is affirmed utterly absurd and miraculous, it rather the more readily admits of such a fact, upon account of that very circumstance, which ought to destroy all its authority. The passion of surprise and wonder, arising from miracles, being an agreeable emotion, gives a sensible tendency towards the belief of those events, from which it is derived (EHU, 117; c.f., 117–119).

Here the explanation is somewhat different from that of the *Treatise*. Even though association still plays a role in order to account for our assent to events that otherwise should provoke our incredulity, its part is a very secondary one. In this case a true primary impression or instinct operates: the passion for the marvelous. The satisfaction of this inclination gives rise to a distinct pleasure that by eventually diffusing and associating itself with the tale about the miraculous event effectively fortifies it, and thus makes it believable. Despite this, "the inclination towards the marvellous" and faith, or "the spirit of religion," as Hume calls it in Section X of the *Enquiry*, are two distinct principles, and it is the absence of conviction typical of the second that explains its customary union with the first and therefore, its ubiquitous influence on human life. Without it, the religious passion, in Hume's own words, would have no "continuance," and hence " would decay away by insensible degrees."

We should briefly dwell on the passions, for they are in a species of dialectical tension with beliefs. Hume's emphasis on such a relationship is one of the reasons that leads him to exclude religious faith from the universe of beliefs which are both genuine and reasonable. It has been noted that authentic beliefs have a superior influence on the passions, and because of it they can become powerful motives of action. Now we must bring forward the converse phenomenon: how the strength of certain passions stimulates the formation of determinate beliefs. In the *Treatise* itself Hume points to this circumstance with the purpose of distinguishing belief in a paradigmatic, or causal, sense from excessive belief, or credulity.

> As belief is almost absolutely requisite to the exciting of our passions, so the passions in their turn are very favourable to belief . . . . A coward, whose fears are easily awaken'd, readily assents to every account of danger he meets with; as a person of a sorrowful and melancholy disposition is very credulous of every thing that nourishes his prevailing passion (THN, 120).

Hence those powerful and "unaccountable terrors with regard to futurity" engender in the religious devotee the credulous attitude towards immortality, a dogma that, as Hume supposes, not only shows no regard for common experience but also appears to oppose the usual course of nature. But there is often another factor that lends additional force to that creed. The belief in an afterlife as well as the fears on which it feeds itself would vanish or at least gradually fade away if it were not because they are "artificially fostered by precept and education." Such an officious indoctrination is provided by ministers and priests who a have a lot to gain in this world by spreading the fears of the other (E, "Of the Immortality of the Soul," 593).

In the same manner, hope and fear, the religious passions *par excellence*, may unquestionably communicate a great degree of liveliness to the conceptions of divinity by means of which human beings seek to represent to themselves those unknown causes of their happiness or misery, causes which are not, except through their supposed effects, immediately present to the senses. But even here, where faith displays manifest doxic vitality, Hume seems to endeavor to show that faith is a weaker form of assent, much closer to the temporary assent we bestow on the characters, actions, and places of dramatic performances than to common belief in matters of fact and existence. But why should this be by force so? If the belief were genuine enough, we should derive no pleasure from being overwhelmed by terror; but in religion and in tragedy we do, and for the same reason, that is to say, because we have no real belief, or have a positive disbelief, in the object that provokes that pleasing, fascinating pleasure:

> In the common affairs of life, where we feel and are penetrated with the solidity of the subject, nothing can be more disagreeable than the fear and terror; and 'tis only in dramatic performances and in religious discourses, that they ever give pleasure. In these latter cases, the imagination reposes itself indolently on the idea; and the passion, being soften'd by the want of belief in the subject, has no more than the agreeable effect of enlivening the mind, and fixing the attention (THN, 115).

Hume's contention is questionable at least for two reasons: First, there is no necessary connection, not even a uniform correlation, between on the one hand, fear and the capacity to cause or not cause pleasure in the conscious subject and on the other, the presence or absence of conviction about the real existence of a feared object; in other words, it seems not to be generally true that the delight experienced by the subject who fears is a reliable index of his or her absence of conviction in the object that elicits such fear. One might object Hume's claim by means of a counterexample. If Hume were right, then the existence of fearful and inveterately credulous masochists would indeed be a rare occurrence; that is to say, there should be very few persons who anxiously expect the appearance of the terrible presence that fascinates them, and who are at the same time totally convinced of the real existence of that awe-inspiring and appealing object. Second, leaving aside the question whether the assent to the objects of religious worship is authentic or not, for a philosopher who stressed that reason is and ought only to be the slave of passion, Hume displays here a somewhat superficial grasp of tragedy; for he almost ignores the important cathartic function which religious rituals and tragic representations perform, and which, as is well-known, Aristotle emphasizes in the *Poetics* and the *Rhetoric*. Finally, one has to add that the claim just examined appears to contradict Hume's own explanation about how we come to place an excessive credit, or credulity, on reports about miracles. Now he presents the pleasurable effect of the fear-provoking account as a reliable sign of the little credit given to it; yet, what he had said in Section X of the *Enquiry* was exactly the opposite: namely, that it was the pleasing effect of miraculous tales, i.e., the passion for the marvelous, the factor which accounts for the over-belief in testimony about miracles.

On the whole, Hume tacitly distinguishes between belief in the broad sense of any strong conception, and belief in the strict sense of genuine conviction; the latter is no only strong, vivid, firm, stable and relevant for action, but also reasonable, in so far as the degree of conviction with which is held is proportional to the empirical evidence in its favor.[18] And with respect to religious faith his conclusion is unequivocally negative:

> This is in the meantime obvious; that the empire of all religious faith over the understanding is wavering and uncertain, subject to every variety of humor, and dependent on the present incidents, which strike the imagination. (NHR, 62).

Consequently, it is very difficult not to conclude that Hume places religious faith out of the set of genuine beliefs, and also takes it to be a conspicuous instance within the genus of irrational or unjustifiable belief, at least in so far as we deal with historical religions. Religious beliefs do not spring out of the causal principle that rests on experience, but from strong passions, such as hope and fear, and from resemblances and contiguities which are capriciously and deliberately associated to very diverse religious representations. And that is the reason why its influence is "wavering and uncertain." For most religious beliefs it applies what Hume explicitly asserted about belief in immortality, that is, if they were not reinforced by diligent and habitual indoctrination, i.e., "precept and education," they would "quickly vanish" (E, 593).

Upon this foundation, Hume goes as far as to uphold that faith in general is apocryphal, "more feigned than real," and Christian faith in particular more so, for by being "most contrary to custom and experience," it is only by the force of a real miracle that it is possible to sustain it at all (EHU, 131). But in doing these two things, Hume is in fact stepping outside the field of the phenomenology of faith and tacitly formulating a normative recommendation: that is to say, he admonishes us to employ the term 'belief' in its restricted sense, which is obviously very different from the way in which it is used in common discourse. And this recommenda-

---

[18] "A wise man . . . proportions his belief to the evidence" (EHU, Section X, "Of Miracles," 110).

tion, with its implication of placing religion out of the sphere of authentic belief, has to be justified. I think that some reasons that Hume might have adduced on the basis of his general theory of belief, are not sufficient to justify his plain rejection of faith. Let us examine them.

Hume suggests that belief founded on sense experience opens to us a coherent and uniform world. Yet, even if we admit that faith is delusive, falsities and vagaries do not necessarily have to be inconsistent. On the other hand, within Hume's epistemological presuppositions, neither is it possible to adhere to empirical belief and reject religious faith because the former corresponds, in contradistinction to the latter, with a world which is external and independent of the believing subject. For the common sense view of the world on which we bestow a "serious conviction" is as much a construction of the imagination as the products of "poetical enthusiasm"; and quite frankly, the latter seem to have, most of the time, more coherence than the former, at least if we are talking about the course of our flesh and blood existence in this world.

In addition, if we forego the question as to what may constitute sufficient evidence to accept any such system among other possible ones, there seems to be no a priori reason for excluding the possibility that a religious faith might provide an outlook of reality totally coherent and consistent with experience thus far, even if this system could not be rationally justified. But, as we have already seen, this also holds true for Hume's system of "judgment," or the system of "reality" and "realities." A set of religious beliefs, even if it were held with sincere conviction, unmistakable force and firmness, would not necessarily exclude doubt, uncertainty, and even agony and anxiety. The presence, perhaps omnipresence, of these is not inevitably a sign of hypocrisy and simulation, any more than for a scientist the trust in experience is eroded because, under the light of new theories, what was originally taken to be a fact of observation may come to be modified or no longer reckoned as such. Likewise within the world of daily life, the trust we place and the candor with which we hold beliefs based on our experience of the behavior of other people is not normally eroded or suspended simply because we may also acknowledge the undeniable fact that such a conduct – human speech, gestures, actions, and events – upon which we found those beliefs is always ambiguous. Hence we come to recognize that our interpretation of its meaning is in principle always open to question or revision, and so our inferential beliefs based on them are also always subject to some degree of uncertainty. But their inherent uncertainty, which Hume knew better than any one else, make these common-sense beliefs neither doubtful, nor weak, nor insincere.

And what about their pertinence for common life? Are religious beliefs dispossessed of pragmatic value? On one occasion or other Hume argues that it is because the have mainly in mind their practical importance that some of the faithful continue to publicly declare their loyalty to dogmas which they do not, or can no longer, sincerely believe: "A religionist . . . may know his narrative to be false, and yet persevere in it, with the best intentions in the world, for the sake of promoting so holy a cause" (EHU, 117–118; see also EHU, 125). Yet his general position is the converse of the former: since the devout person does not in practice take his or her presumed beliefs into account, in the sense that from his or her daily conduct one cannot naturally deduce that he or she actually asserts their truth, then it is evident that these are not uphold with a firm and sincere conviction.

But does not this conclusion appear to be contradicted by a universal experience which shows that dogmas or theological principles are powerful and habitual springs of individual as well as of collective behavior? Obviously Hume does not have any intention to deny this evident and well-established fact. What he will question instead is the claim that the pragmatic efficacy of religious beliefs is due precisely to the clear, firm and sincere assent that devout persons bestow on them. On the contrary, it is rather the symbolic, non-representative, meaning of dogmas, that is, their character as signs or emblems that serve to identify people as belonging to parties or other human groups with distinctive interests, passions and ambitions, what transforms them into real determining foundations of practical action:

> Though theological principles, when set in opposition to passions, have often small influence on mankind in general, still less on princes; yet when they become symbols of faction, and marks of party distinctions, they concur with one of the strongest passions in the human frame, and are then capable of carrying men to the greatest extremities (H, VI, 389).

Thus, for instance, the vigor with which a person proclaims a dogma such as transubstantiation is, in general, more a sign of his or her communion with the interests and purposes of Catholics than of his or her firm and clear assurance of the truth of that principle, even though devotees may of course often invoke the latter in order to sanctify and conceal to themselves those very particular interests:

> Where ambition can be so happy as to cover its enterprizes, even to the person himself, under the appearance of principle, it is the most incurable and inflexible of all human passions (H, I, 207).

Are religious convictions ultimately more useless and harmful than all other beliefs in matters of fact and existence? Although in chapter 8 this matter will be dealt with in detail, it is enough to point at the moment that very often Hume suggests that they are not reliable for the conduct of life, leading to innumerable evils: "errors in religion are dangerous" (THN, 272).[19]

---

[19] Likewise Hume also judges the nature and prejudicial effect of the Puritan zeal that was typical of the soldiers ("saints") of Cromwell's army:

> The saint, resigned over to superior guidance, was at full liberty to gratify all his appetites, disguised under the appearance of pious zeal. And, besides the strange corruptions engendered by this spirit, it eluded and loosened all the ties of morality, and gave entire scope, and even sanction, to the selfishness and ambition, which naturally adhere to the human mind H, V, 493–494).

The alienating effect on character that religious enthusiasm naturally brings about will be discussed in the next chapter.

At this point I only wish to remark that Hume derives a good portion of the dangerousness of religion (in particular its capacity for promoting discord and social strife) exactly from the feigned and self-imposed, or insincere nature of religious faith. The violent effort of believers to silence the voice of those who oppose their faith is really aimed at keeping quiet the unresolved doubts which still besiege their inmost hearts:

> [T]he theological animosity . . . is a certain proof, that they have never reached any serious persuasion with regard to these remote and sublime subjects. . . . But while men zealously maintain what they neither clearly comprehend, nor entirely believe, they are shaken in their imagined faith, by the opposite persuasion, or even doubts of other men; and vent on their antagonists that impatience, which is the natural result of so disagreeable a state of the understanding (H, III, 431–432).

Despite all the precedent considerations, it is manifest that errors, simulation and hypocrisy, along with the sufferings and ills which these commonly bring about, are not, however, exclusive features of religion, but constantly actualized possibilities of any human enterprise, cognitive as much as practical. Even if Hume was aware of this, still it is remarkable that he really took so great care to show that religion, with much more ease than almost any other thing, leads human beings to fall into conceptions and modes of behavior which are absurd, capricious, cruel, in short, immoral. But one would have to be totally blinded by a simplistic ideology not to be able to see that religion is also conductive to much practical and moral goodness. And even if these features remain more or less undisclosed in the *Natural History of Religion*, at the same time one must concede that Hume does not completely ignore them. In the concluding section of that work, he somewhat belatedly came to recognize the positive effect of faith.

> As the good, the great, the sublime, the ravishing are found eminently in the genuine principles of theism: it may be expected, from the analogy of nature, that the base, the mean, the terrifying will be equally discovered in the religious fictions and chimeras (NHR, 75).

Hence, from this brief examination it seemingly follows that the pragmatic test is indecisive. A more definite and less tentative conclusion on this matter will have to wait for the next chapter. Yet before beginning the detailed analysis of Hume's devaluation of the pragmatic and moral worth of faith, I would like formulate two final critical observations of a wider epistemological nature concerning his general theory of belief and its bearing on his account of faith.

First, if both types of beliefs, the ordinary no less than the religious, stem from the same faculty – imagination – , then it has to be conclusively shown, in order to give priority to one over the other, that one is, and the other is not, consistent with sense-experience – the bulwark of "reality" for Hume. One would be the reasonable belief in real matters of fact and existence, the other, simply superstition. But to justify the presumption of reasonableness bestowed upon belief founded on causal inference, one has also to take for granted that Hume shows in a consistent manner that it is possible to gain access to this sense-experience, which is the point of departure and the foundation of such beliefs. This demands from him, among other things, a coherent explanation as to how it is possible for the mind to distinguish consistently between fact and fancy, between memories or faithful copies of past events and pure fictitious accounts. According to many interpreters, Hume actually provides us with such a convincing account. On my part, I have to reiterate the doubts which I expressed in chapter 1, i.e., that one of the greatest difficulties that besets Hume's theory is its seeming inability to formulate a satisfactory explanation of those capital ontological concepts which does not take for granted the very distinctions it seeks to account for, and this is one of the roots of his scepticism. It is for having taken perceptions as point of departure and conceived them as "internal and perishing existences" (some of which are just simply more intense than others) that it becomes controversial whether or not Hume could ever intelligibly establish the "appearance – reality" distinction.

Second, a more general question – which is however linked to the preceding – has been pointed out and discussed at great length by a veritable legion of Hume scholars. Are all the different ways that Hume uses to characterize belief really compatible among themselves? Belief is said to be a lively idea, a manner of conception, a feeling, a custom or habitual disposition, an act of the mind. Is this an heterogeneous collection of expressions which refer to quite different mental phenomena which among themselves exhibit only family resemblances but not a set of strictly universal notes that would justify an unequivocal attribution of the same term 'belief' to each and every one of them? Lastly, can belief be susceptible of being simultaneously described as a lively *conception* and as a *manner* of conception? If the mental phenomena that we call beliefs differ among themselves as do the members of a family, then an affirmative answer to the previous questions becomes more than plausible; but if they are, after all, as Hume appears to suppose, members of the same species or genus of acts, then such a positive answer becomes very problematical.

In brief, these questions, and many others of the same sort, would have to be satisfactorily answered from a gnoseological perspective, for otherwise Hume's treatment of faith in the light of his theory of belief, would be left without a solid base. For the eradication of faith from the field of serious and sensible convictions about reality itself rests on the contrast of religious belief with the paradigm case of reasonable belief, i.e. that which is founded upon sense-experience and the causal inferences that experience supports. And thus at the end we have to suppose something which is truly debatable: namely, that within Hume's philosophy the theoretical integrity of the distinction we commonly made between fact and fancy is reasonably guaranteed. For ultimately this is what bestows intelligibility on our differentiation between the veridical beliefs of common life and experience and the fanciful beliefs, or superstitions, of religious fanaticism.

I have to confess, much to my regret, that I still do not have entirely adequate answers for these two questions.

CHAPTER 8

The Ethical Depreciation of Religion

8.1 INTRODUCTION

It does not cease to produce wonder that Hume, who looks in *The Natural History of Religion* for the origins of religion in human nature, should have been able to reveal such a small amount of humanity to be present in religion. Sympathy, compassion, generosity, gratitude, enlightened self-interest, indeed rationality, these features of the social life, which have such an important place in his analysis of the principles of morality, may also be substantial components of the religious life. Yet if one takes Hume as a guide, it is only by an effort of the imagination that one can conclude that those qualities are conspicuously displayed there, too. Religion all too often degenerates into a furious madness, but the moral life is not exempted from falling into aberrations of its own. Religious foibles he generously describes; the moral ones – although he affirms that his aim is not to promote or recommend morality – he barely touches upon, except for a few mocking remarks directed against the Cynics and Stoics.[1] In the *Natural History* he strongly suggests that religion is the one main factor which invariably leads men astray in the pursuit of the good life; for no other reason he titled Section 14, "Bad Influence of Popular Religion on Morality." The determination of the actual psychological motives and biographical factors which may have inclined Hume to depreciate historical religion does not fall within the scope of our scrutiny.[2] All I shall attempt to show is, first, that Hume's peculiar conception about the origins of historical religion naturally

---

[1] See, for example, I, 272; EHU, 101; EPM, "A Dialogue," 342–343.

[2] This emphasis on the negative may be attributed, at least in part, to the polemical character of the work, perhaps written with the Evangelical wing of the Scottish Church in mind. During the period of publication of *The Natural History of Religion*, the Highflying or Evangelical party conspired to produce the most severe condemnation of Hume's person and writings, i.e. his excommunication from the Church of Scotland. Had it occurred, this would probably have led Hume, as E. C. Mossner convincingly suggests, into his voluntary exile from Scotland. See *The Life of David Hume*, pp. 336–355. On the other hand, the militant attack on religion typical of the deistic controversy, had ceased already at the time Hume chose to publish the *Natural History*. See Sir Leslie Stephen, *History of English Thought in the Eighteenth Century*, I, 77, 136.

leads in the direction of such ethical depreciation; and, second, that such a thesis is not inevitable, even within the framework of Hume's philosophy, and that it appears to be at odds with some basic tenets of his moral theory. We will not examine, however, Hume's famous thesis that morality is independent of religion.[3]

8.2 THE MORAL HARMFULNESS OF RELIGION

But what are precisely the undesirable moral effects of religion? There are major as well as minor evils conjoined with the religious passions, practices and beliefs. As to the lesser, even if and when religion does not promote immorality, the zeal expressed in the strict performance of its rituals produces an indifference towards, and a diversion from, the observance of the genuine moral duties (DNR, 222). In addition, religious faith, when obsessed with hopes and fears of salvation and damnation, not only furthers a spirit of narrow egoism, but also inclines men into a life of simulation and hypocrisy.[4] Even in religions such as Christianity, where God is thought of as supremely good, men immerse themselves in many absurd opinions and frivolous rituals whose specific and almost exclusive purpose is the solicitation of divine favors:

> He considers not, that the most genuine method of serving the divinity is by promoting the happiness of his creatures. . . . But if he fasts a day, or gives himself a sound whipping; this has a direct reference, in his opinion, to the services of God (NHR, 72).

At worst religion, to put it mildly, commands immoral and cruel deeds: dissensions, persecutions, sacred wars, physical and spiritual oppression by and against religious groups and individuals, and other social and historical commotions. This is not the place for us to stop and comment on the quite long list of such evils,

---

[3] Hume's contention is based on two considerations: First, that morality is sufficiently founded upon the constant and universal structure of our human nature, and second, that it is not possible to validly infer any practical and moral conclusions from God's existence. The second point will be analyzed in Part III. Hume discusses the famous "Is – ought" question in Book III of the *Treatise*, Part I, Section I, 467–470, and Appendix I of *An Enquiry Concerning the Principles of Morals*, 283–294. With respect to the actual, not logical, foundations of morality, that Hume bases the latter on human nature is not necessarily incompatible with an ultimate theological foundation. He appears to admit this in Appendix I; for inasmuch as God is taken to be the first cause of all Nature, to that extend morality depends on God (EPM, 294). Yet in what concerns the foundation for the universally binding obligation of ethical rules, morality is effectively divorced from religion: "In restoring a loan, or paying a debt, his divinity is nowise beholden to him; because these acts of justice are what he was bound to perform, and what many would have performed, were there no god in the universe" (NHR, 72).

[4] Hume's doubts concerning the authenticity of religious assent are – as has been shown in the previous chapter – quite unmitigated. See in particular, NHR, 60 and 72.

which Hume offers from section 9 to section 14 of the *Natural History*.[5] But, more importantly, religious attitudes and passions are harmful to the development of moral character. For Hume the superstitious beliefs, practices and feelings endemically connected with religious life simply corrupt our humanity: it is mainly for that reason that the "errors of religion are dangerous" (THN, I, 272). They deaden in us the "constant and universal" although calm voice of sympathy (THN, III, 586, 591). But religious superstition, as he shows in his essay "Of Superstition and Enthusiasm," may also cloud our vision, and by fostering passivity and submission it "fits [men] for slavery" (E, 78), since the unlimited trust in its ministers and priests destroys the freedom of their understanding, their capacity to think by themselves.

Let it be said that for Hume all historical religions inevitably have adverse effects on the moral behavior of their worshipers. This conclusion does not appear in the *Natural History* as an empirical generalization: the product, as it were, of a detailed analysis of the disconcerting variety of forms exhibited by religious life. It seems to be, on the contrary, a deductive consequence of an initial division of that life into two ideal types of a very general nature: polytheism and theism, or [mono]theism. These are poles of a recurrent history, alternating forms connected in a perpetual oscillating movement, which is in itself both the objective expression and the result of a constant and universal human nature.[6] Each of these types of religion has a positive aspect, but each suffers from its own infirmities. For instance, polytheism has, to use Hume's word, the "disadvantage" that it may, and usually does, sanction barbarous, cruel and immoral practices; but as a plus it displays a remarkable spirit of toleration. Monotheism, on the other hand, has on the plus side, the intellectual and moral purity of the object of its worship, an object which should have spurred its devotees to the practice of a perfect morality alone. Yet this has not been the case, because the conception of a sole deity easily produces a spirit of intolerance and hostility towards other sects: "the several sects fall naturally into animosity, and mutually discharge on each other that sacred zeal and rancour, the most furious and implacable of all human passions" (NHR, 49).[7]

Thus polytheism and monotheism oppose each other with respect to the source of both their merits and demerits. However, Hume's comparative study of these is really geared to show that there are significant differences in the degree to which each type of religion exercises a bad influence on morality. And, in this, Hume's in-

---

[5] Gerhard Streminger compiles an almost complete catalogue of these moral infirmities of religion; see "Religion a Threat to Morality: An Attempt to Throw Some New Light on Hume's Philosophy of Religion," *Hume Studies* 15.1 (November 1989): 295–300.

[6] See chapters and 6 above for a detailed analysis of this subject.

[7] About religious fanaticism he says in the essay "Of the Coalition of Parties," that it is:

a principle the most blind, headstrong, and ungovernable, by which human nature can possibly be actuated. Popular rage is dreadful, from whatever motive derived: But must be attended with the most pernicious consequences, when it arises from a principle, which disclaims all controul by human law, reason, or authority (E, 500).

tention is obvious enough: to show that in almost all respects (except rationality, and here even with some doubts) polytheism is definitely superior to monotheism. Furthermore, he goes on to suggest that – morally speaking – ancient polytheism is something more than a lesser evil compared to Christianity. Of the many topics of interest that this relative estimate raises, I shall only consider one: the comparison of Christianity and ancient Graeco-Roman religion "with regard to courage and abasement" (NHR, 51–53), and only because Hume seems here to have formulated, in broad outlines, doctrines which are commonly associated with thinkers from a latter and very different intellectual climate:

> Where the deity is represented as infinitely superior to mankind, this belief, though altogether just, is apt, when joined with superstitious terrors, to sink the human mind into the lowest submission and abasement, and to represent the monkish virtues of mortification, penance, humility, and passive suffering, as the only qualities which are acceptable to him. But where the gods are conceived to be only a little superior to mankind, and to have been, many of them, advanced from that inferior rank, we are more at ease in our address to them, and may even, without profaneness, aspire sometimes to rivalship and emulation of them. Hence activity, spirit, courage, magnanimity, love of liberty and all the virtues which aggrandize a people (NHR, 52).

These acute observations of Hume, brief as they are, have obvious and striking similarities to Nietzsche's well-known doctrine about the origins of moral and religious values in Classical antiquity and in Judeo-Christian tradition.[8] Nietzsche views, in general, the Ancient Graeco-Roman religion as the product of the noble and strong man; Judaism and Christianity, as the offspring of the slave and meek man. Thus in a typical passage he uses a language very reminiscent of Hume's:

> This is a kind of madness of the will in the sphere of psychological cruelty which is absolutely unparalleled: – man's will to find himself guilty and blameworthy to the point of inexpiability . . . his will for rearing an ideal – that of the "holy God" – face to face with which he can have tangible proof of his own unworthiness. . . . The fact is that in itself the conception of gods is not bound to lead necessarily to this degradation of the imagination (a temporary representation of whose vagaries we feel bound to give), the fact that there exist nobler methods of utilizing the invention of gods than in this self-crucifixion and self-degradation of man, in which the last two thousand years of Europe have been masters – these facts can be still perceived from every glance that we cast at the Grecian gods, these mirrors of noble and grandiose men, in which the animal in man felt itself deified and did not devour itself in subjective frenzy.

---

[8] Friedrich Nietzsche, "The Natural History of Morals," *Beyond Good and Evil*, trans. Helen Zimmern, in *The Philosophy of Nietzsche*, The Modern Library (1927; rpt. New York: Random House, 1954), pp. 478–497; see especially the second essay, " 'Guilt,' 'Bad Conscience' and the Like," of *The Genealogy of Morals*, trans. Horace B. Samuel, in *The Philosophy of Nietzsche*, pp. 668–716.

These Greeks long utilized their gods as simple buffers against the "bad conscience" – so that they could continue to enjoy their freedom of soul; this, of course, is diametrically opposed to Christianity's theory of its god.[9]

Hume has certainly grasped the relevant facts which are the ground for Nietzsche's hypothesis.[10] Nonetheless, it can be argued that there remains a significant difference between the two accounts; namely, Hume, when evaluating Graeco-Roman religion and Christianity with respect to the courage and abasement these instill in their respective votaries, reverses the relation of the elements that are brought into play. Whereas Nietzsche derives the pagan and Christian beliefs from the character and passions of the men who entertain them, Hume derives the feelings and attitudes from the respective beliefs.[11] Yet this is indeed a minor point. On the one hand, belief is assimilated – at least in what many have thought to be Hume's final version of his theory of belief – to a determinate, irreducible type of feeling that anyone can introspectively find in himself, but which stands outside any proper definition.[12] On the other hand, Hume has always recognized the reciprocal nature of the relation between passions and beliefs; thus he has established in the *Treatise* that passions, especially strong ones, are effective in the production of beliefs: "As belief is almost absolutely requisite to the exciting of our passions, so the passions are in turn very favourable to belief" (THN, I, 120). For this reason, it seems that Hume would not have opposed in principle Nietzsche's view. Accordingly, in the essay "Of Superstition and Enthusiasm," when analyzing two

[9] "'Guilt,' 'Bad Conscience,' and the Like," *The Genealogy of Morals,* pp. 712–713.

[10] One can say with some justice that in this comparison with regard to courage and abasement, Hume has also anticipated one of the most notorious theses of Ludwig Feuerbach, to wit, that there is an inversely proportional relation between the aggrandizement of divinity and the depreciation of its worshiper:

> This phenomenon is an extremely remarkable one, characterizing the very core of religion, that in proportion as the divine subject is really human, the greater is the apparent difference between God and man; the more, by reflection on religion, by theology, is the identity of the human and the divine denied, and the human, considered as such is depreciated. The reason of this, is that what is positive in the conception of the divine being can only be human, the conception of man, as an object of consciousness, can only be negative. To enrich God, man must become poor; that God may be all, man must become nothing (*The Essence of Christianity*, pp. 75–76).

[11] See Roberto Torretti, *Hume y la religión,* p. 25.

[12] The most emphatic affirmation of this theory occurs in the Appendix to the *Treatise,* (624–625). There he says that "belief consists merely in a certain feeling or sentiment; is something which depends not on the will, but must arise from certain determinate causes and principles of which we are not masters (624, c.f. 625 and *passim*) . . . And this different feeling I endeavour to explain by calling it a superior *force*, or *vivacity*, or *solidity*, or *firmness*, or *steadiness*. This variety of terms, which may seem so unphilosophical, is intended to express the act of the mind, which renders realities more present to us than fictions, causes them to weigh more in the thought, and gives them a superior influence on the passions and imagination" (629). A similar posture is found in EHU, sec. 5, pt. 2, 47–55. J. C. Gaskin, *Hume's Philosophy of Religion*, p. 129, calls it Hume's "final" theory of belief because the passage in THN, 629, is found verbatim in EHU, 49. In the previous chapter, we have seen how problematical Hume's conception of belief is.

different types of Christian sects and the aberrations these fall into, Hume derives the beliefs from the respective passional disposition or character of the believers; in other words, his account is the converse of one he submits in the *Natural History*. He says, for instance, that:

> Weakness, fear, melancholy, together with ignorance, are, therefore, the true sources of superstition. . . . Hope, pride, presumption, a warm imagination, together with ignorance, are therefore, the true sources of Enthusiasm (E, 74).

And it the following passage Hume describes the phenomenon of "bad conscience," or self-deprecation, while also pointing out to its causes and effects, in a manner which is surprisingly similar to the one expressed in the quoted passage of *The Genealogy of Morals:*

> As superstition is founded on fear, sorrow, and a depression of spirits, it represents the man to himself in such despicable colours, that he appears unworthy, in his own eyes, of approaching the divine presence, and naturally has recourse to any other person, whose sanctity of life, or, perhaps, impudence and cunning, have made him be supposed more favoured by the Divinity. . . . Hence the origin of PRIESTS (E, 75).

All this suggests, in short, that the parallel is much closer than it is generally taken to be; that is, Hume anticipates, in substance as well as in manner, Nietzsche's theory.

On the whole, Hume brings into the open the darker features of the religious life: the irrational, the bestial, the malevolent and the hypocritical; he points out that the purest conceptions of divinity and most strict observance of religious ritual are not incompatible with, and in practice have sanctified the most opprobrious, cruel and inhuman deeds. One serious limitation of the *Natural History* is that it easily gives the impression that this is the only side to religion, even if – as Hume himself remarks at the very end of the work – that was not his intention (NHR, 75). It is true that in *The History of England* he takes a more conciliatory position. This more sober ethical appraisal appears in a rectificatory preface that was later relegated to a mere footnote in the text, and finally excised from it.[13]

There is, nonetheless, a wide gap between his description of the moral and the religious man. Why does Hume lay such stress on the negative moral influence of religion?

Perhaps this is linked to his explanation of the origins of religious beliefs. One prominent motive for denying historical religion an instinctual origin may have been Hume's conviction that historical religion – not true theism or philosophical

---

[13] Hume, *History of England*, 8 vols. (Edinburgh, 1792), Vol. II (1756), 449 (Quoted from E. C. Mossner, *The Life of David Hume.*, p. 306). Mossner also transcribes the original draft in full, a MS in Keynes Library, Kings College, Cambridge, and which is endorsed: "Draft of Preface to a volume of D. Hume's History in David Hume's own hand found among my father's papers."

religion – fulfills no basic and indispensable human need, and that its vanishing from human life would not be fatal but beneficial. At any rate, it would not likely follow that upon the removal of religious beliefs "human nature must immediately perish and go to ruin" (THN, I, 225), as he supposes would occur if it were deprived of other "natural" beliefs, such as the belief in causal necessity, in the continuous and independent existence of sensible objects, and in the identity of the self.[14]

But did Hume think that religion is morally harmful because it does not arise out of an original instinct, or did he rather suppose that since religion is morally harmful, then it cannot arise out of an original instinct? It is somewhat difficult to determine this matter; yet I believe the second alternative to be Hume's position. It is true that Hume goes to great lengths at the very outset, in the Introduction to *The Natural History of Religion*, to summarily dispose of such a religious instinct. Instead of dwelling on the innate or inborn origin of instinctive capacities, dispositions, actions and impulses, Hume points out to the features which these must exhibit in order to be called instinctual. These are universality, uniformity in the manner of operation, and irreducibility to more basic factors. Since religious belief does not fulfill any of these conditions, then it "springs not from an original instinct or primary impression of nature" (NHR, 21).

But does it necessarily follow from this denial that religion is not natural and, furthermore, that it is morally harmful? Neither seem to follow. In the first place, although Hume very strongly asserts that religion is not an original but a derivative factor, he does not deny that religion is a natural constituent of human existence. Thus at the conclusion of the *Natural History*, in the "General Corollary," while asserting that the belief in a God or gods is not strictly universal, he recognizes that the predisposition to form such religious representations, that is, the "propensity to believe in invisible, intelligent power" is a "general attendant of human nature" (NHR, 75). In other words, Hume is belatedly granting religious beliefs the universality which he appeared to deny at the beginning. It is noteworthy that he applies the term 'universal' to such a propensity,[15] which is quite close to a belated restitution of its instinctive character.

Second, the practical worthlessness and moral negativity of religious belief does not follow from its not being instinctual. In order to make this plain, it will be necessary to bring forth again the sentiment and virtue of justice. Even though it is not instinctive (THN, 489 and *passim*), Hume considers that justice is, in a broad sense, natural because it is the outcome of the operation of several constitutive principles of human nature (EPM, 307). Yet its natural and non-instinctive being does prevent justice from being the virtue *par excellence* and the most useful for the preservation of society.

---

[14] In chapter 4, I have dealt extensively with the question whether religious beliefs are natural in the same sense in which the preceding beliefs are said to be so.

[15] The passage of the *Natural History* alluded to is ambiguous. J. C. Gaskin derives from it a completely different interpretation; see Hume's *Philosophy of Religion.*, p. 137.

In short, it appears that the negative moral effects of religious beliefs issue neither from their non-instinctive origin nor from their natural character. Whence then do these invariably adverse practical effects come forth, according to Hume? This thesis is not an unavoidable consequence of his sceptical doubts concerning human understanding. Like the other so-called "natural" beliefs mentioned above, the belief in invisible, intelligent power, can neither be rationally demonstrated nor conclusively corroborated by experience. But as the passages just quoted make clear, it is more than plausible to suggest that religious beliefs are natural, too.[16]

If not then from its theoretical uncertainty, whence does Hume derive the intrinsic and invariable moral harmfulness of religion? It stems rather from the exclusively practical view of its origin and permanent nature which he adopts in *The Natural History of Religion*.

Hume's account is narrowly utilitarian. The gods are conceived of as invisible and powerful entities with whom human beings must come to terms in order to preserve their well-being and prevent disaster in the daily struggle for survival in a natural environment; religious rituals are the means to gain the favor and evade the anger of the gods. It seems that, quite inadvertently perhaps, in explaining the genesis of religion, Hume has reduced all its different manifestations to a basic type, to an activity of propitiation and expiation. But this form of religiosity may be, historically speaking, a late product. F. M. Cornford, for instance, calls it "olympianism," and remarks that its characteristic rite is "the commercial sacrifice, regarded as a gift or bribe; in exchange for which benefits are to be returned."[17] Thus the originating and omnipresent motive of religion is self-interest: gods are the objects of our hopes and fears; and we only experience hope and fear before such things as can probably bring us either pleasure or pain, happiness or misery (THN, II, 439).[18]

But even if we grant that Hume is right in noting that self-interest is the original motive or one of the principles at work in the religious life, it does not follow that it is the only one. Concerning the moral life, he acknowledges that there is also sympathy or general benevolence; and it is the latter we have in mind when we praise moral actions and recommend their emulation to others.

---

[16] I only say more than plausible because a sufficient justification of such an assertion has not been given in this chapter. I believe that chapter 4, section 2 above provides such a foundation.

[17] *From Religion to Philosophy*, Harper Torch Books (New York: Harper and Row, 1957), p. 114.

[18] Even in late monotheistic religions like Christianity Hume assumes that the moving force behind the moral commands and the specifically religious practices continues to be, almost exclusively, the prudent pursuit of our own happiness. He says, for instance, that: "By these distinguished marks of devotion, he has now acquired the divine favour; and may expect, in recompense, protection and safety in this world, and eternal happiness in the next" (NHR, 72).

8.3 CRITICAL ASSESSMENT OF HUME'S CLAIM

Why should sympathy or humanity not be as prominent in religions as self-interest seems to be for Hume? We are certainly dealing with the same human nature. Why should religion not develop as easily the altruistic motives and affections? Even virtues that have an indisputable utilitarian origin, are not necessarily, and in most cases are not in fact, practiced because the individual reflects that it is in his best interest to act virtuously. The striking instance is, for Hume, justice. The original motive that led human beings to establish and observe the rules of justice is self-interest, or the material well-being and avoidance of personal injury that only can be provided by common life. But utility is not, according to Hume, the reason why we usually obey the rules of justice, and neither is it the foundation for our liking or moral approval of justice, because, among other things, the observance of the rules of justice is sometimes contrary to the interest of the agent. Utility pleases us because we also have a concern for the happiness of others, and this is precisely what he calls in the *Treatise*, "sympathy," and in *An Enquiry Concerning the Principles of Morals*, "the feeling of humanity":

> Thus self-interest is the original motive to the establishment of justice; but a sympathy with public interest is the source of the moral approbation, which attends that virtue (THN, III, 499–500).

It is by sympathy that I become interested in the welfare of others, through sympathy I feel jubilant in their happiness and saddened by their misery. But how does sympathy operate? In the *Treatise* Hume explains it in terms of the mechanism of association of ideas. I sympathize, so to speak, with another person if the idea I have of any emotion of his or her is converted into the same emotion or impression in myself. But a passion of another is not directly apprehended (THN, II, 317; III, 576), we infer the existence of such a passion "from external signs," from what he does and says. For instance, I see her laugh, and infer that she is happy. The problem is, how does the idea of the other's sentiments and emotions get transformed into an impression in myself? In the *Treatise* Hume accounts for it by an enlivening process, or communication of vivacity similar to that by which he explained in Book I the origin and nature of belief (THN, II, 316–320). In other words, the idea is converted into an impression only if it acquires a sufficient degree of force and liveliness. And whence can it acquire this extra vivacity but from a present impression which, in sympathy, is the "impression of ourselves"? (THN, II, 317)[19]

In *An Enquiry Concerning the Principles of Morals* Hume came to modify this theory, perhaps because it might imply – the self being the enlivening cause of the ideas of the pleasures and pains of other persons – that I could only care or feel con-

---

[19] The difficulties that beset this sort of analogical argument can and will be ignored here. I also pass over the question whether there is a sense in which one could properly say that there is an "impression" of the self.

cern for others because their happiness or unhappiness is transformed into my own happiness or unhappiness in so far as I put myself, as it were, in their place, or refer their happiness to my own. And this may be close enough to the reduction of sympathy – in a way somewhat reminiscent of Hobbes – to a covert species of self-love. And Hume seems, on the other hand, to have recognized that his explanation of sympathy in terms of association, however dear it was to his Newtonian program, was not entirely faithful to the facts of moral life.[20] Consequently, instead of sympathy, Hume talks in the *Enquiry* about an immediate feeling of humanity, that is, the pleasures and pains of others are immediately pleasant and unpleasant to us due to a primary instinct or benevolent impulse of our nature (*EPM*, Appendix II, 301–302). In brief, in the *Enquiry* Hume formulates in a clearer and entirely unambiguous manner a main tenet of his moral philosophy – that altruism is a fact of moral behavior as primary and well-established as self-love certainly is. And it is the immediate concern with the happiness of others, independently of any thoughts about our own welfare, what constitutes "the moral approbation" of justice; the feeling of humanity is the determining ground of the approval and disapproval of all moral characters and actions.

In beginning with the assumption that religious belief and worship are essentially a means for the acquisition of benefits and the avoidance of evils, by the bribing of the gods through prayers and rituals, Hume was not perhaps sceptical enough. He did not examine the religious facts with the same equanimity with which he inquired into the moral ones in order to see whether or not religion can as easily strengthen as it can certainly weaken the motives of morality and humanity. Thus he probably came to diminish the importance of those contemporary practices and historical records of religions available to him that contradicted his initial theoretical outlook. In sum, Hume's "love of simplicity" (EPM, Appendix II, 298), appears to have clouded and narrowed his perception of the love for others which also abounds in religion.

In addition, his purely egotistical conception of religion, with belief as its paramount feature, seems to be one important reason for the paucity of Hume's treatment, or almost lack of treatment, of mysticism. We have a paradox here. On the one hand, we have seen that the belief in gods is analyzed by means of a covert analogy with desires.[21] On the other hand, he glosses over that type of religiosity

---

[20] This is a difficult point of interpretation in which I tend to side with Páll S. Árdal. See his *Passion and Value in Hume's Treatise* 2nd ed., ch. 3, pp. 41–79. For a different and worthy view, see D. G. C. MacNabb, *David Hume: His Theory of Knowledge and Morality*, 2nd ed., pp. 185–197. Two widely different but equally important assessments concerning the relative importance of Newton's influence on Hume's philosophy are found in John Passmore, *Hume's Intentions*; and Nicholas Capaldi, *David Hume: The Newtonian Philosopher*.

[21] Thus, from the very outset, Hume appears eager to show that vulgar belief in a deity is not the product of an innate appetite that would awaken under appropriate circumstances, as it is the case with ordinary bodily and mental impulses: "This preconception [the belief in divine beings] springs not from an original instinct or primary impression of nature, such as give rise to self-love, affection between the sexes, love of progeny, gratitude, resentment; since every instinct of this kind has been found

which is more easily represented under the paradigm of appetite or desire: mysticism, whose aim is not quite the knowledge, but the possession and communion in the life of its blissful object for its own sake. There was too much of the rationalist in Hume, against himself, to pay heed to the famous words attributed to Saint Teresa of Ávila: "No me mueve, mi Dios, para quererte el cielo que me tienes prometido; ni me mueve el infierno tan temido para dejar por eso de ofenderte." (Literally translated: "I am not moved, dear God, to love thee by the heavens you have promised me; nor am I moved by fearful hell to keep from offending you."). Within Hume's own religious tradition, Calvin expressed a similar thought, even if in a more attenuated manner:

> For the pious mind realizes that the punishment of the impious and wicked and the reward of life eternal for the righteous equally pertain to God's glory. Besides, this mind restrains itself from sinning, not out of dread of punishment alone; but, because it loves and reveres God as Father, it worships and adores him as Lord. Even if there were not hell, it would still shudder at offending him alone.[22]

One of the characteristics Hume assigns to instincts is their universality and constancy of operation. He probably thought that mystical experiences are quite unique and extraordinary; so it would be improper to refer them to a primary instinct. As to beliefs, the mystic himself is very frugal indeed. His or her experience, although historically on the fringes of a particular faith, of itself issues into no doctrinal system. By its own admission, the insight the mystic might gain of divinity is ineffable, beyond the possibility of being verbally expressed or communicated. And it is safe to conclude that, for Hume, a belief beyond the possibility of being intelligibly articulated is almost indistinguishable from no belief at all.[23] In fact, in the *Dialogues Concerning Natural Religion*, Cleanthes insinuates that there is basically no ascertainable difference between the mystic and the atheist: "Or how do you MYSTICS, who maintain the absolute incomprehensibility of the Deity, differ from sceptics or atheists, who assert that the first cause is unknown and unintelligible?" (DNR, 158) Still it is noteworthy that Cleanthes, who supports the argument from design, appears to exemplify a peculiar sort of mysticism. In Part III of the *Dialogues*, he propounds the famous analogies of the voice from the clouds and the vegetative library which may also be intended to suggest, in a mosaic fashion, an awareness of divinity different from the indirect one implied by the argument from design; that is to say, a direct encounter with God similar to the experience we have

---

absolutely universal in all nations and ages, and has always a precise determinate object, which it inflexibly pursues (NHR, "Author's Introduction," 21). See chapter 4, section 2 above.

[22] John Calvin, *Institutes of the Christian Religion*, Book I, "Of the Knowledge of God the Creator," ch. 3, sect. 1, p. 43.

[23] In chapter 7 we have seen that to believe is at least, according to Hume, to have a lively idea or conception; on the other hand, what is absurd cannot be conceived by the imagination. Thus it seems to follow that we cannot really believe what is known to be unintelligible. See THN, 95.

of another self, whose mental life is not immediately given to us, but to which we gain some access by "the external signs of his countenance and conversation" (THN, II, 317) or "its causes and effects" (THN, III, 576). Likewise, God may be present to us like another mind, in the sense that we may somehow be able to gain access to God's intelligence and purposefulness through the "visible signs" of order and uniformity inscribed on the "volume of nature."[24]

Another fact that may have narrowed Hume's view of the matter was that he associated mysticism with what he termed "Enthusiasm," or rapturous devotion and furious frenzy. However much he praised the spirit of liberty and tolerance to which "Enthusiasm" gave rise in the end, it remained for him but a form of deluded fanaticism – the kind of fanaticism that the "Levellers" (many of whom belonged to Cromwell's army) and "Independents" of seventeenth-century England exemplified in an extreme form.[25]

All these factors may explain to some degree why Hume did not analyze mysticism in depth. But the single most important cause for this obliviousness is his initial outlook on what religion really is. Religious beliefs are about gods or invisible intelligent powers; before them humankind experiences hope and fear, and thus all religious worship reduces itself to different forms of propitiation and expiation. Hume, I think, has lost sight of one important aspect of religious experience; the gods are not only objects of terror or dread, but also of "fascination" or attraction, to use Rudolf Otto's terminology.[26] It is precisely because the religious object is fascinating that human beings, in seeking possession of God, can surrender to Him. In other words, deities can be loved for their own sake and not only for the favors they may bestow on their votaries. And the mystical or ecstatic dimension is virtually present in the earliest stages of religion. To attribute this omission from Hume's genetic account – which is in so many respects a brilliant psychological and anthropological hypothesis – to the paucity of the historical evidence to which he had access, seems quite implausible. The following words of Otto represent one of the most serious objections to any conception about the origins of religion such as Hume's:

---

[24] "Whatever cavils may be urged; an orderly world, as well as a coherent, articulate speech, will still be received as an incontestable proof of design and intention" (DNR, 155). My reading of Part III of the *Dialogues* has affinities with Stanley Tweyman's interpretation. He asserts that "in presenting the Articulate Voice illustration, Cleanthes is not so much concerned with establishing that it involves a rational inference as he is with emphasizing how we would react to such a voice" (*Scepticism and Belief in Hume's Dialogues*, 56). In addition, I believe with Tweyman against Nelson Pike [*David Hume, Dialogues Concerning Natural Religion* (Indianapolis and New York: The Bobbs-Merrill Company, Inc., 1970), p. 229], that Cleanthes is not thereby abandoning his defense of the argument from design.

[25] E, "Of Superstition and Enthusiasm," 76–77; EPM, 193. His condemnation of the enthusiastic spirit of both Independents and Levellers is even stronger in H, where it is reduced to a self-deluded form of extreme egoism and ambition, which effectively destroys the force of the moral sentiments and constraints, and provokes the disintegration of society (See H, V, ch. 59, pp. 513–514; VI, ch. 60, pp. 53–54).

[26] Rudolf Otto, *The Idea of the Holy*, p. 31.

It can never explain how it is that the 'numinous' is the object of search and desire and yearning, and that too for its own sake and not only for the sake of the aid and backing that men expect from it in the natural sphere. It can never explain how this takes place not only in the form of 'rational' religious worship, but in those queer 'sacramental' rituals and procedures of communion in which the human being seeks to get the numen in its possession.[27]

Against Otto and Saint Teresa (and maybe against Calvin, too), Hume might have retorted that God can never be loved for his own sake simply because God cannot be loved at all. Affection or friendship with respect to God presupposes what Otto affirms and Hume consistently denies, i.e., that there is a genuine religious experience, that we have an impression, however dim, of divine attributes and operations.[28]

Religious beliefs are but a form of self-delusion.[29] In a letter of 1743 to William Mure of Cadwell, Hume expounds such a view in an open and striking manner: God is not an object "either of the senses or Imagination & very little of the Understanding, without which it is impossible to excite any affection."[30] Since God is not "the natural Object of any Passion or Affection," the conclusion that He cannot be loved appears inevitable:

A remote Ancestor, who has left us Estates & Honours, acquir'd with Virtue, is a great Benefactor, & yet 'tis impossible to bear him any Affection, because unknown to us; tho in general we know him to be a Man or a human Creature, which brings him vastly nearer our Comprehension than an invisible infinite Spirit. A man, therefore, may have his Heart perfectly well dispos'd towards every proper and natural Object of Affection, Friends, Benefactors, Countrey, Children & c, & yet from this Circumstance of the Invisibility & Incomprehensibility of the Deity may feel no affection towards him (L, I, 51).

Against such a passage we have, on the one hand, Philo's endorsement, in Part XII of the *Dialogues*, of Seneca's dictum: "To know God . . . is to worship him"

---

[27] Ibid., p. 32.

[28] In the *Dialogues*, Philo appears to assert that we can have any idea of God as a being of infinite perfection. Since according to Hume's theory of perceptions, all impressions are particular and totally determined existences, then it seems nonsense to say that we could have an experience of divine attributes. "Our ideas reach no farther than our experience: We have no experience of divine attributes and operations: I need not conclude my syllogism: You can draw the inference yourself" (DNR, 142–143). In the *Natural History* Hume affirms that traditional polytheism is more reasonable that scholastic monotheism (NHR, 65), and even go as far as to suggest that the idea of an infinite God is an absurd concept (NHR, 43). See in particular note 21 of chapter 5, and the whole chapter, for Hume's account of the genesis of historical ideas of divinity.

[29] See in particular chapter 7, section 3.

[30] L, I, 50–51.

(DNR, 226). Yet, although here Philo agrees with Cleanthes, it is a question open to debate whether this is also Hume's opinion. Anyhow, in what immediately follows, Philo appears to reduce all devotion to God, except the philosophical (such as perhaps Spinoza's intellectual love of God), to the self-interested kind: "all other worship is indeed absurd, superstitious, and even impious" (DNR, 226). On the other hand, Hume's allusion in that letter to "a remote Ancestor" for whom we would not quite be able to feel any affection, is a better example of pseudo-loving than of true friendship; for it is implied that if he were known to us, we would love him for the "Estates and Honours" he may have left us. Yet we do not love our friends because they give us pleasure; they rather give us pleasure because we love them.[31] In this way Hume has elsewhere distinguished "the self-interested commerce of men" from "the more generous and noble intercourse of friendship and good offices" (THN, III, 521). In the same fashion, commerce with the gods is different from love of God. But such commerce may not totally extinguish true love from the "distinguished marks of devotion" (NHR, 72) of religious attitudes and observances, even if we admit with Hume that the self-interested commerce is more prevalent and noticeable. A purely interested worship of divinity is not altogether religion, but, as Calvin remarks about pagan and most actual worship, only "a false shadow of religion, scarcely even worth being called a shadow."[32]

On the whole, this narrowly utilitarian view of religion not only led Hume to dismiss the phenomenon of mysticism, but also made it easier for him to conclude that "popular" or historical religion, by its own nature, invariably has a negative influence on morality.

Nevertheless, one may not lose sight of the enormous (even truculent) facts which Hume emphasizes to make his point, while arriving at a quite different assessment about the moral role of religion. A case in point is that of C. J. Ducasse, American empiricist philosopher and author of a contemporary classic on the philosophy of religion.[33] Ducasse does not deny that religion can and does degenerate into hypocritical adulation, that it does become intolerant and violent; he sees that each sect discharges against others the most virulent hatred and rancor, and also that religion can be, has been and is still used to foster and perpetuate political enslavement and curve the individual's initiative. He grants all these liabilities, yet he considers that they are only natural to religion in the sense that disease is natural to humans; those ills indeed occur, but not because of itself religion necessarily leads to immorality, but only if and when it abandons the exercise of its natural and distinct office. It is noteworthy, though, that in contradistinction to Hume, Ducasse does not define religion in terms of any peculiar kind of belief, and much less as

---

[31] In his essay, "Of the Dignity or Meanness of Human Nature," (E, 85–86), Hume brings the essential disinterestedness of friendship forward in order to refute all those philosophers who defend an egotistical or exclusively self-interested view of human nature.

[32] John Calvin, *Institutes of the Christian Religion*, Book I, chapter 4, section 4, p. 50.

[33] C. J. Ducasse, *A Philosophical Scrutiny of Religion*, (New York: Collier Books, 1965), pp. 130–142.

belief in peculiar entities such as gods. He rather gives an operationalist definition that conceptually delimits religion on the basis of the functions it normally tends to perform. According to Ducasse, "the distinctive social function of religion – however ill performed it often may be – is . . . to develop or strengthen the altruistic impulses."[34]

This definition perhaps would have made Hume shudder. My aim in calling it forth has not been simply to oppose Ducasse's theory to Hume's. Neither has it been to endorse, nor to criticize Ducasse's theory, but only to show that a contemplation of the same historical phenomena may not lead to an ethical devaluation of religion, not even in thinkers such as Ducasse, who are heirs to Hume's empiricist outlook and methodology. One does not by force have to arrive at that conclusion, unless of course one shares Hume's initial assumptions about the origins and permanent nature of religious beliefs. And it has been shown that such account of the origins of religion does not go too well with some basic theses of Hume's own moral philosophy. Herein lie, I believe, the roots of his incomplete historical analysis of the relationship between religion and morality, and which seems to have prevented him from adequately recognizing that sympathy is as prominent a phenomenon in religion as self-interest undoubtedly is:

> Let each of you look not only to his own interests, but also to the interests of others. Have this mind among yourselves, which is yours in Christ Jesus (*Philippians* 2.4–5).[35]

That vibrant exhortation of Saint Paul, which reverberates throughout the centuries, is at once directed to our moral and religious conscience. In *The Natural History of Religion* Hume provides no compelling reason to deny this. On the other hand, his theory of the moral sense and sympathy provides all that is needed to assert that such is the case.

At this point a reasonable objection can be raised against this interpretation. It can be accused of being too narrow and myopic. After all, Hume, speaking through Cleanthes in the *Dialogues*, affirms that the genuine role of religion is to enforce the motives of morality and humanity. Thus he says:

> The proper office of religion is to regulate the heart of men, humanize their conduct, infuse the spirit of temperance, order and obedience; and as its operation is silent, and only enforces the motives of morality and justice, it is in danger of being overlooked, and confounded with these other motives. When it distinguishes itself, and acts as a separate principle over men, it has departed from its

---

[34] Ibid., p. 122; see also, pp. 132–135.

[35] *Revised Standard Version of the Bible.* The rendering of the passage in the *King James Authorized Version* is to some extent less clear: "Look not every man on his own things, but every man also on the things of others. Let this mind be in you, which was also in Christ Jesus."

proper sphere, and has become only a cover to faction and ambition (DNR, 220).[36]

There are, in turn, at least two objections to this reservation. On the one hand, Philo, the sceptic, opposes Cleanthes in very forceful tones, asserting that what Cleanthes takes as an anomaly has been the case with all historical religions (DNR, 222). Thus the *Dialogues* cannot really settle the issue. On the other hand, Cleanthes is pointing to a function that religion *ought* to perform and not to the moral function that it usually performs. And about this Hume explicitly says in the *Natural History* that a historical religion which had as its specific office the regulation of the moral life is something that *never happens;* he emphasizes, on the contrary, its inevitable sinking into absurdity and practical indifference to morality:

> Nay, if we should suppose what never happens, that a popular religion were found, in which it was expressly declared, that nothing but morality could gain the divine favor; if an order of priests were instituted to inculcate this opinion, in daily sermons, and with all the arts of persuasion; yet so inveterate are the people's prejudices, that, for want of other superstition, they would make the very attendance of these sermons the essentials of religion, rather than place them in virtue and good morals (NHR, 71).[37]

---

[36] Peter Jones (*Hume's Sentiments, Their Ciceronian and French Context*, p. 80) mentions the first sentence of this passage and Gerhard Streminger ("Religion a Threat to Morality," pp. 277–278) quotes it in full in order to draw attention to its striking similarity with the suppressed preface of 1756 to Volume 2 of *The History of England*, which was mentioned above.

[37] This passage is a sort of ironical echo of Calvin's resolute denunciation of the hypocritical zeal customarily associated with most religious worship and sacrifices:

> They [men] never consider God at all unless compelled to; and they do not come nigh until they are dragged there despite their resistance. And not even then are they impressed with the voluntary fear that arises out of reverence for the divine majesty, but merely with a slavish, forced fear, which God's judgment extorts from them. . . . Where they ought to serve him in sanctity of life and integrity of heart, they trump up frivolous trifles and worthless little observances with which to win his favor (*The Institutes of the Christian Religion*, Book I, chapter 5, section 4, "Hypocrisy," pp. 51–52).

On the matter of the moral harmfulness of religion, I side with Gaskin (*Hume's Philosophy of Religion,*, ch. 9, "The Causes and Corruptions of Religion," pp. 143–158; see in particular, pp. 151, 154–155). Streminger quotes this passage in order to establish essentially the same conclusion. See "A Reply to Ellin," *Hume Studies* 15.2 (November 1989): 303. Yet he makes no effort to determine the roots of Hume's ethical depreciation of religion and its consistency, or lack of it, with his theoretical and moral philosophy.

8.4 THE POLITICAL AND AESTHETIC RE-EVALUATION OF RELIGION

Without the slightest hint of analogous sarcasm, Hume proposes in *The History of England* exactly what he appears to reject in the preceding passage of *The Natural History of Religion*, namely, the necessity for "an ecclesiastical order, and a public establishment of religion in every civilized community" (H, III, 134).[38] Despite this, what we have here is no belated ethical rehabilitation of religion as an important historical force, but its political and even aesthetic re-evaluation. In *The History of England* Hume will not set aside his hostility against organized religion; far from it, his description of its nefarious effects on the individual and community, its barbarism and cruelty is more detailed and often even more truculent.[39] At the same time Hume recognizes that religion has been a civilizing power, particularly in critical periods of history, such as the early Middle Ages, when the Catholic Church – despite its many incurable constitutive ills – promoted order and peace among the social classes, sanity in the minds of the powerful, and aided in preserving learning and culture (H, III, 137). On the other hand, the wider view of this work maybe furnishes Hume with an optimism concerning the power of the state to eliminate, or at least mitigate, the most prominent social calamities of institutional religion. In this sense, that is, under the authority and employment of the state, "ecclesiastical establishments . . . prove in the end advantageous to the political interests of society" (H, III, 134–135). In other words, the adoration of the sacred, which is typical of religion, becomes a reinforcement of public authority by sometimes legitimizing it and always endowing it with greater efficacy; thus, to cite an instance, "that illusion, if it be an illusion, which teaches us to pay a sacred regard to the persons of princes, is so salutary, that to dissipate it by the formal trial and punishment of a sovereign, will have more pernicious effects upon the people, than

---

[38] The ecclesiastical establishment has to be subsidized by, and subordinated to, the state, for otherwise the private and entirely unrestrained exercise of priestly functions will inevitably corrupt the ministers and impel them to exclusively pursuit their own professional advantage, and thus to neglect the well-being of their flocks: "this interested diligence of the clergy is what every wise legislator will study to prevent; because in every religion, except the true, it is highly pernicious, and it has even a natural tendency to pervert the true, by infusing into it a strong mixture of superstition, folly, and delusion" (H, III, 135).

[39] This happens in particular when he analyses the excesses in which Catholics as much as Protestants fell into during the civil struggles in England:

No character in human society is more dangerous than that of the fanatic; because, if attended with weak judgment, he is exposed to the suggestions of others; if supported by more discernment, he is entirely governed by his own illusions, which sanctify his most selfish views and passions (H, VI, 113).

See also H, V, 493–494, where he dwells on the ferocity that characterized the pious enthusiasm of Independents, which lead them to commit the most horrendous atrocities as if they were divine commands.

the example of justice can be supposed to have a beneficial influence upon princes, by checking their career of tyranny" (H, V, 545).[40]

Yet the fact that religion can be transformed into a unifying political force which solidifies the threads of the social network, strengthens the bonds of subordination, supports stability, peace and concord, is not the only reason on account of which Hume concedes the necessity for some kind of state Church. In the last analysis, it is not only because of its political benefits, but for its general aesthetic effect that Hume approves and recommends organized religion. The reverence for the holy refines and diffuses in society as a whole the taste for beauty; in religions where ritual worship is important, ceremonies, prayers, hymns and temples not only promote the development of the arts, but also are the means by which the beautiful and the sublime, along with the delights which are intrinsic to their enjoyment, come, as it were, to install themselves in the lives of the common people: this is precisely why liturgy is "a more material object to the people" than doctrine (H, III, 385). In this aspect Hume considers that Protestantism is inferior to Catholicism.[41] Finally, it is obvious that the beautiful dimension of religion may also have great political utility. However, Hume distinguishes and separates both aspects of religious worship, and does not, by any means, simply subordinate the aesthetic delight of the devout to the political convenience of the ruler.

Moreover, the Protestant religion, in contradistinction to the Catholic, operates against of the natural predisposition of the human mind (which has been analyzed in chapter 7) to repose on sensible objects and forms, and assent strongly only to ideas associated with the these: "the catholic religion, adapting itself to the senses, and enjoining observances, which enter into the common train of life, does at present lay faster hold on the mind than the reformed, which, being chiefly spiritual, resembles more a system of metaphysics" (H, IV, 14). The Church of England is a happy medium between the extreme ceremonial frugality of the Protestant reformers and the disproportionate liturgical pomp of the Catholic ecclesiastics.

In summary, all the social advantages of religion are political and aesthetic: in other words, their nature is non-moral. And even when organized religion becomes

---

[40] Hume is here alluding to the unfortunate end of Charles I; before he has interpreted the ecclesiastical reform attempted by this king in conformity with the following general principle:

> He had established it as a fixed maxim of policy, to encrease the power and authority of that order [of ecclesiastics]. The prelates, he thought, established regularity and discipline among the clergy; the clergy inculcated obedience and loyalty among the people: And as that rank of men had no separate authority, and no dependence but on the crown; the royal power, it would seem, might, with the greater safety, be entrusted in their hands (H, V, 250).

[41] This is perhaps why, according to Hume, Queen Elizabeth "thought that the reformation had already gone too far in shaking off those forms and observances, which, without distracting men of more refined apprehensions, tend, in a very innocent manner, to allure, and amuse, and engage the vulgar" (H, IV, 122).

a promoter of social ethics, it seldom does it by itself, but on account, and through the operation, of the authority and power of the state.[42]

8.5 CONCLUDING REMARKS

Yet in the end, and in spite of all the misgivings that has been put forward, it is only fair to admit that Hume's philosophy contains all the elements needed to infer, with consistency, a less severe ethical appreciation of religion, and for a more balanced, rich and complex account of the relationship between religion and morality than the one given in the *Natural History*. It certainly allows for these, but only if Hume had paid more attention to some important insights into human nature which were the product of his searching analysis of the moral phenomena. Perhaps then a more sympathetic, less self-interested, treatment of religion would have followed, and exactly for the same reason which made him modify his ethical theory, that is to say, in order to keep his hypothesis less simple, but far more faithful to the facts which it attempts to explain. With a vibrant appeal to moral experience, Hume simply silences ethical egoism:

> What interest can a fond mother have in view, who loses her health by assiduous attendance on her sick child, and afterwards languishes and dies of grief, when freed, by its death, from the slavery of that attendance (EPM, Appendix II, "Of Self-love," 300).

Hume would have probably recognized the same magnificent selflessness in exceptional individuals, such as Mother Teresa and Martin Luther King, Jr., who are moved to act out of their religious convictions. And in *The History of England,* when dealing with extraordinary historical personalities, such as Joan of Arc and Charles I of England, Hume in some sense transcends the excessively negative ethical view of religion. In an eloquent summary to his account of the last days of Charles I he remarks:

> The great source whence the King derived consolation amidst all his calamities, was undoubtedly religion; a principle which, in him, seems to have contained nothing fierce or gloomy, nothing which enraged him against his adversaries, or terrified him with the dismal prospect of futurity. While everything around him bore a hostile aspect; while friends, family, relations, whom he passionately loved, were placed at a distance, and unable to serve him; he reposed himself with confidence in the arms of that being, who penetrates and sustains all na-

---

[42] I must mitigate this assertion, for Hume himself recognizes that superstitious hopes and fears can induce some devotees to perform moral deeds or abstain from committing barbarities: "For superstition can sometimes restrain the rage of men, which neither justice nor humanity is able to controul" (H, II, 252).

ture, and whose severities, if received with piety and resignation, he regarded as the surest pledges of unexhausted favour (H, V, 517–518).[43]

And he describes in a equally sober and appreciative spirit the exemplary deportment of Archbishop Laud before his execution: "Those religious opinions, for which he suffered, contributed, no doubt, to the courage and constancy of his end" (H, V, 457).

It seems as if such instances of noble conduct and strength of character fostered by religious sentiments and beliefs forced Hume, for the moment, to moderate his unmitigated scepticism concerning the moral value of religion. In the final analysis I think it has been shown that his philosophy indeed allows us to see altruistic impulses and actions, courage and fortitude as very prevalent and conspicuous features of the religious face of humankind.

---

[43] For a sympathetic treatment of Joan of Arc, see H, vol. 2, 397–410: "This admirable heroine, to whom the more generous superstition of the ancients would have erected altars, was, on pretence of heresy and magic, delivered alive to the flames, and expiated by that dreadful punishment the signal services which she had rendered to her prince and to her native country" (p. 410).

PART III

Hume's Natural Theology: The Critique of the Presumed Validity of Religious Beliefs

CHAPTER 9

From Historical Religion to Natural Religion

> Hear my prayer, O LORD, and let my cry come
> unto thee. Hide not thy face from me in the day
> *when* I am in trouble; incline thine ear unto me: in
> the day *when* I call answer me speedily. (Psalm
> 102.1–2)

> The heavens declare the glory of God; and the
> firmament sheweth his handiwork. Day unto day
> uttereth speech, and night unto night shewed
> knowledge. (Psalm 19.1–2)

9.1 VULGAR VS. PHILOSOPHICAL RELIGION

In *The Natural History of Religion,* Hume has brought to completion an important
part of that general science of human nature which he programatically anticipated
and set out to achieve very early in the *Treatise*; i.e., to determine the origin of religion in human nature and delineate the manner in which it depends on its permanent structure. Particularly in the *Dialogues*, but also in the *Treatise* and the
Enquiry Concerning Human Understanding, Hume examines its alleged rational
justification. This is a good place from which to cast a glance at the path traversed
and to what still remains ahead of us: First, I shall try to throw some light on the
problematical opposition of "popular," "vulgar," or historical religion and
"philosophical," "natural," or rational religion, that we may be able to answer the
question of whether Hume was right in establishing such a great abyss between
popular and philosophical religion. Second, I shall make a few brief observations
and point out to several principles that will guide our examination of Hume's systematical criticism of the effort to provide a rational foundation for religious faith.

According to an old Spanish proverb, civility does not detract from valor (*Lo
cortés no quita lo valiente*). So even though in multiple instances I have pointed at
the controversial, partial and even implausible character of a few of its principal theses, in all fairness I also have to emphasize that *The Natural History of Religion,*
in spite of its obvious limitations, paves the way for a broader understanding of actual religion. Much of this is due to the fact that Hume made the study of religion a

part of the science of man. In other words, its empirical approach opened to him the possibility of a historical consideration not only of religion, but of all products of the activities of the human mind. This methodological approach makes Hume look at human nature as it is, – or as Philo says concerning religion, such "as it has commonly been found in the world (DNR, 223)," and not as it was thought to be by many theologians of his time, still under the discreet spell of Cartesian rationalism. The latter conceived human nature in an aprioristic manner as thoroughly rational. Thus if and when they deigned to pay any attention to the actual manifestations of the religious life of humanity, to its absurdities, superstitions and barbarities, they customarily tended to interpret these phenomena as a sign of a debased state of humankind, as a degeneration of an original religion, which was supposed to have been both morally and intellectually perfect. These presuppositions were also shared not only by the deists,[1] but even by Newton,[2] who with some difficulty can be classified as one of them. But as it has been made clear in chapter 6, Hume smashed into pieces this simplistic "Golden Age" or "paradisiacal" picture of human nature and history, and of the genesis and development of religion.

If, according to Hume, religion is able to ascend to sublime heights of spirituality, nonetheless it surges out of the turbid depths of human passion, from which cruelty, sinfulness, and folly also spring. Human nature being what it is, only by pure blindness or by a sheer act of self-deceit can the irrational and the barbarous be explained away as extrinsic or purely accidental companions of religion. If in morality itself reason is, in a manner, a slave of the passions, religion is determined by, and bonded to, them to a much greater extent; if the source out of which both spring, i.e., human nature, is not wholly nor principally rational, then neither is religion.

What the empirical perspective may have made obscure to Hume is that religion, even in its earliest and most primitive forms, is not completely irrational either, now interpreting the word 'rational' in a speculative sense. Religion as it is, in the living historical forms that can be the subject matter of empirical science, does not rest, Hume thought, on a rational basis. What is rational is "that speculative tenet of theism" (DNR, 223), a secondary and reflective activity that arises out of the contemplation of the universe: rational theology or "natural religion". Religion in this latter sense, unlike "everything we commonly call religion," consists only in "the Practice of Morality, & the Assent of the Understanding to the Proposition that *God exists.*"[3] But this attitude pertains more to philosophy than to religion, and when united to any historical organized religion, the outcome invariably will be prejudicial to the former, for it "will soon find herself very unequally yoked with her new associate; and instead of regulating

---

[1] See chapter 2 above for a characterization of deism within the historical context of natural religion.

[2] See note 32 on chapter 2 above, which contains a useful reference to the recent polemic about Newton's alleged deism.

[3] L, I, Ltr. 21 (To William Mure), p. 50.

each principle, as they advance together, she is at every turn perverted to serve the purposes of superstition" (NHR, 54). Nevertheless, Hume abundantly shows us the annoying frequency with which philosophy becomes dangerous, and not only ridiculous, by being turned at the hands of superstitious and enthusiastic devotees into a systematic instrument for justifying the "enormities of the blackest dye" (NHR, 72) which they commit in the name of their sacred cause.[4]

The belief in God founded on the disinterested contemplation of the order of nature plays no part in the actual origins and development of religion. Although this thesis occupies a central position in the argument of the *Natural History*, the only reason of some weight which Hume offers is an anthropological presupposition of questionable factual validity. Totally ignorant, impotent against the fluctuations and vicissitudes of a hostile environment, living in equally unstable communities, and full of elemental wants barely satisfied or simply unsatisfied, human beings did not have at first the peace and leisure required for awakening the speculative propensities of their imagination before the uncanny spectacle of an orderly nature:

> But a barbarous, necessitous animal (such as man is on the first origin of society), pressed by such numerous wants and passions, has no leisure to admire the regular face of Nature, or make enquiries concerning the causes of those objects to which from his infancy he has been gradually accustomed (NHR, 24).

In such a fashion, Hume establishes a radical dichotomy between "popular religion," which is truly universal but always superstitious worship, and "natural religion," which is more philosophy than religion, and hence is "always confined to very few persons" (DNR, 223). Even giving due consideration to the scantiness and unreliability of the stock of anthropological and historical evidence that he had available, I think it is difficult to sustain such a strict separation. This opposition is not unlike others that he had established in the *Treatise of Human Nature* and the *Enquiry Concerning Human Understanding* between the attitudes of the "vulgar" and the "wise," or philosophical person." Yet there is a remarkable difference. In the *Treatise* and *Enquiry* Hume admits that his own position is closer to that of the "vulgar": in spite of all his sceptical doubts, he bestows his assent on those fundamental beliefs that are crucial for the constitution of the general outlook of common sense. With regard to popular religion, his rejection is sharp.[5] Since we shall deal later in Part III with the philosophical or natural religion, one may just note here that Hume appears to endorse only a few of the cognitive claims of "true theism" (that is, if one simply accepts at face value Philo's and Cleanthes' agreement in Part XII of the *Dialogues Concerning Natural Religion*). Still, his "philosophical as-

---

[4] "*Generally speaking*, the errors in religion are dangerous; those in philosophy only ridiculous" (T, 271; italics added).

[5] See, for instance, THN, I, Part IV, Sect. II, "Of Scepticism with regard to the senses," 187–218, and Part IV, Sect. VII "Conclusion of this book," 263–274; EHU, Sec. X, "Of Miracles," 109–131, and Sect. XI, "Of academical or sceptical philosophy," 148–165.

sent" is proverbially very hard to pin down, for it is neither unequivocal, nor unconditional.

On the other hand, Hume stresses in his speculative works something that is not quite as manifest in *The Natural History of Religion:* the vulgar and the philosopher are not really two different persons, but rather two different attitudes which can be, and almost always are, conjugated in the same individual, as is the case with Hume himself. For philosophy is an intermittent reflective operation of the mind, and once it ceases the philosopher becomes "a mere plebeian," (EHU, 6). When immersed in practical life, he or she is forced to uphold and make use of those very general beliefs that he or she previously subjected to critical examination, and for which it is not possible, or at least extremely difficult, to find an adequate rational foundation.[6] I have endeavored to show that likewise, in his works on religion, Hume does not establish an excluding distinction between the superstitious and the philosopher. For him they are not two different persons but rather two contrasting attitudes that all of us can assume at one time or another, even though there may be remarkable differences of degree between individuals which may allow us to more easily identify a given person as one or the other.[7]

In short, the "wise" and the "vulgar," the philosopher and the superstitious permanently reside deep in our minds; although these moods may be displayed in numberless ways, they are, nonetheless, alternating mental states which anyone may fall into no matter what, and that somehow are reminiscent of the periodic oscillation in the minds of common devotees between monotheistic and polytheistic beliefs of divinity. If Hume had taken all of this into account, he might have reduced the distance between historical and rational religion, and conceivably given a negative answer to the following questions:

Is the genesis of religion (the religious feelings, and the multiple representations of divinity to which these give rise) exclusively connected with necessity, or what the ancient Greeks called *Ananke* (ἀνάγκη): i.e., with urgencies and scarcity derived from the fact that man is a natural living organism? Can a strict utilitarian, or pragmatically centered theory (such as Hume's thus far considered) be a truthful and satisfactory description of the religious consciousness and its specific mode of being in the world, even if we restrict this account to the experience of human beings in primitive and barbarous communities?

Hume himself, I think, provides all that is needed in order to say that such is not the case, because his own conception of a human nature that is constant and universal joins us with the barbarians and indeed makes us their brothers and sis-

---

[6] A most forceful assertion of Hume's peculiar sort of scepticism is found in THN, I, Part IV, Sect. II, "Of a scepticism with regard to reason," 183. That passage was quoted in chapter 1 above, pp. 17–18.

[7] See chapter 2, section 2 above.

ters: it is what truly enables us to sympathize with them, or to see our own visage reflected on theirs, and so allows us to understand the meaning of their actions.[8]

Hume's explanation about how the ideas of the deities arise in the first human communities reveals particularly well our essential kinship with the barbarians and the primitives, who, in a manner, still are our contemporaries. I have tried to show in chapter 6, section 2, that when Hume refers to our remote ancestors, he is not describing beings much different from us, but rather people like him and us, albeit living in very different circumstances: i.e., within an adverse and inhospitable natural milieu where they are quite ignorant about the way the world works, and hence incessantly besieged by powerful hopes and fears that set in motion those anthropomorphic propensities of our imagination which give rise to the representations of the gods. For no other reason, when Hume points to those earliest religionists, he repeatedly uses the plural of the first person of the personal pronoun (NHR, 28–30). When he dwells on "men" in "rude and barbarous ages," he makes it clear that they form the mental pictures of the gods because "*our* anxious concern" with the invisible and uncertain causes of our happiness or misery "endeavours to form some determinate idea of them" (NHR, 40; italics added).

In conclusion, Hume appears to propound that our participation in one and the same nature cuts short the enormous temporal or spatial distances that may set us apart from the barbarians and the primitives; in short, as the "flux and reflux of polytheism and theism" suggests, we can understand them because we come from them and can permanently become like them again.

Hume's acknowledgment of this essential fellowship may then provide us with a good reason for approximating the popular to the philosophical religion, and to wonder whether Hume's explanation of the origins of historical religions can be amended in order to allow us to recognize that the speculative or disinterested urgency is as primitive, although certainly less noticeable and consequential, as the pragmatically oriented or "anxious" curiosity unequivocally is.

Excluding the teleological underpinning, Hume's outlook on human nature is more akin to Aristotle's than to Descartes'. Yet Aristotle, who viewed the human being, like Hume, as a living dynamic organism within the wider context of nature, did not contemplate such a rift between the religious attitude which forges myths, and that wonder about the world in which humans live that is the prime mover of the philosophical imagination:

And a man who is puzzled and wonders thinks himself ignorant (whence even the lover of myth is in a sense a lover of Wisdom, for the myth is composed of wonders).[9]

---

[8] The most striking declaration of this sort of secular epiphany of the other is found in the frequently labeled "ahistorical" passage of *An Enquiry Concerning Human Understanding*, 83. See chapter 6, section 2 above.

[9] Aristotle, *Metaphysics*, Book I, ch. 2, 982^{b} 17–19, trans. by Sir David Ross, in *The Basic Works of Aristotle*, ed. by Richard McKeon (New York: Random House, 1941), p. 692.

Both the philosopher and the myth-lover experience awe and perplexity; and recognizing their ignorance, both go in search of an explanation. Aristotle simply concluded that, in both cases, their speculation is motivated by something more than practical utility. Indeed, Aristotle was not oblivious to the fact that philosophy is a late cultural achievement. On the contrary, in the first two chapters of the *Metaphysics*, he rightly suggests that theoretical sciences cannot in all circumstances completely flourish and become systematic practices of shared and continuous research. He emphasizes that leisure is needed for them to prosper, and that such unfettered time is provided by the previous appearance of applied knowledge, the practical and productive arts that give human beings a greater control over nature and allow for the formation of more stable communities where the empire of law in turn brings peace and security. All these are pre-conditions for the actual exercise of those mental activities that are not immediately geared to the satisfaction of purely practical, or utilitarian needs.[10]

In contradistinction to Hume, Aristotle stresses that the attraction to the marvelous, the desire to know for its own sake, and the love of wonder are primary ingredients of our human nature, and that they are operative, in one way or another, even in our most rudimentary knowing capacities, such as sense perception. In other words, even in those forms of knowledge that human beings share with other animals what is human in them clearly shows itself:

All men desire to know. An indication of this is the delight we take in our senses; for even apart from their usefulness they are loved for themselves; and above all others the sense of sight. For not only with a view to action, but even when we are not going to do anything we prefer seeing (one might say) to everything else. The reason is that this, most of all the senses, makes us know and brings to light many differences between things.[11]

What Aristotle says seems to be an undeniable statement of fact rather than an expression of any particular intellectualistic prejudices of his own.

Should we then say, in spite of Aristotle and apparently with Hume, that religious origins are entirely irrational? Is it the case that what is rational in religion comes to it from without and quite late in its development, or only with the advent of that turn of mind which we call philosophical? Should we not rather consider that, even in the religious consciousness of primitive humans, there is something

---

[10] Exaggerating a bit, one may say that Hume's argument can be called Aristotelian in what pertains to his explanation of the political and economic conditions necessary for the advent of arts and sciences:

From law arises security: From security curiosity: And from curiosity knowledge. The latter steps of this progress may be more accidental; but the former are altogether necessary. A republic without laws can never have any duration (E, "Of the Rise and Progress of the Arts and Sciences," 118).

[11] Aristotle, *Metaphysics*, Book I, ch. 1, 980[b], 20–28; p. 689.

not altogether unreasonable? Even if Hume is certainly right in denying that the first religious beliefs were the result of a formal and strict mode of reasoning (NHR, 23–26), this does not mean that their origins are totally irrational in the sense of being devoid of disinterested curiosity. Indeed, the curiosity of primitive and almost all religionists most of the time is directed towards the unknown and incalculable causes upon which their happiness as well as their misery totally depend:

> We hang in perpetual suspence between life and death, health and sickness, plenty and want: which are distributed amongst the human species by secret and unknown causes, whose operation is oft unexpected, and always unaccountable. These *unknown causes*, then, become the constant object of our hope and fear: and while the passions are kept in perpetual alarm by an anxious expectation of the events, the imagination is equally employed in forming ideas of those powers, on which we have so entire a dependance (NHR, 28–29).

Despite all of this, if both popular and natural religion are, as James Dye has rightly asserted about superstition and philosophy, "permanent alternative responses to human curiosity about the causes of events,"[12] and if the superstitious and the philosopher, the "vulgar" and the "wise" mostly coexist in all of us, then it may have been the case, that speculative and utilitarian interests also existed together in the minds of the first religionists, albeit in different degrees or proportions.

As I have already pointed out at the conclusion of chapter 4, all in all, there is no systematic reason that may have forced Hume not to concede that even the earliest religious beliefs are elemental forms by which the speculative urge alluded by Aristotle begins to be satisfied. After all, in the *Treatise*, Hume points to the same universal feature of human nature (THN, 266) as one of those principles of imagination which are "permanent, irresistible and universal" (THN, 225). Thus in the same manner that Hume could have more patently acknowledged that sympathy, or the concern for the welfare of others, is present in historical religion as self-interest, or egoism, certainly is, he could have shown in a clearer manner that the practical and the theoretical, the utilitarian and speculative interests are inextricably intertwined in the generation of the first "tremendous images" of the gods. If the human being is, after all, a "curious" animal,"[13] there is nothing to prevent the "vulgar" and the "philosopher" (as well as the barbarian and the civilized) from sharing in the same speculative curiosity that later will fructify into the belief in an intelligent cause of the universe.

Accordingly Hume could have recognized in a more explicit fashion this, as it were, "wonderful" side of religion, for it is not the case that he simply ignores the passion for the marvelous and the innate desire to know. He just assigns them a very limited scope, that is, he mentions them only in order to account for the over-

---

[12] James Dye, "Hume on Curing Superstition," 137.

[13] THN, I, Part IV, Sect. 7, 271: "it is almost impossible for the mind of man to rest, like those of beasts, in that narrow circle of objects, which are the subject of daily conversation and action."

belief concerning incredible reports in the sense of testimony that is improbable or contrary to a regular experience. Thus it is "the passion of *surprise* and *wonder"* that explains the almost inevitable assent to reports about miraculous events (EHU, 117; c.f., 117–119).

Besides, the narrowing of the rift between a theoretically disinterested philosophical religion and a pragmatically self-oriented historical religion does not necessarily contradict Hume's account of the origin of religious beliefs. Idolatrous polytheism is, for Hume, the first religion of humankind; and even granting that polytheism does not arise from reasoning, he shows in the *Natural History* (NHR, 53–54) that it is almost as rational as monotheism. In the *Dialogues* (DNR, 167–168), he suggests, through Philo, that polytheism is even more rational. One can grant Hume that belief in gods is not primarily directed to the satisfaction of a purely intellectual need. At any rate, the dominant pragmatic role of primitive and most historical conceptions of divinity does not necessarily entail that they do not also start to answer an incipient rational demand. For it seems to be more rational to assign causes (however inconstant or capricious) to phenomena than no causes at all, or than to assume that events simply happen by chance. On this particular Hume is indeed quite clear throughout: "chance is nothing real in itself" (THN, 125), or a "mere negative word" (EHU, 95), or "a word without meaning" (DNR, 189).

What is then the main source of Hume's lack of interest in, and even apparent denial of, the speculative dimension of religion? He appears to have been too eager to show that religion (in its popular sense) is not a primary and unavoidable element of human existence. Accordingly he disavows the operation of a universal instinct in the gestation of historical religion, and instead appeals to certain tendencies of our imagination, elementary passions, and circumstances more or less common to all human beings, which may account for the rise of the belief in divinity and the diverse ways we conceive the gods.[14] Against the existence of such an instinct, he maintains that there is quite a large amount of empirical or historical evidence to the contrary (NHR, 21).

Nor is there an innate idea of God, as a kind of mark which the divine workman had set upon his work, so dear to Descartes and many deists. In the *Natural History*, he does not even really argue against this possibility; he just disposes of it at the end of the book with a swift stroke of irony:

But consult this image, as it appears in the popular religions of the world. How is the deity disfigured in our representations of him! . . . You will scarcely be persuaded, that they are any thing but sick men's dreams: Or perhaps will regard them more as the playsome whimsies of monkies in human shape, than the se-

---

[14] As we have seen in chapter 5, these first conceptions are the natural products of an act of reflection or self-awareness and a tendency of sympathetic projection: i.e., the propensity of human beings "to conceive all beings like themselves, and to transfer to every object, those qualities with which they are familiarly acquainted, and of which they are intimately conscious" (NHR, 30).

rious, positive, dogmatical asseverations of a being, who dignifies himself with the name of rational (NHR, 75).

I grant, however, that this passage in Section 15, "General Corollary," of the *Natural History*, may plausibly be interpreted as asserting the opposite: i.e., that the idea of God is innate in a Cartesian sense. However, there are at least two main considerations against this reading. On the one hand, Hume suggests in the passage that what has an innate character is not the idea of the Deity, but the mental predisposition out of which the idea of the God of the philosophers ("the universal Creator") as well as the ideas of the living deities of historical religions arise. It is to that propensity which Hume specifically refers with the striking and well-known Cartesian metaphor of the imprint left by the divine artisan on the human mind:

The universal propensity to believe in invisible, intelligent power, if not an original instinct, being at least a general attendant of human nature, may be considered as a kind of mark or stamp, which the divine workman has set upon his work; and nothing surely can more dignify mankind, than to be thus selected from all other parts of the creation, and to bear the image or impression of the universal Creator (NHR, 75).

On the other hand, Hume consistently denied that the idea of God, in the Cartesian sense of an infinitely perfect Being, were innate. The most striking and well-known passage of such denial occurs in Section 2 of *An Enquiry Concerning Human Understanding*, where the origin of that idea is empirically explained, and thus serves to confirm the principle that all ideas refer to precedent impressions:

The idea of God, as meaning an infinitely intelligent, wise, and good Being, arises from reflecting on the operations of our own mind, and augmenting, without limit, those qualities of goodness and wisdom. We may prosecute this enquiry to what length we please; where we shall always find, that every idea which we examine is copied from a similar impression (EHU, 19).

Yet even if Hume is fundamentally right in his refusal to see religion – in the manner of Auguste Comte – as a kind of proto-science, there is also much to say in favor of a philosophical attempt – such as Comte's theory of the three stages – at establishing a historical continuity between the diverse compartments of living human experience.[15] In the last analysis, it is perhaps because Hume's perspective was not historical enough, that he did not officially assign a place, however modest, to passions like love of wonder and admiration among the elements at work in the historical genesis of religion. But if one recognizes their original presence, then

---

[15] Auguste Comte, *Discours préliminaire sur l'esprit positif (1844)*. In *Traité philosophique d'astronomie populaire, Œuvres d'Auguste Comte*, Tome XI (Paris: Éditions Anthropos, 1970). The *Discours* is the most condensed and clear presentation of Comte's positivistic theory about the intellectual development of humankind.

"popular" religion, too, may properly be called "a species of philosophy" (EHU, 145).

Obviously religion is much more than a search for knowledge. Still, it is not implausible to suggest something that I hopefully will justify latter in Part III: i.e., that religion (the historical as well as the natural kind) and philosophy may be two different modes of extending and radicalizing natural dispositions which Hume recognized to be constantly and universally operative in common life, that is, in the life in which the philosophical person is forced to think and act among, and as one of, the "vulgar." On the one hand, both the ideas of the God of the philosophers or natural religion, and the living gods and God of popular or historical religions arise out of our capacity for self-consciousness and the projective tendency of imagination. The latter is, I believe, just a particular instance of a general and constant propensity of human imagination with which Hume dealt in the *Treatise* and which he brought forward in order to refute Malebranche's occasionalism (God as the sole and immediate power behind all change) and explain the origin of our belief in "power" or causal efficacy – in other words, the propensity of the imagination to "spread itself on external objects and to conjoin with them any internal impressions which they occasion" (THN, I, 165). On the other hand, both religious and philosophical representations of divinity as "invisible, intelligent power" also rise from a natural propensity closely connected with the former, that is, the tendency to give the greatest possible order and unity to our experience of the world (DNR, 134).[16]

This universal propensity, whose importance has been particularly brought forward by Páll S. Árdal,[17] manifests itself as the disposition to let ourselves be guided by the serene affections or "calm passions" which are founded on reflection. In Book III of the *Treatise*, Hume characterizes it as "what, in an improper sense, we call *reason*" (THN, 536; c.f., 583), in order to distinguish it from demonstrative and empirical reason. Thus it appears that, even according to Hume, the "historical" and the "philosophical" religion are not, after all, so much apart.

To almost lose sight of the reasonable element in religion through an overemphasis on the irrational may be as myopic as the deistic attempt to completely excise the irrational from religion. Yet Hume's emphasis is understandable, for he sought to show in the *Natural History* that the real foundations of actual or living religion lie rather in violent feelings and passions, such as hope and fear, and the "trembling curiosity," which is principally interested in our own well-being.

Hume was sometimes called, or mistaken for, a deist. That in the *Natural History of Religion* he more generously dwells on the "folly" and "error"[18] of

---

[16] In chapter 14 below, we will deal with this "reasonable" propensity.

[17] See Páll S. Árdal, *Passion and Value in Hume's Treatise* 2nd ed., and "Some Implications of the Virtue of Reasonableness in Hume's *Treatise*," in *Hume, A Re-Evaluation*, ed. Donald Livingston and James King, pp. 91–106.

[18] This is Hume's own characterization in the *History of England* of the distinctive attitude of deism towards "the various sects," or historical religion, which amounted, according to him, to an absolute and dogmatic rejection of faith and divine revelation. See chapter 2 above.

common faiths, pagan as well as Christian, might have contributed to that wrong impression. Yet to the not-quite-likable Mrs. David Mallet he curtly remarked: "I am no Deist. I do na style myself so, neither do I desire to be known by that Appellation."[19] And faithful to that dictum, Hume attacks in the *Natural History* the typical deistic explanation of the origins of religion in terms of pure rationality. Curiously enough, it is Demea, the "rigid" defender of faith, who in the *Dialogues* best summarizes the main thrust of Hume's argument in the *Natural History:*

> Each man feels, in a manner, the truth of religion within his own breast; and, from a consciousness of his imbecility and misery, rather than from any reasoning, is led to seek protection from that Being, on whom he and all nature is dependent. So anxious or so tedious are even the best scenes of life, that futurity is still the object of all our hopes and fears. We incessantly look forward, and endeavour, by prayers, adoration, and sacrifice, to appease those unknown powers, whom we find, by experience, so able to afflict and oppress us. Wretched creatures that we are! What resource for us amidst the innumerable ills of life, did not religion suggest some methods of atonement, and appease those terrors with which we are incessantly agitated and tormented? (DNR, 193).

On the whole, in making such a sharp emphasis on the irrational and practical side of religion, Hume may have been offering, in the manner of Sextus Empiricus, a sort of dialectical counterpoise to the rationalistic conception which was firmly entrenched in many of the cultured minds of enlightened Europe. For so doing, he is more worthy of our admiration than our indulgence. That he may have been led to stress some detestable and terrible, albeit really omnipresent, features of the true condition of religion does nothing to diminish our appreciation for his intellectual courage. If Hume mitigates, perhaps unduly, the speculative and socially beneficial aspects of religion, it is, nonetheless, because he chose to proclaim some of its dreadful and unpleasant truths before powerful institutions, civil and ecclesiastical authorities, and influential individuals that could easily, as they sometimes did, take reprisals against him.

Philosophers have not always had the courage to remain committed to truth and point to it with simplicity and without fear. As an unmasker of the gloomier, uglier and all too human features of religion, Christianity in particular, Hume behaved according to the motto on his family's coat of arms: True to the end.

After having seen that in general Hume assigns to pure reason a very meager role within actual or historical religion, we shall turn our view to rational religion, that is, to the one he points at with the interchangeable terms of "pure" or "true" theism. How sound really are the rational foundations furnished by natural religion? That is the central question of Part III of the present work.

---

[19] Lord Charlemont, "Anecdotes of Hume," *Royal Irish Academy*, Dublin, MS–12/R/7, f. 523. Quoted in Ernest Campbell Mossner, *The Life of David Hume* (Oxford: Clarendon Press, 1980), p. 395.

9.2 GENERAL REMARKS CONCERNING THE CRITIQUE OF NATURAL RELIGION

In chapter 2, I attempted to capture, from a historical perspective and by means of a succinct analysis of some important doctrines of its most outstanding representatives, the *ethos* or spiritual temper of natural religion. In the next chapter we shall begin to probe Hume's questioning of the chief contention of natural religion: to wit, that it is possible to gain, through the exercise of the natural faculty of reason, without the assistance of any sort of supernatural revelation, actual knowledge of some crucial truths of Christianity, such as the existence of a perfect Creator and other doctrines, both theoretical and practical, which logically depend on the former. In what follows, I will briefly comment on Hume's critique of natural religion and some of the general principles upon which it rests.

In attempting to provide a rational foundation for the truths of religion two approaches have been taken: a priori and a posteriori. An instance of the first kind would be any attempt to establish the truth of the proposition which asserts the existence of God by a purely deductive reasoning, whose validity, not resting on any factual premises, would be independent of experience. Reasoning a posteriori, by contrast, the existence of God would be inferred from a feature or features of the Universe – such as order or change – which we can know about only through experience. Hume offers a critique of both approaches. Yet his analysis of the rational attempt to base the presumed truths of religion upon the evidence of experience was much more direct, thorough and systematic. This disparity in treatment is not casual; it is rather a consequence of Hume's cardinal partition of the objects of human enquiry and reasoning into "relations of ideas" and "matters of fact and existence." It follows from this division that the legitimacy of the a priori approach in rational theology is excluded in principle.

Propositions about relations of ideas are "discoverable by the mere operation of thought, without dependence on what is anywhere existent in the universe" (EHU, 25), in other words, a priori. "Of the first kind are the science of geometry, algebra and arithmetic; and, in short, every affirmation which is either intuitively or demonstratively certain" (EHU, 25). Mathematical propositions can be demonstrated because they cannot be denied without self contradiction; but through these our knowledge of the world is not extended, since these propositions assert only the relations between ideas or concepts (here the relations of quantity and number), independently of whether or not there exist in the world any objects which correspond to the concepts: "Though there never were a circle or triangle in nature, the truths demonstrated by Euclid would for ever retain their certainty and evidence" (EHU, 25).

Propositions about matters of fact and existence, on the other hand, are known only by experience, and can be denied without self-contradiction. "That the sun will not rise tomorrow is no less intelligible a proposition, and implies no more contradiction than the affirmation, that it will rise" (EHU, 25–26). Consequently matters of fact and existence, which are the subject matter of all sciences except mathematics, "are incapable of demonstration" (EHU, 164).[20]

In brief, the cash value of this doctrine is that if we reason a priori, we can indeed discover truths which state necessary connections between our concepts, but we shall pay the price of never being able to demonstrate the existence of any being. The reason why this is so is epigramatically expressed by Hume at the end of the first *Enquiry:*

> Whatever is may not be. No negation of fact can involve a contradiction. The non-existence of any being without exception, is as clear and distinct an idea as its existence. The proposition which affirms it not to be, however false, is no less conceivable and intelligible, than that which affirms it to be (EHU, 164)

The propositions of theology obviously claim to be valid beyond the sphere of our ideas; on the contrary, it is presumed that they have factual significance, as for example, that they prove the existence of the universe to be a necessary effect of an intelligent cause or God. But if propositions like these are to retain factual significance, they should be something more than the conclusions of a purely deductive a priori reasoning; that is, they should have to appeal to experience as their foundation, for a priori we can never be assured that anything must be the cause or effect of any other thing. Since "the existence of any being can only be proved by arguments from its cause or its effect, and these arguments are founded entirely on experience" (EHU, 164), and since God has been traditionally conceived to be the Supreme Cause, it must also be true of divine causes and effects that they should be "discoverable, not by reason, but by experience" (EHU, 24).

The preceding statements makes one immediately appreciate why Hume's critique of a priori argumentation in theology is so elusive in character, and why, on the contrary, he took with such seriousness the famous argument from design, even going as far as to devote perhaps his greatest book, the *Dialogues Concerning Natural Religion*, almost exclusively to its philosophical analysis and critique.

The main reason for this choice is that the argument from design was for Hume a quite apt representative and the most promising of all the a posteriori arguments by means of which the existence of God was claimed to be demonstrated. If these (and the argument from design in particular) were genuine experimental reasonings concerning matters of fact and existence, then they would save the books of rational theology from Hume's express design of throwing them into the flames (EHU, 165). However, Hume's critique is not confined to this specific argument; if it were

---

[20] We have bypassed for the moment Hume's doctrine of philosophical relations and his distinction between constant and inconstant relations. Hume does not mention these in the first *Enquiry* although they – I think – constitute the ground for the distinction of "relations of ideas," and "matters of fact." We shall come back to this topic in the following chapter when examining the critique of the ontological argument.

valid, then it would be fatal against all theological arguments from experience.[21] In that case "Divinity or Theology" would be only a summary of errors and delusions, since it "has a foundation on reason, so far as it is supported by experience" (EHU, 165). The argument from design was, as we shall see later in chapter 14, unduly anthropomorphic; but Hume's attack is not mainly centered upon any anthropomorphic way of formulating it.

I think that Hume rather chose this argument as the subject matter of his investigation due to several motives: On the one hand, it was the most ancient, well-known and popular of all traditional proofs. On the other hand and more importantly, it could claim a consent almost universal: it could receive the assent of common people *(the vulgar)* – with the supplement of traditional faith – , of deists – without appealing to any supernatural help – , and of cultured and sensible persons *(the wise)*, who were deeply impressed by the amazing success of Newtonian science, and saw in it a reasonable means to harmonize their moderate Christianity with the new science to which they also lent their resolute consent. And it also could be willingly assented to – without appealing to divine revelation – by the most orthodox Calvinist divines within the Church of Scotland, that is, the members of the Evangelical or "High Flying" Party. After all, had not Calvin himself, when arguing that the divine wisdom is shown everywhere and so can be seen by all, availed himself of the same argument? In fact, Calvin formulated this claim with a force and eloquence comparable to Hume's rendition of the same contention in the *Dialogues Concerning Natural Religion:*

> There are innumerable evidences both in heaven and on earth that declare his wonderful wisdom; not only those more recondite matters for the closer observation of which astronomy, medicine, and all natural science are intended, but also those which thrust themselves upon the sight of even the most untutored and ignorant persons, so that they cannot open their eyes without being compelled to witness them. Indeed, men who have either quaffed or even tasted the liberal arts penetrate with their aid far more deeply into the secrets of divine wisdom. Yet ignorance of them prevents no one from seeing more than enough of God's workmanship in his creation to lead him to break forth in admiration of the Artificer.[22]

And finally, Hume perhaps also selected the argument from design because it drew attention – without any sort of reticence – to the multiple cases of functional organization in nature (especially in living organisms), precisely those features of our experience of the world which *prima facie* seem to offer the strongest evidence

---

[21] See, for instance, Anthony Flew, *Hume's Philosophy of Belief,* p. 220–223, and Norman Kemp Smith, Introduction to Hume's *Dialogues*, pp. 25–30.

[22] John Calvin, *Institutes of the Christian Religion,* Book I, "Of the Knowledge of God the Creator," ch. 5, p. 53.

for design by an intelligent cause. As Kemp Smith[23] has said, so much was its persuasive force, that it was taken to participate more of intuitive than of demonstrative certainty, excluding in the mind of Hume's contemporaries the serious consideration of other possible theoretical accounts of the order of nature.

In what follows we shall discuss Hume's critique of a priori and a posteriori theological argumentation. Following Hume, we shall treat in more detail the second topic, which is the decisive one for determining the extent to which religion has a foundation other than faith, that is, a rational justification. Although Hume's critique of the ontological proof and his argument about miracles have given rise to a truly gigantic and ever growing bibliography, their examination will be relatively brief indeed, for my purpose is mainly to connect his critique of rational theology with those doctrines of the *Treatise* that in some sense support them, such as Hume's notion of existence and his analysis of causality, in order to determine their actual compelling force and implications.

I have not given a strictly, nor predominantly, historical treatment to those two issues. On the one hand, I have not felt the need, and it is also beyond my power, to duplicate several excellent historical studies on both subjects.[24] On the other hand, a broadly conceived philosophical consideration of the sort I have attempted, not only complements the historical outlook, but might even provide other equally valuable insights on these perennial topics of speculative and practical curiosity. The several historical observations which have been made in the next two chapters are intended, either in order to clear up the import of Hume's key ideas, or to explicate the theoretical foundations of his main arguments as well as the problems they pose. At other times, I have simply attempted to show the curious fate of sound arguments, which even though they seemingly demolish important philosophical and theological doctrines, are mostly forgotten or ignored by great contemporary thinkers who either take for granted, or even promote to the rank of self-evident principles, exactly those tenets which Hume's critique has, I think, effectively refuted.

---

[23] Norman Kemp Smith, *Introduction to Hume's Dialogues*, pp. 25–30.

[24] There are many good anthologies and comparative analyses on both subjects. See especially, about the ontological argument, Alvin Plantinga, ed., *The Ontological Argument* (Garden City, N. Y. : Doubleday, 1965), and Graham Oppy, *Ontological Arguments and Belief in God*, (Cambridge: Cambridge University Press, 1995). On the argument from miracles, see Stanley Tweyman, ed., *Hume on Miracles* (Bristol: Thoemmes Press, 1996), and R. M. Burns, *The Great Debate on Miracles: From Joseph Glanvill to David Hume* (London and Toronto: Associated University Presses, 1981).

CHAPTER 10

The Impassable Path of A Priori Reasoning: Analysis of Hume's Critique of the Ontological Argument and Its Foundations

10.1 PIETY AND THE PROOF

Hume's criticism is not specifically directed against the ontological argument, but rather against all attempts to demonstrate a priori the existence of God. But as Kant saw, this argument occupies a central position within this species of proof, for if it were valid, it would at once solve two problems which are inseparable for religious consciousness.[1] As its name suggests, it would establish simultaneously the essence and existence, not of any God or first cause, but of a Being that a religious person can always unconditionally accept as the genuine object of worship.

We have good reasons to suppose that Hume could not have been oblivious to this unrenounceable religious demand. When Philo, the sceptic of the *Dialogues* and the character more akin to Hume's own philosophical position, says that "to know God . . . is to worship him," he is not only using Seneca's dictum to emphasize – as we have already seen in chapter 8 – the self-conceited nature of most actual religious adoration, but also echoing a central theme of the Calvinistic tradition in which Hume himself was raised: to wit, that knowledge and adoration of God are inseparable, for the disclosure of his existence to us as the inexhaustible source of all perfection, gives us an unmistakable assurance that we must worship him. Calvin's description of "piety" eloquently expresses this conviction:

> Although our mind cannot apprehend God without rendering some honor to him, it will not suffice simply to hold that there is One whom all ought to honor and adore, unless we are also persuaded that he is the fountain of every good, and that we must seek nothing elsewhere than in him . . . no drop will be found either of wisdom and light, or of righteousness or power or rectitude, or of genuine truth, which does not flow from him, and of which he is not the cause. Thus we may learn to await and seek all these things from him, and

---

[1] Immanuel Kant, *Critique of Pure Reason*, trans. Norman Kemp Smith (London: Macmillan, 1929), Dialectic, II, III, sect. 4, "The Impossibility of an Ontological Proof of the Existence of God," (A 596–597, B 624–625), p. 503.

190

thankfully to ascribe them, once received, to him. For this sense of the powers of God is for us a fit teacher of piety, from which religion is born.[2]

And there is no doubt that the God to whom the ontological argument refers is, as Calvin says, such a "One whom all ought to honor and adore," by virtue of being, in Kant's words, an *ens realissimum*, a being of infinite perfection; it is not merely the most perfect being that there is, but in Saint Anselm's formulation, "something-than-which-nothing-greater-can-be-thought," that is, the most perfect being that it is possible to conceive, so perfect that it is inconceivable that it should not exist.[3] J. N. Findlay expresses remarkably well this vital demand of the religious attitude which the ontological argument seems directed to satisfy: "And hence we are led on irresistibly to demand that our religious object should have an unsurpassable supremacy along all avenues, that it should tower *infinitely* above all other objects."[4] This unsurpassable superiority of the object of religious worship ultimately demands that "not only must the existence of other things be unthinkable without him, but his own not-existence must be wholly unthinkable in any circumstances." [5]

10.2 HUME'S CRITIQUE AND ITS FOUNDATIONS

Hume's refutation of the ontological argument seems to me to be definitive.[6] But curiously, this critique is one which is made by implication; in no place does he explicitly mention the ontological proof; instead he leaves to the reader the job of drawing the negative consequences which some of his doctrines have for the validity of this argument. For this reason we shall examine his critique of the ontological argument by relating it to the tenets of the *Treatise* and the *Enquiry Concerning Human Understanding* upon which it rests.

Hume's refutation is cogent, I think, under the presupposition of the truth of the following three principles: first, that no bridge can be built that would enable us to pass from "relations of ideas" to "matters of fact and existence," or that it is not possible to prove a priori the existence of any being, including God's: "there is an evident absurdity in pretending to demonstrate a matter of fact, to prove by arguments a priori" (DNR, 189); second, that the idea of a necessarily existent being is

---

[2] John Calvin, *The Institutes of the Christian Religion*, Book I, chap. 2, sect. 1, pp. 40–41.

[3] *St. Anselm's Proslogion, with a Reply on Behalf of the Fool, and The Author's Reply to Gaunilo*, ch. 3, p. 119.

[4] J. N. Findlay, "Can God's Existence Be Disproved?," in *New Essays in Philosophical Theology*, ed. A. N. Flew and A. MacIntyre (London: SCM Press and New York: The Macmillan Co., 1955), p. 51.

[5] Ibid., p. 52.

[6] It is conclusive, that is, only if one subscribes his ontological commitments, in particular his conception of being and existence.

unintelligible – "the words 'necessary existence' have no meaning" (DNR, 189); and third, that existence is not a property or characteristic among others, which could form part of the definition of anything – "We have no abstract idea of existence distinguishable and separable from the ideas of particular objects" (THN, Appendix, 623); "That idea, when conjoin'd with the idea of any object, makes no addition to it" (THN, 67).

Hume discusses the first and especially the second principle not while directly referring to the ontological argument, but to another a priori proof: the cosmological argument. But as Kant clearly pointed out, these two proofs are inextricably intertwined, having a common thread, that is, the concept of a being whose existence is absolutely necessary or unconditional.[7] Hence, since the idea of necessary existence is a foundation of the ontological argument, and Hume rejects such idea while examining the cosmological proof and, furthermore, since there are plausible but different interpretations of necessity when united with existence, then we shall have to spend some time, in section 10.3, analyzing the latter proof before attempting to unfold the full implications of Hume's critique of the ontological argument.

Since the language employed by Hume seems to suggest that he had Descartes especially in mind, I shall reproduce only Descartes' version of the proof, and shall discuss Hume's critique as it applies to it. Yet what Hume says applies also to Saint Anselm's formulation, since on the whole what Descartes does is to bring clearly into the open the main presupposition of such proof, namely, that existence is, using Kant's terminology, conceived as a real predicate. In Part IV of the *Discourse on Method* Descartes argues as follows:

> I saw very well that if we suppose a triangle to be given, the three angles must certainly be equal to two right angles; but for all that I saw no reason to be assured that there was any such triangle in existence, while on the contrary, on reverting to the examination of the idea which I had of a Perfect Being, I found that in this case existence was implied in it in the same manner in which the equality of its three angles to two right angles is implied in the idea of a trian-

---

[7] Immanuel Kant, *Critique of Pure Reason*, Dialectic, II, III, sect. 5, "The Impossibility of a Cosmological Proof of the Existence of God," (A 596–597, B 624–625), p, 508: "The cosmological proof . . . retains the connection of absolute necessity with the highest reality, but instead of reasoning, like the former [ontological] proof, from the highest reality to the necessity of existence, it reasons from the previously given unconditioned necessity of some being to the unlimited reality of that being." Usually the cosmological is taken to be an empirical, or a posteriori, argument because it has as premise a factual proposition: the existence of something in general. But, like Kant, Hume asserts the a priori character of this proof, probably because it is a demonstrative reasoning whose conclusion would exclude the possible truth of its contradictory. In this sense it differs from the design argument, which is an analogical and probable argument. Hume might have given, I think, his approval to the following explanation offered by Kant of why the cosmological proof is a priori: "Both the above [ontological and cosmological] proofs were transcendental, that is, were attempted independently of empirical principles. For although the cosmological proof presupposes an experience in general, it is not based on any particular property of this experience but on pure principles of reason, as applied to an existence given through empirical consciousness in general. Further, it soon abandons this guidance and relies on pure concepts alone" [(A 613, B 641), p. 514; see also (A602, B 630), p. 508].

gle; or in the idea of a sphere, that all points on its surface are equidistant from its centre, or even more evidently still. Consequently it is at least as certain that God, who is a Being so perfect, is, or exists, as any demonstration of geometry can possibly be.[8]

In the *Meditations* it is not only from the idea but also from the essence of God that he argues to the necessary existence of such a Being:

I clearly see that existence can no more be separated from the essence of God that can its having its three angles equal to two right angles be separated from the essence of a [rectilinear] triangle, or the idea of a mountain from the idea of a valley; and so there is not any less repugnance to our conceiving a God (that is, a Being supremely perfect) to whom existence is lacking (that is to say, to whom a certain perfection is lacking), than to conceive of a mountain without a valley.[9]

What would Hume have to say about all this? In the first place, he would have objected to Descartes' procedure of reasoning from a definition (even if existence were an attribute or perfection) to the existence of a thing, that is, of arguing from an analysis of the constitutive notes of the concept 'God' to the actual existence of God. For Hume, the existence of no being can be demonstrated a priori, namely, merely by disclosure and analysis of the relations which hold necessarily between ideas. The proposition which states the existence of any being states a matter of fact, something that can only be known by experience, either directly through immediate observation, or indirectly, through causal inference based on some observation.

Accordingly there is no valid way that would enable us to deduce from propositions which merely explicate the meanings of the terms into which a definition can be composed ("relations of ideas") that there must exists somewhere an entity to which that definition applies ("matters of fact"). So long as the meanings of the words remain the same or "so long as ideas remain the same," the first sort of propositions are necessarily true, namely, cannot be denied without self-contradiction, whereas "that Caesar, or the angel Gabriel, or any being never existed, may be a false proposition, but still is perfectly conceivable, and implies no contradiction" (EHU, 164). Hume would have said, along with Descartes, that he can see no reason to be assured that there is any such triangle in the world; against Descartes, he would probably have emphasized that there is no reason to suppose that such a God exists so long as we remain within the domain of ideas. Against Hume assault,

[8] René Descartes, *Discourse on Method*, in *The Philosophical Works of Descartes*, trans. Elizabeth S. Haldane and G. R. J. Ross (2 vols., Cambridge: Cambridge University Press, 1970), I, 103–104; *Ouvres de Descartes*, ed. Charles Adam and Paul Tannery (13 vols., Paris: Cerf, 1897 and 1913) VI, 36.

[9] René Descartes, *Meditations on First Philosophy*, Haldane-Ross, I, 181; Adam-Tannery, VII, 52.

Descartes, like any other defender of the ontological argument, should justify the claim that in this case, and only in this case, can we make the leap form ideas to things, from essence to existence.

But before going on to examine this topic, it is necessary to trace this important dichotomy of "relations of ideas" and "matters of fact" (which gives intelligibility to the contention that the existence of anything cannot be demonstrated a priori) to the doctrines of the *Treatise* which ground it or – if this is denied – at least are the original tenets from which it rises. First of all, I admit that this procedure might appear to be an idle digression. It may be justified, though, as an instrument for helping us to determine in a clear manner whether or not Descartes can successfully withstand Hume's challenge and if at the same time Hume is able to sustain his attack on the ontological argument on firm logical ground. For in defense of the ontological argument it could be argued that Hume's dichotomy must be abandoned. One could, for instance, adduce that its foundation is either unintelligible, or that it rests upon doctrines which, theoretically speaking, fail to lend adequate support to such a critique, in other words, that the latter cannot be deduced from them as a logical consequence.

Although this interpretative position is not unobjectionable, I think that the distinction between "relations of ideas" and "matters of fact" is a development of Hume's theory of philosophical relations. In the *Treatise* Hume employs the word 'relation' to refer to two different things. First, by relations he means the quality or qualities "by which two ideas are connected together in the imagination" (THN, 13). These qualities are resemblance, contiguity in time and place, and causation; Hume calls them "natural relations." They are natural because what connects ideas together is the natural "gentle" force of association, that is, by custom one idea is associated with another, and the thought of the one makes the mind naturally recall the other. This connection, being habitual, is consequently involuntary or automatic. But secondly, ideas may be connected in the mind not through customary association only, but also by a conscious, voluntary act of comparison, provided there is some similarity between them. The relations thus established Hume calls "philosophical relations," and defines them as "any particular subject of comparison without a connecting principle" (THN, p. 14). In short, they are not the result of a passive association but of an "arbitrary" or premeditated act of conscious reflection.

The philosophical relations play a role of considerable importance, since knowledge depends on the discovery of relations between objects. Philosophical relations are those which a methodical search for knowledge seeks to disclose. There is an infinite number of relationships that the human mind can establish upon reflection. Hume classifies these relations into seven general categories. The degrees of certainty that pertain to the different sciences will depend on the kind of relationship upon which each one of them is based. Because each science studies its subject matter from the point of view of certain basic relationships, there is perhaps no exaggeration in saying that philosophical relations are conditions of the possibility of scientific knowledge.

Hume divides these relations into two kinds: constant (invariable) and inconstant (variable) relations. Resemblance, contrariety, degrees in quality, and proportions in quantity and number are invariable relations. These are constant in the sense that they depend entirely on the objects compared, and cannot be changed unless the objects themselves change. This can be made clearer by means of the proverbial Cartesian example: the sum of the angles of a triangle will be equal to two right angles as long as our idea of a triangle remains the same. Since resemblance, contrariety and degrees in quality are, according to Hume, discovered at first sight, they have an intuitive certainty: proportions in quantity and number are, on the contrary, discovered by demonstrative reasoning. Thus in mathematics we have demonstrative certainty, but only because mathematical truths state relations between our ideas, which cannot be altered without at the same time altering those ideas.

The inconstant relations are identity, relations of time and place, and causation these are inconstant because they can change without there being any change in the objects or their corresponding ideas. For instance, the distance between two objects can change while the objects remain the same. Hume says that these relations "depend on a hundred different accidents, which cannot be foreseen by the human mind" (THN, I, 69). For this reason the propositions that state these type of relations have probable, not absolute, certainty. That "John is the father of little Annie" may be a true proposition but of a certainty quite different from "the sum of the angles of a triangle is equal to two right angles." Paternity – here taken as an instance of a particular kind of causation – can be denied without self-contradiction; of course, it has to be established by other means.

Hume also divides the inconstant relations into two types; identity and space and time relations are more a matter of perception rather than reasoning, in these two cases: "both the objects are present to the senses with the relation" (THN, 73). Causation, on the other hand, involves reasoning, since in moving from effect to cause or from cause to effect the mind proceeds to infer from an object given to the memory or senses the existence of another which is not immediately experienced or observed. Precisely because of the inconstant character of this relation, causal inference is not the same as demonstrative reasoning; this is so, according to Hume, because "the power by which one object produces another is not discoverable from their idea." (THN, 69). Consequently, the only relation that enables us to make inferences about the existence of objects which are not immediately observed must be based on experience: " 'Tis evident cause and effect are relations, of which we receive information from experience, and not from any abstract reasoning or reflexion" (THN, 69).

On the whole, "constant relations" appear to be equivalent to "relations of ideas" of the first *Enquiry*, and "inconstant relations" to "matters of fact and real existence." The most significant difference seems to be that the formulation of the *Treatise* is more psychological, putting the emphasis on the sorts of perceptions, whereas in the *Enquiry* the emphasis is on the logical side, on the formal structure of the propositions which state the different relationships. For this reason, most commentators believe that the formulation of the *Enquiry* is, from a theoretical point of view, much less objectionable.

This provision, however, does not precludes anybody from questioning Hume's sharp division from a phenomenological standpoint, that is, in a Husserlian fashion: If this dichotomy of "relations of ideas" and "matters of fact" were a truly logical consequence of the doctrines of the *Treatise*, there would be little reason to maintain it. Why, if in the last analysis all relations are relations between perceptions, ideas being no more than faint copies of precedent perceptions or impressions, do not all propositions (including mathematical propositions) reduce themselves to factual statements? As is well known, this is what John Stuart Mill, one of Hume's more celebrated successors, maintained when he came to view even mathematical theories as some sort of empirical hypotheses. What are, after all, impressions and ideas but psychological states in a Heraclitean flux? They are mental events which unceasingly come to be and pass away, different and interrupted, none of them – however resembling – exactly identical to any other. If we take all of this seriously, is it not the case then that no knowledge whatsoever can ever be more than probable? If ideas are continuously evanescent temporal events, can the absolute certainty of the truths about "relations of ideas" be really guaranteed solely because these relations depend entirely on the ideas compared? Can we say, within this conception of mental life, that an idea, when fulfilling the role of logical subject in any proposition, remains identically the same idea independently of the different times in which the proposition is asserted? Hume says that we have certain knowledge about propositions which assert constant relations "so long as the ideas remain the same" (THN, 69); yet it is very difficult to see just how they could ever remain thus, since he says, on the other hand, that the impressions of which ideas are copies are only "internal and perishing existences, and appear as such (THN, 194)." It is not a coincidence that in Part IV, Section I of the *Treatise*, "Of scepticism with regard to reason," Hume was prepared to go as far as to reduce all knowledge to probability.[10]

One may reasonably conclude, in sum, that the validity of the dichotomy can be eroded if all propositions are reduced ultimately to empirical or factual statements. But under such a supposition, could we also say that Hume's critique of the ontological argument is thereby substantially weakened? In other words, if the dichotomy could not be sustained (for it would imply an absurd consequence), then the critique of the ontological argument which is founded upon it, could not be maintained either, and hence the defender of the proof would have no reason to

---

[10] Many commentators minimize the import of this conclusion, and explain it away as due to Hume's idiosyncratic penchant for skeptical paradoxes, and so also dismiss his enigmatically Cartesian argument for complete scepticism as a sophism. I think it is of Cartesian inspiration, because it starts from the possibility of committing error even in demonstrative sciences. Perhaps that specific argument is a sophism; but Hume's sceptical conclusions do not depend exclusively on its validity; they appear to be a consequence of his point of departure, i.e., that the objects of immediate awareness are impressions and ideas. Perhaps Husserl was closer to the truth than a sizable number Hume scholars when he sought to disclose the sceptical consequences and to disprove the kind of psychologism whose spiritual father Hume was. A reluctant father, we may add, since in his actual convictions he was closer to the common-sense view. See Edmund Husserl, *Logical Investigations*, trans. J. N. Findlay (2 vols., New York; Humanitie: Press, 1970), I, "Prolegomena to Pure Logic," pp. 53–247.

abandon it. However, it seems that such a negative rehabilitation of the proof is not feasible. What the defender of the proof needs is perhaps the opposite, viz. to ultimately reduce truths of fact to truths of reason, to use the language and famous conclusion of Leibniz. At the very least anyone who subscribes the argument should uphold the intelligibility of the distinction at all costs, albeit of course allowing room for one important exception, the idea of God. In this case, and only in this case, it would be possible to move from ideas to facts. In fact, this seems to have been the position taken from the beginning by Saint Anselm, the inventor of the proof, against his earliest important objector, Gaunilo; and such a stance is instanced by Descartes, too.[11]

In the case of the triangle there is nothing, Descartes will repeatedly say, which can give us any assurance of the existence of a corresponding object. The same holds true for the ideas and definitions of other entities. However, on examining the idea of a perfect being, Descartes concludes that this being must exist, since existence is necessarily implied in that very idea, whereas it is not implied in the idea of a triangle or of anything else. God is a supremely perfect being; existence is a perfection; God must consequently exist. This is the way in which he usually argues in the *Meditations;* his statement that there is no less absurdity in thinking of a God who lacks existence than in thinking of a mountain without a valley seems to imply that he conceives of God as a "necessarily existent being." If this were the case the proposition which asserts God's existence would be a necessary truth, and it would not be possible to deny it without self-contradiction. This interpretation receives support from the fact that Descartes has said that all ideas contain existence.[12] But why? Simply because he thought, just like Hume, that "we can conceive nothing except as existing."[13] The difference between the idea of God and all other ideas is that the latter contain possible existence only, whereas to the idea of God pertains necessary existence: "in it [the mind] recognizes existence not merely a possible and contingent existence, as in all the other ideas it has of things which it clearly conceives, but one which is absolutely necessary and eternal."[14] We can al-

---

[11] Saint Anselm, *The Author's Reply to Gaunilo*, in *Proslogion*, p. 179: "whatever exists, save that-than-which-a-greater-cannot-be-thought, can be thought as not existing even when we know that it does exist." René Descartes, *Meditations on First Philosophy*, Meditation V, Haldane-Ross, I, 183; Adam-Tannery, VII, 55: "For is there anything more manifest that there is a God, that is to say, a Supreme Being, to whose essence alone existence pertains?"

[12] René Descartes, *Reply to Objections II*, "Arguments Demonstrating the Existence of God and the Distinction Between Soul and Body, Drawn up in Geometrical Fashion," Axiom X, Haldane-Ross, II, 57; Adam-Tannery, VII, 166.

[13] Ibid. "Existence is contained in the idea or concept of everything, because we can conceive nothing except as existent, with this difference, that possible or contingent existence is contained in the concept of a limited being, but necessary and perfect existence in the concept of a supremely perfect being."

[14] René Descartes, *The Principles of Philosophy*, Part I, "Of the Principles of Human Knowledge," Principle XIV, Haldane-Ross, I, 224; Adam-Tannery, VIII, 10. See also *Notes Directed against a Certain Programme*, Haldane-Ross, II, 444–445, Adam-Tannery, 361–363.

ways say about whatever we can clearly and distinctly conceive that it is possible for it to exist. But we can and must say that God certainly exists, since in this case we conceive clearly that actual existence is necessarily and always united with the other attributes of God.[15]

Hume would not accept Descartes' demonstration; yet at first it is not easy to see why he should not, for he accepts Descartes' claim, at least in the *Treatise*, that all the ideas which we distinctly and clearly conceive contain the idea of possible existence:

> 'Tis an establish'd maxim in metaphysics. That what the mind clearly conceives includes the idea of possible existence, or in other words, that nothing we image is absolutely impossible. We can form the idea of a golden mountain, and from thence conclude that such a mountain may actually exist. We can form no idea of a mountain without a valley, and therefore regard it as impossible (THN, I, 32; c.f., 43, 89).

For Hume, it is certain that whatever can be conceived by a clear and distinct idea necessarily implies the possibility of existence (THN, 43), in such a manner that to think of any thing is *ipso facto* to think of it as possibly existent. But the acceptance of that principle does not entail the rehabilitation of the ontological argument; for merely because one includes existence among the contents of an idea, one cannot *ipso facto* say the idea implies the necessary existence of the object which corresponds to it. In order to take this step, we need first a clear idea of "necessary existence"; but this is exactly what we can never have, for the concept of "necessary existence" seems to be as logically absurd as the concept of "a mountain without a valley."

10. 3 THE SEVERING OF THE COMMON THREAD OF THE ONTOLOGICAL AND COSMOLOGICAL ARGUMENTS: THE IDEA OF NECESSARY EXISTENCE

Curiously, Hume does not argue in the manner just described when criticizing the ontological argument; this thesis appears rather as the conclusion of an argument in Part IX of the *Dialogues Concerning Natural Religion*, which is expressed by Cleanthes, the defender of the a posteriori argument, against a common version of the cosmological proof, which is proposed by Demea, the "rigid" defender of ortho-doxy. On the other hand, the same argument, almost identically formulated, appears as one of the principal conclusions of the last section of the *Enquiry Concerning Human Understanding* (EHU, Sect. XII, 163–164) The fact that Hume immediately adds here that "Caesar, or the angel Gabriel, or any being never existed, may be a false proposition, but still is perfectly conceivable, and implies no contradiction" (EHU, 164), appears to suggest that he is also, and maybe principally, having in

---

[15] René Descartes, *Reply to Objections I*, Haldane-Ross, II, 20; Adam-Tannery, VII, 117.

mind the ontological argument. Be that as it may, the immediate object of Cleanthes' critique is another a priori proof of God's existence, whose starting-point is the contingency of things in the world. Like the ontological argument, the cosmological proof makes use of the idea of a "necessarily existent being who carries the REASON of his existence in himself, and who cannot be supposed not to exist without an express contradiction" (DNR. 89). Precisely because of the momentous implications that Cleanthes' scrutiny of this idea has for the logical integrity of the ontological argument, it is imperative for us to briefly examine some principal and puzzling aspects Hume's critique of the cosmological argument in Part IX of the *Dialogues*.

Those who support the latter argument claim that it demonstrates conclusively the existence of God by arguing that to deny its conclusion, namely, to deny the existence of the necessarily existent Being is to fall into self-contradiction. In what seems to be a calculated Cartesian language, Cleanthes refutes this claim:

Nothing is demonstrable unless the contrary implies a contradiction. Nothing that is distinctly conceivable implies a contradiction. Whatever we conceive as existent we can also conceive as non-existent. There is no being therefore, whose existence implies a contradiction. Consequently there is no being, whose existence is demonstrable (DNR, 189).[16]

If the non-existence of any and every being, including God himself, is an intelligible possibility, the expression 'necessary existence' is a purely arbitrary combination of words: "the words 'necessary existence' have no meaning, or what is the same, none that is consistent" (DNR 189–190). This declaration of Hume (I obviously suppose that here Cleanthes speaks for Hume) deserves some explanation. If we could rightly say that there is no interpretation in which it is possible to ascribe a coherent meaning to the expression 'necessary existence,' then Hume would not be able to say, as Cleanthes affirms a few lines after the passage just quoted, that it is not only possible that God exists, but even that he possesses some peculiar and extraordinary qualities by virtue of which it may not be possible for him not to exist, or stop from existing. There are two possibilities: 1. Either Cleanthes' reasoning is a mere *ad hominen* argument that Hume does not have by force to subscribe, and whose purpose is – as we will immediately see – to illustrate that the conclusion of the ontological argument, even if one concedes its validity, does not demonstrate everything that the religious consciousness demands; 2. Or Hume, in fact, is affirming here that the concept of a necessarily existent being is not by force nonsensical.

To my mind, the previous dilemma is apparent, because both sides are right. Concerning necessary existence, we must indeed amend Cleanthes' declaration in order to admit of one exception: if 'necessary existence' is equivalent to exist, paro-

---

[16] A worthy and different, albeit perhaps complementary, interpretation of this passage and the whole of Part IX of the *Dialogues* is offered by Stanley Tweyman in "Drama and Arguments in Hume's Dialogues Concerning Natural Religion," *Diálogos* 71 (1998): 7–24.

dying Handel, 'forever and ever', that is, without beginning nor end, and in this sense eternally, then one cannot exclude the possibility that in virtue of certain characteristics at present unknown to us, God cannot refrain from existing in this sense. But it is here that the sting of Hume's objection becomes visible: How, or under what conditions, would we be able to say this? Only if we first knew that God exists, is that afterwards we could say that he exists necessarily; that is to say, we should have to know beforehand through some kind of direct experience that God exists, and of course that he possesses those extraordinary properties, in order to be able to assert later that he is incapable of not existing. At any rate we can never gather this information from a mere inspection of the definition of the term 'God'. Despite this, is Hume not conceding after all that there is a possible definition – albeit unbeknownst to us at present – out of which it might be possible to infer the necessary existence of God? Yes and no. If we refer to an a priori definition, or what Hume calls a proposition about "relations of ideas," then there is no way for us to go from ideas to things, from essence to existence. But the present case is about a definition founded on a matter of fact: i.e., our hypothetical experience of God and some of the divine attributes. "God exists" would be then a factual proposition, and it would be contradictory to deny the necessary existence of God provided that we first agree to the fact that he exists; in short, God's necessity would be conditional, not absolute.[17]

At this point, we must remember that in the Anselmian and Cartesian versions of the ontological proof the contradictory character of God's non-existence is derived from the absolute perfection which the mind is forced to attribute to the Deity. Because of this is that, for Descartes, in the idea of God "existence absolutely necessary and eternal" is eminently contained. We must also take into account that Descartes is not identifying necessity with eternity, but rather disclosing the latter as a consequence of the inconceivability of the non-existence of God, and making it dependent upon the absolute perfection of the divine Being. In the Humean interpretation of what may be called the factual and conditioned necessity of God's existence, it rather appears first, that 'eternal existence' is transformed in a synonym for 'everlasting and boundless existence'; and second, that the latter becomes the conclusion of a causal inference based on a direct, empirical acquaintance of those private qualities of the divine Being upon which the uninterrupted exercise of the power that always keeps him in existence is dependent.

On the other hand, if we reason along the lines of the argument from contingency from existing things to their necessary cause, neither it immediately follows that the necessarily existent being has to be everything which the religious consciousness understands God to be:

---

[17] It is only be appealing to such a conditional necessity, I think, that a paradoxical thesis that J. N. Findlay formulates in *Ascend to the Absolute* (London: Allen & Unwin, 1970), becomes intelligible. Findlay asserts both that the Absolute exists by virtue of a necessity which arises out of its own nature and that it has a contingent side. Otherwise, the following claim would become trivial: "If there is an Absolute of a certain essential sort, then there cannot *not* be an Absolute of that certain essential sort" (p. 24).

[W]hy may not the material universe be the necessarily existent being, *according to this pretended explication of necessity?* We dare not affirm that we know all the qualities of matter; and for aught we can determine, it may contain some qualities, *which, were they known,* would make its non-existence appear as great a contradiction as that twice two is five (DNR, 190; italics added).

The *ad hominen* character of the objection is manifest, for this passage emphasizes that such necessity is not genuine, but "pretended." In accordance with this, Philo, the sceptic, at the end of Part IX of the *Dialogues*, reaffirms the same thing by insinuating that neither physicists nor theologians can legitimately claim the same kind of necessity to which mathematicians appeal in their demonstrations (DNR, 191–192). Besides, the contradiction involved in asserting the divine non-existence is such only under a factual conditioning: the effective knowledge of those properties from which the necessary existence of the divine Being follow.

At this point we can go back to Hume's critique of the ontological argument, because all of these further inconvenient consequences, however fatally they may afflict the validity of the cosmological proof, do not seem to follow from the ontological argument.

10.4 THE ONTOLOGICAL ARGUMENT
AND THE REJECTION OF THE PROPERTY OF EXISTENCE

It is obvious that – unlike the argument from contingency – the ontological proof does not make us fall into the predicament of establishing that there exists a necessary being at the cost of having to relinquish its worship: for there is no doubt that a being of infinite perfection must be God, and thus, in Calvin's words, "One whom all ought to honor and adore."

The defect of the ontological argument lies elsewhere, and it is of such a magnitude that it would not be remedied even if we admit that the expression 'necessary existence' (in the conditioned and factual interpretation) is meaningful and suppose that the proposition 'God exists necessarily' could conceivably be true. Even then, one would not be able to say that the ontological argument thereby establishes the truth of that proposition. If the actual existence of God is to be deduced from an analysis of the defining characteristics of his being, then 'God exists' must be true because it would rightly assert of that subject a property, that is existence, that pertains to it. In other words, existence must be one among the positive attributes that a thing can possess.

But this is what Hume exactly denies. It is essential to emphasize this point because here lies the foundation of Cleanthes' declaration to the effect that the concept of 'necessary existence' is incoherent. Such inconsistency is not apparent to those who conceive existence as a property or characteristic; however, it is manifest to those who deny this tenet. From Hume's viewpoint, existence is not a note which could conceivably be included in the definition of a possible object. In other words, existence cannot be part of the meaningful contents of any idea because it is not a distinct idea which could be united to, or separated from, any other idea.

In what follows Hume expresses this thesis quite tersely and insuperably, and in a way which draws attention – if only by implication – to this basic presupposition of the ontological argument:

> 'Tis also evident, that the idea of existence is nothing different from the idea of any object, and that when after the simple conception of any thing we wou'd conceive it as existent, we in reality make no addition to our first idea. Thus when we affirm that God is existent, we simply form the idea of such a being, as he is represented to us; nor is the existence, which we attribute to him, conceiv'd by a particular idea, which we join to the idea of his other qualities, and can again separate and distinguish from them. . . . When I think of God, when I think of him as existent, and when I believe him to be existent, my idea of him neither encreases nor diminishes (THN, 94; c.f., 66–67, 96, 623 footnote).

If the idea of existence is not a distinct idea, if existence is not a distinct property, then the ontological argument cannot establish its conclusion. If existence cannot be a property, it can be even less a necessary property of anything. But if the idea of existence is not a distinct idea which can be joined with, and separated from, the idea of any object, what is it then? Existence is not an idea different from the idea of the object; the idea of the existence of an object is rather the very same with the idea of the object. To think of X, and to think of X as existent are the same thing:

> Whatever we conceive, we conceive to be existent. Any idea we please to form is the idea of a being; and the idea of a being is any idea we please to form (THN, I, 67).[18]

As corollary of this conception of existence, Hume could have said with Descartes that when we think of God we necessarily think of Him as existent, although for reasons very different from Descartes'. This is so, but not because of the logical impossibility of thinking the non-existence of the divine Being, but rather because to think of something as existent is a *sine qua non* condition for being able to think of it. And this is a condition which applies to any thing, if it is to be conceived at all; by no means it is an exclusive prerogative of the idea of God. I have to confess, though, that if one excludes the dogma about the attributive character of existence, then Hume's position that to think of something is to think of it "as it might exist" is almost indistinguishable from the Cartesian position that to every thing about which we can have a clear and distinct idea pertains possible existence.

---

[18] In the *Abstract* to the *Treatise* Hume's expresses this in a more cautious and enigmatic manner: "When we simply conceive an object, we conceive it in all its parts. We conceive it as it might exist, tho' we do not believe it to exist" (THN, A, 632).

On the whole, we believe that Hume's refutation of the ontological argument is conclusive (at least against the formulations of St. Anselm and Descartes) if ultimately existence is not a predicate or positive quality (*realitas*). Hence any attempt to rehabilitate the argument must provide an alternative, coherent and tenable philosophical interpretation of being and existence. Such an account would have to intelligibly show not only that existence is indeed somehow a genuine attribute, but also that being can, as it were, be enjoyed, or partaken of, in different degrees. At present, I do not really see just how existence might be conceived as something that is to be possessed by an entity, and am inclined to think that Hume's critique – and likewise the more systematically expounded one of Kant (which, as we have seen, Hume almost entirely anticipated) – does in fact refute the cognitive claims of the argument.

10.5 SOME QUESTIONS ABOUT HUME'S ACCOUNT OF EXISTENCE AND NON-EXISTENCE

Despite my previous verdict of reasonable success, I do not intend to give the impression that Hume's critique is free from all ontological difficulties. Do Hume initial presuppositions allow for placing that idea within his inventory of the contents of the human mind? If any idea we please to form is the idea of a being, how could there be something like an idea of a non-being, or non-entity? To put it otherwise, if "no ideas are in themselves contrary, except those of existence and non-existence" (THN, 26) and if we cannot think of anything except as existent, then can we really think of it as non-existent? John Passmore is the commentator that has more persuasively and concisely maintained that Hume truly gives no adequate explanation of the idea of non-existence:

> Hume's original doctrine, in fact, leaves him open to the Eleatic criticism of 'not being'. If to think of anything is to think of it as existing, it follows that 'not-being' can never be thought of.[19]

Yet Hume must account for the idea of non-existence in order to give meaning to his distinction between "relations of ideas" and "matters of fact and existence," which is itself one main foundation of his critique of the ontological argument.

---

[19] John Passmore, *Hume's Intentions*, pp. 26–27, 97–99. He attributes the defect of this doctrine to the undue interference of Hume's psychology in his logic: "The obscurity of Hume's theory derives from his attempt, in the interests of a logic in which the only links are psychological, to avoid this contrast between formal and non-formal, a contrast which is also implicit in his description of existence and non-existence as the only 'ideas' which are 'in themselves contrary'" (p. 27). F. Zabeeh, in *Hume: Precursor of Modern Empiricism* pp. 103–105, fundamentally agrees with Passmore. D. G. C. MacNabb, "David Hume," *Encyclopedia of Philosophy*, ed. Paul Edwards, IV, 78–79, even admitting that Hume conceived of ideas as images, and specifically as visual images, offers a defense of Hume's position in terms of a psychological account of non-existence which seems to be, frankly speaking, very cumbersome and artificial.

"The non-existence of any being, without exception, is as clear and distinct an idea as its existence" (EHU, 164). This Hume has said immediately after asserting that no negation of fact can involve a contradiction. But one might as well ask, how is it possible to conceive a negation of fact if whatever we conceive, we conceive to be existent? That does not seem possible unless we first had a clear and distinct idea of non-existence.[20]

How much truth is there in Passmore's reproach? On the one hand, one cannot deny that there is a difficulty with the idea of non-existence, even though it is also true Hume was well aware of such an objection,[21] and tried to meet it. On the other hand, the verbal expression in which Passmore formulates this critique makes it easier for him to impute incoherence to Hume. Since it of lesser import, let us immediately pass to the second point. It is noteworthy that even if Hume initially says that whatever we conceive, we conceive to be existent (THN, 67), he later expresses himself more precisely by asserting that to conceive an object is to conceive it as it might exist (THN, A, 632). But Passmore simply paraphrases Hume thus: to think of anything is to think of it as existing. Although this latter gerund grammatical form takes in the indicative mode of Hume's first formulation, it is nonetheless very far from being equivalent to the subjunctive mode in which Hume casts his final version in the *Abstract* to the *Treatise*. Hume's employment of this derived grammatical form should give us warning, and even lead us to suspect that he is deliberately trying to evade the Eleatic dilemma. In short, before ascribing to him a view which is at first sight absurd, we should first endeavor to see whether there is a possible Humean explanation of how is it possible for us to think of non-being or non-existence, even though such an account may perhaps be a tacit one, and anyway more complex and derived in an epistemological sense.

The truth of the matter is that Hume did attempt to account for this curious idea of non-existence. When analyzing the philosophical relation of contrariety or opposition, he says:

> But let us consider that no two ideas are in themselves contrary, except those of existence and non-existence, which are plainly resembling, as implying both of them an idea of the object; though the latter excludes the object from all times and places, in which it is supposed not to exist (THN, 15).

In that passage Hume seems to reaffirm first of all that the fact that we may have an "clear and distinct" idea of existence as well as of non-existence does not

---

[20] More recently, Phillip D. Cummins, in "Hume on the Idea of Existence," *Hume Studies* 17, no. 1 (April 1991): 78, has elaborated, in detail and in a more systematic fashion than Passmore, the same reproach to Hume's theory about the idea of existence: "His meagre positive account put misplaced emphasis on the items on which an operator would operate, leaving it incapable of the distinctions required of an adequate account of how various positive and negative existence claims would be thought."

[21] Hume explicitly concedes that "the ideas of *existence* and of *external existence* . . . have their difficulties" (THN, 66).

imply that we have an abstract, that is, distinct and separable, idea of the object that is conceived of as existent or non-existent, because the idea of existence when it is joined to the idea of any object "makes no addition to it" (THN, 67). Are both ideas then the products of a "distinction of reason" *(distinctio rationis)*? Yes indeed. Hume uses this term to designate a great number of ideas that the mind is able to form out of a complex act, which he tries to explain in the section of the *Treatise* dedicated to abstract ideas (THN, I, Part I, Section VII, 17–25). By its means the mind can come to distinguish that which it is unable to differentiate nor separate from a particular thing, such as the movement from the thing that moves, or the figure from the figured object, or the color from the shape over which it extends.[22] Although the figure cannot be separated from the colored thing that exhibits it, as it happens with a globe of white marble, we can somehow distinguish that which we cannot separate in reality – the figure – if we compare the first object, that is, the sphere of white marble, with a sphere of black marble, and fix our attention in that aspect in which they resemble each other; in the same fashion we may distinguish color from the figure, for instance, by directing our view to the resemblance that a globe of white marble has with a cube of white marble (THN, 24–25).

Could not the mind come to distinguish, or somehow mentally separate, in a similar manner the existence or non-existence from the thing that it conceives to exist or not to exist? There is a lot to say in favor of this interpretation, for if it were correct, Hume's theory about the ideas of existence and non-existence would become more intelligible. Unfortunately, there is also a crucial, albeit perhaps not decisive, passage of the *Treatise* in which Hume appears to deny that we come to form an idea of existence by means of a distinction of reason:

> That kind of distinction is founded on the different resemblances, which the same simple idea may have to several different ideas. But no object can be presented resembling some object with respect to its existence, and different from others in the same particular; since every object that is presented, must necessarily be existent (THN, 67).

Hume's argument is obscure, and thus it is not strange that it had been accepted as well as rejected with plausible reasons by perspicacious scholars of this question. From the positive side, Philip Cummins emphasizes that in order to extract a distinction without a difference and be able to assign a common quality to a group of objects, it is necessary to have an "experience of an object which does not resemble the objects in the group in the way they resemble one another." But since no perceivable object differs from the rest with respect to existence, therefore "no idea of existence (understood as a quality of objects) can be generated by the required com-

---

[22] I think that Hume's admission of these distinctions of reason, although necessary in order to lend intelligibility to his account of the ideas of existence and non-existence, throws serious doubts on his own explanation of abstract ideas. For instead of being a corollary of this theory, the *distinctio rationis*, rather appears to be incompatible with a principle that provides the foundation for his account of abstraction: to wit, that it is possible to separate only that which is distinguishable (THN, 18).

parisons."[23] It seems as if, according to the Humean argument that Cummins subscribes, in order to be able to form a distinction without a real separation, it is not only necessary to be aware of other objects which are similar to a particular object in one aspect and different in other respects, but it is also indispensable for us to be conscious of other objects which are dissimilar to the first object in this same aspect: thus, for instance, in order to be able to mentally separate a particular figure (a sphere) from the color with which it presents itself (white), we need to perceive or imagine some other objects with the same shape and different color, but also some objects with other shapes, such as white triangles. But since no perceivable object (idea or impression) can differ from any other for lacking existence, then it is not possible that we should form the idea of existence distinct from that which we conceive as existent by virtue of a distinction of reason. Although Stanley Tweyman agrees with this conclusion, he considers, however, that it cannot be established by the preceding argument, which is – in his opinion – obviously wrong.[24] "Now, if existence were related to whatever can be conceived, as colour is related to figure, then it would be possible to distinguish existence from what can be conceived, provided that we perform the relevant contrasting comparison required for a distinction of reason."[25] To put differently, if existence were a characteristic common to all things that can be conceived and hence inseparable from them, we still could distinguish it by a distinction of reason, provided we contrast it with some of the many traces in virtue of which those things differ among themselves: the common trace would stand out in comparison with, and under the light provided by the immense multiplicity of characteristics which differentiate things one from the other.

Even though I can well perceive the merit of Tweyman's argument, at the moment I think that Hume's argument is more persuasive. First, what makes plausible Tweyman's position is a presupposition that Hume rejects and which is what leads him to question whether the idea of existence is a distinction of reason or not: to wit, that there is no distinct impression from which the idea of existence ("entity") is derived, and which is inseparable from every perception that we believe to be existent (THN, 66–67). Second, and very linked with the preceding consideration, Hume introduces the distinctions of reason in order to account for that species of abstract ideas which result from comparing objects among which there are no strictly universal similarities, or resemblances common to all of them. I think that the examples Hume employs (a globe of white marble, a globe of black marble, and a cube of white marble) are intended to stress this point. On the other hand, both in the section on abstract ideas and in the cited passage (THN, 67), Hume points out that he is considering those resemblances that "simple ideas" can have with other ideas; and in this respect, one may even ask whether there can be strictly universal resemblances among simple things. The fact that the examples Hume offers of dis-

---

[23] Phillip Cummins, "Hume on the Idea of Existence," 77.

[24] Stanley Tweyman, "Some Reflections on Hume on Existence," *Hume Studies* 28, no. 2 (November 1992): 137–149.

[25] Ibid., 141.

tinctions of reason are complex ideas, as even Tweyman himself concedes, does not invalidate this point, but rather supports it.[26] Finally, even if we admit that distinctions of reason explain how we come to form the idea of existence, I do not see what exactly they can contribute to explain the idea of non-existence.

Concerning this polemical matter, I would like to accentuate two points. First, that Hume's argument is not wrong, and it really succeeds in showing that the idea of existence is not a first order distinction of reason, that is, an aspect which is abstracted from the characters of a given thing and the resemblances and differences that are disclosed when we compare it with other things. I rather suggest that it is distinction of reason of a higher order. Even though it definitively runs against an immediate identification of the idea of existence with such a kind of *distinctio rationis*, the passage is not, I think, decisive against those who identify that distinction of reason with the "act" by means of which the mind, according to Hume, comes to distinguish the existence of any thing from its non-existence. What Hume emphatically establishes again and again is that the difference between thinking of something and thinking of something as existent does not consist in the contents of what is thought, but in the way in which it is thought, or its "manner of conception." Hence if we could provide an account of the idea of existence in terms of the mode of conceiving that idea, and not in terms of its identification with some of the its constitutive characters (in the same manner that Hume attempts to explain the difference between thinking that something exists and believing that it does exist),[27] then it would be possible to give a workable explanation of the idea of existence as well as non-existence; that is to say, it would be feasible, but only in terms of a distinction of reason of a higher order. This second-order mental separation would be based on the resemblances and differences that the manner of conceiving the object we affirm to exist or not to exist has with many other possible modes of conceiving the same mental datum. This is the reason why Hume goes to say – as we have seen – that the ideas of existence and non-existence are "plainly resembling" (THN, 15). In this case, the distinction of reason is not performed on the datum, which is the same (idea or impression), but on the peculiarities of the mental activity or manner of conceiving the same datum.[28]

---

[26] Ibid., 138.

[27] Hence Tweyman is right when he asserts that "[f]or Hume, a satisfactory account of belief also provides a satisfactory account of reality or existence" (Ibid., 142). Yet in spite that Tweyman also correctly maintains that "[f]or Hume . . . the modalities of possibility and actuality are analyzed in terms of the *way* in which perceptions are apprehended, rather than in terms of *what* is apprehended" (Ibid., 142), I believe that he places a wrong emphasis on the role of the "force and vivacity" of perceptions in Hume's account of those ontological and epistemological distinctions, and I suspect this is why he denies that existence can be separated from the idea of something by means of a distinction of reason (Ibid. 143).

[28] See THN, Book I, Part III, Sect. VII, "Of the nature of the idea, or belief," in particular pp. 94–95: "But as it is certain there is a great difference betwixt the simple conception of the existence of an object, and the belief of it, and as this difference lies not in the parts or composition of the idea which we conceive; it follows, that it must lie in the *manner* in which we conceive it." See also THN, Appendix, 624–625.

Second, Hume explains – in the cited passage (THN, 15) – what is involved in the existential predication. To assert the existence of an object is to say that it occurs at certain times and places, to assert the non-existence of the same object is to exclude it from those same times and places. To think of something as existent seems to be, in general, to refer it to, or place it in, a spatio-temporal horizon; to think of it as non-existent is to remove it from, or place it outside, that same spatio-temporal field. Probably the field Hume has in mind is the one provided the system of belief, namely, the system of causally interconnected perceptions which he divides into the system of the memory and senses (*reality*), and that of judgment (*realities*) (THN. I, 108).[29]

An apparent corollary – and for some also an unfortunate consequence – of Hume's theory of existential predication is that in accordance with it we should have to say, as Paul Tillich does,[30] of an eternal God (that is, intemporal and not merely sempiternal, or everlasting) that He does not exist. At the very least, we should have to assert (supposing that it is meaningful to say so) that God is, like Plato's idea of the Good, beyond being and not-being.[31] I think that such a consequence follows from a principle to which Hume, as it were, arrives through several argumentative avenues in Book I, Part I of the *Treatise*, to wit, that if it is not possible for us to think of something absolutely different from our perceptions, then it also impossible to conceive the existence of any object specifically different from those things that are perceived by us (THN, 67).[32]

Again and for the last time, I have to concede that Hume's account is, as I have just tried to show, beset by serious ontological difficulties, although these may not

---

[29] There is an striking resemblance between this Humean theory and that of Kant. For the latter, to say that something exists is not to affirm that it has an additional attribute (i.e., existence) to all the rest, but to place it in the real world, which is, in Kants's language, "to posit an object . . . in relation to my concept" (*Critique of Pure Reason*, A 601, B 629; p. 505). This means, generally speaking, that we connect the concept with an object within the world of experience, since, according to Kant, all our knowledge of existence entirely belongs to the sphere of experience (Ibid.). At the end of the section, Kant affirms that even though the existence of an entity outside that domain cannot be declared absolutely impossible, it is, however, an hypothesis that we have no means of establishing (Ibid.).

[30] Paul Tillich, *Systematic Theology*, (3 vols.; Chicago: The University of Chicago Press, 1951; London: James Nisbet & Co. Ltd., 1953), I, Part II, Sect. II. B. 3: "God as Being," pp. 235–241.

[31] It is somewhat surprising that J. N. Findlay, one of the sharpest critics of the ontological argument in the 20th century, had migrated – in a manner reminiscent of Berkeley – to a Neo-Platonic position. In *Ascent to the Absolute*, he maintains that it is essential for God, if he is to be at the same time a necessary being and a fitting object of worship, to share in the nature of a Platonic Form: "I give it as a verdict of my feeling that only a form, something basically universal, though uttering itself in the individual and the specific, can be truly adorable, can in any way deserve the name of 'God'" (p. 267).

[32] Later on, he qualifies that doctrine: "The farthest we can go towards a conception of external objects, when supposed *specifically* different from our perceptions, is to form a relative idea of them, without pretending to comprehend the related objects" (THN, 68). One may even interpret Hume's declaration as approaching the Kantian doctrine according to which although non-sensible objects cannot be known, they can, nevertheless, be thought of. This principle is implicitly operative in the passages quoted in the preceding note about Kant.

perhaps be entirely insurmountable. But what else is to be expected when, after all, the subject Hume deals with (even though he may appear to shy off and walk away from it) is the recalcitrant problem of Being?

10.6 THE DISCREET HISTORICAL EFFECT OF HUME'S CRITIQUE

With all its limitations (most of them probably self-confessed), Hume's critique of the ontological argument is, I believe, substantially right. This, however, has not prevented – and of course will not prevent – from multiplying the efforts to set up a formally impregnable version of the proof. Of the innumerable and relatively recent attempts to reformulate the argument in a coherent manner, those of Norman Malcolm and Charles Hartshorne deserve special mention because they place great emphasis on the notion of "necessary existence." In essence, they both take as point of departure the disjunction "Either the existence of God is necessary, or impossible."[33] From it, and assuming that the concept of God as a logically necessary being is meaningful, they go on to establish the first clause of the proposition. Alvin Plantinga follows them in this respect, but his reasoning is different from theirs in that he employs the resources of modal logic, and in particular because for him the Leibnizian notion of 'possible worlds' plays a central role.[34]

The celebrated and already cited essay of J. N. Findlay, "Can God's Existence be Disproved," may be presented as fair evidence that the polemic around the proof is destined, by a sort of internal dynamics, to end in an impasse. In contradistinction to the former thinkers, Findlay adheres to the second clause of the dilemma. Arguing in a manner that appears to be entirely *ad hominen,* and starting with the presupposition that the concept of a being of infinite perfection is incoherent, he fabricates an a priori "disproof," or ontological counter-argument. In order to bring out its uncanny likeness to Cleanthes' argument in Part IX of the *Dialogues,* I outline the main steps of Findlay's "disproof" like this: 1. If the concept of an X does not imply a contradiction, the existence of x is possible; 2. If the concept of an X implies a contradiction, the existence of X is impossible; 3. The concept of God implies the concept of necessary existence; 4. The concept of necessary existence is contradictory; 5. Therefore, the existence of God is impossible. It is noteworthy that when Findlay explains why he thinks that the concept of an object whose non-existence is inconceivable is incoherent, he mentions Kant's critique, but not once does he hint at Hume, even though Findlay's own argument shares, albeit con-

---

[33] Norman Malcolm, "Anselm's Ontological Arguments" in *Knowledge and Certainty: Essays and Lectures* (New Jersey: Prentice Hall, 1963), pp. 141–162; Charles Hartshorne, *Man's Vision of God* (Chicago: Willet, Clark and Co., 1941), ch. ix, "The Necessarily Existent", pp. 299–341; and *The Logic of Perfection* (La Salle, Illinois: Open Court Publishing Co., 1962), chs. 2–4. Hartshorne's outlook is more historical in *Anselm's Discovery: A Re-Examination of the Ontological Proof for God's Existence* (La Salle, Ill., Open Court, 1965). Although in this work Hartshorne dedicates a section to Hume (pp. 201–208), yet I honestly think that he mostly ignores the essentials of Hume's critique.

[34] Alvin Plantinga, *The Nature of Necessity,* (Oxford: Clarendon Press, 1974).

versely, remarkable family resemblances with the latter's. Findlay has later admitted that his argument is flawed.[35] For this reason, I have called it *ad hominen;* viewed under this light, it may still retain some philosophical value.[36]

Some other defenders of the argument not only take as tacit presupposition, but even as axiomatic truth precisely the principle which Hume's critique provides us with better reasons to reject: namely, that existence is an object or a property of an object. The most conspicuous case of this indifference to Hume (I have no reason to impute ignorance in this case) is that of Kurt Gödel, who left among his papers a rough draft of a sort of "ontological demonstration" *(Ontologischer Beweis)* of God's existence. Afterwards the proof has been reconstructed and commented by scholars of his work.[37] In Gödel's system, not only being or existence is a positive property, but – according to one of its axioms – necessary existence itself is a positive property: P (NE). It is interesting to note in passing that two of the most serious objections that Jordan Howard Sobel formulates to Gödel's proof are – even if he does not mention Hume – of unmistakable Humean ancestry. In the first place, for Sobel it is "obvious" – obvious after Hume, one might add – that even if we include existence in definitions of kinds of things, from these we cannot possibly deduce the real existence of things of those kinds, that is, "we cannot thereby define into existence things of any kinds we *please*."[38] Second, Sobel maintains that even if one concedes that within the formal demands of Gödel's axiomatic system it follows as a valid conclusion that there is a being whose existence is necessary, by any means it also follows that such a being is God, at least in the religious sense of being an appropriate object of worship: "the God of that system – its God-like being – could not, by anyone who would speak in ordinary terms, be called God."[39]

Verily, the vivid image of Kurt Gödel, the most brilliant mathematical logician of the twentieth century, late in his life, cerebrally officiating in two blurred pages a sort of logical resurrection of the ontological argument, makes one think of the end of Part IX of the *Dialogues Concerning Natural Religion.*[40] There Philo, the scep-

---

[35] J. N. Findlay, *Ascend to the Absolute*, p. 13.

[36] Other later attempts to refute the ontological proof, which follow the same argumentative pattern employed by Findlay, strike me as too contrived to be either philosophically or theologically persuasive. See, for instance, David and Marjorie Haight, "An Ontological Argument for the Devil," *The Monist* 54 (1970): 218–220.

[37] See Jordan Howard Sobel, "Gödel's Ontological Proof," in *On Being and Saying: Essays for Richard Cartwright*, Judith Jarvis Thomson, ed. (Massachusetts: MIT Press, 1987), pp. 241–261.

[38] Ibid., p. 248.

[39] Ibid., p. 250. Graham Oppy essentially repeats Sobel's objections to Gödel's proof in *Ontological Arguments and Belief in God*, p. 225. When dealing with "Hume's Objections" to the Ontological Argument Oppy sides with – among others – J. C. A. Gaskin, by claiming that the argument Hume voices through Cleanthes is question-begging, and with John Passmore, by adducing that Hume cannot account for the idea of non-existence (Ibid., pp. 226 – 227). Based on what has been said in this chapter, I believe that he is wrong on both counts.

[40] The manuscript is dated February 10, 1970. Gödel died in 1978.

tic, reflects on the almost irresistible attraction which a priori proofs, such as the ontological argument, have always exerted on people of a mathematically inclined mind and essentially speculative temper, and says that:

> Other people, even of good sense and the best inclined to religion, feel always .some deficiency in such arguments, though they are not perhaps able to explain distinctly where it lies; a certain proof that men ever did, and ever will derive their religion from other sources than from this species of reasoning (DNR, 192).

As far as I am concerned, I feel still that no other thinker has been able to explain in a more lucid, profound and vibrant manner than Hume what are the failings which inevitably afflict the ontological argument.

CHAPTER 11

The Rejection of Miracles: An Attempt to Elucidate the Import of Hume's Critique

11.1 HISTORICAL NOTE

Hume highlights, while explaining in *The Natural History of Religion* the actual origins of religious beliefs, that it is when confronted with astonishing and altogether unusual events that common people are disposed to suppose that the causes of such extraordinary phenomena before their eyes are personal, that is, invisible and intelligent beings. It should not appear strange then that, viewed from a historical standpoint, the practice of invoking extraordinary or privileged kinds of experiences as confirmation of the divine origin of very diverse religious beliefs, had been very common. Prominent among these have been miracles conceived as alterations to the natural course of events. Hence it should not surprise us that Hume decided to look into this presumably empirical foundation of religion. Accordingly, in Section X of the *Enquiry Concerning Human Understanding,* he asks whether there is any testimonial evidence which can conclusively prove that a miraculous event has occurred so as to validate the claims to truth of a historical religion.

This section of the *Enquiry* is by far the most widely read and controversial of all Hume writings. And it was, during Hume's lifetime, the most polemical of his philosophical productions and the one that provoked the most tenacious and virulent opposition from the religious apologists of those days.[1] Hume himself hinted at the reason for this violent hostility against him in a letter to Rev. George Campbell (1719–1796), the author of *A Dissertation on Miracles,* which was the most discerning contemporary response to Hume's argument and the only one he

---

[1] Hume's *Of Miracles,* Section X of *An Enquiry Concerning Human Understanding,* appeared when the deistic controversy in England was coming to an end. This book was first published in 1748 with the title of *Philosophical Essays Concerning Human Understanding.* Hume had originally intended to include the section about miracles in the *Treatise of Human Nature,* Books I and II, (1739). In anticipation of the "clamour of the zealots," Hume proceeded to "castrate its more nobler parts." He was not mistaken; even without those parts, the *Treatise* was employed by the "zealots," i.e., the Evangelical wing of the Church of Scotland, to deny him in 1745 the chair of Moral Philosophy at the University of Edinburgh.

deigned to answer.[2] In that letter he asserts that the argument first occurred to him in his youth, during his stay in the little town of La Flèche, France, when he was writing his first and fundamental philosophical work, the *Treatise of Human Nature*. It was while walking with a learned Jesuit through the cloister of the famous College of La Flèche that Hume made it known to another for the first time. Hume's companion was apparently confounded by the reasoning; but at last he replied to him that "it was impossible for that argument to have any solidity, because it operated equally against the Gospel as the catholic miracles." Hume found that observation to be a "sufficient answer."[3]

In spite of the almost universal assessment among Hume's contemporaries that his reasoning was worthy of the most unabashed enemy of the established Church, it is also true that the source which inspired it – if one is right in believing Hume in this respect (EHU, 109) – had the most respectable orthodox credentials: i.e., John Tillotson (1630–1694), preacher of the Anglican Church, who not only became Archbishop of Canterbury, but was one of the most able and reasonable defenders of religious orthodoxy during his age. Tillotson's polemical argument, to which Hume refers at the beginning of the section, is an attack on the Catholic dogma of transubstantiation. The reasonableness of Tillotson is plainly manifested in the foundation upon which the premises of his argument rest, and which is the same presupposition that guides *The Reasonableness of Christianity*, by the orthodox Locke, as well as *Christianity Not-Mysterious,* by the deist Toland: "Nothing ought to be received as a Revelation from God which plainly contradicts the Principles of Natural Religion, or overthrows the certainty of them."[4] Tillotson's reasoning, as Hume reformulates it at the beginning of the section, may be synthesized in six steps, which I immediately itemize so that it may be possible for us to judge whether Hume's argument is, as it were, its legitimate logical offspring: 1. Sensible evidence is the only thing (excluding revelation) that justifies our assent to the occurrence of any event whatsoever; 2. Direct (first person) experience is stronger (has greater credibility) than indirect experience (the testimony of third persons); 3. We ought always to assent to the stronger evidence when it is opposed to a weaker; 4. Sensible (direct) evidence is the foundation of the credit we give to the Gospel (in this case, the Apostles' testimony). 6. Therefore, even if the doctrine of transubstantiation were to be found in the Gospel, we should not assent to it, for

---

[2] *A Dissertation on Miracles* (Edinburgh, 1762; rpt. New York and London: Garland Publishing, Inc., 1983).

[3] L, I, Letter no. 194, 360–361.

[4] John Tillotson, *The Works of the Most Reverent Dr. John Tillotson, late Lord Archbishop of Canterbury* (London, 1696), Sermon 21, Sect. 4., p. 227. In Sect. 5, he asserts that "nothing ought to be received as Divine Doctrine and Revelation, without good evidence that it is so" (Ibid., p. 228). From the conjunction of these two principles Tillotson justifies his acceptance of miracles (as based on sensible evidence) and rejection of transubstantiation (because of its absurd and contradictory character) (Ibid.)).

the evidence in its favor, although it is of the same kind (that is, sensible), is weaker than the one that lead us to reject it.[5]

By proceeding in this manner, it is obvious that we start with an arguable presupposition: to wit, that Hume's representation of Tillotson's argument, even if it is not a mere paraphrase, is at any rate a formally faithful and true reconstruction of it. This is, however, a highly debatable question. Important commentators, such as J. C. A. Gaskin, think that Hume's argument is quite different from Tillotson's.[6] Even though I find very enlightening almost all Gaskin says about Hume's essay on miracles, I think that he is wrong in this particular point. At the outset one must concede that Hume's rendering does not textually correspond with any of the versions that Tillotson offers in the most extensive text, *A Discourse against Transubstantiation*, pp. 31–40. But it is also true that Hume parodies in an amplified manner the earlier versions that appear in *The Rule of Faith*, pp. 274–275, and in particular, in *Sermons Preach'd Upon Several Occasions*, pp. 313–317. Because the latter is the version which is materially more similar to Hume's reconstruction, I allow myself the liberty of quoting a most striking passage from it:.

> If the testimony of *sense* be to be relied upon, then *Transubstantiation* is false: If it be not, then no man is sure that Christianity is true. For the utmost assurance that the Apostles had of the truth of Christianity, was the testimony of their own senses concerning our Saviours miracles; and this testimony every man hath against *Transubstantiation*. From whence it plainly follows, that no man (no not the Apostles themselves) had more reason to believe *Christianity* to be true, than every man hath to believe *Transubstantiation* to be false. And we who did not see our Saviours Miracles (as the Apostles did) and have only a credible Relation of them, but do see the *Sacrament*, have less evidence of the *truth* of *Christianity* than of the *falshood* of *Transubstantiation* (*Sermons Preach'd Upon Several Occasions*, pp. 315-316).

Clearly, even if the preceding argument were formally identical to Hume's reformulation, it would, however, continue to be materially different from it. In all its different versions, Tillotson's argument expressly puts forward a doctrine which Hume does not insist upon, and does not even mention, when he rephrases it: in the words of Tillotson himself, i.e., "that miracles . . . are certainly the best and highest external proof of Christianity."[7] This is so perhaps because Hume's argument is designed precisely to subject that major claim to critical scrutiny.

A less debatable question is whether the reasoning on miracles that Hume ironically proclaims as "an everlasting check" to superstition is of the same type as

---

[5] Tillotson's argumentation against this Catholic doctrine is found in *Sermons Preach'd Upon Several Occasions*, 2nd ed. (London, 1673), *The Rule of Faith*, 2nd ed. (London, 1676), and is developed in detail in *A Discourse against Transubstantiation*, 2nd ed. London, 1685 (first published 1684).

[6] J. C. A. Gaskin, *Hume's Philosophy of Religion*, 2nd ed., p. 152.

[7] John Tillotson, *A Discourse against Transubstantiation*, p. 40.

Tillotson's. I believe a careful perusal of the texts of Tillotson's works already cited amply justifies an affirmative stance. Yet, we shall not deal here with this historical question. I shall rather attempt to determine to what extent Hume's argument is a corollary of his own empiricist philosophy. The truly amazing fact is that his famous argument about miracles has produced a verily prodigious bibliography, composed on the one hand, of replies and refutations, and on the other, of defenses and new formulations of it.[8] Strangely, perhaps the greatest part of this long dispute has centered around a question which at best one can say that Hume dealt with by implication only, namely, whether or not miracles can possibly happen. A plain and direct reading of the text makes one conclude that Hume not only granted that possibility, but also admitted that the occurrence of miracles may possibly be established by human testimony:

> For I own, that otherwise, there may possibly be miracles, or violations of the usual course of nature, of such a kind as to admit of proof from human testimony (EHU, 127).

Not to dismiss a priori the existence of miracles appears, in addition, to be more compatible with one main foundation of his analysis of causality, viz. that, since no negation of fact involves a contradiction, no matter of fact and existence can ever be demonstrated:

> [I]t implies no contradiction, that the course of nature may change, and that an object, seemingly like those which we have experienced, may be attended with different or contrary effects (EHU, 35).

Apart from that, Hume himself admits that the occurrence of phenomena contrary to the ordinary succession of physical as well as of historical events, is not precisely a rarity: "irregular and extraordinary appearances are frequently discovered in the moral, as well as in the physical world" (E, "Of Some Remarkable Customs," 366).

In sum, if miracles are events contrary to the usual course of nature, and miracles are impossible, it seems then that Hume must renounce the preceding principle. But I must confess that the choice is not so clear cut. Hume's more usual way of referring to miracles as "violations of the laws of nature," conjoined with the further implicit thesis that of such universal laws of nature it is not meaningful to say that

---

[8] Out of this immense number of writings, I singularize only those of Antony Flew and Richard Swinburne. The former author, *Hume's Philosophy of Belief* (London: Routledge & Kegan Paul, 1961), ch. 8 "Miracles and Methodology", pp. 166–213, and "Miracles", *Encyclopedia of Philosophy*, ed. Paul Edwards, V, 346–353, has by general consent produced the most lucid contemporary defense and reformulation of the critique of miracles typical of Hume's philosophical tradition. Richard Swinburne's, *The Concept of Miracle* (London: Macmillan, 1970), is, on the contrary, the most vigorous attempt to rehabilitate the notion of miracle within the realm of natural theology against the Hume-Flew kind of objections.

they have exceptions, has led many[9] to conclude that Hume asserts, in the last analysis, that miracles are impossible, i.e., that the notion of miracle is a pseudo-concept which can have no application. This interpretation finds enough support in the confident manner in which Hume summarily and outrightly dismisses as impossible events which seem *prima facie* miraculous, without considering it necessary to stop and examine the character and nature of the testimony which supports them. His remarks about the miracles supposedly wrought at the tomb of the Abbé Paris, the famous Jansenist, are illustrative:

> And what have we to oppose to such a cloud of witnesses, but the *absolute impossibility or miraculous nature of the events*, which they relate? And this surely, in the eyes of all reasonable people, will alone be regarded as a sufficient refutation (EHU, 125; italics added).

According to this second interpretation, it would be true by definition that evidence can prove extraordinary events, but never strictly miraculous ones. For if a proposition is a true law of nature, then there is no kind of evidence that could possibly contradict it. Let us say that we are confronted with an alleged miracle. In this situation there are only two courses of action open to us. We must either discard the law (i.e., admit that it is not such a law of nature, since the fact in question falsified it) or reformulate the law in a way that this novel fact could be subsumed under it. Or we must, on the other hand, simply disbelieve the alleged miracle, instead of believing in the existence of something which, if the universal law of nature is true, must be physically impossible.[10] Furthermore, this view seems to gather additional force from the following statements Hume made in the *History of England* :

> It is the business of history to distinguish between the *miraculous* and the *marvellous*; to reject the first in all narrations merely profane and human; to doubt the second; and when obliged by unquestionable testimony . . . to admit of something extraordinary, to receive as little of it as is consistent with the known facts and circumstances (H, II, 398).

However, what Hume does in this Section "Of Miracles" is to probe and assess the trustworthiness of the particular sort of testimony which is invoked in favor of miracles. And this task seems quite pointless, if one assumes from the start that the concept of miracles is impossible or incapable of being instantiated anyhow. We must rather say with R. C. Wallace that "either the concept is a possible one, in which case one's assessment of the relevant evidence is vitally affected; or else it is

---

[9] See, for instance, Stanley Paluch, "Hume and the Miraculous," *Dialogue*, 5 (1966–1967): 61–65. A view even more extreme than Paluch's, is that of Alastair McKinnon, "Miracle," *American Philosophical Quarterly* 4, 4 (October 1967): 309–310.

[10] Antony Flew, *Hume's Philosophy of Belief*, pp. 186–187, 200–209.

not, in which case consideration of the nature of the evidence becomes superfluous."[11]

11.2 ANALYSIS OF HUME'S ARGUMENT

On the strength of what I have said at the beginning, it seems to me that those who affirm that the concept of miracle is coherent are right; yet my principal goal is not to adjudicate the victory to any of the contenders in this controversy. Our focal point will be instead on the examination of what I take to be the main issue of this section of the *Enquiry*, which is the argument by which Hume seeks to establish the truth of a substantial proposition, viz. that "no human testimony can have such a force as to prove a miracle, and make it a just foundation for any such [that is, "popular" or historical, not philosophical] system of religion" (EHU, 127). This problem is logically independent of the question we have just called attention to. Obviously if miracles are impossible, it follows *ipso facto* that no testimony can prove them; but even if miracles do occur, it does not necessarily follow that they can be so proved.

It is noteworthy that the problem of miracles is focused from a confined perspective. What is asked is not whether any sort of evidence can establish the occurrence of a miracle, but whether one specific sort, testimonial evidence or the reports of "witnesses and historians," can do it. Except maybe by way of implication, Hume nowhere poses the question: Granted that our perceptive apparatus is operating normally, can I, or any other person, possibly witness a truly miraculous event in contradistinction to a mere marvelous one; how can one be sure that one has witnessed it? In this sense his standpoint is different from Locke's, who in his *Discourse of Miracles* analyzes these from the spectator's or bystander's point of view. Locke supposes this to be the chief one even for those cases in which we assert the existence of a miracle on the strength of the testimony of others: "He that is present at the fact, is a spectator: he that believes the history of the fact, puts himself in the place of a spectator."[12]

Hume's question seems rather to be: what conditions must the testimony of a presumed witness satisfy for us to accept his or her claim that a miraculous event has in fact occurred? Since Locke analyzes the problem almost entirely from the spectator's perspective, he mostly disregards the problem about the nature of the recorded or documental evidence that may establish the occurrence of such events. It is also the case that Locke simply takes for granted that no reasonable person can doubt the fundamental credibility of the *Scriptures*, which was something that deists such as Matthew Tindal immediately denied against him, Clarke, and Newton.[13] Thus Locke confidently asserts:

---

[11] R. C. Wallace, "Hume, Flew and the Miraculous," *Philosophical Quarterly*, 20 (1970), 230–243.

[12] John Locke, *A Discourse of Miracles*, in *The Works of John Locke*, IX, p. 256.

[13] See chapter 2 above for a discussion of Tindal's outlook on this matter.

I think the most scrupulous or sceptical cannot from miracles raise the least doubt against the divine revelation of the Gospel.[14]

This overriding interest of Hume in testimonial evidence may have at least two sources. First, Hume was after all a historian, and miracles do offer him an occasion for examining problems of the methodology of historiography. According to Antony Flew, Hume offers here a set of evidential canons for the guidance of historical research in general.[15] Second, Hume's argument is one of the concluding chapters in the famous deistic controversy in England during the seventeenth and eighteenth centuries. The orthodox divines, pushed into a corner by the deists ("those dangerous friends or disguised enemies of the *Christian Religion*, who have undertaken to defend it by the principles of human reason"),[16] were led ultimately to assert very emphatically that the fundamental truths of religion were essentially mysterious, incapable of being disclosed to natural reason. Our only means of access to them is through divine revelation. But if human reason is impotent in these matters, how are we to distinguish which, among several different doctrines, is the true revelation? One of the answers was that true religion is accompanied by miracles; in other words, that the occurrence of miracles proved the divine nature of the revelation. Since in the Christian religion the most important miracles are indirectly known, that is, they are known through the Scriptures and tradition, any appeal to miracles itself rested upon the trustworthiness of scriptural and historical testimony. Thus the real truth-value of such sources became the central and most lively issue of discussion. What Hume seeks to show was the insufficiency of any such sort of approach to provide a just foundation for any popular system of religion, that is, its failure as a means of establishing the claims to truth of religion.

Mysteries can be proved by revelation alone; and revelation was to be proved by miracles. To consider the value of this method of proof is therefore, the final task for Hume's ingenuity.[17]

---

[14] John Locke, *A Discourse of Miracles*, p. 258

[15] Antony Flew, *Hume's Philosophy of Belief*, pp. 187–188. C. D. Broad claims, in his classical article, "Hume's Theory of the Credibility of Miracles," *Proceedings of the Aristotelian Society* (1916–1917), 77–94, that the concern with the methodology of the historical sciences is Hume's dominant interest.

[16] EHU, 129–130. Hume seems to refer to the deists in particular, and not, I think, to the Newtonian philosophers or the friends of the Royal Society, as A. E. Taylor supposes in "David Hume and the Miraculous," *Philosophical Essays*, (London: The Macmillan Co., 1934), p. 348. See the discussion about deism in chapter 2 above. One may add to this that John Toland presents himself, in an explicit manner and with apparent sincerity, as being much more than a mere friend of Christianity: "The only religious Title that . . . I shall ever own, for my part, is that most glorious one of being a *Christian*" (Christianity not Mysterious, xxx).

[17] Sir Leslie Stephen, *English Thought in the Eighteenth Century*, p. 287. See especially ch. 4, Sect. V, "The Argument from Miracles," pp. 192–213, and Sect. VI, "The Historical Argument,"

Hume's argument has two definite stages. First, he proceeds to ask about what conditions any report about a miracle should have to satisfy so that a reasonable person – the "wise," who "proportions his belief to the evidence" (EHU, 110) – may be justified in bestowing her or his assent on it with the exact degree of assurance that it deserves. Second, Hume then goes on to examine whether the particular kind of testimony for presumed miracles associated with religion does, in fact, fulfill those conditions; only if it does, can the testimony be brought forward as evidence – independent of revelation – for the truth of religion.

Hume begins by asserting once more that all our inferences about matters of fact are founded upon experience. But he cautions that experience is not an infallible guide: our expectations about the future, based on what has happened in the past, can be and are frequently frustrated. Some sorts of events are always and everywhere found to be constantly conjoined together. However, not all events follow their supposed causes with the same degree of regularity. Experience teaches us to expect, in the universal succession of causes and effects, regularity in some cases and irregularity in others. Hence "in our reasonings concerning matter of fact, there are all imaginable degrees of assurance, from the highest certainty to the lowest species of moral [that is, probable] evidence" (EHU, 110). An expectation about the occurrence of an event, if founded on an infallible or completely uniform experience, has the greatest possible degree of certainty, and it is considered to be a proof of the future existence of the event. If an inference is founded, however, upon an experience which is contrary or not entirely regular, it is probable only. Since it is not supported by all the evidence, that is, only by some "past observations and experiments," but not by all, in order to determine the exact degree of probability of our inference, "we must balance the opposite experiments, where they are opposite, and deduct the smaller number from the greater" (EHU, 111).

In brief, no reasoning concerning matters of fact should be invested with a higher degree of certainty than what is guaranteed by the evidence gathered for it from past experience. And this applies also to reasonings based on human testimony or "the reports of eye-witnesses and spectators," for the assurance we repose upon them is derived exclusively from experience,[18] that is, from "the observation of the veracity of human testimony and of the usual conformity of facts to the reports of witnesses" (EHU, 111):

No man can have any other experience but his own. The experience of others becomes his only by the credit which he gives to their testimony; which proceeds from his own experience of human nature (L, I, No. 188, 349).

---

pp. 213–230. Most of the authors I have read and who deal with this controversy have a debt – sometimes explicitly recognized but more usually unacknowledged – with this classic work of Stephen.

[18] Hume suggests here that testimony is a species of the genus causal arguments. John Passmore, *Hume's Intentions*, pp. 32–34, points out the difficulties that this assimilation encounters.

The evidence for a particular testimony will be considered either as a *proof* or as a *probability*, depending on whether it is founded on a regular or irregular experience, in other words, "according as the conjunction between any particular kind of report and any kind of object has been found to be constant or variable" (EHU, 112).

If the testimony is of such kind that it has not infallibly established the fact in the past, its degree of probability will be determined, as in all cases where there is contrariety in the evidence, by subtracting the favorable cases from the unfavorable ones (that is, those cases or circumstances which cause doubt or uncertainty). After "this opposition and mutual destruction of arguments," we assent to the superior side, "but still with a diminution of assurance, in proportion to the force of its antagonist" (EHU, 112). The circumstances which can diminish the certainty of testimony depend not only on the nature of the reporters (the opposition of contrary testimony) the character or number of witnesses, their manner of delivering their testimony, etc.), but also – and this is the crucial assumption, without which Hume's argument cannot move ahead – on the nature of the event which is reported. The certainty of the testimony will vary proportionately with the degree of probability of the event that the testimony attempts to establish. The more improbable the event, that is, the more extraordinary or marvelous it is, the less the degree of assurance of the testimony, for the amount of evidence against the occurrence of the event gathered from past experience is proportionally greater; "in that case the evidence resulting from the testimony admits of a diminution, greater or less, in proportion as the fact is more or less unusual" (EHU, 113). The report should be accepted (always with a correspondingly diminished degree of certainty) only if experience shows that the falsity of the report is more probable than the occurrence of the event.

But the probability that testimony should establish the occurrence of a miracle is "from the very nature of the fact," that is, from the very definition of a miracle, even less. A miraculous event is not merely marvelous or extraordinary. The latter is not conformable to our past experience, in the sense that our knowledge of the past did not lead us to expect that it might occur. A miracle is an extraordinary event, but something else in addition: it is a "violation of the laws of nature" (EHU, 114).[19] Hume seems to be saying thereby that miracles are "contrary to experience" (EHU, 114) in the sense that the testimony which affirms that a miraculous event has occurred is contradicted by a general law which is supported by or "founded upon a firm and unalterable experience" (EHU, 114) which is exactly contrary to it. The record of regularity or uniformity is, in the case of a law of nature, complete; thus it is equivalent to a proof. If a miracle, on the other hand, is to be established by testimony, this testimony must be supported by an even stronger proof than that of the law which the presumed miracle breaches. But even in this case the certainty of the report should be diminished in a degree proportional

---

[19] This definition is from a general point of view clearly defective, but, as I will try to show further on, its employment is amply justified within the ensemble of problems from which Hume approaches the notion of miracle.

to the force of the contrary proof. If the fact is "really miraculous; and . . . the testimony considered apart and in itself, amounts to an entire proof, of which the strongest must prevail, but still with a diminution of its force, in proportion to that of its antagonist" (EHU, 114).

The "plain consequence" of this is that the occurrence of a miracle can therefore only be established or proved if the falsity of the testimony in its favor would be even more improbable, that is, even more miraculous, than the presumed miracle (EHU, 115).

Such is the substance of the first part of the argument. Hume formulates it in a markedly abstract language, with few really useful examples, and devoid of the usual literary nimbleness and brilliance that always elucidate the sense of his philosophical discourse. No wonder that to posterity the consequences of this argument did not appear to be as plain as to Hume himself.[20]

The force of Hume's argument may be avoided by those who refuse to accept his definition of miracle as a violation of a law of nature. God – they could say – may perform miracles both in irregular and indirect ways, as well as in regular and direct, that is, without having to breach any natural law. This may well be the case. But the capacity to detect the immediate activity of God through the occurrence of insignificant and perfectly usual events seems to be one very difficult to acquire apart from a package of doctrines offered by a particular religious faith. Thus, for instance, it is only because he already believed in the spirit of the LORD and trusted his word that the prophet Elijah was able to become aware of God's presence, not in a strong wind, nor in an earthquake, nor in a fire, but in a still small voice (1 Kings 19:11–13). Furthermore, that set of doctrines should also include a well-defined criterion, or some kind of theological semiotics, by means of which to sort out the miraculous from the non-miraculous events. Yet it seems at first sight that it is only because of their uniqueness that miracles can be taken as revelatory

---

[20] Even though Anthony Flew's position is complex and occasionally ambiguous, I think that he is right in the following claim:

> What he is trying to demonstrate a priori in Part I is: not that, as a matter of fact, miracles do not happen, but that from the very nature of the concept – 'from the very nature of the fact' – there must be a conflict in the evidence required to show that they do (*Hume's Philosophy of Belief*, p. 176).

Robert Fogelin, "What Hume Actually Said About Miracles," *Hume Studies* 16, no. 1 (April 1990): 81–86, has questioned this interpretation. According to Fogelin, Hume not only offers an a priori argument against the existence of miracles but also "an priori argument . . . to show that testimony, however strong, could never make it reasonable to believe that a miracle has occur" (Ibid. 81). Flew refutes this thesis, shortly and convincingly, in "Fogelin on Hume and Miracles," *Hume Studies* 16, no. 1 (November 1990): 141–145. Other relatively recent and interesting works about this issue are the following: Dorothy Coleman, "Hume, Miracles and Lotteries," *Hume Studies* 14, no. 2 (November 1988): 277–304; Barry Gower "David Hume and the Probability of Miracles," *Hume Studies* 16, no. 1 (April 1990): 17–32; Bruce Langry, "Hume, Probability, Lotteries and Miracles," *Hume Studies* 16, no. 1 (April 1990): 67–74; Kenneth G. Fergunson, "An Intervention into the Flew-Fogelin Debate," *Hume Studies* 18, no. 1 (April 1992): 105–112.

signs of a reality beyond.[21] This is why Nicodemus, the Pharisee, says to Jesus: "Rabbi, we know that thou are a teacher come from God: for no man can do these miracles that thou doest, except God be with him" (John, 3:2).

This element of the supernatural (and specifically supernatural causation) is emphasized by Hume in his more accurate definition of a miracle as a "transgression of a law of nature by a particular volition of the Deity, or by the interposition of some invisible agent (EHU, 115).[22] The last clause takes note of the proverbial maxim that the devil also can work miracles.[23] Whatever deficiencies this definition may have if viewed within a purely theological context provided by a particular faith, it seems that one must fall back on it in order to give substantial meaning to the claim that the occurrence of miracles can endorse a particular revelation. To try to provide a theological context for such a definition – as R. C. Wallace[24] tries to do – is, I believe, to beg the question whether a miracle can be proved so as to make it a foundation for a particular religion. In that case a miracle would already be a part of a faith, and not something that could justify our assent to a particular revelation.

In summary, it seems to me that Hume's argument is not directed to prove either that miracles cannot occur, or that their occurrence can never be proven by human testimony: What he has shown are the enormous difficulties which any attempt at establishing them must encounter, even under the best of circumstances, due to the radically conflicting evidence. In addition, he has also tried to show that the confidence that anyone can reasonably bestow upon such testimony is very small; probably it is very similar to the degree of assurance conferred upon "the lowest species of moral evidence."

The second part of Hume's argument is directed to disprove what he has conceded in the first part: i.e., he tries to demonstrate that the evidence upon which the testimony for miracles is based has never, in fact, amounted to a full proof, that it is instead a very conflicting evidence, amounting to a very low probability, and that for this reason miracles cannot serve to conclusively authenticate the truth of any religion. I shall not dealt at length with this part of Section X of the *Enquiry*, but

---

[21] "If miracles were not known to be contrary to the laws of nature, how could they suggest the presence of the supernatural? How could they be surprising unless they were seen as exceptions to the rules?" C. S. Lewis, *Miracles*. London: (Collins Fontana Books, 1960), pp. 52, 36, 64. The opposite view is expressed with comparable force by authors such as G. Van der Leeuw, *Religion in Essence and Manifestation*, trans. J. E. Turner (New York: Harper & Row, 1963), chap. 85, pp. 565–572 [German edition: *Phänomenologie der Religion*, 2d. ed. (Tübingen: J. C. B. Mohr, 1933)], and Paul Tillich, *Systematic Theology*, Vol. I, pp. 128–131.

[22] If one dispenses with this type of cause, and suspects that the uncanny event in question arose out of mere chance or occurred by sheer coincidence, then there is no miracle and no violation of a law of nature.

[23] Anthony Flew has conclusively shown that Hume's definition is not arbitrary. He points out that it substantially agrees with the definitions offered by St. Thomas Aquinas and Samuel Clarke (*Hume's Philosophy of Belief*, pp. 188–191).

[24] R. C. Wallace, "Hume, Flew and the Miraculous," pp. 230, 238–241.

only bring forward the four observations Hume offers to justify this thesis, and later try to determine the real import of his critique.

First, no religious testimony for miracles has ever satisfied minimal criteria of objectivity and impartiality: Either the witnesses have been too few in number, or too ignorant, or not above moral reproach. All to frequently, for instance, they have had an interest of their own in the establishment of the alleged miracle.

Second, the affections of surprise and wonder are irresistible, and when associated with religious fervor, often produce excesses of credulity and imposture.

Third, miracles have been reported mostly among ignorant and barbarous nations.

Fourth, "in matters of religion, whatever is different is contrary" (EHU, 121), that is, the truth of one religion, Hume seems to say, excludes that of all others. Miracles are considered to be proofs of a truth of one religion, yet miracles abound in all religions; "thus, all the prodigies of different religions are to be regarded as contrary facts, and the evidences of these prodigies . . . as opposite to each other" (EHU, 122). In other words, the evidence for the miracles of one religion must cancel the evidence for the miracles of every other religion, so that the truth of none can be established by an appeal to miracles: "It is impossible the religions of ancient Rome, of Turkey, of Siam, and of China should all of them be established on any solid foundation" (EHU, 121).

Frankly speaking, these four considerations have a very uneven refutative value. We shall only dwell on the last one, because it is, from a logical point of view, the most interesting one.

Obviously Hume is not saying that the occurrence of a miracle within one system of religion precludes, of itself, the actual occurrence of other such events in other religions. The different would-be miracles are "contrary events" only under the supposition that they are brought forward as a guarantee of a religion whose truth is logically incompatible with that of every other religion.[25] Hume makes this clear in a letter to his friend Hugh Blair, who had previously send him a copy of the manuscript of *A Dissertation on Miracles* by George Campbell, a work mentioned at the beginning of this chapter:

> If a miracle proves a doctrine to be revealed from God, and consequently true, a miracle can never be wrought for a contrary doctrine. The facts are therefore as incompatible as the doctrines (L, I, No. 188, 350–351).

Hume then makes various assorted observations apparently intended to weaken the certainty and credibility of the historical testimony about miracles. Against the

---

[25] One should also note that Hume's critique presupposes that we are dealing here with the meaning that the doctrines actually have for the common believer, and not with the sense these might come to have for a theological or philosophical reinterpretation of them. The latter may reconcile apparently different religious beliefs, either by discovering a core common to all faiths, or by reinterpreting all other doctrines in terms of one's own. See with regard to this Ninian Smart, *The Philosophy of Religion* (New York: Random House, 1970), ch. 1, "On Understanding the Concept of Religion," pp. 3–39.

vociferous, contradictory, and often fraudulent testimonies for miracles we have the unanimous voice of a completely uniform experience supporting the laws of nature. Before such disparity of evidence Hume concludes that it is always more probable that a miracle has been fabricated than that it has actually happened: it is always easier to account for such a presumed event in terms of "the known and natural principles of credulity and delusion" (EHU, 126) than to suppose that a law of nature has momentarily ceased to operate. The pertinent question, and one for which an answer may be forthcoming, is not so much whether or not miracles do occur, but rather how does it occur that people come to believe in them. And so Hume proceeds to give the causal account of the excessive credulity usually ascribed to reports about miracles that we have already examined in chapter 7, section 3.

On the whole, in this second part Hume's conclusion establishes two points: In general, that since the contrary empirical evidence "annihilates" the certainty of the religious testimony about miracles, it is not possible to base upon it the claims to truth of any historical religion, i.e., that a miracle cannot be proved so as to serve as a foundation or endorsement for any "popular" or historical religion (EHU, 127). And in particular, that even though Hume admits that miracles, considered as violations of the usual course of nature, could be established by testimony, he however denies that in practice there has been any such testimony sufficiently convincing to do it.[26]

11.3 VARIOUS OBJECTIONS TO HUME'S PROCEDURE

However shocking it may have appeared to Hume's contemporaries, the preceding conclusion is a view with which many modern orthodox theologians could comfortably live with. But Hume, in addition, asserts something which is not perhaps warranted by his argument:

> But should [a] miracle be ascribed to any new system of religion; men, in all ages, have been so much imposed on by ridiculous stories of that kind, that this very circumstance would be a full proof of a cheat, and sufficient, with all men of sense, not only to make them reject the fact, but even reject it without farther examination (EHU, 128–129).[27]

Yet when Hume first stated his argument, he established as a condition that in the computation of the probability of a miracle, the testimony favorable to it should be assessed "apart and in itself," that is, for the evidential value that it has on its

---

[26] In order to clarify the latter point, Hume offers only a few ironical and ingenious, although merely hypothetical, examples, such as the unanimous and uncontested report by historians about the resurrection of Queen Elizabeth in 1600 (EHU, 105).

[27] In the same mood he suggests that the tales about the miracles attributed to Joan of Arc were only frauds with the aim of discouraging the warlike spirit of the invaders: "This is certain, that all these miraculous stories were spread abroad, in order to captivate the vulgar" (H, II, 399).

own, and not necessarily as a member of a larger group or class. But here Hume seems to be lumping together all religious testimony under one class, which as a whole has a very low degree of reliability. We just do not know whether this is a sound thing to do, or even compatible with his initial assumptions in the first part of the argument. Furthermore, Hume's actual procedure with regard to religious testimony for miracles is at odds with a fundamental methodological attitude of "philosophical" or moderate scepticism which Hume formulates, in the *Dialogues Concerning Natural Religion* with distinctive eloquence and force through Cleanthes, and with which Philo, the sceptic in the *Dialogues*, entirely agrees:

> Wherever evidence discovers itself, you adhere to it, notwithstanding your pretended scepticism . . . . *These sceptics, therefore, are obliged, in every question, to consider each particular evidence apart, and proportion their assent to the precise degree of evidence which occurs.* This is their practice in all natural, mathematical, moral, and political science. And why not the same, I ask, in the theological and religious? (DNR, 136–137; italics added).

Moreover, if we were to follow Hume's usual practice (exemplified by his hasty rejection of a considerable number of reports of extraordinary phenomena which later knowledge has shown to have occurred),[28] many presumed laws of nature might have never been falsified by the contrary testimony of "eye-witnesses and historians."[29] George Campbell appears to have been the first to put this objection to Hume in the following *ad hominen* argument:

> Now I insist, that as regards the author's argument, a fact perfectly unusual, or not conformable to our experience, such as for aught we have had access to learn, was never observ'd in any age or country, is as incapable of proof from testimony, as miracles are; that, if this writer would argue consistently, he could never, on his own principles, reject the one and admit the other. Both ought to be rejected, or neither.[30]

---

[28] It is very probable that some of the miracles attributed to Abbé Paris, the Jansenist, and Vespasian, the emperor, did in fact occur. Hume hurriedly dismisses them. See Antony Flew, *Hume's Philosophy of Belief*, pp. 183–186. In contrast to Hume, George Campbell, even though he also rejects the occurrence of those presumed miracles, does it after a thorough and detailed analysis of the documented evidence accessible to him. See George Campbell, *A Dissertation on Miracles*, pp. 200–210 (on Vespasian's miracles), and pp. 225–247 (on Abbé Paris').

[29] I think that Hume himself recognizes, at least implicitly in what follows, that such is one of the most important advantages of the study of history; and it is also a corollary of his conception of history, which has been discussed in chapter 6. Hence for Hume "*history* is not only a valuable part of knowledge, but opens the door to many other parts, and *affords materials to most of the sciences*" (E, "Of the Study of History", 566; italics added).

[30] George Campbell, *A Dissertation on Miracles*, p. 51

Campbell even employs Hume's distinction between the two senses of experience: our own, or direct sense experience, and human experience in general, which we mostly appropriate through the testimony of other persons. Similarly Campbell distinguishes the conclusions about a particular event deduced from generalizations based on a uniform experience, from those which are grounded on a trustworthy testimony. The assertions of the second class are founded on a "personal" experience; those of the first type, on a experience which is "derived."[31] Experience of the second class is not, according to Campbell, necessarily opposed to miracles, since it provides us with reports about them as well as with accounts of uniformities within the natural course of events.[32] In a crucial aspect, that is to say, with regard to the evidence which it provides about the occurrence (especially in the past) of particular facts, experience which is based on testimony even vastly exceeds those inductive generalizations which are founded on past experience: "A general conclusion from experience is in comparison but presumptive and indirect; a sufficient testimony for a particular fact is positive and direct evidence."[33]

Campbell was likely right when he pointed out that Hume's offhand rejection of biblical tales about miracles typifies a disposition that is alien to the true philosophical spirit; this habitual propensity, a sign and product of "laziness" according to Campbell, is the ancestor of excessive credulity as well as of excessive incredulity, which "always inclines us to admit or to reject in the *gross*, without entering on the irksome task of considering things in *detail*."[34]

But leaving aside the question of the reasonableness or non-reasonableness that pertains to such an attitude, it must be emphasized, against Campbell, that Hume's summary and expeditious rejection of religious testimony about miracles is not the offspring of a peculiar sort of historiographical indolence; nor should it be necessarily or exclusively ascribed to his personal antipathy to popular religion. It is rather the result of Hume's deep conviction about the absolute uniformity of nature with which the occurrence of miracles, as true exceptions to natural laws, would clash. These laws, Hume believed, are universal and necessary. I said that he *believed* them to be thus, because in so far as we are dealing with questions of fact, it is not possible to demonstrate, strictly speaking, that these laws must have such a character. In other words, the belief that all events must be caused and that they must be

---

[31] Ibid. pp. 30–37. Campbell acknowledges, in pp. 30–31 of his *Dissertation,* that in making such a distinction he is following the "pious Bishop of Durham," Joseph Butler, *The Analogy of Religion,* Part 2, ch. 2, sect. 3.

[32] Hume seems to admit the same thing as Campbell with respect to testimony, or experience in the second sense. For on the one hand, Hume asserts that "such events, as bear little analogy to the common course of nature, are also readily confessed to be known only by experience" (EHU, Sect. IV, I, 28), and on the other, that "all the laws of nature, and all the operations of bodies without exception, are known only by experience" (EHU, Sect. IV, I, 29).

[33] George Campbell, *A Dissertation on Miracles*, p. 46.

[34] Ibid., p. 149.

inexorably connected with their causes is beyond the possibility of a purely logical proof. The next passage very aptly illustrates this point:

> While we cannot give a satisfactory reason, why we believe, after a thousand ex-
> periments, that a stone will fall, or fire burn; can we ever satisfy ourselves con-
> cerning any determination, which we may form, with regard to the origin of
> worlds, and the situation of nature, from, and to eternity? (EHU, 162).

As to universality, under Hume's conception of causality we can only say that a law of nature is but a compendium of propositions about particular past observations; but however large that collection, they continue to be a set of particular propositions, devoid of strict universality. As Flew has put it, "statements of lawful connection are reduced to merely numerical universal conjunction."[35] And as to necessity, Hume repeats in this section his fundamental position that "no objects have any discoverable connexion together" (EHU, 111); in other words, that no events logically imply either their causes or their effects.

On the whole, it appears that under these presuppositions Hume cannot deny in principle that miracles may occur as exceptions to these laws.[36] But on the other hand, it seems also true that Hume did not seriously contemplate this possibility (and in practice denied it, although not in theory) because he still continued to share the rationalistic faith in universal determinism. Nature is completely regular, irregularities are seeming irregularities, not real; that is, they are due to the operation of other causes, unknown to us yet:

> It is true, when any cause fails of producing its usual effect, philosophers
> ascribe not this to any irregularity in nature; but suppose, that some secret
> causes, in the particular structure of parts, have prevented the operation (EHU,
> 58).

> From the observation of several parallel instances, philosophers form a maxim,
> that the connexion between all causes and effects is equally necessary, and that
> its seeming uncertainty in some instances proceeds from the secret opposition of
> contrary causes (EHU, 87).

---

[35] Anthony Flew, *Hume's Philosophy of Belief*, p. 204.

[36] See, for instance, Anthony Flew: "But if that were indeed all that a law of nature asserted then it would give no ground at all for saying that the occurrence of an exception to such a law is physically impossible" (*Hume's Philosophy of Belief*, p. 204). C. D. Broad says: "we have no right to say off-hand with Hume that no possible evidence could make it reasonable to suppose that a miraculous exception to some law of nature had taken place" ("Hume's Theory of the Credibility of Miracles," 94). The difference between Broad and Flew is that the latter believes that Hume's law of nature could be reformulated in such a way as to exclude in principle the possibility of miraculous events. I do not know whether this is really feasible under any theory.

It is noteworthy that the postulate of the uniformity of nature is not for Hume the result of a metaphysical deduction, nor even a dogma; it is a maxim, a general rule of procedure for actually determining cause-effect relationships;[37] it is, generally speaking, a kind of an *implicite Faith,*[38] which because it is rooted in the constitution of our human nature, operates inevitably, "by an absolute and uncontrollable necessity,"[39] and hence cannot be overthrown by any doubts. Still, it is also true that in the *Treatise,* although not in the *Enquiry,* Hume's scepticism engulfed the rules by which to judge of causes and effects, and even eroded the trustworthiness of this fundamental belief:

> [T]he sceptics may here have the pleasure of observing a new and signal contradiction in our reason . . . . The following of general rules is a very unphilosophical species of probability; and yet it is only by following them that we can correct this, and all other unphilosophical probabilities (THN, I, 150).

In other words, the general rule that lead us to trust only in regular connections arises out of the same propensity of human nature that gives rise to other general rules, like prejudices, which we never ought to trust. Our preference for regularity may indeed be really inevitable, but can it be rationally justified?

In spite of those sceptical objections, perhaps a scientist cannot seriously contemplate the occurrence of a genuine exception to the laws of nature; when confronted with startling new phenomena, she must look for their natural causes. He must either discard or amend the law. After all, are we not too fully aware of our ignorance of nature to declare a fact not yet explained to be totally inexplicable? This often reiterated observation may be true after all, and it may also capture an essential trait of actual scientific research. But this is one thing, and it is quite another to transform such a methodological requisite of scientific procedure into a precondition for actuality, that is, into a sort of ontological postulate. Only thus can the possibility of miraculous events be denied. At the very least, it is doubtful that Hume had done this in the section on miracles; I think that substantive reasons have been presented that make it clear that he could not do it. In any case, his other

---

[37] See THN, I Part II, Sect. XV, "Rules by which to judge of causes and effects," especially rules 4, 5, 6, and 7. The difficult question is: can these rules be derived as logical consequences of his analysis of causality in terms of "constant conjunction"? Authors such as Nicholas Capaldi, in *David Hume, The Newtonian Philosopher,* pp. 49–70, 95–129, and J. L. Mackie, in *The Cement of the Universe* (Oxford: Clarendon Press, 1974), pp. 1–58, give an emphatic yes to it. These are ingenious attempts to show the intelligibility and essential soundness of Hume's theory about causality, and defend it against the serious objections that John Passmore had posed much earlier with clarity and conciseness in *Hume's Intentions,* pp. 42–64. More recently, R. Harré and E. H. Madden, in *Causal Powers* (Totowa, New York: Roman & Littlefield, 1975, pp. 1–69), have developed in a more detailed fashion an outlook akin to Passmore's.

[38] *A Letter from a Gentleman to his Friend in Edinburgh* (1745), p. 21.

[39] THN, I, Part IV, Sect. I, 183.

contention, namely, that testimony for miracles cannot by itself legitimate the claims to truth of any historical religion, seems very sound.

What could be more plausibly objected against Hume's general outlook (and this has been the most usual objection that since the eighteenth century has been leveled against it) is that it segregates miracles from the religious experience within which they can only occur. For only a person who is, as it were, open to the supernatural can discover in miracles (be these extraordinary or perfectly ordinary facts) signs of the supernatural. The Gospel passage about the healing of Bartimaeus, the blind man, pointedly illustrates this other view of miracles:

> Thou son of David, have mercy on me. And Jesus stood still, and commanded him to be called. And they call the blind man, saying unto him, Be of good comfort, rise; he calleth thee. And he, casting away his garment, rose and came to Jesus. And Jesus answered and said unto him, What wilt thou that I should do unto thee? The blind man said unto him, Lord, that I might receive my sight. And Jesus said unto him, Go thy way; thy faith hath made thee whole. And immediately he received his sight, and followed Jesus in the way (Mark, 10:48–52).

According to this conception which Hume presumably would have ignored, a miracle is not so much a guarantee of the divine credentials of the person who works it and thereby a sort of porch towards faith for the person who witness it, but rather one of the fruits of faith, namely, an event that cannot happen and hence cannot be attested without the belief in the divinity of its cause.

The preceding criticism of Hume's treatment of miracles has been expressed in an immense variety of forms.[40] Yet, however reiterated, it is simply misplaced, for

---

[40] With some frequency Hume is charged with a religious shortsightedness which would itself be a consequence of his presumed adherence to a kind of metaphysical imperialism. The latter would presuppose that there is only one way of truly referring to, and interpreting the world: i.e., that of positive or empirical science. According to such a critique, the question of miracles cannot be properly dealt with without recognizing that there are, either two different ways by which the meaning of reality comes to be constituted for the human subject, or two types of languages that are different in so far as they disclose the conceptual structure of two heterogeneous life forms, the scientific and the religious, both of which are legitimate ways of seeing and describing the world, and valid within their own spheres, although incommensurable between themselves. Thus Richard Swinburne typically says in *The Concept of Miracle*, p. 71:

> With one *Weltanschauung* ('world view') one rightly does not ask much in the way of detailed historical evidence for a miracle since miracles are the kind of events which one expects to occur in many or certain specific situations. . . . With another *Weltanschauung* one rightly asks for a large amount of historical evidence, because of one's general conviction that the world is a certain sort of world, a world without a god and so a world in which miracles do not happen.

Many of these contemporary defenses of faith seem to be new versions, dressed up in analytical or phenomenological garb, of the old doctrine – which was probably falsely attributed to the medieval Islamic philosopher and theologian, Averroës – of "double truth," that radically opposes faith and reason, without relinquishing the claims to truth made on behalf of both. This would not apply, though, to

its proponents quite simply assume that Hume intends to demonstrate the incoherence of the concept of miracle, while at the same time they disregard in a very convenient fashion the conclusion of this section, where Hume explicitly grants what they reproach to him. His contention is that miracles are not independent evidence in favor of the truth of any faith, but on the contrary, that belief in miracles is itself an ingredient of faith.

> I am the better pleased with the method of reasoning here delivered, as I think it may serve to confound those dangerous friends or disguised enemies to the *Christian Religion*, who have undertaken to defend it by the principles of human reason. Our most holy religion is founded on *Faith*, not on reason (EHU, 130).

In conclusion, Hume's conception of miracles seems to be more subtle than those we have just examined. And with regards to their relationship with faith, it is also similar in substance to Locke's, whom Hume does not mention in Section X. This is what I will immediately attempt to show.

11.4 LOCKE'S POSITION ON THE EVIDENTIAL VALUE OF MIRACLES AND ITS AFFINITY WITH HUME'S

It is almost commonplace to reduce Locke's contribution to the early modern debate about miracles to a single point, to wit, that miracles, taken in isolation, offer insufficient evidence to command assent from reasonable and impartial persons. And since most proponents of the argument from miracles readily conceded this, Locke's caveat would have been a very minor and perhaps dispensable addition to that discussion. What gets lost in this usual way of portraying the *Discourse of Miracles* is much of the subtlety of Locke's approach. He is not simply repeating the truism that miracles in isolation are not a complete ground for assent, but rather explicating the concrete conditions that would make it possible to isolate or identify particular and extraordinary events as miracles, which, as such, then may provide some evidence for the truth of a particular religious revelation. If viewed from this perspective, then one can say that Locke's account is akin to Hume's.

On the one hand, Locke, like Hume, does not question the possibility of miraculous occurrences, and admits them as violations of natural laws; accordingly he defines a miracle as "a sensible operation, which, being above the comprehension of the spectator, and in his opinion contrary to the established course of nature, is taken by him to be divine."[41] But on the other hand, the reality of a miracle is, as this passage seems to suggest, similar to the type of reality that Locke ascribes to sensible qualities such as color, taste, odor, etc. Locke calls them secondary quali-

---

Swinburne, for he believes he has given good reasons for choosing one *Weltanschauung* over the other.

[41] John Locke, *A Discourse of Miracles*, p. 256.

ties, for he supposes that they do not exist in themselves, or in the object, as do primary qualities (extension, figure, bulk, and the like), but only in relation to a percipient subject.[42] Similarly one could say that there are not miracles in themselves, or miracles absolutely speaking; they exist only in relation to the knowledge and expectations that a given spectator has about what nature can do and cannot do.

If something is actually a violation of a natural law, then it will be taken as a divine intervention. But since opinions with respect to the former are most diverse, in other words, since what is within or beyond the powers of nature is always established from our presumed knowledge of those laws, then a certain event could be a miracle for a person but not for another. In addition, one could never exclude the possibility of finding an spectator for whom no fact whatsoever would ever count as a miracle. Locke himself admits these apparently strange consequences that follow from his relative conception of miracles, but he adds on the one hand, that they do not invalidate his definition of miracle, and on the other, that they can be avoided under no conceivable definition.[43] At any rate, what still holds true for the definitions of miracle offered by Locke and Hume is: first, that miracles must be taken as events contrary to the usual course of nature (this would hold as their necessary condition),[44] and second, that such a violation is brought about by God or an agent who works on his name or with his acquiescence.

In short, miracles have to be occurrences outside of the ordinary so that they may become precipitant motives or effective inducements of the conviction that these events are real sensible signs or manifestations of a divine power. However, it is evident that such a conviction presupposes some kind of previous belief in God and his relation with nature; and this belief cannot be gathered out of the miraculous event itself, because such an occurrence, in effect, presents itself as, or is adduced to be, a certification of the divine credentials of the person who brings it about. This is made plainly evident by Locke's rule for determining, among contending "extraordinary operations" brought about by different miracle-workers, which is the actual miracle that confirms the divine inspiration of its worker. The miraculous occurrence is none other but the prodigy which exhibits "the marks of a greater power than appears in opposition to it."[45] But why should we confidently rely on such a practical criterion, even when it is clear that we can never fathom the limits of the force of finite beings, nor the extent of the Creator's power? Simply because we antecedently know that God exists, and is omnipotent: "What is the uttermost power of natural agents or created beings, men of the greatest reach cannot discover; but that it is not equal to God's omnipotency, is obvious to every one's

---

[42] See John Locke, *An Essay Concerning Human Understanding*, I, Book II, ch. 8, pp. 168–177. In the case of the goodness and beauty, or the moral and aesthetic qualities, Hume expressly affirms that their reality is akin to that of secondary qualities; see E, "The Sceptic," 163–165.

[43] John Locke, *A Discourse of Miracles*, pp. 256–257.

[44] Ibid., p. 264, Locke says that miracles are "*at least* operations contrary to the fixed and established laws of nature" (italics added).

[45] Ibid., p. 259

understanding; so that the superior power is an easy as well as sure guide to divine revelation, attested by miracles, where they are brought as credentials to an embassy from God."[46] Yet that God is omnipotent, we know by Scripture, for reason can prove only the existence of "a most powerful being."[47]

Once something counts as a miracle, then it is unreasonable, according to Locke, to mistrust the divine mission of the miracle-worker and the truth of the doctrine which the miracle allegedly confirms: "it is plain, that where the miracle is admitted, the doctrine cannot be rejected; it comes with the assurance of a divine attestation to him that allows the miracle, and he cannot question its truth."[48] Still, it is also plain for Locke that no one can proclaim this truth without faith:

> For example, Jesus of Nazareth professes himself sent from God: he with a word calms a tempest at sea. This one looks on as a miracle, and consequently cannot but receive his doctrine. Another thinks this might be the effect of chance, or skill in the weather, and no miracle, and so he stands out; but afterwards seeing him walk on the sea, owns that for a miracle, and believes: which yet upon another has not that force, who suspects it may possibly be done by the assistance of a spirit.[49]

All in all, it seems to me that Hume's position is – even though I do not claim any direct influence – essentially the same as that of his eminent empiricist predecessor, Locke.[50]

11.5 HUME'S CONCLUSION AND
THE RELATION OF SECT. X TO SECT. XI OF THE ENQUIRY

The basic affinity between the theories of Locke and Hume is, I think, also emphasized (of course, if we for the moment overlook the dominant irony and mockery of the passage) by the famous or notorious conclusion of Section X, "Of Miracles":

> So that, upon the whole, we may conclude, that the *Christian Religion* not only was at first attended with miracles, but even at this day cannot be believed by any reasonable person without one. Mere reason is insufficient to convince us of its veracity: And whoever is moved by *Faith* to assent to it, is conscious of a continued miracle in his own person, which subverts all the principles of

---

[46] Ibid., 261; see also p. 262.

[47] *An Essay Concerning Human Understanding*, II, Book IV, ch. 10, p. 308.

[48] *A Discourse of Miracles*, p. 259.

[49] Ibid.

[50] R. M. Burns persuasively argues for such an influence of Locke on Hume. See *The Great Debate on Miracles: From Joseph Glanvill to David Hume*, ch. 3, especially pp. 59-64. For his views on Hume's "Of Miracles," and his critique of Hume's arguments see chs. 6, 7 and 8.

his understanding, and gives him a determination to believe what is most contrary to custom and experience (EHU, 130)

The sharp irony and sarcasm directed in this passage against the worth of faith itself is understandable; Hume had probably in mind, as Norman Kemp Smith suggests, "the teaching of the Reformed Churches, that Faith . . . is impossible save with the aid of a divinely conferred Grace, and that Faith is then operated in a sheerly miraculous manner."[51] However, by treating Faith with such an apparent contempt, Hume is not simply dismissing the possibility that it may be true after all, but joyously playing the role of the sceptic, that is, really turning the tables on the Calvinistic tradition in which he was brought up. From the time of Calvin on to his own day, Presbyterian divines had dispensed a steady and robust regiment of sardonic wit and ridicule on the traditional Catholic recourse to miracles to authenticate and strengthen that faith. Thus Calvin characteristically thunders against Catholic priests:

But compared to us they have a strange power: even to this day they can confirm their faith by continual miracles! Instead they allege miracles which can disturb a mind otherwise at rest – they are so foolish and ridiculous, so vain and false![52]

In the same letter in which he reacts to Campbell's critique, Hume slyly echoes Calvin's sarcasm:

I wonder the author [Campbell] does not perceive the reason why Mr John Knox and Mr Alexander Henderson did not work as many miracles as their brethren in other churches. Miracle-working was a Popish trick, and discarded with the other parts of that religion (L, I, 350).

In brief, if one asserts that a faith, like the Roman Catholic, which relies on miracles to justify its truth, is no more than delusion and enthusiasm, then one should also say that a miraculously engendered and sustained faith, like the Calvinist, is, for that matter, no less so. In addition, Hume is emphasizing in that conclusion, once again, that the conflicting and doubtful evidence for miracles does not permit the sensible person, or "the wise," who proportions his or her belief to the evidence, to bestow a rational assent upon them; "the vulgar" will not cease to believe in miracles anyhow.

Irony allowed for, the main point is transparent enough: Without faith not even miracles can be acknowledged and attested, and this is why the appeal to testimony about miracles provides no rational, independent inducement to religious belief. In

---

[51] Hume's *Dialogues Concerning Natural Religion*, Introduction, p. 47.

[52] John Calvin, *Institutes of the Christian Religion*, I, Prefatory Address to the King Francis I of France, p. 16.

that sense too, Hume's discussion of miracles confirms a more general proposition: faith is the only foundation for a popular system of religion.

But if the existence of God could be proved empirically, could we not then bring God forward to prove the occurrence of miracles? Not at all, according to Hume. Miracles are rather arguments against the existence of God: "And such events, as, with good reasoners, are the chief difficulties in admitting a supreme intelligence, are with him [the vulgar] the sole arguments for it" (NHR, 41–42). If we can only infer the existence of God from our experience of order in the universe, we cannot look for God in the fringes of order, that is to say, we cannot at the same time infer the existence and attributes of God from the alterations or ruptures to the natural order of events. In summary, these two apologetic strategies cancel each other out:

> Though the Being to whom the miracle is ascribed, be, in this case, Almighty, it does not, upon that account, become a whit more probable; since it is impossible for us to know the attributes or actions of such a Being, otherwise than from the experience which we have of his productions, in the usual course of nature (EHU, 129).[53]

For this reason one cannot disconnect Section X, "Of Miracles," from the next section, "Of a Particular Providence and a Future State," where Hume analyzes the "chief or sole argument for a divine existence," which is derived from the order of nature. The God of infinite perfection, the one that the religious person can and must always worship, can be proved by no priori reasoning, like the ontological argument. The friendly and close God, whom the believer can trust to occasionally intervene to alleviate his or her sufferings, and sometimes to mortify his or her enemies, cannot be proved by testimony favorable to miracles. In Section XI, Hume, as it were, concludes his act. Here – and in a much more detailed manner in the *Dialogues Concerning Natural Religion* – he will endeavor to show that the argument founded on genuine and real evidence, that is, founded on the uniformity of nature (and for that matter, the only rational foundation of religion), cannot demonstrate the existence of the God of revelation, that is of the God who is worshipped in historical religion, and who works miracles.

---

[53] The negative implications that Hume's terse declaration has for rational theology are more obvious if one reads this passage against the background of Locke's preceding assertions about the relationship between miracles and God's omnipotence.

CHAPTER 12

The Uncertain Path of Empirical Reasoning, Part I: The Unfolding of Hume's Critique of the Argument from Design

12.1 INTRODUCTION

In the previous chapter we have examined, among other matters, Hume's negative opinion about the attitude of common people (*the vulgar*) who appeal to extraordinary experience to justify the truth of their religious beliefs. In the present chapter we shall dwell instead on the philosophical calling, namely, the appeal of the reasonable or sensible person (*the wise*) to ordinary experience. Indeed, the analysis of Hume's critique of the argument from design will be the principal task of Part III of this book. It might appear to be a contradiction in terms, but I shall try to trace a sort of logical history of this critique. Hume's thorough analysis of the argument in the *Dialogues Concerning Natural Religion* is the last stage in the development of a theoretical position that has its roots in the *Treatise of Human Nature*, is succinctly outlined in the *Enquiry Concerning Human Understanding* (especially in Section XI), obliquely suggested but cautiously toned down in the *Natural History of Religion*, and finally unfolded in all its ramifications in the *Dialogues*. Yet the purpose of this journey is not only to clarify Hume's diagnosis of the logical fitness of this particular argument, but to determine what his final position concerning the supposed rational foundation of religion really is. In the next section we shall deal with the first inklings of the critique in the *Treatise*.

12.2 THE CRITIQUE IN A TREATISE OF HUMAN NATURE

The validity of the argument from design appears to be explicitly held in this work:

> The order of the universe proves an omnipotent mind; that is, a mind whose will is *constantly attended* with the obedience of every creature and being. Nothing more is requisite to give a foundation to all the articles of religion; nor is it necessary we should form a distinct idea of the force and energy of the Supreme Being (THN, Appendix, 633).

235

But the way in which this argument is constructed may lead us to think that it is true, simply because the argument is tautological.[1] Our suspicion may grow stronger, since the above argument is expressed in strikingly similar terms to an argument of Cartesian origin that Hume, by unmasking its tautological character, effectively disposed of. This argument intended to demonstrate that only in the case of God we do have a clear and distinct idea of power:

> As to what may be said, that the connexion betwixt the idea of an infinitely powerful Being and that of any effect, which he wills, is necessary and unavoidable; I answer, that we have no idea of a Being endowed with any power, much less of one endowed with infinite power. But if we will change expressions, we can only define power by connexion; and then in saying that the idea of an infinitely powerful Being is connected with that of every effect which he wills, we really do no more than assert, that a Being, whose volition is connected with every effect, is connected with every effect; which is an identical proposition, and gives us no insight into the nature of this power or connexion (THN, 248–249).

These two arguments are not really identical. In the second one Hume is repeating his charge against those philosophers who disguise their profound ignorance about the nature of causation by defining it in terms of other expressions which are only synonymous: "the terms of *agency, power, force, energy, necessity, connexion,* and *productive* quality are all nearly synonymous; and therefore 'tis an absurdity to employ any of them in defining the rest" (THN, 157; c.f., 82, 90, 91). Probably what Hume is saying here is that in the case of God, as in the case of any other cause, efficacy or power cannot be defined by connection; but he is not saying that the Deity lacks such a power, or that it is improper to consider the Divine Cause as an intelligent will and the Universe as the effect of such a will. What he certainly denies is that in the case of the Deity, as with every other being, we have a distinct idea of causal efficacy in the sense of a metaphysical necessity, that is, a complete knowledge of those ultimate qualities by which a cause must necessarily produce its effects. Since "the power by which one object produces another is not discoverable from their idea" (THN, 69), it is inevitable to conclude "that there is no such thing in the universe as a cause or productive principle, not even in the deity himself" (THN, 248).[2]

We are thus led to the following dilemma: Either nothing can be the cause of any other thing unless the idea of the one logically implies that of the other, or else constant conjunction between these things is a sufficient condition for declaring them to be causally connected (THN, 248). Under the first supposition, nothing,

---

[1] See Fargang Zabeeh, *Hume: Precursor of Modern Empiricism*, p. 52.

[2] In chapter 5 we have already discussed Hume's account of the idea of "necessary connexion," which is presumably essential to the causal relationship, and its bearing on the account about the genesis of the idea of the divine.

"not even the Deity," can be a cause. Yet Hume does not deny that God could be conceived as a cause in the second sense. It is noteworthy that in the passage of the Appendix he refers to God as a mind whose will is *constantly attended* with the obedience of every creature or being. He does not say "constantly connected," which would certainly be circular, but "constantly attended." It appears that Hume is attempting here to understand the relation between God and the world in terms of his own conception of causality as "constant conjunction." On the whole, the two arguments are not – it seems to me – logically equivalent.

External evidence against such an identification is the fact that Hume, who delivers the clearest and more serious objections to the argument from design in the first *Enquiry* and the *Dialogues*, did not there dwell upon its tautological character. This suggests that Hume very early saw that the argument, as an argument from experience, could be formulated in a manner not open to the critique of vacuity, making it necessary to bestow upon it a closer and more detailed examination. Furthermore, to say that in the *Treatise* Hume took the argument from design to be tautological would be incompatible with his express acceptance of the same argument in *A Letter from a Gentleman to his Friend in Edinburgh*, a pamphlet he hastily wrote to defend his candidacy to the Chair of Moral Philosophy at Edinburgh University against those who publicly had attempted to extract from the *Treatise* consequences allegedly impious and hostile to religion. There he says:

> Wherever I see Order, I infer from Experience that there, there hath been Design and Contrivance. And the same Principle which leads me into this Inference, when I contemplate a Building, regular and beautiful in its whole Frame and Structure; the same Principle obliges me to infer an infinitely perfect Architect, from the infinite Art and Contrivance which is display'd in the whole Fabrick of the Universe (*Letter*, pp. 25-26).

This formulation is highly important, because Hume makes almost an exactly similar version the direct target of his criticism in Section XI of the first *Enquiry*. God is not an immediate object of experience. Thus he has to be inferred solely through his effect: the whole universe. Is this a valid or even a possible inference? However, he did not question in the *Treatise* the logical validity of the argument from design as an inference from analogy. He suggests rather the contrary: that the argument is compatible with his account of causality. Perhaps Hume was not fully aware of the great difficulties that such reconciling project implied; perhaps he knew about these and did not see fit to publish them at the time.[3]

---

[3] This seems more probable; in 1737, writing to Henry Home, he said: "Having a frankt letter, I was resolved to make use of it; and accordingly inclose some *Reasonings concerning Miracles,* which I once thought of publishing with the rest, but which I am afraid will give too much offence, even as the world is disposed at present. . . . I am at present castrating my work, that is, cutting off its nobler parts; that is, endeavouring it shall give as little offence as possible . . . This is a piece of cowardice, for which I blame myself, though I believe none of my friends will blame me" (L, I, 24–25).

Hume's definition of causality as a philosophical relation (which is the one that ought to guide us in all reasoning concerning matters of fact) implies the fulfillment of a set of conditions which puts in serious jeopardy the possibility of predicating a causal relationship in the case of God and the world.

> We may define a CAUSE to be "An object precedent and contiguous to one another, and where all the objects resembling the former are plac'd in like relations of precedency and contiguity to those objects, that resemble the latter" (THN, 170, 172)

The greatest difficulty is not so much what sense to make out of the relations of "precedency" and "contiguity" in the case of God and the Universe. An analogical twist may perhaps give rise to an interpretation which might dissolve such problems. The telling point is the generality or universality which inherently pertains to the relation of cause and effect. It holds not between particular objects as such, but rather between species of objects. And here lies the explanatory gain of the causal inference: the particular object is made intelligible by being subsumed under a universal.[4] The following passage particularly well illustrates this aspect and also the problems which unavoidably beset the argument from design:

> We remember to have had frequent instances of the existence of one species of objects; and also remember, that the individuals of another species of objects have always attended them, and have existed in a regular order of contiguity and succession with regard to them. Thus we remember to have seen that species of object we call *flame*, and to have felt that species of sensation we call *heat*. We likewise call to mind their constant conjunction in all past instances. Without any further ceremony, we call the one *cause*, and the other *effect*, and infer the existence of the one from that of the other (THN, 87).

If we predicate the relation analogically of instances which do not, or cannot, fall under our observation, it is only because we subsume those instances under known species of objects. But in the case of God as cause and the universe as effect, those conditions which would make the predication meaningful seem to be absent, because God and the world are such exceptional objects. In the *Treatise* Hume had already said that analogy is a species of probable reasoning whose certainty proportionally decreases with the diminishing of the resemblance between the cases compared:

> Without some degree of resemblance, as well as union, 'tis impossible there can be any reasoning [from causes or effects]: but as this resemblance admits of

---

[4] Catherine S. Frazer gives a good and concise assessment of the importance of this feature of Hume's account of empirical inferences in "Hume's Criticism and Defense of Analogical Argument," *Journal of History of Philosophy* 8 (1970): 173–179.

many different degrees, the reasoning becomes proportionally more or less firm and certain (THN, I, 142).

It is precisely from this angle that Hume will attack in the *Enquiry* the logical coherence of the argument from design.

But before passing on to the *Enquiry*, it is perhaps important to point out another feature connected with the formulation of the argument in the *Treatise*, which remained unchanged throughout Hume's critique. He seems to suggest that, even if the argument were valid, we should not thereby expect to have acquired "a distinct idea of the Supreme Being" (THN, Appendix, 633). This is a consequence of Hume's Newtonian approach. The human mind can never legitimately claim to know ultimate causes; we must simply reject hypotheses about occult entities and qualities; at best we must look for the most universal principles of explanation that still can be subjected to some empirical test. (THN, xxi–xxii; EHU, 12–13). But these principles or laws only describe the most general sequences or conjunctions between phenomena; they do not disclose their ultimate causes (if there are such), that is, those which would explain why things must necessarily behave the way they do. And this holds true for matter as well as for mind. Concerning the former he says: "the ultimate force and efficacy of nature is perfectly unknown to us, and . . . 'tis in vain we search for it in all the known qualities of matter" (THN, I, 159). It is the same with mind: "as to those impressions, which arise from the senses, their ultimate cause is, in my opinion, perfectly inexplicable by human reason" (THN, I, 84). If we cannot penetrate the essence of particular objects (THN, I, 84), much less can we expect the essence of the Divine Being to be disclosed to us. Yet this is an orthodox conclusion, one to which St. Thomas Aquinas, for instance, might have given his approval. The problem to which Hume directs his attention is a different one: how much, based on our knowledge of the world, are we justified in asserting about its author?

12.3 THE CRITIQUE IN AN ENQUIRY CONCERNING HUMAN UNDERSTANDING

Here Hume offers in a nutshell, but only by way of suggestion, the main outline of the criticism of the argument from design which he will fully develop later in the *Dialogues Concerning Natural Religion*. This criticism – as we have tried to show in the preceding section – was implied by the conception of causality expounded in the *Treatise*. In the earlier work, Hume's emphasis on the requisite of constant conjunction between things causally related may naturally suggest that he was having in mind the cosmological, rather than the traditional teleological argument. And this is in fact the case, although he is from the outset criticizing the design argument. For the latter is a teleological proof in the sense that its point of departure is the observation of means to ends relationships especially in the parts of natural organisms, such as plants and animals. But it is cosmological, rather than teleological, in the structure of its reasoning, for its starts from our observation of certain features of the universe in order to infer the existence and nature of God, i.e. that first cause capable of producing those sensible effects. As an empirical hypothesis to account for the actual order of the natural world, the design argument dispenses with final causes; it is rather an inference to God as the efficient cause of the intelligible structure of the universe.

Most probably, the argument from design is presented in this cosmological mold, as a reasoning from efficient causality, in order to thwart the principal criticism deployed by many different modern philosophers against the common teleological proofs. Descartes is a typical case in point. In the *Reply to Fifth Objections* made to the *Meditations*, which were posed by Pierre Gassendi, he forcefully rejects the teleological argument which the latter proposes to him as a viable alternative to his two cosmological proofs of the *Third Meditation* :

> The arguments you adduce on behalf of final causality are to be referred to the efficient cause; thus it is open to us, from beholding the uses of the various parts of plants and animals to regard with admiration the God who brings these into existence, and from a survey of these works to learn to know and glorify the Workman [*opificem, ouvrier*],[5] but that does not imply that we can divine the purpose for which He made each thing.[6]

It should come as no surprise then that Hume vaguely echoed Descartes' criticism in the *Enquiry* and the *Dialogues*. It is more noteworthy that in the *Enquiry* he criticizes a version of the argument from the design that almost paraphrases Descartes' own in the above passage. And finally, it is also somewhat ironical that his main argument pits Descartes against Descartes, since he will employ the well-known Cartesian maxim of efficient causality against a design argument in which God emerges as the first efficient cause ("workman") of some of the sensible things which exhibit teleological relationships.

In the *Enquiry* Hume seriously questioned for the first time the validity of the argument. Can "the chief or sole argument for a divine existence" (EHU, 135) from the observed order and beauty in nature establish that there is "project and forethought in the workman?" (EHU, 136). Can experience offer to us sufficient grounds for drawing, by way of analogy, any conclusions concerning completely unique objects such as God and the universe? In brief, is the argument from design

---

[5] I have modified the translation by Haldane and Ross here, were it reads "the Author of these works" instead of "Workman". On the one hand, even though the Latin word *"opificem"* permits such a translation, the fact that Descartes is demanding that we should consider God as an efficient – not a final – cause, makes that choice of words somewhat inappropriate. On the other hand, there is no similar ambiguity in the French translation of the *Objections and Replies* by Claude Clerselier, which was approved by Descartes himself; for there is no doubt that a workman, (*ouvrier*) acts at any rate as an efficient cause: "il est juste d'admirer la main de Dieu qui les a faites, et de connaître et glorifier l'ouvrier par la inspection de ses ouvrages, mais non pas de deviner pour quelle fin il a créé toutes choses" [*Méditations Métaphysiques*, présentés par Florence Khodoss, Cinquième édition (Paris: Presses Universitaires de France, 1968), p. 247].

[6] *Reply to Fifth Objections*, HR, II, 223; AT, VII, 374–375.

a genuinely cogent argument from analogy? To all of this Hume suggests a negative answer.

Hume, however, did not make the logical cogency of the argument the central target for his criticism in the *Enquiry*. He chose instead to show that, even if the validity of the argument were not questioned, that is, even if it is allowed that the argument proves the existence of an intelligent author of the Universe, it is still impossible to validly infer from it some of the dearest conclusions of traditional religious thought, such as the immortality of the soul and an ultra-mundane eschatology corresponding to that future state. It is certainly possible that God may exercise a perfect moral government over the world, and that he will also punish those who have contravened his commandments and reward those who have obeyed them. However those practical consequences cannot be drawn from the "religious hypothesis," or the design argument.

Hume substantiates these objections in Section XI, "Of a Particular Providence and of a Future State." This section is conducted in dialogue form between Hume and a friend who assumes the task of defending Epicurus against the accusation that his atheistic doctrines have dangerous moral consequences for society. Hume's friend, taking the role of Epicurus, argues that it is instead in the best interests of the State to permit total freedom of philosophical discussion, and that speculative opinions are in no way dangerous, since anyhow they have no practical consequences. And this holds true even for the extreme case of Epicurus, who supposedly denies "a divine existence, and consequently a providence and a future state" (EHU, 133).

We ought to stress that "Epicurus" does not question the validity of the argument; he rather analyzes its form in order to clarify the nature of its conclusion and of the other consequences which can be drawn from it. The argument from a particular effect, the universe, infers a cause, God, sufficient to produce it. The present case is quite exceptional, since the cause is known solely through its effect; yet, the same rule that holds with respect to any other causal inference must also apply here – we should never attribute to the cause any qualities in excess of those which are strictly requisite to produce the effect. "A body of ten ounces raised in any scale may serve as a proof, that the counter-balancing weight exceeds ten ounces but it can never afford a reason that it exceeds a hundred" (EHU, 136). Since the cause must be proportioned to the effect, we cannot infer from the cause other effects, beyond those by which alone it is known to us. Had we seen just one of Zeuxis' pictures, we could not infer that he was a sculptor and an architect. It is likewise with the divine architect, whom we know through one single work (EHU, 136).

In brief, even if the inference that God is the author of the universe were valid, we could only ascribe those qualities to Him which at present we observe in his product, that is, that he possesses that precise degree of power, intelligence and benevolence, which appear in his workmanship, but no more. We cannot validly infer that he possesses higher qualities or that he will produce further and more perfect effects, unless "we call in the assistance of exaggeration and flattery to supply the defects of argument and reasoning" (EHU, 127).

But this is precisely what the adherents of the argument from design do. They, as it were, "mount up from the universe, the effect, to Jupiter, the cause; and then descend downwards, to infer any new effect from that cause; as if the present effects alone were not entirely worthy of the glorious attributes, which we ascribe to that deity" (EHU, 137). They view this world as a "porch" or "prologue" to another where He shall produce something greater and more perfect than "the present scene of things which is so full of ill and disorder" (EHU, 137). But all these supposed corollaries of the "religious hypothesis," these presumed "practical consequences of natural theology,"[7] like immortality and eschatology, are arbitrary suppositions only. If we know of the divine cause solely from its effects, then "they must be exactly adjusted to each other; and the one can never refer to anything farther, or be the foundation of any inference and conclusion" (EHU, 137). In other words, the argument from design is completely inane; we can never draw from it any novel inference concerning matters of fact additional to those which could have been drawn from the observation of the usual course of nature. Natural theology has, in short, no practical consequences. From the existence of God, the conclusion of the argument from design, we cannot infer any new principles of conduct and behavior.

> The experienced train of events is the great standard, by which we all regulate our conduct. Nothing else can be appealed to in the field, or in the senate. Nothing else ought ever to be heard of in the school, or in the closet (EHU, 142).

But at this stage of the argumentation, what we ought to note is that Hume's critique of the argument from design rests upon the certainty of the principle that the cause must be proportional to the effect. For Descartes, this principle (stated by him in the language of scholasticism) had intuitive certainty: "it is manifest by the natural light of reason that there must at least be as much reality in the total and efficient cause as in its effects."[8] Hume obviously cannot, and will not, claim this sort of certainty for that principle. On the other hand, that the cause must be proportional to the effect is something which cannot be demonstrated; the contrary proposition is intelligible and implies no contradiction.[9] This is but a corollary of Hume's thesis that one can never demonstrate, without begging the question, that there must be a cause for everything that begins to exist in time; in short, if one cannot prove the necessity of a cause for every event, then *a fortiori*, much less can one prove that a cause must always be proportional to its putative effects. On the other hand, it is not necessary to suppose that Hume ever in fact admitted the unconditional validity of the Cartesian maxim of efficient causality. What Hume is doing here is rather employing this principle in a limited and conditional, or *ad*

---

[7] This was the original title of Section XI.

[8] René Descartes, *Meditations on First Philosophy, Third Meditation*, Adam-Tannery VI, 40; Haldane-Ross, I, 162.

[9] THN, I, Part II, Sect. II, "Why a cause is always necessary," 78–82.

hominen, manner: in other words, as an inference rule whose validity has to be taken for granted, not only by Descartes, but even by the proponents of the design argument, for otherwise this proof would cease to be a genuine instance of the species arguments from analogy.

Despite these difficulties, Hume formulates the principle of efficient causality with a universality that presupposes a degree of regularity and uniformity of experience which his own theory of knowledge may not be able to justify. Hume, however, has to retain this principle, and even with its character of universal law, in order, as it were, to castigate the logical excesses of natural theologians. He might perhaps have said in its defense that this principle is a rule (or "maxim," as he asserts about the principle of the uniformity of nature) for judging of causes and effects. Moreover, Hume might have claimed that the maxim according to which causes must be proportioned to their effects, even if it cannot be demonstrated by experience, is a principle thus far conformable to it. But in my opinion, he would not have judged such a defense as entirely appropriate. On the one hand, the presumed universal validity of the maxim (since it holds for every possible case of causal union) presupposes that the future will be similar to the past, but on the other, one cannot justify the universal validity of the principle by an appeal to past experience without presupposing the same thing, i.e., that the future will be similar to the past. For, in effect, the past can never be a proof for what will happen in the future unless one tacitly presupposes a resemblance between the two. In summary, if the principle of efficient causality were the product of an inductive generalization, then any attempt to justify it empirically would be invariably circular. We again find ourselves before a rule about which Hume might have said that we have an "implicit Faith" backed up by a *fundamentum in re,* which even if it is equivalent to a history of complete uniformity disclosed by past observation, it is not, however, a strict proof of its unexceptionable validity.

But to come back to the argument that Hume voices through "Epicurus," why is it that we cannot, from a mixed and imperfect state of things, infer the existence of an infinitely perfect Creator, who eventually will complete his work, bestowing upon it all the perfection that it lacks at present? This is precisely what we do when, in the presence of a half-finished building, we infer that the building will soon be completed. We can, for instance, if we see upon the seashore the print of one human foot, conclude that a man has passed by, and that he has also left the traces of the other foot, though now effaced (EHU, 142); why can we not conclude that God possesses more goodness, power, and wisdom with which he will complete the half-finished building of the Universe?

The infinite difference between the two subjects forbids us to reason concerning the works of nature in the same manner. In works of human art we can advance from the effect to the cause, and from this in turn make new inferences concerning the changes the effect has undergone and may probably undergo. But this is possible only because we have seen many previous instances of such art; furthermore since we "are otherwise acquainted with the nature of the animal, we can draw a hundred inferences concerning what may be expected from him; and these inferences will be founded in experience and observation" (EHU., 144). That is to say, we have had enough experience of the constant conjunction between two kinds of fact, human activities and its products. Thus when we are before one of those works, it is only custom which leads us to presume that the present one is an effect of the kind of cause which usually accompanies it; in other words, the effect of an intelligent human activity. Furthermore, it is the same habit that makes us anticipate new effects from the inferred cause; for example, not only that such an object is a human product which is unfinished, but also one that, as has been the case in the past, will probably be completed in the future. If we knew man by only one of his products, no new inference whatsoever could be legitimately drawn concerning his further productions. And this is what happens in the case of God.

> The Deity is known to us only by his productions, and is a single being in the universe, not comprehended under any species or genus, from whose experienced attributes or qualities, we can, by analogy, infer any attribute or quality in him (EHU, 144).

God is an unique cause, known to us only through an equally unique effect, the universe; since we lack experience of what other beings like God might otherwise do (there are none; there is but one God), it is not possible to attribute to him anything additional to what he has accomplished thus far in the universe. For that reason the religious hypothesis suffers from an incurable predictive sterility:

> No new fact can ever be inferred from the religious hypothesis; no event foreseen or foretold; no reward or punishment expected or dreaded, beyond what is already known by practice and observation (EHU, 146).

Simply put, the existence of the God of "popular" or historical religion, specifically of the Hebrew-Christian tradition, cannot be established by the argument from design. Here lies the connection between this section and the preceding one on miracles.

Finally Hume, speaking in his own person, formulates an objection that is directed not so much against the practical consequences which are frequently drawn from the argument, but against the validity of its main conclusion, that is, against the possibility of proving the existence of an intelligent author of the universe:

> In a word, I much doubt whether it be possible for a cause to be known only by its effect (as you have all along supposed) or to be of so singular and particular a nature as to have no parallel and no similarity with any other cause or object, that has ever fallen under our observation. It is only when two *species* of objects are found to be constantly conjoined, that we can infer the one from the other; and were an effect presented, which was entirely singular, and could not be comprehended under any known *species*, I do not see, that we could form any conjecture or inference at all concerning its cause (EHU, 148).

These closing observations of the *Enquiry* constitute the starting point of the *Dialogues*. Is the argument from design a genuine reasoning from effects to causes? What is its real import, that is, how much can we really conclude about the cause of the whole from such premises, if anything at all? In a word, Hume draws, for the first time, the negative consequences that his analysis of causality (as we have already seen when dealing with the *Treatise*) have for the argument from design. Hume seems to imply that the argument goes wrong not only because the conclusion that it establishes is less determinate, more ambiguous than it is usually taken to be, but, more importantly, because the case in question is so exceptional that no definite conclusion can really be drawn concerning the cause of the universe. The conditions that could make the argument from design a true specimen of an analogical argument (i.e., constant conjunction and the similarity of those objects to other kinds of objects of which we have experience) are not given in this case.

To try to infer a cause for the universe – a completely singular object which cannot be comprehended under any *known* species – is like trying to determine the cause of a completely new object from the mere inspection of it, without consulting experience. But "there are no objects, which by mere survey, without consulting experience we can determine to be the causes of any other; and no objects, which we can certainly determine in the same manner not to be the causes." (THN, 173).

Likewise in the case of the universe there is no conceivable experience for us to fall back upon. As Philo, the sceptic of the *Dialogues*, says, "to ascertain this reasoning, it were requisite that we had experience of the origin of worlds." (DNR, 149). And before experience, anything may be the cause or effect of any thing. It is only experience and observation that can give more weight to one hypothesis, or to one possibility, over all others. By merely surveying the universe as a unique object we cannot even know if it is really an effect, that is to say, if it is really dependent upon any other object, that is, if a cause for the whole is also necessary.

In short, Hume appears to imply that the argument from design can infer nothing precisely because everything can be inferred from it. Thus the conclusion of this argument is not only useless but uncertain: "It is uncertain because the subject lies entirely beyond the reach of human experience" (EHU, 142).

But in spite of it, how do we explain the striking conviction which the argument nonetheless produces in most people? Hume refers this undeniable effect to the same tendency of sympathetic projection which is, as we have seen, at the root of the genesis of historical religion: "We tacitly consider ourselves as in the place of the Supreme Being" (EHU, 147). It does not matter much that the empirical evidence does not justify the inference to a divine existence, since at the point where experience fails us, imagination takes over, and by an analogical leap supplies us with a "fancied experience." In other words, we suppose that the similarity of the works of nature and the productions of human artifice is sufficiently obvious or well-established so as to enable us to assert that the universe also has an intelligent cause or Creator.

In another section of the *Enquiry* Hume merely suggests the reason why this method of procedure is not logically sound:

And however we may flatter ourselves that we are guided, in every step which we take, by a kind of verisimilitude and experience, we may be assured that this fancied experience has no authority when we thus apply it to subjects that lie entirely out of the sphere of experience (EHU Sect. VII, Pt. I, 72).

In the *Dialogues* he will take quite seriously the analogy on which the argument from design is based; there he will subject it to a minute and searching analysis in order to establish exactly how far it really leads us, that is, in order to determine whether it can really support such a momentous conclusion.

12.4 THE CRITIQUE IN THE NATURAL HISTORY OF RELIGION

The central question which Hume examines in this work is not the one concerning the rational foundations of religion, but that of its origin in human nature. Probably with the intention of preventing, or at least minimizing, possible misunderstandings and misconstructions as to the nature of his argument and its consequences, Hume from the very beginning asserts that the first question "admits of the most obvious, at least, the clearest solution," and he produces thereupon what seems to be a version of the argument from design:

> The whole frame of nature bespeaks an intelligent author; and no rational en-quirer can, after serious reflection, suspend his belief a moment with regard to the primary principles of genuine Theism and Religion (NHR, 21).

Obviously this theistic declaration is not an unequivocal endorsement of the claims of historical or "popular" religion, and even less of the common representations of divinity, for "*barbarity, caprice* . . . form the ruling character of the deity in popular religions" (NHR, 73). On the other hand, in the above statement the omission of the moral attributes of the deity is conspicuous, and the questions as to whether God is omnipotent or limited in power, and about which other attributes – if any – is necessary or possible to ascribe to him, are left open. Moreover, in other passages he suggests doubts about the alleged simplicity of God, at least with respect to the God of scholastic theology.[10] Even though the latter may be only an *ad hominen* argument, it does anyhow question the coherence of such an idea. But even more, in the following passage Hume strongly suggests that the concept of an infinite deity is unintelligible:

> Thus they [the idolaters] proceed; till at last they arrive at infinity itself, beyond which there is no farther progress: And it is well, if, in striving to get farther, and to represent a magnificent simplicity, they run not into inexplicable mys-

---

[10] See, for instance, NHR, 26–27.

tery, and *destroy the intelligent nature of their deity*, on which alone any rational worship or adoration can be founded (NHR, 43; italics added).[11]

In this case, the invocation of mystery is to no avail; it does not make the concept more intelligible, but only offers "the devout votaries . . . an opportunity of
subduing their reason, by the belief of the most unintelligible sophisms"
(NHR, 54).

Despite this sporadic questioning of the infinity and unity of God, it is also
true that almost every time Hume compares monotheism with polytheism, he
points out that even if the latter is not altogether an absurd hypothesis, it is still a
groundless supposition (NHR, 65); monotheism is, on the contrary, more
conformable with the nature of our understanding. But in general, Hume does not
dispute in the *Natural History* either the validity or the truth of the conclusion of
the argument from design. He seems rather to give it his qualified approval.

And here precisely lies the great puzzle of the *Natural History*. We have, on the
one hand, his presumed assent to the design argument, which he repeats again and
again throughout the book, and on the other, we also have his remarks at the end of
the book, which *prima facie* at least seem to contradict such approval, or are at least
very difficult to reconcile with it. The latter appear to lend support to a different
sort of conclusion; and one that, if not atheistic, seems rather to be agnostic:

> The whole is a riddle, an aenigma, an inexplicable mystery. Doubt, uncertainty,
> suspense of judgment appear the only result of our most accurate scrutiny, con-
> cerning this subject. But such is the frailty of human reason, and such the irre-
> sistible contagion of opinion, that even this deliberate doubt could scarcely be
> upheld; did we not enlarge our view, and opposing one species of superstition
> to another, set them a quarrelling while we ourselves, during their fury and con-
> tention, happily make our escape into the calm, though obscure, regions of phi-
> losophy (NHR, 76).

We shall assume that we are confronted with an apparent, not an irreducible,
contradiction. Accordingly we shall attempt to find a point of view from which the
above assertions could be seen as compatible and complementary. The *Natural
History* itself offers some grounds for this reconciling project. At the very beginning of the section where Hume's supposed confession of agnosticism is found, he,
paradoxically enough, reiterates his theistic assent:

> [I]t scarcely seems possible, that any one of good understanding should reject
> that idea, once it is suggested to him. A purpose, an intention, a design is evi-
> dent in everything; and when our comprehension is so far enlarged as to con-

---

[11] It is curious that in the *Dialogues*, it is Demea, the inflexible defender of orthodoxy, the character that brings forward considerations such as these, with the purpose of establishing, against Cleanthes,
who exposes the argument from design, that it is wrong to attribute to the Deity an intelligence similar
to our own. See DNR, 155–157.

template the first rise of this visible system, we must adopt with the strongest conviction, the idea of some intelligent cause or author (NHR, 73).

Anyone of "good understanding" cannot but assent to the thesis that the cause of the universe is intelligent. But one can, and one must, suspend judgment concerning the further inferences that historical or popular religions draw concerning the attributes of the deity; these are but superstitions. Accordingly he will say a few paragraphs below that the actual doctrines or principles to which men usually lend their conviction "are anything but sick men's dreams . . . playsome whimsies of monkies in human shape, than the serious, positive, dogmatical asseverations of a being, who dignifies himself with the name of rational" (NHR, 75). Thus, even if Hume dramatically acknowledges the essentially mysterious character of reality, his flight into philosophy is not to linger in utter silence concerning the whole and its cause. It is rather, as he explicitly remarks, a way to escape from superstition.

This is, I think, the conclusion of the *Natural History*. However, it would be rather risky and premature to infer that it constitutes Hume's definitive position with respect to the claims of a knowledge of God made on behalf of natural religion, unless one of course could also reasonably say that in the *Dialogues* too he arrives at basically the same conclusion. In short, a thoroughly justified answer, unlike a merely reasonable guess, to this question will have to wait for the analysis of the *Dialogues*, that is, for the assessment of what is the definite theoretical position that its author establishes in this masterpiece both of philosophical and theological speculation.

CHAPTER 13

The Uncertain Path of Empirical Reasoning, Part II: The Critique of the Argument from Design in the *Dialogues Concerning Natural Religion*

13.1 PRELIMINARY REMARKS

It is a widespread opinion that the *Dialogues Concerning Natural Religion* are a demolishing critique of natural theology, that is, of the attempt to rationally justify, with complete independence from any special revelation, the presumed truths of the Christian faith, in particular the belief in the existence of a creator God of infinite perfection. At the same time it is paradoxical that the study of Hume's philosophy of religion has not reached a historical consensus about what is the positive doctrine that the *Dialogues* really establish, especially about what foundation in human reason – if any – the belief in the divine Being actually has. For some interpreters, Hume's stance is frankly atheistic, or even materialistic; for most of them, it is agnostic. From the affirmative side the usual move has been to identify Hume with the finite and heterodox theism that is defended by Cleanthes, one of the main characters of the dialogue; yet, disparate positions that go from orthodox fideism to pantheism have been attributed to him. Finally, there are other interpreters who even affirm that in the *Dialogues* Hume offers no conclusion about the problems of rational theology, and hence that it is a hermeneutic mistake to suppose that one or some of the characters express a definitive opinion on behalf of the author of that work.

It what follows I shall outline an interpretation of the *Dialogues* which seems to me to formulate the most plausible Humean conclusion that can be derived from them. With it, I certainly do not presume to have unraveled the enigma of the *Dialogues*; but anyhow, I consider that this alternative reading deserves attention because it takes very seriously three important points: First, that the *Dialogues* are an eminently negative examination of the validity of the reasoning which derives the existence of God from our experience of the immanent order displayed by the universal course of events (the famous argument from design); this is but the culmination of a critique merely suggested in the *Treatise of Human Nature*[1] and in

---

[1] These suggestions are contained, it seems to me, in THN, Book I, Part III, Sect. XIV, and the *Appendix*, p. 663.

the *Natural History of Religion*,[2] and which he began to develop in the *Enquiry Concerning Human Understanding.*[3] Second, that Hume does not deny in any of his philosophical works, but on the contrary affirms, the truth of the conclusion of the design argument. And finally, that any interpretation of the *Dialogues* must be at the least compatible with Hume's peculiar philosophical outlook, namely, with the scepticism which in the *Enquiry Concerning Human Understanding* he qualifies as "mitigated."[4]

But before analyzing the arguments of the *Dialogues* in order to justify such an interpretation, we must examine and refute the view that presents itself as a kind of insurmountable obstacle against it: namely, that this book provides no clue which might permit us to extract a definite conclusion about the questions of natural religion. If such an interpretative approach were correct, i.e. if it were true that the text of the *Dialogues* does not allow us to enter into the unitary theoretical intention of its author, then the task which I have proposed to undertake in this chapter, that is to say, to determine whether Hume establishes in the *Dialogues* any rational foundation for religion, would be but the product of a sort of hermeneutic misunderstanding.

13.2 HERMENEUTIC DIFFICULTIES OF THE DIALOGUES

The apparently unresolved hermeneutic dispute around the *Dialogues* has its origins, to a great extent, in the literary form of the work, that is, in the fact the Hume's critique is not expounded in a systematic discourse, but rather flows from the dramatic setting provided by the lively confrontation of the different points of views of the main speakers in that work. These are: Cleanthes, the heterodox theist, whom Hume called the "Hero of the Dialogue,"[5] and who defends the argument from experience and the conception of a finite deity; Demea, the exponent of religious orthodoxy, who at the same time, exemplifies a curious mixture of a mystic – since he postulates the absolute impenetrability of God's nature to the human intellect – and a believer in our capacity of proving a priori the existence of God, which is a possibility which Hume criticizes here only in passing;[6] and Philo, the "careless" sceptic. Furthermore, this dialectical contest is not presented by Hume, in the first person, as we have already seen that he does in Section XI of the first *Enquiry*, where in an explicit manner and for the first time, he criticizes the argument from design. In the *Enquiry* we witnessed a dialogue between "I" and a friend who assumes the role of "Epicurus." In the *Dialogues*, by contrast, we have a ficti-

[2] In the NHR the Introduction and section 15 are particularly relevant.

[3] EHU, Section XI, is the most important part in this respect.

[4] EHU, Section XII, Part II, 161–162.

[5] L, I, 153, Letter to Gilbert Elliot of Minto, 18 February, 1751.

[6] DNR, Section IX, 188–192.

tious character, Pamphilus, who reports to his friend Hermippus, a conversation which Cleanthes, Demea and Philo had some time ago, and of which he was a silent auditor. And it will also be Pamphilus who will have the last word of the *Dialogues*, which, however, one cannot expeditiously attribute to Hume, since Pamphilus is a disciple of Cleanthes. In brief, all this explains, up to a certain point at least, on the one hand the origin of the ambiguity and enigma that surrounds the *Dialogues,* and on the other the diversity and contraposition between the interpretations that the study of this masterpiece has generated and continues to give rise to.

In "Theatre and Religious Hypothesis,"[7] Maria Franco-Ferraz offers an eloquent and reasoned argument in favor of a fresh and different sort of hermeneutic approach to the *Dialogues Concerning Natural Religion* as a suitable means to disentangle the web of proverbially difficult philosophical questions posed by Hume in that work. For her the key point of the *Dialogues* lies in the fictional setting in which the theological discussion takes place. She goes on to show that the literary form of the *Dialogues* is intrinsically connected with its philosophical content[8] so as to serve to elucidate the precise nature of the conclusion which is established at the end, in Part XII. In other words, the theatrical structure facilitates a more profound and detailed investigation of the problems dealing with the existence and nature of God; in fact, Hume offers no final solutions to these problems and thereby none of the characters of the *Dialogues* can properly he said to present the victorious point of view or the one counting with the complete authority of the author of the play:

> The most important aspect of this text is the interaction between the different characters' points of view, which by being in confrontation with each other, undergo reciprocal transformations (Franco-Ferraz, 228).

With this one cannot but agree. In addition she shows that there is a profound relation between this theatrical form and some substantive philosophical theses which Hume developed in the *Treatise*, the first *Enquiry*, and *The Natural History of Religion*. In reality the theater metaphor clarifies the sense of those philosophical doctrines, which in turn throw light on and corroborate her main contention about the conclusion of the *Dialogues*. For according to her, any definitive solution to the

---

[7] Maria Franco-Ferraz, "Theatre and Religious Hypothesis," *Hume Studies* 15, no. 1 (April 1989): 220–235.

[8] Some recent authors have taken notice of the connection between the dramatic form and the philosophical argument: "In the *Dialogues* Hume's dialectical intelligence finds its true literary form, a form the analogues of which are discerned from the *Treatise* on." Thus argues Donald Livingston in *Hume's Philosophy of Common Life*, p. 39. Peter Jones, in *Hume's Sentiments, Their Ciceronian and French Context*, p. 69, asserts that "Hume valued the dialogue form because it allowed the full expression of rival views." And according to Peter Gay, in *The Enlightenment: An Interpretation*, I, 414–415, the *Dialogues* is a book "almost unique in the literature of theological disputation in its felicitous marriage of form and substance – a drama, cerebral but exciting [which is] a genuine confrontation of ideas."

problems of natural theology is not presented at the end by any of the characters on behalf of a God-like author (*Dieu auteur*), and furthermore this *deus ex-machina* solution would conflict especially with Hume's conception of the mind as being "une pièce sans théâtre," a drama without a stage. (Franco-Ferraz, 234). In the same manner that the self is a theater without substantial support, i.e., a manifold of perceptions in flux and mutual opposition lacking any substantial unity, so the theatrical structure of the *Dialogues* is an indication that the essence of this work lies in the plurality and dramatic tension in which the expressed opinions stand to each other, and hence that no theoretic unitary intention should be attributed to its author.

Such is the substance of this interesting thesis. I think that such interpretation provides a novel outlook and one fruitful means of access to an adequate understanding of the *Dialogues*. But I am quite unable to subscribe to the most important aspect of that reading of the text – the absence of a definite conclusion on the part of the author – for the "inconveniences," in Philo's sense of the word, which seem to follow from it.

The main textual support for such an interpretation is a passage from Part III of the *Dialogues* in which Demea objects to Cleanthes' claim, defended by two very ingenious analogies, that an orderly world like a coherent, articulate speech will always be taken as a sign of intelligent design:

> When I read a volume, I enter into the mind and intention of the author: I become him, in a manner, for the instant; and have an immediate feeling and conception of those ideas which revolved in his imagination while employed in that composition (DNR, 155–156).

What are Demea's "naive" and "false" premises? In short, that a written text may enable a reader to enter into the mind of its author, thus gaining access to the author's ideas and intentions, "becoming," as Demea puts it, "him, in a manner, for the instant" (DNR, 155). Franco-Ferraz seems to categorically deny this. Although perhaps her overall interpretation would stand even if she were wrong about Demea's contention, it seems to me that there are more reasons to approve of Demea's premises than to call them naive and false.

I think it is safer to follow here as a maxim for interpretation Peter Gay's observation that Demea is certainly a foil but not a fool.[9] On the one hand, it is precisely Demea who will voice at the end of Part III (DNR, 156–157) Hume's conception of the mind as a flux of fleeting and successive perceptions in order to deny the resemblance between the human and the divine mind. On the other hand, it is curious that in the passage she quotes, Demea is relying, in order to retort to Cleanthes' almost Platonic-like allegories of the voice from the clouds and the vegetative library, on another and complementary aspect of Hume's theory of the mind, which instead of emphasizing the flux and plurality of the mind, stresses those principles which allow for the mind being a bundle, or for the systematic

---

[9] Peter Gay, The *Enlightenment*, I, 415.

union between the perceptions which constitute it. Hume would have said about the human mind what Aristotle asserted about a world governed by Mind (*Noûs*), i.e., that it is not a bad tragedy.[10] Not in vain did he also compare it to a republic or commonwealth:

> [T]he true idea of the human mind, is to consider it as a system of different perceptions or different existences, which are linked together by the relation of cause and effect, and mutually produce, destroy, influence, and modify each other (THN, 261, italics added).

When Hume is describing those other principles which make the mind a system and which also render the communication of emotions and ideas between different persons possible, he elucidates them through another fine metaphor, that of the mirror:

> [T]he minds of men are mirrors to one another, not only because *they reflect each other's emotions*, but also because those rays of *passions, sentiments, and opinions*, may be often reverberated, and may decay away by insensible degrees (THN, 365; italics added).

Thus it seems as if religious hypotheses can reflect back at each other in an infinite "jeu de miroirs," as Franco-Ferraz has splendidly put it, only because human minds are themselves mirrors which reflect each others emotions and opinions.

I do concede, of course, that Demea's presuppositions may be wrong after all. But to put it mildly, it is debatable that they were so for Hume, who in the *Treatise* went to such pains to give a causal explanation – in terms of the mechanism of association – of the principles which lie at the basis of our access to the world of common life, intersubjective communication, and sympathy. He says accordingly that association is a "gentle force which *commonly prevails* [among thoughts] and is the *cause why, among other things languages so nearly correspond to each other*" (THN, 10, italics added). And furthermore "so far as regards the mind, these [associative connections] are the only links that bind the parts of the universe together or *connect us with any person or object exterior to ourselves*" (THN, 662, italics added).[11] Neither can I view Demea's premises as naive except in the sense that they are tacitly believed to be true by everybody (even by the philosopher when he is not in his closet). But the context of Demea's strictures against Cleanthes' hypothesis makes clear that they are not naively held. It is certainly through sympathy that we gain some access into the passions, sentiments, and opinions of another person, but Demea is careful to add that we only become the other, or sympathize with him, "in a manner," that is, I think, by analogy. Let

---

[10] Aristotle, *Metaphysics* 1090b 19–20: "Observation shows that nature is not episodic, like a bad tragedy."

[11] See also EHU, 23, 67–68.

us remember what we have pointed out more than once: no passion (as well as no intention) of another is ever directly apprehended; it is inferred rather from "external signs" (THN, 317–318) or "its causes and effects" (THN, 576); in other words, we become aware of his or her feelings and thoughts from what the other person does or says. In turn what makes this knowledge possible is that there is a specific resemblance between human minds:

> The minds of all men are similar in their feelings and operations; nor can any one be actuated by any affection of which all others are not in some degree susceptible (THN, 575–576; see also THN, 316–318).

If sympathy with another person's passions, sentiments and opinions is grounded upon a causal sort of inference, and if it is a well-established Humean doctrine that valid causal claims rest on the experienced union between species of objects, then although hearing (the voice from the clouds) or seeing (the vegetative library) a coherent, articulate speech would certainly enable one to pick up the intelligent thoughts and intentions of its author, the same inference cannot be made from the experienced order of nature to its presumably intelligent cause or God. Here we lack the required specific resemblance to other experienced types of objects that would legitimate the inference from the effect, the Universe, to its cause, God. This is what Demea, I think, is really pointing at immediately after the last sentence of the passage quoted by Franco-Ferraz:

> *But so near an approach we never surely can make to the Deity.* His ways are not our ways. His attributes are perfect, but incomprehensible. And this volume of nature contains a great and inexplicable riddle, more than any intelligible discourse or reasoning (DNR, 156; italics added).

If one does not split Demea's argument, then it appears to be *ad hominen*. Demea is not saying that our access to the other person's ideas and intentions is perfect; he is just establishing a comparative relation between it and our presumed knowledge of God's intelligent nature. He seems to assert that – once granted – our access in the first case is easier, and that there are great, if not insuperable, difficulties in the second case, that is, concerning our access to God's intelligence based on the "visible signs" on the "volume of nature."

In the end one wonders whether or not Franco-Ferraz (or any author for that matter) should share Demea's assumption that a text can enable a reader to enter into the mind of its creator. For even Pamphilus, through whom Hume himself would, according to her, be giving the clue for understanding the *Dialogues*, seems to share Demea's objectionable principles:

> [I]f the subject be curious and interesting, *the book carries us, in a manner, into company;* and unites the two greatest and purest pleasures of human life, study and society (DNR, 128; italics added).

Yet the author's most daring and up-hill claim is that it is a "mistake" to search in the *Dialogues* for clues as to who Hume's spokesman really is. I will not dispute that assertion, since I believe that it comprises a sound methodological principle for the interpretation of the *Dialogues*. Yet one could say that she is, as it were, rowing against the main current of almost two centuries of Hume scholarship. It may be argued that Hume himself has encouraged at least some Hume scholars to fall into that "mistake," since in a letter of 1753 to James Balfour he asserted that "in every Dialogue, no more than one person can he supposed to represent the author."[12]

On the whole, though, one can earnestly concede that it would be a mistake, and also an unprofitable philosophical exercise, to approach the *Dialogues* looking for clues as to who Hume's authentic voice is. This can be at best a secondary issue. However, even allowing for the justified criticism of those who are obsessed with finding Hume's complete spokesman and also for the interplay of the many voices which in the course of the debate criticize, influence and modify each others' opinions, I still believe that it does not thence follow that the text of the *Dialogues* as a whole does not offer a definitive position on behalf of its author about the substantive theological issue under discussion as his main theoretical intention. For that reason, now that we have cleared that hurdle, we can begin to analyze the main arguments of the *Dialogues*.

13.3 THE CRITIQUE OF THE DESIGN HYPOTHESIS (INTRODUCTION, PARTS I–V)

The reasoned pleas, ingenious illustrations, and counterexamples of Philo are geared to undermine the logical validity of the argument from design, and thereby to cast serious doubts on the truth of its conclusion, i.e., that the order of nature offers undeniable evidence of the existence of its perfect Creator.

I cannot offer here a complete enumeration, and much less a detailed determination of the true import, of Philo's arguments. We shall dwell only on some remarkable aspects of the criticism to the design argument in so far as this is indispensable for elucidating, and maybe for making convincing, our answer to the central question: What Hume's definitive position about the rational foundations of religion really is?

Who of the three participants speaks for Hume? One of them or all of them in varying degrees? Certainly the type of overall appraisal of Hume's philosophy of religion which is finally offered, will depend in great measure on whom one considers to be Hume's mouthpiece. But the consideration of this question can be postponed, since the relevant passages, those which offer the greatest difficulties of interpretation, are found in Part XII, the final section of the *Dialogues*. Hopefully, this question will be more manageable after the implications of Philo's attack – and also of Demea's – on the argument and Cleanthes' defense of it have been brought into the open. It must be emphasized once more, that, even though it is not neces-

---

[12] L, I, 173.

sarily an absurd task, the identification of the author's mouthpiece or mouthpieces is but a minor issue. In any case, we shall select and uphold at the end, among the most viable possibilities of interpretation which the *Dialogues* as a whole suggests, that hermeneutic alternative which is also more compatible with the general philosophical outlook that Hume has developed in the *Treatise*, the *Enquiries* and the *Natural History of Religion*. But now we shall turn to Hume's examination of the argument from design.

The first problem ahead of us is: what is the true subject-matter of Hume's critique? Is Hume questioning the possibility of establishing the existence of God? Or is he merely questioning our capacity for determining what his attributes (that is, God's essence or nature) really are? If we follow a literal reading of the *Dialogues*, we shall have to conclude that his critique concerns the second point only. Thus in the prologue to the *Dialogues*, Pamphilus, Cleanthes' disciple and the actual narrator of the conversation between Philo, Demea, and Cleanthes, is made to say that there is no truth so obvious as the being of God, whereas there is no question more obscure and uncertain than the one concerning the nature of the divine being (DNR, 178). Furthermore, both Philo and Demea apparently concur in the same conclusion, "that the question can never be concerning the being but only the nature of the Deity" (DNR, 142). On the other hand, Cleanthes' defense of the argument, as Demea promptly points out to him, proceeds as if the issue in question were also the existence, not merely the essence, of God. "By this argument a posteriori, and by this argument alone, we do prove at once the existence of a Deity and his similarity to the human mind and intelligence" (DNR, 143).

Generally speaking, this controversy appears to be purely verbal. If one defines God, as Philo does, as an "original cause of the universe," or, as an original "principle of order," it seems quite idle to say of such a being that it does not exist. For all we know, the universe might be its own cause; there must be "an original, inherent principle of order somewhere, in thought or in matter" (DNR, 174). But if we are talking about the God of traditional theology, at least of a wise, powerful and good Creator, the problem concerning his existence cannot be separated from that concerning his essence. To say that God exists in this sense, would be incompatible with saying that God exists because there is an original principle of order in the unguided force of matter. For this reason I suggest that what is truly at stake is the problem of the existence of God, in a sense that, although not identical, is quite close to the common religious understanding of the term 'God.'[13] Let us remember that Hume, or at least the "Epicurus" of Section X of the *Enquiry Concerning Human Understanding,* straightforwardly presented the argument as the "chief or sole argument for a divine existence," and also that there Hume, or at least the "I" of the dialogue, presents "Epicurus" as "denying a divine existence, and consequently a providence and future state" (EHU, 133). And finally, if there ever was a

---

[13] William H. Capitan defends a contrary interpretation, "Part X of Hume's Dialogues" in *Hume: A Collection of Critical Essays*, ed. V. C. Chappell, Modern Studies in Philosophy (London: Macmillan, 1968) pp. 384–395. A. P. Cavendish asserts an opinion similar to our own; *David Hume* (New York: Dover Publications, 1968) pp. 105–106.

philosophy wherein the problems of existence and essence could not be separated, such a one was Hume's.[14] As we have already seen when analyzing the ontological argument, the idea of existence is the same with the idea of the object; i.e., whatever we conceive, we conceive to be existent. In general, the *Dialogues* bring to its ultimate conclusion the line of criticism that Hume sketched in Section XI (Of a particular providence and a future state) of the *Enquiry*. The former will carefully illustrate the uncertainty and vagueness of the argument from design as a theory intended to account for the existence and order of phenomena, even if the argument itself is formulated within the limiting conditions set by "Epicurus" in the *Enquiry*. In order to be consistent with these, Cleanthes, the defender of the argument, will accordingly pretend to assert of God no more than what the empirical evidence guarantees and never to infer from that hypothesis any purely imaginary suppositions which might throw us into a scheme of things totally alien to that which experience presents to us. For that reason, Cleanthes will neither assert the infinite attributes of God, nor immortality and an ultramundane eschatology. What now comes to the center of the stage in Cleanthes' version of the argument is, as the fundamental condition for the establishment of an intelligent cause of the universe, the analogy of the products of nature (especially living organisms as plants and animals) to the works of human artifice, especially machines:

> Look round the world: contemplate the whole and every part of it: you will find it to be nothing but one great machine, subdivided into an infinite number of lesser machines, which again admit of subdivisions to a degree beyond what human senses and faculties can trace and explain. All these various machines, and even their most minute parts, are adjusted to each other with an accuracy which ravishes into admiration all men who have ever contemplated them. The curious adapting of means to ends, throughout all nature, resembles exactly, though it much exceeds, the productions of human contrivance; of human designs, thought, wisdom, and intelligence. Since, therefore, the effects resemble each other, we are led to infer, by all the rules of analogy, that the causes also resemble; and that the Author of Nature is somewhat similar to the mind of man, though possessed of much larger faculties, proportioned to the grandeur of the work which he has executed (DNR, 143).

Perhaps in less emphatic terms than Spinoza, Hume will not accept Descartes' mechanical model of explanation for the behavior of living organisms as the only or more adequate theoretical alternative. Like Spinoza, Hume rejects Descartes' geometrical, static concept of matter, which was the one main factor that gave verisimilitude to the hypothesis that living organisms were merely the products of

---

[14] This is a point which is emphasized by Ronald J. Butler, although in order to support a very different interpretation, in "Natural Belief and the Enigma of Hume," *Archiv für Geschichte der Philosophie* 42 (1960): 94.

an external mechanical design.[15] Hume, through Philo, emphasizes again and again the remoteness of that analogy and the great uncertainty that attaches to it when we transform it into a model for the explanation of the origin and generation of the whole of nature.

In the *Dialogues* it is Philo who is in charge of pointing out the theoretical difficulties that stand in the way of establishing the hypothesis of design as a coherent cosmogonical hypothesis, and he continues the same line of criticism of Sect. XI of the *Enquiry*, implying that it is possible to uphold such an hypothesis because the difference between the two cases has not been sufficiently remarked and because for the evidence that experience denies us we arbitrarily supply an imaginary reconstruction of the whole, which owes its plausibility to an analogy which is more imperfect and ambiguous than it seems at first sight.

[W]herever you depart, in the least, from the similarity of the cases, you diminish proportionably the evidence; and may at last bring it to a very weak *analogy*, which is confessedly liable to error and uncertainty (DNR, 144).

First of all, Philo shows how gratuitous and self-serving is the nature of the analogy between the products of nature and machines in the case in question. From the contemplation of plants and animals we derive striking examples of the order and regularity in the operations of nature. These are bodies composed of innumerable parts in which each part is necessarily related to the others, and all of them to the whole, making it possible for a particular configuration or structure to be relatively preserved. But from the undeniable fact of order in the universe one cannot *ipso facto* infer that there must exist an external intelligent orderer; that is, one cannot immediately go from unitary design to intelligent design unless one begs the question.[16] And this is what Cleanthes, the defender of the argument from design, seems about to do by hurriedly assimilating vegetables and animals to machines. It is obvious that a mechanical aggregate of inert particles of matter cannot create and re-create itself as a definite whole continuously; it has, so to say, to be put together by an external mechanic.

---

[15] This aspect of Spinoza's philosophy is brought forth by Hans Jonas, "Spinoza and the Theory of Organism," in *Spinoza: A Collection of Critical Essays*, ed. Marjorie Greene, Modern Studies Philosophy (New York: Anchor Press, 1973), pp. 259–278.

[16] This is uphold by George J. Nathan in "Hume's Immanent God," *Hume: A Collection of Critical Essays*, ed. V. C. Chappel, p. 339: "In arguing that the universe resembles a machine, Cleanthes has ensured the conclusion that it must have an external cause." Stanley Tweyman, in *Scepticism and Belief in Hume's Dialogues concerning Natural Religion*, pp. 36–39, has attempted to absolve Cleanthes from the charge of circularity: "My reading of Cleanthes' argument makes clear that the machine-like character of the world is a *conclusion* which the argument as whole supports, rather than a *premise* which is employed in the argument" (p. 39). They are both right up to a certain point. The manner in which Cleanthes initially formulates the argument provides a ground for the circularity charge; yet, Cleanthes does not subscribe the Cartesian mechanism and materialism, which is typical of principal deists: this is brought forward by the allegory of the vegetative library.

In other words, this analogy completely disregards the crucial fact that makes living bodies essentially different from mechanical artifacts, i.e., that living organisms are in a continuous process of self-creation, of self-generation, and self re-generation; an individual living organism is in a continual process of interchange of matter with its environment, whereby its own material constituents are being constantly replaced by others; it is, on the other hand, a particular structure or configuration, not the stuff or substance, which constitutes the identity of the organism, that is, which remains the same throughout a process which is not brought about by any external agency, but which is rather the necessary development of the inner possibilities of the entity in question.

Cleanthes' answer to Philo's objection is but the seemingly dogmatic assertion that the similarity between the universe and a machine admits of no proof simply because it is self-evident (DNR, 152). The best one can do, according to him, is first, to offer illustrations of other possible cases (in fact rather strange instances), which even if they are not analogous to those we find in our ordinary experience, would, in spite of their rarity, be immediately considered as the works of some design, and second, to show that the case with respect to the actual universe is not much different.

In this part of the work Cleanthes propounds the ingenious and intriguing analogies of the voice from the clouds (a voice that simultaneously addresses all humankind and which is understood by all humans beings, in spite of their different tongues, that is, something like an ironical version of Pentecost), and the living library (books that propagate themselves as organic beings, such as plants or animals). These fantastic illustrations do not have a perfect analogy with ordinary experience; but this would not weaken our response when hearing such a strange voice and when seeing those organic books. We would instinctively and instantly believe that their cause is intelligent, although that inference would not certainly be the product of a strict reasoning; it would rather be an "irregular" argument, and for that reason logically objectionable:

Whatever cavils may be urged, an orderly world, as well as a coherent, articulate speech, will still be received as an incontestable proof of design and intention (DNR, 155).

But, as we have seen in section 13.2, Demea will object to Cleanthes' defense in the same terms as the "I" and "Epicurus" in Section X of the *Enquiry*. Even conceding that the inference holds for the bizarre cases proposed by Cleanthes, because of the infinite difference between the cases here involved, that is, due to the uniqueness of God and the universe or their absence of specific similarity with the kinds of objects of which we have experience, the inference from the experienced order within the universe to a divine intelligence is not legitimate (DNR, 156). However, this reproach is not a satisfactory refutation of Cleanthes, for by means of the argument from design he does not presume to establish the existence of an intelligent and infinite cause. It will be Philo, not Demea, who will point to the "inconveniences" or strange consequences that follow from the hypothesis about the finiteness of the intelligent cause.

We shall examine only the most remarkable among the multitude of clever objections of Philo. First of all, he questions the alleged self-evidence of the analogy between the universe and a machine, and he again remarks that it seems to beg the question. The universe cannot be considered to be the effect of an intelligent orderer unless Cleanthes can prove either of two things; that is, either that it is possible to prove a priori, from the very essence of thought and of matter, that order is an attribute that pertains necessarily to the constitution of thought and not of matter (DNR, 179); or that experience conclusively shows that thought is the only cause of order in the world. Concerning the first case, it is impossible, within Hume's premises, to demonstrate a priori that something can or cannot be the cause of any other thing; and Cleanthes himself has already admitted that the only possible proof of God's existence is a posteriori, or empirical. Furthermore, the fact that we have observed many instances of thought without order, as in madness, and equally of matter without order, as in corruption, (DNR, 163), perhaps suffices to show that order as such is not an essential attribute of either of the two. With respect to the second possibility, Philo points at the arbitrariness of our choice of thought, among many other principles, as the principle for the explanation of the universal order of things. But why thought? On one hand, experience – which is the only guide that Cleanthes allegedly follows – does show us many instances of entities that produce order without knowing it, as in the case of plants and animals, and hence that thought is not the only, nor the more extensive, cause of order in the world (DNR, 147); in addition to reason, we are acquainted with "instinct, generation, vegetation, which are similar to each other, and are the causes of similar effects" (DNR, 147). If, on the other hand, we had gained an explanatory advantage by postulating such a principle, then perhaps the selection of reason would have been justified. But this is by no means the case, because we are not offering a genuine explanation, that is, we are not referring a particular effect to more general causes, but referring a particular effect, the universe, to another particular and unique cause, the divine intelligence (DNR, 149).

This is indeed, a repetition of the critique suggested at the end of Part XI of the *Enquiry* (EHU, 147–148). The uniqueness of the objects involved forbids us to legitimately assert any conclusion concerning the whole. However interesting these enquiries may be, none of the hypotheses that spring from them can be subjected to empirical verification (DNR, 177):

[W]e have no data to establish any system of cosmogony. Our experience, so imperfect in itself, and so limited both in extent and duration, can afford us no probable conjecture concerning the whole of things (DNR, 177).

Cleanthes, on the other hand, pretends to bring the argument from design in line with this empirical requirement so as to bestow a greater degree, or at least a semblance of probability on its conclusion. This is why he attributes to God no more than what is presumably necessary for bringing about the world that our limited experience opens to us. It may well be that Philo only intends to show the inherent and insuperable difficulties of Cleanthes' position; yet, it is still significant that he gives to that hypothesis the name of "experimental theism."

The first momentous consequence that his fidelity to experience has for Cleanthes' position is that it makes it quite impossible for him to affirm that God is a being of infinite perfection. And in this consists his heterodoxy: God may be, judging by the scene of things contemplated by us, the most perfect being that there can be, but not the most perfect being that can be conceived. Obviously, to the orthodox this position is indistinguishable from idolatry, and Demea immediately makes this reproach to Cleanthes. His answer to Demea is not less forceful and abrupt: To worship an infinite God whose nature is absolutely incomprehensible to us is an obscure form of atheism, it is virtually to say that we do not know God at all (DNR, 158). And then, what sense there is in a complete abandonment to ignorance, or in worshipping a mystery which perhaps is just a cloak for sheer absurdity?

To say that God is incomprehensible, that our ideas in no way correspond to his real nature, is the same as saying that the word 'God' is meaningless, that is, to say that we really have no idea of the Deity. If our ideas refer to no conceivable feature of our experience, if they refer in no way to impressions of sensation or of reflection, then, according to Hume's first principle that all ideas are copied from impressions, what should really be concluded is that we have no idea of God: "If we abandon all human analogy . . . we abandon all religion and retain no conception of the object of our adoration" (DNR, 203). This is a corollary of a principle which Hume formulated thus in the *Treatise,* and to which we have referred when examining the ontological argument:

> Now since nothing is ever present to the mind but perceptions, and since all ideas are deriv'd from something antecedently present to the mind, it follows, that 'tis impossible for us so much as to conceive or form an idea of anything specifically different from ideas and impressions (THN, 67).

It seems to follow then that the real idea which we have of God, according to Cleanthes, is – like the idea of external existence – a "relative" one. Cleanthes' anthropomorphic or relative conception of God is, in fact, an attempt to maintain religious belief within the boundaries of intelligible discourse, within the limits of a doctrine that, in contradistinction to mysticism, could be comprehended by all and be communicated and be the subject of controversy, of acceptance or rejection, of confirmation or refutation. Perhaps this is one reason why Hume gives the epithet of "hero" to Cleanthes. Anyway, the presumed accusations of meaninglessness against traditional religious orthodoxy are themselves clothed in Hume's own theories of perception and of meaning. And these the orthodox and mystic alike could choose to reject. But under these presuppositions both Cleanthes' refusal to affirm the infinite nature of the Deity as well as his questioning whether to the concept of a Divine mind there pertains a perfect simplicity, are totally consistent. On the one hand, all impressions are particular and totally determined existences; thus it does not seem possible that we could have experience of infinite attributes. Philo had already mischievously put this forward in the following reasoning:

> Our ideas reach no further than our experience. We have no experience of divine attributes and operations. I need not conclude my syllogism. You can draw the inference yourself. And it is a pleasure to me (and I hope to you too) that just reasoning and sound piety here concur in the same conclusion, and both of them establish the adorably mysterious and incomprehensible nature of the Supreme Being (DNR, 142–143).

As we have seen, Cleanthes concludes quite straightforwardly that if God's nature is infinite, we really do not have any idea of Him. This appears to be a consequence of Hume's theory of ideas. But from it follows neither that God's nature is not infinite, nor that there is no infinite God.

Concerning the nature of the divine mind, Hume had already suggested in the *Natural History* that the idea of a perfectly simple mind is an absurd conception: "in endeavoring to represent a magnificent simplicity they run into inexplicable mystery, and *destroy the intelligent nature of their deity*, on which alone any rational worship or adoration can be founded" (NHR, 43; italics added). In the *Dialogues*, Cleanthes forcefully declares this concept to be inconsistent:

> [T]hose who maintain the perfect simplicity of the Supreme Being . . . are compleat Mystics. . . . They are, in a word, Atheists, without knowing it. For though it be allowed, that the Deity possesses attributes of which we have no comprehension, yet ought we never to ascribe to him any attributes which are absolutely incompatible with that intelligent nature essential to him. A mind, whose acts and sentiments and ideas are not distinct and successive; one, that is wholly simple, and totally immutable, is a mind which has no thought, no reason, no will, no sentiment, no love, no hatred; or, in a word, is no mind at all. It is an abuse of terms to give it that appellation; and we may as well speak of limited extension without figure, or of number without composition (DNR, 159).

In short, it is impossible to attribute perfect simplicity to the Deity if one holds Hume's conception of the self as a "bundle" or "collection" of different perceptions in perpetual temporal flux. Yet, curiously enough, this is what the orthodox Demea does the *Dialogues,* for he expounds both doctrines. The difficulties which this conception of mental life presents for any attempt to explain the undeniable fact of the identity of the knowing self throughout the whole succession of perceptions, are, as Hume himself came to recognize, enormous and perhaps insuperable (THN, Appendix, 633–636). However, with all its self-confessed shortcomings, Hume's analysis of the self effectively annihilated the last stronghold of the old inert or static idea of substance as an ultimate substratum or stuff, and thereby paved the way for a dynamical understanding of things and selves which would stress the features of real process and constant relations.

Precisely because of this positive accomplishment the religious orthodox cannot ignore Hume, at least so long as she or he remains within this traditional conception of substance he cannot assert the existence of a perfectly simple substance and at the same time reject the "hideous hypothesis" or "atheistic" hypothesis of Spinoza of one infinite substance. In the *Treatise*, Part IV, Section V, "Of the immateriality of the soul," Hume produces an *argumentum ad hominen* to show that all the logical absurdities which the orthodox theologian detects in Spinoza's conception of one extended substance can equally be found to beset the theologian's conception of a perfect simple spiritual substance. Hume concludes here that, either both conceptions are equally tenable or both are equally unintelligible. It is not surprising the Cleanthes arrived in the *Dialogues* at the second conclusion concerning the supposed simplicity of the divine mind. On the other hand, if what the orthodox refers to when taking about such a mind is, borrowing Locke's phrase, an unknown something in which the divine thoughts simultaneously inhere, Hume would probably take this as a learned way of confessing ignorance or as a concept as vacuous as that of an unobserved external object: "a certain unknown, inexplicable *something*, as the cause of our perceptions; a notion so imperfect, that no sceptic will think it worth while to contend against it." (EHU, 155). It seems, though, that in the *Dialogues*, Cleanthes (although not Philo) does consider it worth the trouble to argue against the idea of an absolutely simple divine mind.

But Cleanthes' experimental theism is plagued by difficulties of its own, which Philo is not slow to enumerate. Part V of the *Dialogues* is, in fact, devoted to a sort of *reductio ad absurdum* of Cleanthes' thesis. God's perfection, Cleanthes has agreed, cannot be proved a priori. But if God is finite and his perfection has to be inferred from experience, we cannot even say that he is finitely perfect: On the one hand, our limited experience does not permit us to judge whether his workmanship, notwithstanding the limitations that are imposed upon God's will, is relatively perfect, or the best that there can be; "it is impossible to say whether this system contains great faults, or deserves any considerable praise, if compared to other possible, and even real systems" (DNR, 167). In addition, even if the world were really perfect, this in itself would not prove that its cause must also be perfect; perhaps the world is the product of a process of slow development from very simple and imperfect beginnings. Philo brings this point forth by means of a simile, which likens the visible world to a ship:

> If we survey a ship, what an exalted idea must we form of the ingenuity of the carpenter who framed so complicated, useful, and beautiful a machine? And what surprize must we feel, when we find him a stupid mechanic, who imitated others, and copied an art, which, through a long succession of ages, after multiplied trials, mistakes, corrections, deliberations, and controversies, had been gradually improving? Many worlds might have been botched and bungled, throughout an eternity, ere this system was struck out; much labour lost, many fruitless trials made; and a slow, but continued improvement carried on during infinite ages in the art of world-making (DNR, 167).

Once the admission of finitude has been made, we cannot establish monotheism, or at least exclude polytheism. Perhaps the universe was the product of different deities either working in a concerted action or aimlessly. Whereas in the *Natural History* Hume founded the superior rationality of monotheism on the uniformity and harmony of natural events, in the *Dialogues* he changes the emphasis, and suggests that polytheism is more rational and not precisely an idle multiplication of causes; contrary effects or irregularities, which abound in nature, point to the existence of contrary causes. In fact he wants to out-do Cleanthes in his anthropomorphism: polytheism is, once we have excluded infinity, both more rational and simple than monotheism.

[W]hy may not several deities combine in contriving and framing a world? This is only so much greater similarity to human affairs. By sharing the work among several, we may so much further limit the attributes of each, and get rid of that extensive power and knowledge, which must be supposed in one deity, and which, according to you, can only serve to weaken the proof of his existence (DNR, 167–168).

And if we follow more closely the analogy with experience, there is no reason for us to deny such gods a bodily existence or even sexual differentiation. We could likewise ascribe to them many other attributes that may bring them nearer to our condition. To all this Cleanthes answers that, although he sees the far-fetchedness of all these suppositions, it is no less certain that by none of them Philo ever gets rid of the hypothesis of design. This gives Philo the opportunity to make his first serious assault on the theory of design.

13.4 THE NATURALISTIC ALTERNATIVES TO THEISM: HYLOZOISM AND MATERIALISM (PARTS VI–IX)

Although Philo reaffirms that no analogy can be conclusive concerning the origin of the world, he also maintains that if we follow Cleanthes' principle that like effects prove like causes, then hylozoism, and not theism, is the more probable hypothesis. The universe resembles more an organized body or a living organism than a mechanical artifact or any other product of human intelligence.

The world, therefore, I infer, is an animal; and the Deity is the SOUL of the world, actuating it, and actuated by it (DNR, 171).

With all its limitations, this hypothesis is more conformable to our common experience. First, it does not suppose the artificial separation between mind and body, which is never observed in experience. Second, it recognizes that order and arrangement are an inherent attribute of matter as well as of thought. And third, it takes notice of the reciprocal influence of mind upon matter and of matter upon mind. These may be vulgar prejudices, but they are such as Cleanthes cannot disregard, since they are founded on "vulgar experience, the only guide you profess to follow in all these theological enquiries" (DNR, 172).

But if we admit vulgar experience as a true standard, then Cleanthes' method turns against the existence of an intelligent author, who made the world according to an ideal plan:

> If the universe bears a greater likeness to animal bodies and to vegetables, than to the works of human art, it is more probable that its cause resembles the cause of the former than that of the latter, and its origin ought rather to be ascribed to generation or vegetation, than to reason or design (DNR, 176).

To refer generation and vegetation to reason is to beg the question, unless order were an intrinsic and private characteristic of intelligence. Furthermore the supposition that generation owes its origin to a rational scheme or plan leads to an infinite regress, since such a mind might perhaps have its origin in a divine generation, etc.

> [A] mental world, or universe of ideas, requires a cause as much, as does a material world, or universe of objects; and, if similar in its arrangement, must require a similar cause (DNR, 160).

If it were the case that, by referring the organization of animals and vegetables to the working of a superior reason, we were in fact explaining the unknown by the familiar, or reducing the complex to the elemental, not much could be said against such procedure. But both generation and intelligence are enigmatical principles: "reason in its internal fabric and structure is really as little known to us as instinct or vegetation" (DNR, 178). It is noteworthy that Hume had said already in the *Treatise* that "the uniting principle among our internal perceptions is as unintelligible as that among external objects, and is not known to us any other way than by experience" (THN, 169). That the order of actual happenings in the visible universe follows according to a system of ideas or a plan created by an external intelligence is no more intelligible than surmising that the world attains this order by itself. After all, we do not even understand how ideas do organize themselves in a plan which is adequate for the fulfillment of a purpose; and much less do we know how it is possible afterwards to mold things according to this plan. Either we look for a cause of the arrangement of ideas, which implies an infinite regress, or we say that ideas spontaneously fall into order. But if we follow the second alternative there is no good reason for denying the possibility that the material things may also of, and by themselves, fall into order, without the intervention of an intelligent orderer (DNR, 164).

Hence, the teleology of intelligence is neither the only, nor by force the best or most simple theoretical alternative to account for the organization inherent in animals and plants. Experience shows otherwise, that is, that generation always precedes reason. What the theistic hypothesis does, in supposing the material, visible universe to emerge from an ideal world, is to reverse the empirical order:

In all instances which we have ever seen, ideas are copied from real objects, and are ectypal, not archetypal, to express myself in learned terms: you reverse this order, and give thought the precedence (DNR, 186).

If we were to stop somewhere, better stop at generation instead of reason; this supposition is more conformable to our experience, since "we see every day the latter arise from the former, never the former from the latter" (DNR, 180).

In general, Philo concludes that of all the candidate hypotheses none of which can be established by experience, that which assigns an inherent principle of order to the world is the least unsatisfactory (DNR, 174). What Philo seems to be really saying is that both hylozoism and materialism are more plausible hypotheses than that of an eternal and external (that is, ontologically distinct) creator, in other words, than the theological hypothesis of the Christian God. Even if thought were if the ordering principle, the mind involved would be far from being the Divine creative mind of traditional Christian theology; at most this is pantheism, not theism.

The theoretical viability of hylozoism and materialism is justified in the *Treatise*. Hume's conception of causality gave him the advantage of not having to deny a priori that interaction can occur, or that matter may be the cause of thought. A priori anything may produce anything, and it is but a "systematical prejudice" to say that matter and motion cannot give rise to thought under the pretext that matter and thought are radically different, and that no intelligible connection exists between them. Yet this rationalistic bias is opposed by the "vulgar prejudice," that is, by the universal experience that bodily changes affect our mental states: "every one may perceive, that the different dispositions of his body change his thought and sentiments" (THN, 248). In addition, if we follow rationalism, we would have to conclude that nothing can be the cause of any other thing, since such intelligible connection between causes and effects can never be grasped. But if, on the other hand, what is requisite to declare objects to be causes and effects is the experience of their constant conjunction, it is then indubitable that matter and thought mutually influence each other, and that matter can and frequently is the cause of thought (THN, 250).

This is one of the reasons that led Hume to give such serious attention to those cosmogonical theories that make the active principle of order immanent to the world itself. He already remarked in the *Treatise* that this theory of causality "gives the advantage to the materialists above their antagonists" (THN, 250). Perhaps what he meant by this was that it exploded Descartes' static and geometrical conception of matter.

In summary, once the possibility that matter may have within itself the principle of its own becoming is granted, then the door is open for a materialistic account of the order in the universe. Philo presents it merely as a revised version of the Epicurean hypothesis, "the most absurd system, that has yet been proposed" (DNR, 182), but in reality it contains the seeds of an evolutionary, almost Darwinian, outlook on natural processes. Philo revises the hypothesis by supposing that the total of material constituents is finite, that the quantity of movement throughout the universe is preserved constant, and more important, that movement, activity, is an intrinsic and eternal property of matter itself, that is, that matter is not dead, having its own dynamics. In an infinite duration all possible arrangements or combination will be tried by a finite number of particles in perpetual motion. It is plausible that from initial chaotic conditions matter may eventually arrive at some stable state or uniform disposition, which would maintain itself amidst the continuous exchange of the parts:

> This we find to be the case with the universe at present. Every individual is perpetually changing, and every part of every individual; and yet the whole remains, in appearance, the same. May we not hope for such a position, or rather be assured of it, from the eternal revolutions of unguided matter; and may not this account for all the appearing wisdom and contrivance which is in the universe? (DNR, 184).

In other words, the contemplation of order in the universe is not an undeniable proof of the workings of an ordering intelligence. On the contrary, "unguided matter," through a purely mechanical process, may lead to the establishment of a certain structure or order which preserves itself; that is, the process itself starting from the initial conditions could necessarily produce such a result. The stable individual configurations are the necessary outcome of the process because they arise out of the peculiar characteristics possessed by the entities making up the process.

But the existence of order in individual natural entities, that is, the fact that their parts have a relation to each other and to the whole, and that the latter itself has a relation to other complex individuals and ultimately to the universe as such, does not necessarily show that these organisms were created by a purposeful intelligence; this organization is rather the very condition without which they would not exist and persist at all as individual entities. Hume advances in what follows the typical Darwinian answer to the problem of the nature of functional adaptations in living organisms:

> It is in vain, therefore, to insist upon the uses of the parts in animals or vegetables, and their curious adjustment to each other. I would fain know, how an animal could subsist, unless its parts were so adjusted? Do we not find, that it immediately perishes whenever this adjustment ceases, and that its matter corrupting tries some new form? It happens indeed, that the parts of the world are so well adjusted, that some regular form immediately lays claim to this corrupted matter: and if it were not so, could the world subsist? (DNR, 185).

During the last few years Philo's modified Epicurean materialistic hypothesis has received the polemical attention of important scholars[17] of the *Dialogues*, who

---

[17] Thus Leon Pearl, in "Hume's Criticism of the Design Argument," *The Monist* 54, (1970): 283, considers that the Epicurean hypothesis cannot be an empirically founded hypothesis such as the design hypothesis, and he seems to assimilate it to an ideal model or a priori possibility. Stanley Tweyman, in

have not reached an agreement about its formal character and the material role it plays in Hume's questioning of rational theology. So this may well be a fitting moment for us to stop and place it in sharp focus in order to determine what kind of hypothesis it really is, whether it contains hidden and problematical presuppositions that fatally nullified it, and what is its precise relationship with Hume's overall critique of the "religious hypothesis." My initial conviction is simply that this naturalistic hypothesis is not merely an episodic interlude of the philosophical imagination, and as such an accessory and disposable item in Hume's refutation, but rather an essential and decisive constituent of Hume's logical strategy for the demolition of the citadel of speculative theism.

Is the modified Epicurean hypothesis the only naturalistic explanation of the universe proposed by Hume in the *Dialogues,* and is that explanation itself the only or at least a sufficient justification of his position, namely, his rejection the argument from design? Let us turn to the first point. Even giving due allowance for the elusive meaning of the term 'nature,'[18] it amounts to an error of fact, to assert that the so-called Epicurean materialism of Parts VII and VIII of the *Dialogues* is the sole naturalistic hypothesis, for Philo's hylozoistic hypothesis of Parts V and VI of the *Dialogues* seems to merit, no less than the materialistic-mechanical hypothesis, the epithet of naturalistic. It is true that hylozoism is not anti-theistic, but pantheistic; yet it is no less naturalistic for that matter; at most one must bestow on it the title of naturalistic pantheism. The universe is in both theories its own cause (*causa sui*), the principle of order lies within the nature and potentialities of the world, as distinct from the operations of an eternal and external (that is, ontologically distinct) intelligence.[19] And let us not forget that Philo laboriously tries to show to Cleanthes that the animistic hypothesis is much more conformable to experience than even that of a finitely perfect designer. Even more important is that hylozoism seems to have been brought forward to show that the consideration of sub-systems within the universe, especially living beings like plants and animals, when and if taken as a "norm" or "model" for the whole, make the hypothesis of a designer cumulatively less probable. This other kind of naturalism underlines a crucial and de-

---

Scepticism and Belief in Hume's Dialogues Concerning Natural Religion, pp. 111–112, argues against Pearl to the effect that the Epicurean hypothesis is a genuine empirical explanation. In this I think Tweyman is right.

[18] See DNR, 178: "that vague, undetermined word, nature, to which the vulgar refers every thing."

[19] Thus Philo says:

And were I obliged to defend any particular system of this nature (which I never willingly should do), I esteem none more plausible than that which ascribes an eternal, inherent principle of order to the world; though attended with great and continual revolutions . . . . How could things have been as they are, were there not an original, inherent principle of order somewhere, in thought or in matter? And it is very indifferent to which of these we give the preference (DNR, 174).

George J. Nathan even supposes that Hume adheres to a sort of hylozoism, defending the position that in the *Dialogues* Hume is a pantheist rather than an agnostic. George J. Nathan, "Hume's Immanent God," pp. 396–423.

cisive consideration against the design argument, i.e., that the analogy upon which the causal inference that the argument from design pretends to be is incurably ambiguous and uncertain. Hylozoism makes clear that living organisms, commonly taken as paradigmatical cases of purposeful or teleological arrangement, cannot be readily equated with systems of material parts in mechanical interactions. By contrast, the atomistic hypothesis perhaps was historically inspired by the use of mechanical models to explain natural phenomena,[20] or at any rate it takes very seriously the analogy of the world to a machine.

In short, if the universe more closely resembles a living being, then design is a less probable hypothesis than a cosmic principle of generation or vegetation, but if the universe is really like a mechanical artifact, then the Epicurean hypothesis, suitably revised and freed from some "systematical prejudices" (like Descartes' static and purely geometrical conception of matter), is a cosmogonical hypothesis as likely as that of an intelligent author.

One cannot give, however, a similarly expeditious answer to the second question: How fundamental is this materialistic hypothesis within the overall critique of design which Hume develops in the *Dialogues*? Although it has been fairly shown that it is not the only refutation of classical theism, one may still ask whether Hume does propose it as a complete and self-sufficient reply to it, and if, with such character, this hypothesis is not itself exempted from dubious presuppositions that reduce it to the absurd, and hence make the critique of design not compelling. And, finally, if naturalism were found to be contrary, and theism conformable, to our experience of the world, then the cogency of the design argument would have been justified and the probability of a designer reasonably established. Such protagonistic interpretation – an even tragic, since the protagonist would self-destroy – of the naturalistic hypothesis, in spite of its obvious appeal to those who sympathize with the design argument, is not sufficiently supported by the *Dialogues*, as I shall attempt to show in what follows.

The naturalistic hypothesis certainly is an important part, even a climatic point, in Hume's attack of the argument; it is one of the two major Epicurean challenges[21] to the claim that the order of the universal course of events, as it appears to our experience, testifies to the existence of a perfect Creator. However, instead of being the justification of the other arguments, the Epicurean hypothesis is itself supported by them and in fact made into a credible theoretical alternative only after the cumulative effect of Philo's searching criticism (substantially the same of Section XI of the first *Enquiry*) of Cleanthes' "experimental" theism has made us realize that the existence of a designer is not a self-evident proposition but the conclusion of a causal and analogical inference of a logically suspect or "irregular" kind.

---

[20] According to Robert S. Brumbaugh "Anaximander's 'models' were, of course, the strongest argument in favor of this new approach to physical reality; for the atomic theory could explain the fact that nature behave like a machine because it really was a complex mechanism." Robert S. Brumbaugh, *The Philosophers of Greece* (Albany: SUNY, 1981), p. 87.

[21] In Part X Hume formulates the classical Epicurean challenge to the moral attributes of God (DNR, 198), which will be examined in section 14.5.

The theoretical and refutative self-sufficiency of the naturalistic hypothesis is put into question by the carefully hesitant and tentative manner in which Philo first proposes it: "commonly, and I believe, justly, esteemed the most absurd system that has yet been proposed" (DNR, 182). He is not justifying its truth, or even its verisimilitude, but establishing it with "a faint appearance of probability" (DNR, 182). Besides, it is not possible to simply thrust on to Hume the kind of mechanistic materialism which Philo proposes. This is clarified by the following passage of the *History of England*, in which Hume apparently rejects, or at least gives a very conditional approval to, the mechanistic philosophical dominant in his time, which received its inspiration from Newton:

> While Newton seemed to draw off the veil from some of the mysteries of nature, he shewed at the same time the imperfections of the mechanical philosophy; and thereby restored her ultimate secrets to that obscurity, in which they ever did and ever will remain (H, VI, 542).

By means of this theoretical alternative Hume appears not to be challenging the likelihood of a designer but rather remarking that the scantiness of the empirical evidence does not allow the definitive exclusion of other sorts of cosmogonical accounts.

But, just how binding is the insufficient data claim? Does it really precludes us from making a licit inference to design? We could think, after all, that this objection is not decisive, for it is itself based on the same hidden and quite questionable premises of the naturalistic hypothesis, i.e., that there is only one universe. Is this really so? I believe not. Of course, if 'universe' means 'all that is,' then the precedent thesis becomes quite uninteresting. But in the *Dialogues* Hume more frequently uses the word 'universe' interchangeably with words like 'this system', 'the whole', 'position', 'arrangement' or 'adjustment of the world', 'the whole of nature' and so forth. This usage rather suggests the ancient meaning of *kosmos*, a particular configuration or reunion of the many beings into one. In this sense the assertion that this universe is the only there is, is not a truism; in the former sense, however, it becomes quite preposterous to entertain the idea of comparing "this system to other possible, or even real systems" (DNR, 167).

What precludes any theoretically satisfying answer to the riddle of the origin of the whole is not so much the unavailability of data from other universes but the imperfect and partial view we have of this one (DNR, 177). That is why we cannot say that the one known universe is really perfect. But even if we knew this to be the case, it would not then follow with necessity, as Philo's metaphor of the ship (DNR, V, 167) is intended to show, that its author should possess the same degree of perfection which we see his handiwork to display at present.

Still, it must be admitted that one can rightly assert that the design argument really needs but one universe which must manifest some order. The insufficient data claim does not eliminate the possibility of a designer or makes its existence less likely. The function which this objection thoroughly fulfills is another: it effectively disposes of the claim that the available evidence makes it reasonable for us to assert the existence of an infinitely perfect designer.

But is it not possible that the Epicurean hypothesis is beset by presuppositions even more objectionable than the former? Is it not based on the assumption that any stable universe has to be totally ordered? This objection seems reasonable enough, because Philo propounds that the universe, if we give it enough time, will attain some order without the intervention of any external agent. And once this is presupposed, does it not also follow that the presence of even a single instance of disorder in this universe would refute the naturalistic hypothesis? I believe one should answer both questions in the negative. Even if one concedes that Hume indeed holds the total order thesis, it does not follow that he also assumes that once the universe reaches such total order, it will keep it forever and ever. He rather suggests that the cosmogonical movement is one of periodical alternation of chaos and order, somewhat similar to "the flux and reflux of polytheism and theism" (NHR, 46–51). It is true that Cleanthes argues against the likelihood of abrupt, frequent and total convulsions in the natural history of the world (DNR, 172–174). But Philo's reply to Cleanthes is not that disorder of material beings is impossible; he rather asserts that matter cannot remain totally disordered, not that it has to be totally ordered (DNR, 174–175). This cyclical view is supported by the following:

> And though order were supposed inseparable from matter, and inherent in it; yet may matter be susceptible of many and great revolutions, through the endless periods of eternal duration (DNR, 174).

The necessity of order in the universe is a hypothetical one: if the universe, like any other whole of constantly changing constituents, remains structurally the same, then the ordered relationships between its moving parts must remain constant:

> [T]his adjustment, *if* attained by matter of a seeming stability in the forms, with a real and perpetual revolution or motion of parts, affords a plausible, if not a true solution of the difficulty (DNR, 185; italics added).

Under these assumptions I think that the presence of particular instances of disorder would be a very likely occurrence. Total order or total disorder would be limiting cases in a cosmogonical flux and reflux.

Of course, our stable universe is known to be not totally ordered. Does if follow then that it is not really the Humean system of a finite number of indivisible particles? Not necessarily. Perhaps our world is insensibly ascending towards, or slowly falling from, such a state of absolute order.[22] In either case it would be difficult not to say that the actually experienced universe is a reasonably to be expected result of the perpetual revolutions of "unguided matter." Although Hume would probably

---

[22] In "Of the Populousness of Ancient Nations," Hume says: "though it were allowed, that the universe, like an animal body, had a natural progress from infancy to old age; yet as it must still be uncertain, whether, at present, it be advancing to its point of perfection, or declining from it" (E, 378).

say that this conjectured atomistic universe is not sufficiently confirmed by experience (DNR, 185–186), I think he would reject the claim that our experience of disorder disproves it. Thus, when Cleanthes attempts to falsify the Epicurean hypothesis, instead of dwelling on particular instances of disorder, he points to several features of functional adaptation in living organisms and in humans which appear to be disproportional to the mere natural necessity of subsistence or self-preservation which they are, according to the Epicurean hypothesis, geared to satisfy (DNR, 185). Cleanthes objection is the exact opposite of the present one: It is the superabundance of order over disorder (which suggests the workings of a benevolent designer) what the naturalistic hypothesis fails to account for.

Besides, to claim that Hume upholds that any material stable universe has to be totally ordered, is to transform what is, I believe, an *ad hominem argument* against design into a position which Hume himself would totally endorse. Yet Philo states that to defend such hypothesis is something "which I never willingly should do" (DNR, 174; see also, DNR, 186–187). Such claim is also incompatible with Hume's tenet that it is not possible to prove a priori or a posteriori that order is an essential attribute of thought or of matter (DNR, 162–63, 179). The fact that we have observed many instances of thought without order, as in madness, and equally of matter without order, as in corruption, perhaps suffices to show that order as such is not an essential attribute of either of the two (DNR, 162).

And what are we to say about the correspondence of both hypotheses with fact and reality? Should Hume deny that the epistemic superiority of the design argument lies in its greater conformity with our actual experience of the world? I believe that Hume is not attempting to deny the following assertion: "the one great advantage of the principle of theism, is, that it is the only system of cosmogony which can be rendered intelligible and complete, and yet can throughout preserve a strong analogy to what we every day see and experience in the world" (DNR, 216). Thus speaks Cleanthes, and if one could prove beyond reasonable doubt that in this Philo substantially agrees with him, then one would have to conclude that Hume, without reservations, bestows his assent on the preceding proposition.

More than once we have seen that disorders in nature can, and frequently are, taken as putative evidence for the workings of some designer. In fact, this is noted, with a certain irony, by Hume through Philo: "the many inexplicable difficulties in the works of nature perhaps will be insisted on, as new likeness to human art and contrivance" (DNR, 167). But the moment we assume that the existence of no being whatsoever can be proved a priori, and once we decide to infer the existence of God from our experience of order in the universe, from the uniformity of nature, then we cannot simultaneously look for God in the fringes of order, that is, we cannot then impute to him the ruptures of such order, or the alterations of the usual course of nature. As we have already observed in the chapter on miracles, extraordinary events, prodigies, presumed miracles, have to be counted not so much as corroboration but rather as factual counter-examples of the hypothesis of design: "And such events, as, with good reasoners, are the chief difficulties in admitting a supreme intelligence are with him ["the vulgar"] the sole arguments for it" (NHR, 41).

Certainly, designers can – and occasionally do – create disordered works. But within the admittedly conventional, historical and even aesthetic constraints under which the argument and Hume's critique are formulated, simplicity and lawfulness, beauty and order are taken as the most natural and unequivocal signs of intelligent design, "of project and forethought in the workman" (EHU, 136). Conversely, you cannot bring God forward in order to establish the probable occurrence of miracles in the sense of violations to the uniform course of nature (EHU, 129).

Hume may have not gone as far as to suggest that the religious hypothesis is compatible with any state of affairs, and that it looses, on such account, any valid pretensions to cognitive significance.[23] He does not quite contend with the claim that a cosmic designer is compatible with our actual experience of the universe. At most, what he questions is the consistency of the argument which, based upon the experience of the latter, infers the existence of the former:

> [H]owever consistent the world may be, allowing certain suppositions and conjectures, with the idea of such a Deity, it can never afford us an inference concerning his existence. The consistence is not absolutely denied, only the inference (DNR, 205; see also 201, 211).

At the same time one must not forget that in passages such as these Philo is criticizing Cleanthes' attempt to empirically establish the moral attributes, and not so much the intelligence, of the designer.

Yet let us suppose that Hume has been guilty, in the framing of his naturalistic hypothesis, of all the mistakes and confusions that have been attributed to him. Let us further assume that experience is really against it. Since we are dealing, after all, with probable hypotheses about the origin of the world, those liabilities by themselves would not increase the probability of the design hypothesis: "a hundred contradictory views may preserve a kind of imperfect analogy" (DNR, 182).

Ultimately, this is why Philo, as befits his sceptical outlook, pretends not that this hypothesis solves at once all the difficulties, but only that, taking into consideration the uncertainty of all conjectures about the whole, it is as plausible as theism, and even retains a greater analogy with experience. But in any case, he reaffirms that the proper attitude is not to embrace any system: "A total suspense of judgment is here our only reasonable resource" (DNR, 186–187).

13. 5 THE ANTI-THEODICY (PARTS X AND XI)

In contradistinction to Philo's outlook thus far considered, Cleanthes' thesis of a finite deity is a recourse to escape such a suspense of judgment, and an attempt to confront directly, without flight into the realm of mystery, the major difficulties

---

[23] The most formidable and lucid exponent of this typical reading of Hume's critique is Antony Flew. See his *Hume's Philosophy of Belief*, pp. 231–233.

which militate against the existence of a benevolent God, facts such as the existence of pain, suffering, and evil in the world. This is something which the religious person, at least within the Hebrew-Christian tradition, cannot simply close his or her eyes to; the acknowledgment of the goodness of God is correlative with the recognition of evil in the world, and with the conviction that God is not indifferent to the outcome of the conflict between good and evil, that God does not want him or her to remain indifferent with respect to such a struggle.

The exclusion of infinity from the attributes of God makes it possible, according to Cleanthes, to reconcile God's benevolence with the mixture of evil in the universe, and permits the religious person to answer the last Epicurean challenge to his or her faith: "Is he willing to prevent evil, but not able? then is he impotent. Is he able, but not willing? then is he malevolent. Is he both able and willing? whence then is evil?" (DNR, 198). Maybe this is another reason why Hume called Cleanthes "the Hero" of the *Dialogues*.

For Cleanthes, moral and natural evil can be accounted for if God is finitely perfect, for "benevolence, regulated by wisdom, and limited by necessity, may produce just such a world as the present" (DNR, 203). At any rate Cleanthes' God is very far from being the God of traditional Christian theology; he is nearer the conception of a Platonic Demiurgue.

But it is very difficult – both Philo and Demea note – to construct, with the materials provided by misery and suffering, human as well as animal, an argument in favor of the existence of a good God, as at the beginning of Part X Cleanthes seems intent on doing. There is no possibility of computing good against evil and showing that, grief notwithstanding, the balance is in favor of good. Even more preposterous, not to say insensible, is Cleanthes' attempt to take the actual condition of human existence within the world as the starting point for such an empirical proof of God's benevolence. This is why Philo rejects such a device. Only if the divine goodness could be demonstrated a priori, could the picture of suffering and privation which experience discloses be reconciled in a definitive way with the moral attributes of divinity, not only with finite but even with infinite attributes, provided, as Philo remarks, that we first renounce the claim that we properly comprehend these attributes:

> None but we Mystics, as you were pleased to call us, can account for this strange mixture of phenomena, by deriving it from attributes, infinitely perfect, but incomprehensible (DNR, 199).

Now we begin to see that the mixture of mystic and a priori reasoner that Demea exemplifies is not so strange after all. Although Cleanthes rejects, and Philo accepts, the logical legitimacy of Demea's mysticism, both of them refuse in Part XI to follow the a priori path towards the divine. Cleanthes "experimental theism," in effect, excludes such a possibility from the start; and as we have seen when we examined the ontological proof, Hume's philosophy, out of sound reasons, invalidates it in principle.

With regard to mysticism, it seems that Cleanthes rejects it because ultimately if nothing can be asserted of God, then nothing can be denied of Him either; and the theist surely wants to affirm his goodness, however limited by necessity. Philo's position, which Demea has so far shared with gusto, namely, that an infinite God is for us perfectly incomprehensible (or mysterious, in traditional religious language), logically leads not to say that God is incomprehensibly good, but rather to affirm something which horrifies Demea, the fideistic orthodox theologian, and that finally makes him abandon the conversation altogether: namely, that judging from our experience of the world and human life, it is more likely that God is indifferent to good and evil (DNR, 202).[24]

Philo does not concern himself with the problem as to which is the proper attitude that the worshipper ought to assume towards the moral attributes of God; yet he observes that even Cleanthes' revisionist theism cannot establish empirically the goodness of the Deity. At best it can show that the present scene of things is compatible with that goodness, but it can never legitimately infer the latter from the former (DNR, 201, 205, 211). And if experience is taken as our only guide, the divine purpose seems to be oriented towards the preservation of the species rather than towards the happiness of the individual He presses this point with a naturalistic metaphor about the whole, which is completely contrary to the comparison of the world to a great machine used by Cleanthes at the beginning of his defense of the argument from design:

> Look round this universe. . . . The whole presents nothing but the idea of a blind Nature, impregnated by a great vivifying principle, and pouring forth from her lap, without discernment or parental care, her maimed and abortive children! (DNR, 211).

But Philo goes even further. Even if the Deity were finite, for all we know it is not inconceivable that He could have prevented the evils and sufferings which at present endemically plague his creation. In this sort of inventive challenge to traditional apologetics, he goes on to enumerate four causes of evil in the world, and then proceeds to suggest ways by means of which those evils might have disappeared without significantly altering the uniform panorama of nature. In Part XI (DNR, 205–210), Philo describes an utopian universe in which: 1. although animals can experience pleasure, they are deprived of the sensation of pain, but still have enough forethought and steadfastness to be moved to act, not by actual pain, but simply by the absence of pleasure; 2. the particular or occasional intervention of the Deity would thwart the usual negative and painful consequences of natural events as well as of human decisions and actions; 3. animals would be more generously endowed with those capacities which they need to cope with their natural en-

---

[24] Nelson Pike's "Hume on Evil," [*David Hume, Critical Assessments*, ed. Stanley Tweyman (London and New York: Routledge, 1995), vol. 5, pp. 300–314], and Stanley Tweyman's "Hume's Dialogues on Evil," [Ibid., pp. 315–322] not only present persuasive, albeit contrasting views on this subject, but also are the best analyses of Parts X and XI that I know of.

vironment with consistent success, and 4. this milieu would always behave in a strictly regular and predictable manner, that is, without those sudden and unmerciful commotions produced by events very common in our world, such as earthquakes, hurricanes, draughts and floods, etc. If those four conditions were satisfied, the majority of evils that torment humans and the rest of living beings would disappear from the face of the earth. By means of Philo, Hume manifestly strives to show that such earthly paradise is a distinct and perfectly conceivable possibility, i.e., that it implies no contradiction, and hence is not beyond the capacity of a Deity with good intentions, although with much more might and sagacity than us, and much less exceeds that of an infinitely good, wise, and powerful God. But we shall not follow Hume in this hasty *tour de force* (DNR, 205–210).

More substantial than the preceding are his critical comments about the arguments of traditional theodicy, or the justification of God before the apparent ills and disorders of the world. One usual line of defense consists in arguing that due to the limited experience we have of the world we cannot really say whether what seems to us to be an evil is not, viewed from the perspective of the whole, a good or at least something absolutely indispensable for the achievement of the perfection and beauty of the universal scheme. In the *Enquiry Concerning Human Understanding* (EHU, 101–102), Hume had already examined this argument of Stoic provenience, remarking that whatever conviction it may produce in a person of a speculative frame of mind, it seems rather incredible and offers little comfort to anyone actually suffering any of those unavoidable evils. In the *Dialogues* he summarily dismisses it by means of a very acute metaphor:

> Did I shew you a house or palace, where there was not one apartment convenient or agreeable; where the windows, doors, fires, passages, stairs, and the whole economy of the building, were the source of noise, confusion, fatigue, darkness, and the extremes of heat and cold . . . . The architect would in vain display his subtilty, and prove to you, that if this door or that window were altered, greater ills would ensue. . . . But still you would assert in general, that, if the architect had had skill and good intentions, he might have formed such a plan of the whole, and might have adjusted the parts in such a manner, as would have remedied all or most of these inconveniences. His ignorance, or even your own ignorance of such a plan, will never convince you of the impossibility of it. If you find any inconveniences and deformities in the building, you will always, without entering into any detail, condemn the architect (DNR, 204–205).

We might also argue for the Deity, in a way similar to the author of *The Book of Job*, that man cannot bring God to reckoning, that God does not have to give humans any account for His actions. Hume seems to suggest that this answer is conclusive against Job, since what is at stake there is God's benevolence and justice, not God's existence, which is obviously taken for granted by Job, his faithful servant. But in the case of Cleanthes, where faith is not involved – and in fact dismissed – and where the possibility of finding some rational ground for God's existence is at stake too, such an answer is not proper. If human understanding is so uncertain a guide that we cannot trust it to adequately judge the moral propriety of God's actions, neither can we rest any confidence in that same judgment when it seeks to establish the existence of God. If it is incompetent in one case, it is equally incompetent in the other. And this is a very difficult argument to be evaded by any non-fideistic approach. A corollary of this reasoning, in truth its converse, is what led Hume to assert with striking consistency throughout all his works that if we recognize God as the ultimate cause of the whole, then it is not possible to say that He is not the author of evil, unless we declare at the same time that these are matters which transcend the limits of our knowing capacities.

> If nothing be active but what has an apparent power, thought is in no case any more active than matter; and if this inactivity must make us have recourse to a Deity, the Supreme Being is the real cause of all our actions, bad as well as good, vicious as well as virtuous (THN, 249).

Let us remember that in the *Treatise* Hume has defined God as a mind whose will is *constantly attended* with the obedience of every creature and being. In the *Enquiry* he says thus: "Human actions . . . either can have no moral turpitude at all, as proceeding from so good a cause; or if they have any turpitude, they must involve our Creator in the same guilt, while he is acknowledged to be their ultimate cause and author" (EHU, 100). And Part XI of the *Dialogues*, Philo affirms essentially the same:

> You must assign a cause for it [vice], without having recourse to the first cause. But as every effect must have a cause, and that cause another; you must either carry on the progression in infinitum, or rest on that original principle who is the ultimate cause of all things (DNR, 212).

In short, it seems as if we found ourselves before an irresolvable dilemma: If we cannot say that God is good, then neither can we say that He exists; but if we know that He exists, then there is no way to clear Him up from evil.

A very common defense that Hume does not explicitly examine is the one according to which evil and suffering are the price to be paid for human freedom. But this does not mean that his arguments have no important consequences for that question. Anthony Flew, a very acute commentator of Hume's thought, has indicated that the hidden meaning of the preceding dilemma is not – as Hume and Philo suggest in the alluded passages of the *Enquiry* and *Dialogues* respectively – that the question about divine omnipotence and moral evil is enclosed in the deepest mystery, but to suggest that there is an inevitable contradiction between divine omnipotence and human freedom.[25] Because God is creator in an absolute sense, it

---

[25] See Anthony Flew, "Divine Omnipotence and Human Freedom," *New Essays in Philosophical Theology*, pp. 144–169. The same opinion is held by J. L. Mackie, "Evil and Omnipotence," *Mind* 64, 254 (April 1955): 200-212. Mackie's rendering of this dilemma is clear, eloquent, and urgent:

is not possible for Him to create beings which are genuinely free, or in other words, being that could by themselves make choices against the will of God, for nothing, absolutely nothing, occurs that is not in conformity with the divine will. Flew's reading is credible, since Hume voices his reflections about evil, free will and omnipotence within the context of his critique of Malebranche's occasionalism. This doctrine proclaims, on the one hand, that God is, as creator, the single and immediate cause of everything that happens in the world, and on the other, that no other being is, in a strict sense, a real cause. Creatures simply do not act; they are not effective causes, but only the occasions which the Supreme cause avails himself of in order to exert his power.[26] But if God is the only cause, then it appears that one cannot deny that He has to be the power behind the actions of some of his creatures, that is, the real cause even of the determinations of our will. In short, if God is omnipotent the human will cannot be free, but if we freely choose, then God cannot be omnipotent.

One must, however, attenuate the previous proposition. What would be incompatible with omnipotence is the assertion that human choices are uncaused and unpredictable, that is, that they occur in conformity to what Hume calls in the *Treatise*, the liberty of *indifference*. This kind of free will would be absolutely irreconcilable, not only with the existence of divine predetermination, but even with the existence of a universe subjected to laws which are strictly universal, regular and necessary, and where the ultimate responsibility for this feature is ascribed, not to God, but to nature itself. It is not surprising then that Hume tried to reconcile freedom with his belief in universal determinism, or the "maxim" of the uniformity of nature. This is the liberty of *spontaneity*, which is contrary to violence, or external constraint, but does not imply – as the liberty of indifference does – the absence of necessity or of causes antecedent to the decisions of the will (THN, 407–408). In this sense, free actions would not be uncaused and unpredictable in principle, since they would be the products of the nature of the agent (that is to say, those actions would follow from the character of the agent), and because of it they would still be compatible with the existence of a world ruled by casually necessary laws. In the *Enquiry* Hume qualifies this capacity for acting according to the determinations of the will, without external coercion, as *hypothetical* liberty, in order to distinguish it from the liberty which would have to be characterized as unconditional, that is, freedom uncaused and unpredictable: "hypothetical liberty is universally allowed to belong to every one, who is not a prisoner and in chains" (EHU, 95). I think Hume

---

I should ask this: If God has made men such that in their free choices they sometimes prefer what is good and sometimes what is evil, why could he not have made men such that they always freely choose the good? If there is no logical impossibility in man's freely choosing the good on one, or several occasions, there cannot be a logical impossibility in his freely choosing the good on every occasion. God was not, then, faced with a choice between making innocent automata and making beings who, in acting freely, would sometimes go wrong: there was open to him the obviously better possibility of making beings who would act freely but always go right (p. 209).

[26] This is why Hume says that this theory rob "second causes of all force or energy" (EHU, 73, footnote 15).

would also have acknowledged that freedom of spontaneity is not only reconcilable with natural determinism, but *a fortiori*, with divine omnipotence and predestination. Yet, this is precisely what Flew has emphatically denied in his own, and in Hume's, name.[27]

But before analyzing this opinion, one should ask why Hume does not expressly cope in his anti-theodicy with the question whether by appealing to human freedom one could in fact free God from the ultimate responsibility of evil. Is it not perhaps because he thought that he had implicitly refuted this apologetic line by refuting the last two arguments, which do seem to be sorely needed in order to cogently establish the free will defense? For it is only if one contemplates it within the framework of totality that freedom – which seems to have so many and painful inconveniences for the entity that attempts to exercise it – can appear as a second order good, that is to say, as a condition which, like courage and generosity, presuppose the existence of certain antecedent evils – risks, dangers, privation, scarcity, for instance – in order to come into being and produce the goods which are both intrinsic to them and greater than the liabilities and misfortunes which they sometimes also give rise to. It is only if we are reasonably convinced of the existence of an omnipotent and good God, that we can point at freedom in order to show that the spectacle of the countless sorrows of human life is the reasonably to be expected result of the operation of such a deity. But if we do not yet know that God exists, is it not the case, as Flew suggests, that liberty appears as an irrefutable argument, if not against God's existence, at least against his omnipotence?

Is the hidden purpose of Philo's allegation that the known causes of evil in the world could conceivably have been rendered inoperative by God, even by a finitely perfect deity, is to show that the exercise of human freedom is not by force incompatible with a world without evil, i.e., with a universe in which human beings – as Flew suggests – would always freely (without coercion) choose to do good and their decisions would never bring about any adverse and painful consequences? No, Philo's utopia is not designed to deal with moral evil, and thus to refute the free-will defense, but to show that even a mighty, albeit good-intentioned deity, could have eliminated the factors upon which "all or the greatest part of natural evil depend" (DNR, 210).

What would Hume have said about the claim of philosophers such as Flew and Mackie that God could have created free persons who at the same time would never sin? Would it be really possible to call any one good in a world peopled exclusively by beings who, without any loss of liberty, would never engender even a single instance of a morally incorrect deed or a vicious action, and hence where egoism, injustice, untruthfulness, and violence would never come to pass? In this hypothetical world, if we were to predicate freedom and goodness of any and each one of its inhabitants it would have to be because, despite the fact that they always do

---

[27] Antony Flew, *God and Philosophy* (New York: Dell Publishing, Co., 1966), p. 56: "there seems to be no contradiction in suggesting that he could have ensured that all his creation always, and freely, did what they should. Our actual wickedness therefore remains intractably a major part of the evil which has to be reconciled with the thesis of creation by an infinitely good Creator."

the right thing, there would be no reason to deny them the capacity, propension, or disposition to act wrongly. Why so? Because it would always be possible for us to image or clearly conceive that they could have followed a course of action opposed to the one they invariably follow, which is to do good. Although this possibility appears plausible at first sight, when we examine the case more closely, we should conclude that in such a world the predication of the potency or power to do evil would neither have any definite sense, nor really be possible. Even if we follow Aristotle and acknowledge that potency is a genuine ontological category, it still remains a derivative mode of being: in other words, one cannot predicate a potentiality of any being if it is not from the knowledge of an actual case of that kind of being; thus, for instance, we could not say that a tadpole is a frog in potency, if we have seen no single instance of the transformation of the one into the other. Likewise, if we accept the Aristotelian principle of the priority of the actual over potential being, it would not be possible to say of any being that it is free and good (that it is a being who always chooses the good although is capable of doing what is evil) if in that supra-angelic world (for some angels, like Lucifer, do sin) there never will occur a single actual determination of a will which is really evil, or morally wrong.

Hume, who goes so far as to question the Aristotelian distinction of potency and act, could not have said less. In the *Treatise*, he affirms – as a corollary of his definitions of causality – that "the distinction, which we often make betwixt *power* and the *exercise* of it, is . . . without foundation" (THN, 171). According to it, for example, it would make no sense to assert that there is in the flame a power to produce heat, unless we have had the experience of their accustomed union, that is, unless we have actually observed the constant conjunction between objects similar to flame and heat. In like manner, it would make no sense to affirm that a being has the capacity or potential to do evil if we have had no experience of even a single instance of the exercise of that evil power by that being or by beings similar to it. A mere logical possibility that is empty of any real contents does not quite provide us with a sufficient warrant to assert the presence of a potency or real power.

In contemporary analytical philosophy, Ninian Smart has refuted, with an argument similar to the preceding consideration which I have formulated in Hume's name, the thesis propounded by Flew and Mackie.[28] According to Smart, even though God can create many kinds of beings, he would not create what is absurd, because, following St. Thomas Aquinas, he presupposes that nothing which implies a contradiction can be a real limitation to God's omnipotence. Hence, God would not create free beings, who infallibly and always do what is good, because they would not properly be persons or beings about which one could say in a clear and precise sense that they are morally good, for instance, forceful and resolute in resisting evil, truthful, loyal, courageous, generous, etc. Smart devises several ingenious utopias about various possible worlds, some similar to, others quite distinct from, our world, whose aim is to show that moral concepts would loose their

---

[28] Ninian Smart, "Omnipotence, Evil and Supermen," *Philosophy* 36, 137 (1961): 181–195.

sense in worlds which, unlike our own, humans would have been made entirely good, or where we would have been constructed so that we would never have, nor succumb to, the temptations which pleasure, power, riches, or fame amply afford. At the least it would be questionable or "unclear" to say of such "men" that they are wholly good, or even that they are "men." The idea of human beings which are wholly good is, according to Smart, an abstract possibility without any definite contents, whose real possibility – at least until their proponents specify it – can be reasonably challenged. But once we begin to specify it, we become aware that it has to be rejected as absurd, since the sort of reconstruction of our humanity that would have to be done in order to be "immunized against evil," would also eliminate the concrete conditions which make possible for persons to display their goodness or badness, and which permit us to identify them as such: "the reasons why men are called good and bad have a connection with human nature as it is empirically discovered to be."[29] With this appraisal Hume, the moral philosopher, would, I think, heartily concur.

In addition, Smart thinks that it is questionable that a world peopled by beings totally good would be necessarily superior to our actual world. This brings us back to Philo's utopia of Part XI of the *Dialogues*, because he has put it together as a world much better than ours, and apparently as a work more worthy of the good and omnipotent will of the Creator. For John Hick, another renowned contemporary philosopher of religion, in this "hedonistic paradise" which Philo depicts the divine purpose would be to endow living beings with the greatest quantity of pleasure and a minimum of pain. Yet at least for Christianity, God's purpose is rather to create a world in which persons can exercise their freedom, cultivate the moral virtues or vices, in short, which is propitious for human beings to enter into a relationship with God, so that they may be able to freely love him or hate him. In a manner which resembles Smart's, Hick argues that in Philo's utopian world human beings would be incapable of developing the character traits and modes of behavior which would make them good and thus worthy of being loved by God.

> Consequently, such a world, however well it might promote pleasure, would be very ill adapted for the development of the moral qualities of human personality. In relation to this purpose it would be the worst of all possible worlds.[30]

How adequate is this response against Philo's hypothesis? I believe it does not apply to the present case, however strong it might be against other opponents of traditional theodicy. We must remind ourselves that with it Philo replies to Cleanthes, who precisely upholds the conviction that Hick criticizes, namely, that the best of all possible worlds must contain an excess of pleasure over pain. But in arguing thus, Cleanthes is closer to deism, which rejects faith and the conception of this life as a waiting room or antechamber to a better one. Demea, the orthodox

---

[29] Ibid., pp. 190–191.

[30] John Hick, *Philosophy of Religion*, (Englewood Cliffs, N. J.: Prentice Hall, Inc., 1963), p. 45.

Christian, emphasizes the opposite, that is, the countless and diverse evils which we encounter in this world. Let us remember too, that Philo himself remarks that, judged from Cleanthes' perspective, the divine purpose seems more oriented towards the preservation of the species than towards the happiness of the individual. At any rate, to empirically show, taking as point of departure the present scene of the universe, that God's aim is to foster, not the happiness, but the moral personality of human individuals (a condition which is only attainable within a universe where they could fully exercise their freedom), is not possible as a valid causal inference. This Hick himself seems to admit, because even though the exercise of freedom is the condition without which inestimable moral goods would not emerge, very frequently, however, it is also the condition for rise of terrible evils.[31] And again, out of the terribly mixed condition of goods and evils within this world, be these the products of liberty or not, one cannot legitimately infer an infinitely good and powerful Cause. With respect to this world it is clear that we can not say that "no evil occurs which is not offset by the advent of a corresponding good,"[32] and not even – in spite of the old saying – that "evil is so often turned to good." Demea, along with traditional Christianity, will supplement the assessment about the sorrowful present state with a "future state" or ultramundane eschatological scheme. But, in the last analysis, Philo's intention is not to deny that the present universe has much in common with a world made by God with the purpose of fostering freedom and the qualities of character which depend upon it. This has been willingly conceded by Philo, even for an infinitely good and powerful deity; what he rather challenges is the logical propriety of inferring that such is the nature of the Creator's design, if we have to judge exclusively from the empirical knowledge we have of the world inhabited by his creatures:

> I am Sceptic enough to allow, that the bad appearances, notwithstanding all my reasonings, may be compatible with such attributes as you suppose; but surely they can never prove these attributes. Such a conclusion cannot result from Scepticism, but must arise from the phenomena, and from our confidence in the reasonings which we deduce from these phenomena (DNR, 211).

In summary, Philo concludes his challenge to the argument from design by confidently asserting that concerning the moral, although perhaps not the natural, attributes of the Deity, Cleanthes' experimental theism can be conclusively refuted:

---

[31] John Hick, *Philosophy of Religion*, pp. 46–47: [A]lthough there are many striking instances of good being triumphantly brought about out of evil through a man's or a woman's reaction to it, there are many other cases in which the opposite has happened. Sometimes obstacles breed strength of character, dangers evoke courage and unselfishness, and calamities produce patience and moral steadfastness. But sometimes they lead, instead, to resentment, fear, grasping selfishness, and disintegration of character." Hick has developed this theodicy, inspired by Irenaeus, in *Evil and the God of Love* (New York: Harper & Row, 1966).

[32] This is my literal, and somewhat awkward, rendering of the old Spanish proverb, "No hay mal que por bien no venga."

Here I triumph. . . . there is no view of human life, or of the condition of mankind, from which, without the greatest violence, we can infer the moral attributes, or learn that infinite benevolence, conjoined with infinite power and infinite wisdom, which we must discover by the eyes of faith alone (DNR, 202).

Up to this point, Philo's critique of the argument from design has shown that this reasoning is founded on an analogy between the works of nature and the products of human art. He has remarked that the analogy is remote, in fact imperfect, for it is far from being a specific similarity, and that the certainty of the conclusion that the world has been created by an intelligent God is reduced in proportion to the remoteness of the analogy. Hence it is impossible to prove the "religious hypothesis" beyond reasonable doubt. Furthermore, his careful analysis of the analogy has led him, without renouncing the guidance of experience, to frame a naturalistic alternative which, either in its hylozoistic or materialistic version, is equally plausible with theism. He has gone so far as to suggest that the analogy of experience is more favorable to naturalism than to theism, while at the same time he has admitted that the former theory also confronts serious, even perhaps insuperable, difficulties. But on the other hand, he has asserted, more than once, that the more reasonable alternative is the sceptical, that is, a suspense of judgment concerning the enquiries about the causes of the whole. However, he seems to go beyond this suspense with respect to the moral attributes of God, where his answer seems to be openly negative.

On the whole, Philo's conclusion looks strikingly similar to that found at the conclusion of the *Natural History*, which at first sight seemed to be agnostic. Does this mean then that the belief in an intelligent author of the universe, for Hume the nucleus of theism, lacks all grounds in human reason?

13.6 HUME'S MITIGATED THEISM (PART XII)

Part XII of the *Dialogues* gives a completely new turn to the whole discussion. Philo's reasoned pleas do not culminate in the purely agnostic position (even atheistic, if one takes seriously enough his revised Epicurean hypothesis). On the contrary, he makes a profession of faith in which he gives, although in a much qualified manner, an assent to the proposition that Cleanthes has been defending. Thus at the beginning of this part he says:

[N]o one has a deeper sense of religion impressed on his mind, or pays more profound adoration to the Divine Being, as he discovers himself to reason, in the inexplicable contrivance and artifice of nature. A purpose, an intention, a design, strikes every where the most careless, the most stupid thinker; and no man can be so hardened in absurd systems, as at all times to reject it (DNR, 214).

Yet this assent is not unrestricted; it is not an assent to the God or gods of popular religion, which Hume invariably classed as superstitious worship. In fact, eight of the fifteen pages of this part are devoted to a condemnation of popular religion in terms quite similar to those employed in *The Natural History of Religion*, that is, as leading to impiety, barbarity, caprice, intolerance, and at best to indifference towards the true motives of morality. His assent is not practical, but theoretical or rational, to that God who "discovers himself to reason," not to abstract reason, we may add, but to experimental reason, or the understanding in its function of making causal inferences or establishing causal connections between matters of fact. Furthermore, the intelligence referred to here discovers itself "through the inexplicable contrivance of nature." Philo has conclusively shown that there are very considerable differences between natural products and machines. Hence, the similarities between them do not guarantee any hasty speculations about what the divine purpose might be, and even less justify the consideration of this presumed purpose, as had been traditionally done, in purely anthropomorphic terms: i.e., that the universe was made for the sake of human beings, for their benefit and enjoyment.

Philo's apparent turnabout was not, however, completely unexpected. There is one point in Cleanthes' argument to which Philo has not yet paid direct attention: the strong impression that the contemplation of the order and uniformity of nature produces in us, which sensibly forces us to assent to theism, or at least to the existence of an intelligent Author of nature. For instance, Cleanthes asks in Part III:

> Consider, anatomize the eye; survey its structure and contrivance; and tell me, from your own feeling, if the idea of a contriver does not immediately flow in upon you with a force like that of sensation (DNR 154).

To this Philo does not really answer until Part X where he, for the first time, recognizes the force of Cleanthes' contention:

> Formerly, when we argued concerning the natural attributes of intelligence and design, I needed all my sceptical and metaphysical subtilty to elude your grasp. In many views of the universe and of its parts, particularly the latter, the beauty and fitness of final causes strike us with such irresistible force, that all objections appear (what I believe they really are) mere cavils and sophisms; nor can we then imagine how it was ever possible for us to repose any weight on them (DNR, 201–202).

On the other hand, the agreement between Philo and Cleanthes appears more unexpected than it really is because Hume, up to Part XII, has mostly been emphasizing their differences. Cleanthes' theism has a rational foundation precisely because of its heterodox character, i.e., its distance from the traditional Christian conception of one infinitely wise, omnipotent, and good Creator; in fact, Cleanthes' position appears to be more deistic than theistic, and from the start, very close to Philo's own. For example, after Philo has disclosed some of the logical paradoxes to which the hypothesis of design arrives, he says that at most Cleanthes can only "assert or conjecture that the universe, sometime *arose from something like design*" (DNR, 169; italics added). Now let us compare this with the conclusion Cleanthes asserted when he formulated for the first time the argument from design. There he made the memorable comparison of the universe with a machine, whose adequacy is what Philo most strongly questions throughout. However apt or inapt the analogy may be, Cleanthes asserts only that "the Author of nature *is somewhat similar to the mind of man*; though possessed of much larger faculties, proportioned to the grandeur of the work, which he has executed" (DNR, 143; italics added).

On the whole, the differences between Philo and Cleanthes are far from being abysmal. The main one, however, concerns the moral attributes of God. Cleanthes thought these could be inferred from experience, at least for a finite Deity. Philo, on the other hand, denied this strongly, although he admitted that experience is not incompatible with such a supposition, not even with Demea's fideistic hypothesis, who affirms the infinite perfection of God.

In spite of the previous considerations, the manner in which Philo agrees with Cleanthes in Part XII is not itself without ambiguity or paradox. First, after his confession of faith, Philo suggests that it is not possible to decide, in the controversy between theist and atheist, which of the two contenders is right. But the conclusion to be drawn from this is not that their differences are irreconcilable, but that their dispute is "merely verbal," and that they fundamentally agree with each other. The disputes about the degrees of any quality can never be settled; it is not possible to determine the exact degree of similarity between the human and the divine mind for the same reason that we cannot decide any controversy about the degree of Hannibal's greatness or of Cleopatra's beauty. Neither the analogies, nor the similarities can be measured with precision; it is not even possible in such disputes to agree upon an acceptable usage of terms; thus most of the time the contenders are in fact closer to each other than their words make us suspect:

> I ask the Theist, if he does not allow, that there is a great and immeasurable, because incomprehensible difference between the human and the divine mind: the more pious he is, the more readily will he assent to the affirmative, and the more will he be disposed to magnify the difference: he will even assert, that the difference is of a nature which cannot be too much magnified. I next turn to the Atheist, who, I assert, is only nominally so, and can never possibly be in earnest; and I ask him, whether, from the coherence and apparent sympathy in all the parts of this world, there be not a certain degree of analogy among all the operations of Nature, in every situation and in every age; whether the rotting of a turnip, the generation of an animal, and the structure of human thought, be not energies that probably bear some remote analogy to each other: it is impossible he can deny it: he will readily acknowledge it. Having obtained this concession, I push him still further in his retreat; and I ask him, if it be not probable, that the principle which first arranged, and still maintains order in this universe, bears not also some remote inconceivable analogy to the other operations of nature, and, among the rest, to the economy of human mind and thought. However reluctant, he must give his assent. Where then, cry I to both these antagonists, is the subject of your dispute? The Theist allows, that the

original intelligence is very different from human reason: the Atheist allows, that the original principle of order bears some remote analogy to it (DNR, 218).

This agreement between the theist and the sceptic has been viewed, by those who stress the importance of the preceding passage above all others, as saying one of two things. Either it asserts that these disputes necessarily end in an agnostic conclusion, or it says that they lead to no conclusion whatsoever, because they are totally meaningless enquiries. The first interpretation, the agnostic, ignores the fact that both Cleanthes and Philo have repeatedly remarked that suspense of judgment is scarcely possible in these matters (DNR, 216). If agnosticism is an attitude which excludes assent, then this interpretation is wrong. However, if what is meant by agnosticism is only the recognition that we should deny cognitive significance to enquiries about the cause of the whole, in the sense that neither empirical evidence nor demonstrative reasoning can conclusively rule out any of the alternative hypotheses, then Hume's conclusion is agnostic. Natural Theology or Religion is not a science like mathematics and physics. This is the position taken by many interpreters, including James Noxon in his excellent article "Hume's Agnosticism";[33] this interpretation finds support in many passages of the *Enquiry Concerning the Human Understanding*. Nonetheless, we have to confess that this second sense of 'agnosticism' seems unnatural and strained, because the degree of evidence is not what determines the assent. In a footnote in which Hume comments on the nature of this verbal dispute, he notes that the dogmatist admits that the difficulties concerning the senses and science are "in a regular, logical method, absolutely insolvable." The sceptic, on the other hand, asserts that we are under an absolute necessity of thinking, believing, and reasoning concerning these. The only difference is that the sceptic from "habit, caprice, or inclination" stresses the difficulties and the dogmatist, for the same reasons, the necessity (DNR, 219). Noxon thinks, interpreting this passage, that Hume says that the dogmatist, because of habit, caprice, and inclination is "fated" to believe in God, where as the sceptic, for like reasons, is equally disposed not to believe.[34] This interpretation is, I think, not quite accurate. It seems, on the contrary, that Hume is here saying that the dogmatist and the sceptic both necessarily believe or make an assent to that proposition, but by inclination, etc., the sceptic points to the evidence against, whereas the dogmatist points to the evidence in favor of such a belief.

According to the other interpretation, Hume is really declaring such disputes about the cause of nature totally unintelligible. This interpretation has been maintained by those who want to establish a strict parallelism between Hume's philoso-

---

[33] James Noxon, "Hume's Agnosticism," in *Hume: A Collection of Critical Essays*, ed. V. C. Chappell, pp. 361–383.

[34] Ibid., p. 383. The "regular, logical method" which Hume seems to refer to are the reasonings that he presented in the *Treatise*, Book I, Part III, Sects. I and II: "Of scepticism with regard to reason," and "Of scepticism with regard to the senses." He concludes there that the dogmatic as well as the sceptic are compelled to believed, to put their trust in reason and the senses due to "an absolute and uncontrollable" natural necessity (THN, 183).

phy and contemporary logical empiricist or positivist doctrines.[35] Yet this sort of reading of Hume seems much more implausible than the first. Its main fault is its ahistorical orientation, and the tendency of its proponents – even when they profess to be anti-metaphysical – to thrust upon Hume a more positive metaphysical outlook on reality than his own "mitigated scepticism" permitted him. Hume did say that these disputes could not be settled by experience and that therefore they were futile, and practically useless. But he never said, in so many words, that they were meaningless. At the beginning of the *Dialogues Concerning Natural Religion,* Pamphilus, the narrator of the whole conversation, remarked that "such topics are so interesting, that we cannot restrain our restless enquiry with regard to them" (DNR, 128). This position is consistent with Section XI, of the *Enquiry,* where the "Epicurus" of the dialogue asserts that such enquiries are "and these magnificent, but perhaps fruitless" (EHU, 134). On the other hand, these enquiries are the extension of the natural ways of reasoning which people employ in common life, where philosophy itself has its starting point (DNR, 134). That experience itself, however indecisive its evidence for the drawing of a fully satisfying theoretical conclusion, leads us to draw inferences concerning the cause of the whole and even to suppose that the latter is intelligent, is something which cannot seriously be doubted. So Philo, the sceptic, is, with the rest of mankind, constrained to assert. "No man," he says, "can deny the analogies between the effects: to restrain ourselves, from enquiring concerning the causes is scarcely possible" (DNR, 217). Philo had already said that we ought not to assent to any absurdity (DNR, 186); if the positivistic interpretation is right he would be violating this norm. Furthermore, it is not the verbal network of the hypothesis which is defective, but rather the insufficiency of the evidence to support one against the other hypotheses. If Hume had in fact said that an hypothesis is meaningless if it cannot be verified conclusively by experience, then the positivistic interpretation would be right. But then, it is only with the greatest anachronistic bias that we can extract such a conclusion from Hume's writings. Furthermore, even his naturalistic explanation, the revised Epicurean and incipiently Darwinian hypothesis, should also have to be considered meaningless according to such interpretation.[36]

---

[35] This is the attitude which permeates the work of Farhang Zabeeh, *Hume: Precursor of Modern Empiricism,* which, apart from this, is excellent in its treatment of other aspects of Hume's philosophy, such as his philosophy of mathematics.

[36] Curiously enough, Hume did not even declare unintelligible the question about immortality. The latter will be an unreasonable fancy, but it is still possible. See "An Account of my Last Interview with David Hume," by James Boswell, Appendix A, in Norman Kemp Smith's edition of *Hume's Dialogues,* pp. 76–77. It is somewhat paradoxical that the character who maintains views which are more akin to logical positivism is Cleanthes. Concerning the concept of an infinite God, he implies that it is an absurd one. When the infinite moral attributes of God are brought forward, he suggests that the concept implies the coexistence of incompatible predicates (See DNR, 203). While discussing the ontological argument we have seen that contemporary analytic philosophers, such as J. N. Findlay, have attempted a refutation of that proof based upon an identical supposition. Cleanthes, more cautiously, only rejects the concept, and while at the same time he affirms the existence of a finitely perfect Being, a conception

But to return to the main issue, what is the real import of Philo's assent; what sort of deity could we reasonably say that natural theology permits us to affirm? Concerning this, Philo expresses himself as follows:

> If the whole of Natural Theology, as some people seem to maintain, resolves itself into one simple, though somewhat ambiguous, at least undefined proposition, *That the cause or causes of order in the universe probably bear some remote analogy to human intelligence:* if this proposition be not capable of extension, variation, or more particular explication: if it affords no inference that affects human life, or can be the source of any action or forbearance: and if the analogy, imperfect as it is, can be carried no further than to the human intelligence, and cannot be transferred, with any appearance of probability, to the qualities of the mind; if this really be the case, what can the most inquisitive, contemplative, and religious man do more than give a plain, philosophical assent to the proposition, as often as it occurs, and believe that the arguments on which it is established exceed the objections which lie against it? (DNR, 227).

Natural religion permits us to assert that the author of the universe is somewhat similar to human intelligence. This is but what Cleanthes and Philo had agreed upon. But reason by itself can never lead us to say anything more. Whatever else we may affirm is a matter of faith. All the threads of Hume's argument are reunited into this final conclusion; in this the *Treatise*, the *Enquiry* the *Letter from a Gentleman to his Friend in Edinburgh*, the *Natural History* and the *Dialogues* coincide.

What separates Demea from Philo and Cleanthes is that he affirms both the infinite and perfect, although incomprehensible, simplicity of the Deity; and, by doing so, he destroys, borrowing the words of the *Natural History*, the intelligent nature of the deity, on which alone any rational worship or adoration can be founded (NHR, 43). This is confirmed by the *Dialogues*: "To know God, says Seneca, is to worship him. All other worship is indeed absurd, superstitious, and even impious" (DNR, 226).

But Philo's affirmation is also, and more conspicuously, a negation. The remoteness of the analogy does not warrant the assertion that the cause of the universe is unique: polytheism is not in principle ruled out. In addition, the possibility that the divine intelligence could be immanent in the world, and not necessarily a creator, is not excluded either. Furthermore, the moral attributes cannot be asserted of God; and for that reason, no divine commands for the regulation of moral conduct can ever be given. Thus Philo's assent is purely theoretical, having no practical consequences. This specification of the theoretical contents of natural theology is at the same time a denial of a rational foundation to the historical or "popular" conceptions of divinity, like the Christian notion of a perfectly omnipotent, wise, and

that strongly reminiscent of the view defended by John Stuart Mill in *Three Essays on Religion* (London: Longmans, Green and Co., 1875).

good Creator. For this reason Norman Kemp Smith[37] concluded that Philo's assent is equivalent to a learned confession of ignorance, similar to the concluding paragraph of *The Natural History of Religion:*

> The whole is a riddle, an enigma, an inexplicable mystery. Doubt, uncertainty, suspence of judgment appear the only result of our most accurate scrutiny, concerning this subject. But such is the frailty of human reason, and such the irresistible contagion of opinion, that even this deliberate doubt could scarcely be upheld; did we not enlarge our view, and opposing one species of superstition to another, set them a quarrelling; while we ourselves, during their fury and contention, happily make our escape into the calm, though obscure, regions of philosophy (NHR, 76).

The agnostic interpretation of Kemp Smith is not only wrong with regard to the *Dialogues*, but even more so with respect to the *Natural History*. On the one hand, that concluding passage is opposed by many others in which Hume embraces the conclusion of the design argument. Thus in the same Introduction to the work, he asserts:

> The whole frame of nature bespeaks an intelligent author; and no rational enquirer can, after serious reflection, suspend his belief a moment with regard to the primary principles of genuine Theism and Religion (NHR, 21).

Obviously, the preceding statement is not an unequivocal endorsement of the claims of historical or "popular" religion. Nothing at all is said about the moral predicates of the deity; nor about whether it is omnipotent or limited in power and in its other attributes.

On the other hand, Kemp Smith loses sight of the fact that at the beginning of that section in the *Natural History* where Hume makes his allegedly agnostic confession, he himself asserts that such a suspension of judgment about the cause of the whole is not viable, at least for persons of a rational disposition:

> *[I]t scarcely seems possible, that any one of good understanding should reject that idea*, when once it is suggested to him. A purpose, an intention, a design is evident in every thing; and when our comprehension is so far enlarged as to contemplate the first rise of this visible system, we must adopt, with the strongest conviction, the idea of some intelligent cause or author (NHR, 73; italics added).

The use of the terms 'some intelligent cause' emphasizes that the philosophical assent is less definite than it at first seems to be; but it is no less of an assent for that matter.

---

[37] Introduction to *Hume's Dialogues*, pp. 20–24, 57–75.

Anyone of "good understanding," or any rational enquirer cannot but assent to the thesis that the cause of the universe is intelligent. But he or she can, and must, overcome the unaccountable hopes and fears which plague our uncertain life within this world, and so suspend judgment concerning the further inferences that are drawn concerning the attributes of the deity by historical or popular religions: they are more "the playsome whimsies of monkies in human shape, than the serious, positive, dogmatical asseverations of a being, who dignifies himself with the name of rational" (NHR, 75).

Reality is certainly mysterious; we cannot claim to have penetrated into the essence of God when we recognize that the whole possibly has an intelligent cause; whenever we try to specify this claim, we invariably fall either into absurdities (like Demea) or impieties (like Cleanthes). And philosophy can and must make us aware of these ever-present dangers. But this is not the same as saying that nothing can be philosophically asserted about God, or that it is necessary or even possible to sustain a philosophical suspense on these matters. Such is, contrary to Kemp Smith's very influential interpretation, the conclusion which the *Natural History* establishes, and the *Dialogues* too.

Since Kemp Smith identifies Hume with Philo (for good reasons, I believe), he concludes, in general, that Hume's true position is agnosticism. Certainly Philo's confession of faith appears colorless and neutral when compared to the claims of traditional religion. But for that matter, Cleanthes' own is also very pale; and Kemp Smith does not say that Cleanthes is an agnostic. The only ascertainable difference between their positions is that Cleanthes, against Philo, believes that experience offers some ground for inferring the limited benevolence of God. But he does not draw from this any moral and practical consequences, additional to those which we could have known by consulting experience; he rejects Demea's outlook on the human existence as a preamble for a better one, and the possibility of inferring immortality as a necessary consequence of the existence of God. On the other hand, Kemp Smith is very sceptical of the repeated assertions of Philo about the impossibility of suspending judgment. However much we may disagree with this totally agnostic interpretation, we nonetheless must acknowledge that if one understands by agnosticism only the denial of knowledge, or the denial that a rational demonstration of divine existence can be given, then Kemp Smith, and James Noxon too, are right. But if agnosticism excludes assent, then they are wrong. The *Dialogues* have shown that a belief remains, which, even if it does not exclude all uncertainty, receives some ground from our experience, and thereby becomes a reasonable belief.

For my part, I believe that Philo and Cleanthes (up to a point too) speak for Hume. Yet, as has been stressed in section 2 of this chapter, the choice of a mouthpiece is not the main issue. And it is not so, because it does not necessarily lead us to a particular position concerning the conclusion of the *Dialogues*. For instance, both Kemp Smith and Noxon think that Hume's final position is agnostic. For Kemp Smith this is the case because the philosophical position most germane to Hume's own is, according to him, that of Philo, the sceptic. Noxon, perhaps uneasy with Philo's confession of faith and his affirmations against suspense of judgment, dissociates Philo from Hume. He founds instead his agnostic interpretation of the *Dialogues* upon the supposed agreement of the contents of the footnote of page 219 of the *Dialogues*, ("the single paragraph of this work in which Hume quite clearly speaks for himself") with the sceptical doctrines of the *Enquiry Concerning Human Understanding*[38] George J. Nathan,[39] assuming that Philo substantially agrees with Hume, submits, on the contrary, a pantheistic conclusion. And these are but a few paradigmatic cases.[40]

Philo, I think, speaks for Hume, that is to say, Philo's conclusion that the cause or causes of order in the universe probably bear some remote analogy to human intelligence, is the mitigated theism which naturally issues from Hume's mitigated scepticism. This scepticism makes us aware of the powers and limitations of human understanding in all its determinations, practical as well as theoretical. But its function is not to prevent us from judging and believing, because nature has not left this to our choice. This is something which we shall always instinctively do; "nature by an absolute and uncontrollable necessity, has determin'd us to judge as well as to breathe and feel" (THN, 183). What philosophy can and should do is only to "correct and methodize" those judgments by showing us those subjects, where assurance and conviction are more likely to be expected; thereby we may perhaps be able to be wise; that is, we may at last habituate ourselves to proportion our assent to the evidence presented to us in each case.

Philo's profession of faith is indeed an example of the assent of the wise, who, conscious of the logical difficulties involved, is not at the same time obstinately oblivious to the demands of our own nature. Reason cannot ignore the logical paradoxes and the ambiguous nature of the evidence which stand against any conclusion about the whole; thus Philo's assent is far from being a dogmatical pronouncement. But on the other hand, the contemplation of the remarkable order of nature, produces in us an irrepressible inclination for the hypothesis of an intelligent author. Thus ultimately, like Cleanthes and the rest of humankind, he too assents, although in a manner suited to his sceptical principles; that is, he assents in the qualified and vague manner which is calculated to make clear that he is not advocating the constitution of a science of theology, but only giving expression to the sediment of reasonable belief that is left after a critical scrutiny has revealed that such exaggerated cognitive pretensions cannot be satisfied.

In the end Philo advocates the mitigated theism that fits the nature of the person whom Cleanthes calls the reasonable sceptic:

The declared profession of every reasonable sceptic is only to reject abstruse, remote, and refined arguments; to adhere to common sense and the plain in-

---

[38] James Noxon, "Hume's Agnosticism," p. 365.

[39] George J. Nathan, "Hume's Immanent God," pp. 420–423.

[40] A very good recent summary of the great diversity of interpretations about the conclusion of the *Dialogues*, is offered by William Lad Sessions, "A Dialogic Interpretation of Hume's *Dialogues*," *Hume Studies* 17, no. 1 (April 1991): 15-40.

stincts of nature; and to assent, wherever any reasons strike him with so full a force that he cannot, without the greatest violence, prevent it (DNR, 154).

Cleanthes and Philo express in strikingly similar terms the belief in an intelligent cause, and in doing so they give voice to Hume's own opinion. But in so far as they disagree concerning the possibility of asserting the moral attributes of God, it is Philo who seems to be closer to Hume's own point of view, as it is expressed in his previous works. Concerning God's benevolence, Hume can be classified as an agnostic. Although he goes as far as admitting the compatibility of such a supposition with our view of the world and the present condition of human life, he vigorously denies the possibility of validly inferring God's benevolence from the present scheme of things. On the other hand, both the *Dialogues* and the *Natural History* make clear that we should not, and does not really have to, give our assent to the further suggestions of our human nature, that is, we should give no heed to our superstitious hopes and fears. These all too frequently make us impute partiality, caprice, and barbarity to God. The worship that naturally issues from such violent emotions "depresses the Deity far below the condition of mankind; and represents him as a capricious Daemon, who exercises his power without reason and without humanity" (DNR, 226).

This interpretation may, of course, be wrong after all, but it has the obvious virtue of not having simply to explain away the fact that in the *Treatise*, the *Letter from a Gentleman to his Friend in Edinburgh*, the *Enquiry Concerning Human Understanding*, and the *Natural History* Hume assents, however guardedly, to the conclusion of the argument from design, even if at the same time he points at the flaws of such a reasoning. Furthermore, this approach is not incompatible with the plain fact that Hume repeatedly denied that natural theology could ever become a science. Reason can say that the cause of the universe probably resembles human intelligence, but only that. Here lies the sole rational foundation of religion; all other gaps in our belief have to be filled up by faith.

Let us remember that at the end of the *Enquiry Concerning Human Understanding*, Hume had already established the same conclusion:

> Divinity or Theology . . . . has a foundation in reason, so far as it is supported by experience. But its best and most solid foundation is faith and divine revelation. (EHU, 165).

Although Philo's final words in the *Dialogues* may be susceptible of an ironical interpretation which would expel religious faith from the universe of rational discourse, their explicit sense is basically the same as that conveyed by the conclusion of the *Enquiry;* in other words, even though faith may not be rational in the sense that one could prove its truth by reasoning from experience, as Cleanthes attempts to do, yet it does not necessarily have to be irrational, because the heart of theism, the idea of an intelligent author of the universe, receives some empirical support. Thus to assent by faith to much more than what experience guarantees – which is something that philosophical scepticism makes us aware – is, for Hume, a reasonable alternative, or at least one which is not irrational, provided that we do not ascribe to the Deity anything absurd, impious, or unmerciful. However far Hume's position might appear to be from that of an orthodox thinker, such as Thomas Aquinas, the outlook of the "infidel" is not, in this instance, so much different from that of the saint. According to the latter, religious faith does not have by force to be irrational either; although it may lead us to assert things which are above reason, these can never be contrary to reason.[41] But this interpretation is feasible only under a non ironical reading of the following part of Philo's last words:

> A person, seasoned with a just sense of the imperfections of natural reason, will fly to revealed truth with the greatest avidity: while the haughty Dogmatist, persuaded that he can erect a compleat system of Theology by the mere help of philosophy, disdains any further aid, and rejects this adventitious instructor. To be a philosophical Sceptic is, in a man of letters, the first and most essential step towards being a sound, believing Christian (DNR, 227–228).

Hume thought of himself as a man of letters, and endeavored to live fully as such in an autonomous fashion, without the assistance of noble or rich godfathers. There is but one exception to this policy of personal self-sufficiency, which was, however, in fact acknowledged by Hume himself as such. Irked and disappointed at the apparent lack of success of Lord Hertford, the British Ambassador to France, in his campaign in London to get him the formal appointment as Secretary to the Embassy, Hume wrote letters to a few of his intimate and influential friends asking them to second Lord Hertford's efforts. Thus in a letter, dated 27 March 1764, to Gilbert Elliot of Minto, at the time a prominent member of Parliament, he said:

> I believe I need not inform you how little I have been always inclin'd to sollicit the Great, or even my Friends, for any thing that regards my own Fortune. I may venture to say, that, hitherto, I have never once made any Applications of this Nature (L, I, 427).

Elliot, even though he immediately intervened on his friend's behalf, was taken aback by the uncharacteristic tone of despondency, excessive self-pity and protestation of Hume's letter. He apparently felt compelled to awaken his friend to the fact that his situation was far from desperate (Hume was officially appointed Secretary to the Embassy on 3 July, 1765), being rather the kind of opposition and delay which the appointment of a controversial figure in many circles should naturally be expected to receive. And in his reply of 25 April 1764, Elliot, as it were, incisively put his finger on his friend's wounded self-pride, and proceeded to make the reproach he well knew would be most deeply felt by Hume, who treasured his independence above much else:

---

[41] Saint Thomas Aquinas, *The Summa contra gentiles*, I, chaps. 7–8, pp. 14–17.

Your Lokes, Newtons & Bacons, had no great matter to boast of during their lives, & yet they were the most orthodox of men, *they required no Godfather to answer for them*, while on the other hand did not Lord Hertford spread his sevenfold shield, over all your transgressions, pray what pretentions have you either in Church or State, for you well know you have offended both (italics added).[42]

As this short episode of Hume's life makes clear, from a historical perspective there are few reasons, probably none, to assert that he was eager to escape to revealed truth and embrace a heavenly godfather. In spite of this, and even if "the leap of faith" was not the alternative chosen by Hume – although it was the one invariably taken by the literary friends[43] with whom he shared the "unreserved intimacy" (DNR, 214) typical of Philo's friendship with Cleanthes – , Philo's final declaration establishes that such an alternative is compatible with "consequent" scepticism, which is the result of a philosophical meditation about the cognitive powers of the human mind. In short, it is a legitimate option to assent by faith to those "magnificent" and "interesting" theological questions whose enigma, however, human understanding will never be able to decipher. Likewise, it must be emphasized that we are not dealing here with "brutish" scepticism, which is the instrument of the dogmatic believer, or the proponent of extreme fideism, who employs it, not as a method for subjecting his or her own beliefs to critical scrutiny, but as a tool for defending them and as a weapon for attacking the beliefs of others. Thus by disavowing reason and undermining our trust in it, the dogmatist remains fixed in the theological principles in which he or she has been brought up. Cleanthes' points at this species of scepticism, which is antecedent to philosophical investigation, when he remarks, with good reason, that it is natural for men to adhere to those principles by means of which they are able to best defend their doctrines (DNR, 140).

The alternative represented by a faith that has been enlightened by the understanding is, from a logical perspective, as valid as a suspension of judgment, and much more natural too. But even in this case, the flight to revealed truth is made possible, and confined, by the rational character of the assent: one will affirm nothing which is unworthy of the divine perfection. In the end, the person who escapes into the obscure regions of faith should do it with the same aim with which Hume, at the conclusion of *The Natural History of Religion*, throws himself into "the calm, though obscure, regions of philosophy," that is, to in like manner fly from superstition, absurdity, and cruelty. Any one who chooses to traverse this road left open by Hume's scepticism might suitably be called a "moderate" or reasonably mitigated fideist.

---

[42] MS 23151, folio 12, National Library of Scotland; also published in L, II, Appendix C, 35.

[43] See Richard B. Sher, *Church and University in the Scottish Enlightenment: The Moderate Literati of Edinburgh* (Edinburgh: University Press, 1985), pp. 156, 159, on Hume and the "moderate" clergy.

PART IV

General Conclusions

The Natural and Reasonable Character of the Belief in an Intelligent Author of the Universe

Hume's critical analysis of natural religion severely limits the excessive claims that have traditionally been made in favor of the argument from design. The belief in an intelligent author of the world survives such a critical scrutiny, however. What is the origin of the tenacious and recalcitrant hold that such a belief exercises on our minds?

I think that Hume would say that such a belief is a natural one, and that from this it derives its irresistible character. Its truth cannot be rationally demonstrated; and although it naturally arises in the course of our experience of the world, neither can it be conclusively justified by the empirical evidence. But this is no reason for us to discard it, since this is something which it has in common with other fundamental beliefs such as, for instance, the belief in the existence of an independent, external world and that in the identity of the self. The objects of immediate awareness are not external things, but perceptions (impressions and ideas). This conviction was a part of the Cartesian heritage that Hume never explicitly rejected. Since nothing is ever present to the mind but its own perceptions, and these objects are, in Hume's words, "distinct and separate" (THN, 222), and "internal and perishing existences" (THN, 194), it is easy to see that there is no possible way (from such a point of departure at least) to prove either the existence of a continued and independent external world or the identity of the self. Hume's problem is another; how to account, starting from an experience which is built up of a multiplicity of internal perceptions in perpetual temporal succession, for our belief in the existence of those objects.

Neither the causal energy, nor the identity of the self, for instance, are properly given to experience; they are rather the constructions of the imagination out of the material provided by perceptions. In the *Treatise* Hume goes so far as to declare that the objects of such beliefs are illusions; the difference between them and the other normally called fictions, being only of degree. "The question is, how far we ought to yield to these illusions" (THN, 267).

Nonetheless, Hume recognized two types of fictions: one may denominate the first type as disposable fancies, and the second, as unavoidable illusions. Hume distinguishes between these two purely in terms of the characters intrinsic to these mental contents and the functions they discharge in human life, but not in terms of their reference or non-reference to any extramental reality. The first type are the products of principles of the imagination which are "changeable, weak, and irregular." Among these fictions he includes the products of madness, of superstition, of education (when it is synonymous with mere indoctrination) and the vagaries of metaphysicians. These we can, and should, reject, "since they are derived from principles, which however common, are neither unavoidable to mankind, nor necessary, or so much as useful in the conduct of life; but on the contrary are observ'd to take place in weak minds, and being opposite to other principles of custom and reasoning, may easily be subverted by due contrast and opposition" (THN, 225). Probably most of the religious beliefs which Hume described in the *Natural History* would fall under this category. The second species of fictions are generated by principles of the imagination which are "permanent, irresistible, and universal," and "are the foundation of all our thoughts and actions, so that upon their removal human nature must immediately perish and go to ruin" (THN, 225).

The former fictions are thus characterized by arbitrariness, disorder, opposition, and contrariety; to the latter pertain instead constancy, uniformity, order, and consistency. Here lies their main difference. But we may note that universality and consistency are after all, rational criteria; and they make Hume give his approval to the latter kind of fictions and his disapproval to the former. The unavoidable fictions constitute the beliefs which are essential to humankind. By means of natural beliefs (such as the beliefs in the continued and independent existence of sensible objects and the identity of the self) we bestow order and consistency to our perceptual experience; that is, out of discontinuous and fleeting perceptions we gain access to one coherent world, the world where our "common life," or daily cognitive and practical dealings take place.

Perhaps that is why Hume calls the coherent ensemble of interconnected perceptions, which is the work of the imagination, or that configured by the natural beliefs, the system of *judgment* or of *realities* (THN, 108). The beliefs which constitute the framework of that system, or the general horizon within which all of our other particular beliefs find their place, can be said to be regulative fictions. These give much more unity, continuity, and completeness to our perceptual experience than what it in fact has, or at least more than what an ulterior philosophical reflection discovers to be present in the sense-contents out of which this experience is constituted. Hence, for instance, "whenever we infer the continued existence of the objects of sense from their coherence, and the frequency of their union, it is in order to bestow on the objects a greater regularity than what is observed in our mere perceptions" (THN, 197).

But the fact that they bestow order and coherence on experience, does not take away from the objects of natural beliefs their character of illusions. Compelling evidence that such is the case is the manner in which Hume alludes to the common-sense belief in the continued and independent existence of sensible objects:

> It is a gross illusion to suppose that our resembling perceptions are numerically the same; and it is this illusion which leads us into the opinion that these per-

ceptions are uninterrupted, and are still existent, even when they are not present to the senses (THN, 217).

The identity of the self will be, for the same reasons, equally "fictitious" (THN, 254–259), and causal efficacy, or the necessary connection between causes and effects is reduced to an "illusion of the imagination" (THN, 267).

If we take all of this into consideration, then one would have to say that the general belief whose irresistible character is recognized at the end of the *Dialogues* derives this character precisely from the sources from which the other natural beliefs also spring. That is to say, this belief has its origin in the nature and manner of operation of the human understanding, which Hume identified with "the general and more establish'd properties of the imagination" (THN, 267), and which could also be called experimental reason. The tacit operation of that belief finds its most striking exemplification in the sort of fundamental regulative presuppositions which guide our search for knowledge of reality; in other words, it manifests itself in the specific sort of methodological attitude which the scientist assumes before the subject-matter of his enquiry, in a general sense, the world. It is not surprising then that when Philo acknowledges the irrepressible character of the belief in an intelligent author of the universe, he immediately points to the experiences of the scientist in the disinterested contemplation of the order and simplicity by which nature proceeds in all of its operations, a regularity which permits the scientist to unify his or her knowledge of the world under principles of ever-increasing generality:

> A purpose, an intention, a design, strikes every where the most careless, the most stupid thinker; and no man can be so hardened in absurd systems, as at all times to reject it. *That Nature does nothing in vain,* is a maxim established in all the schools, merely from the contemplation of the works of Nature, without any religious purpose; and, from a firm conviction of its truth, an anatomist, who had observed a new organ or canal, would never be satisfied till he had also discovered its use and intention. One great foundation of the Copernican system is the maxim, *That Nature acts by the simplest methods, and chooses the most proper means to any end;* and astronomers often, without thinking of it, lay this strong foundation of piety and religion. The same thing is observable in other parts of philosophy: and thus all the sciences almost lead us insensibly to acknowledge a first intelligent Author; and their authority is often so much the greater, as they do not directly profess that intention (DNR, 214–215).

The irony with which Hume refers to the "purpose," to the "design" is obvious. Its aim is to highlight once more and in passing the insufficient evidence upon which the absolute and systematical cognitive claims of Natural Theology are, in fact, founded. But the main point is a different one. I think we do no violence to the above text by concluding that Hume, through Philo, is there decisively pointing to the fundamental function which the belief in God fulfills. That is to say, this belief enables us to think of Nature as a universal realm absolutely determined or

ruled by regular laws. This belief in God would be, according to the present interpretation, the ultimate resting point of an inherent movement generated by the very
nature and structure of human understanding, or experimental reason, which guides
it in the drawing of causal connections and in the framing of general principles.

In the last chapter of the best recent commentary of the *Dialogues*, Stanley
Tweyman quotes the preceding passage and the paragraph immediately after it, in
order to justify an interpretation akin to the one presented here. Philo's point, according to Tweyman, is that "by observing the adaptation of means to ends and coherence of parts throughout nature, we are struck with a belief in purposiveness.
Hence, this belief in purpose is prior to the investigation of nature."[1] In short, "the
observation of nature . . . impresses us with the needed beliefs required to provide
those maxims for science which will prove to be its most dependable guide."[2] Even
though I agree in general terms with this view, I cannot, however, subscribe his interpretation of the relationship between the observation of nature and the belief in an
intelligent cause: the former is, according to Tweyman, "followed by an anthropomorphic conception of God as the cause of design, which explains why the world is
believed to be purposively designed."[3] In my opinion, to interpret in such a way
Philo's confession of faith seems not to be compatible with Tweyman's previous
suggestion, which is indeed right, that the belief in purposiveness (and thus in an
intelligent cause of it) is prior to the investigation of nature.

It seems to me, on the other hand, that such a conception of God, instead of being an effect of the inquisitive observation of nature, is rather a condition which
makes it possible. Even conceding that the contemplation of teleological relations
in natural objects is a causative factor and necessary condition for the formation of
the belief in an intelligent cause – in the same way as the constant conjunction between observed similar pairs of events is the cause and condition without which the
belief in the necessary connection between them does not emerge – , here too, we
need something more. In order to ascribe causal powers to perceived objects, the
mind has first "to spread itself on external objects," that is, it must project into objects a necessity which is subjective, felt, or internal. Likewise, it is possible to
discover the purposiveness of natural objects as means or ends, only because we
have also from the start spread on, or projected ourselves into, them, in other
words, because from the beginning we tacitly or implicitly view them as if they had
been produced by the artifice of an intelligent cause.

This is accentuated by Philo's example: Galen, the famous pagan physician.
When Galen devoted himself to the task of detecting and explaining the purposiveness in the structure of living bodies for the fulfillment of a varied ensemble of
complex functions, in spite of his "infidelity," he "could not withstand such striking appearances," nor could he avoid conceiving them as if they were the products

---

[1] Stanley Tweyman, *Scepticism and Belief in Hume's Dialogues Concerning Natural Religion*,
p. 131

[2] Ibid., p. 132.

[3] Ibid., p. 134.

of an inventive mind, although, of course, his purpose as a natural philosopher had never been to present them as evidence in favor of the existence of a "supreme intelligence" (DNR, 215). It is true that a theologian or a devout person can always transform that methodological guideline into a theoretical conclusion, i.e., into a causal inference to the existence of an intelligent cause founded on our experience of the natural order, or intelligible design in the world. But at this stage in the conversation Philo is no longer laying emphasis on the incurable uncertainty of such analogical and causal inference, whose fallacious character has been abundantly shown in the first eleven parts of the *Dialogues*.

To sum up, with regard to Galen, it is not the case that an anthropomorphic conception of God supports or lays the foundation for the belief in intelligent artifice. He was an infidel. What this case does illustrate is that, by following the maxims which guide scientific research, we, and anyone who does science like Galen, "lay this strong foundation of piety and religion," because without having that intention, or "without thinking of it," those maxims will "almost lead us insensibly," that is, unawares, "to acknowledge a first intelligent Author" (DNR, 215). Why? Because those methodological precepts presuppose that nature behaves in accordance with ends, and hence, that the search for an intelligible connection between the structural design and the specific function will be rewarded, for nature exhibits an ordered and intelligible structure such as if had been made by an intelligent artificer. Yet, when we try to prove the existence of a such a Being, we just simply transform a subjective principle, based on the manner in which our understanding operates, into an objective or ontological principle about the first cause of the objects known to us. But such a transformation is an inevitable illusion.

That belief may be dubbed an illusion, since its object can never be instantiated in sense experience.[4] But it is nonetheless an unavoidable illusion, a necessary belief arising from the same principles of the understanding from which philosophy and in fact all our theoretical as well as practical determinations arise. Hume had long before pointed at the foundation of this general and regulative belief, without exploring it in full. When drawing the sceptical conclusion of Book I of the *Treatise*, he thus says:

> Nothing is more curiously enquir'd after by the mind of man than the causes of every phenomenon; nor are we content with knowing the immediate causes, but push on our enquiries till we arrive at the original and ultimate principle (THN, 266).

And at the beginning of the *Dialogues*, Philo, the sceptic, again dwells upon the same phenomenon:

---

[4] Tweyman has very clearly seen this point too, that is, that with such a belief "we go beyond" the data of experience (Ibid., p. 134). However, he does not sufficiently explain why we transcend what is immediately perceived: that is to say, to bestow more unity and order on our experience of the world.

[F]rom our earliest infancy we make continual advances in forming more general principles of conduct and reasoning; that the larger experience we acquire, and the stronger reason we are endued with, we always render our principles the more general and comprehensive; and that what we call philosophy is nothing but a more regular and methodical operation of the same kind (DNR, 134)

It seems to me, in summary, that the belief in an intelligent author of the universe is, like the other natural beliefs, an unavoidable illusion, which remains even in the face of ambiguous or insufficient factual support. This should come as no surprize to us; for is it not, after all, a striking feature of illusions that even after we have detected their deceptiveness, they, nonetheless, continue to appear before us? But in this particular case, it is an illusion that arises as a result of the natural movement of the understanding in its attempt to give the greatest possible unity and order to its knowledge of reality. Thus this belief, like all the other natural beliefs, would be another example of that "regular and established" tendency of the imagination which puts much more unity, coherence, and continuity into the sense contents than what, as Hume himself recognizes, philosophical reflection is able to find in them.

Inasmuch as they are offspring of the same impulse of imagination, one might say about the idea of God the same thing Hume asserted about the idea of causal necessity, namely, that it "is an operation of the soul, when we are so situated, as unavoidable as to feel the passion of love, when we receive benefits: or hatred, when we meet with injuries" (EHU, 47).

One may even speculate in a plausible manner that under different ontological presuppositions Hume is adumbrating the same phenomenon which led Kant to formulate his doctrine of the "transcendental illusion" in the *Critique of Pure Reason*, and which appears to be the starting point of his attempt to give a different, regulative interpretation to the teleology of nature in the *Critique of Judgment*.[5] In a famous passage of chapter 1 of the Transcendental Dialectics, Kant verily approaches the doctrine which we have seen Hume expounding in the passages of the *Treatise* cited in the present chapter, and he even employs the term 'natural and inevitable illusion':

---

[5] Immanuel Kant, *Critique of Judgment*, trans. J. H. Bernard (New York: Haffner Press, and London: Collier Macmillan Publishers, 1951), Second Part, "Critique of the Teleological Judgment." In § 75, Kant expounds a view very similar to that developed in Part XII of Hume's *Dialogues*, as one may reasonably appreciate in the following passage:

> But what now in the end does the most complete teleology prove? Does it prove that there is such an intelligent Being? No. It only proves that, according to the constitution of our cognitive faculties and in the consequent combination of experience with the highest principles of reason, we can form absolutely no concept of the possibility of such a world [as this] save by thinking a *designedly working* supreme cause thereof. Objectively, we cannot therefore lay down the proposition – there is an intelligent original Being; but only subjectively, for the use of our judgment in its reflection upon the purposes in nature, which can be thought according to no other principle than that of a designing causality of a highest cause (pp. 246–247).

For here we have to do with a *natural* and inevitable *illusion* which rests on subjective principles, and foists them upon us as objective; whereas logical dialectic in its exposure of deceptive inferences has to do merely with an error in the following out of principles, or with an illusion artificially created in imitation of such inferences. There exists, then, a natural and unavoidable dialectic of pure reason – not one in which a bungler might entangle himself through lack of knowledge, or one which some sophist has artificially invented to confuse thinking people, but one inseparable from human reason, and which, even after its deceptiveness has been exposed, will not cease to play tricks with reason and continually entrap it into momentary aberrations ever and again calling for correction.[6]

In general, this overall interpretation of Hume's philosophical reflection on religion is, from my perspective, a most plausible one. But I am sceptical enough to offer it only as a reasonable alternative which is undeniably supported by Hume's philosophical works. I do not pretend to say that it is the definitive, and much less the only, solution to all these problems. Far from it, I readily acknowledge that it is not itself free from difficulties. At least two main objections can be brought against it:

First, we have been supposing all along that, as a natural belief, the theistic belief must have some instinctual basis. Yet this assumption appears to be incompatible with Hume's introductory remarks in the *Natural History*. He there says that the belief in gods "springs not from an original instinct or primary impression of nature" (NHR, 21); in addition, such belief, he says, "has not been uniform in the ideas which it has suggested" (NHR, 21). These assertions lend enough plausibility to the suggestion that we should better say that it springs from "changeable, weak, and irregular" principles of the imagination, instead of arising from principles that are "permanent, irresistible and universal."

To meet this objection one could say (as I have asserted in chapter 4) that Hume himself seems to have fairly modified his position at the end of the *Natural History*. There he remarks that such a belief is "at least a universal attendant of human nature" (NHR, 75), something which is, by the way, very difficult to distinguish from an instinct. Furthermore, in that same chapter and in chapter 9, I have endeavored to show that Hume really did not have very powerful reasons for denying an instinctual basis (even in his sense of 'instinct') to religious beliefs. Besides, if one closely examines the conditions which for Hume are required to be able to say about any propensity, predisposition, impulse, or appetite that it arises out of an instinct (i.e., universality, uniformity in the manner of operation, and irreducibility to more basic factors), then one will see that the reasons why he asserts that religious belief is not instinctive could also apply to cases which for him are clear and unequivocal examples of the operation of instinctive tendencies, such as

---

[6] Immanuel Kant, *Critique of Pure Reason*, Transcendental Dialectic, Introduction, I, "Transcendental Illusion," (A 298, B 354–355), p. 300.

"self-love, affection between the sexes, love of progeny, gratitude, resentment" (NHR, 21). Finally, I have also attempted to establish, with debatable success, that there is no need to identify 'instinctive' and 'natural', so that even if the belief in invisible, intelligent power were not instinctive, it might well be, after all, an authentic natural belief, provided that it had a share in the most important notes possessed by those beliefs upon which nobody doubts to confer the epithet of 'natural'. This is, I think, the case with respect to the belief in the divine.

The second objection is somewhat more complex. Even if it is certain that the natural beliefs are imaginative devices for unifying and ordering our experience of the world, it is no less true that these beliefs have an eminently pragmatic significance. Consequently, Hume says that the "permanent, irresistible, and universal" principles of the imagination from which they rise are "the foundation of all our thoughts and actions, so that upon their removal, human nature must immediately perish and go to ruin" (THN, 225). But in addition, human understanding, or experimental reason, or the faculty of making causal inferences about matters of fact and existence, is basically a practical faculty, which is necessary for securing the welfare of the individual and of the species within the realm of nature. Obviously, causal prediction has an incalculable survival value for men and other living organisms; in accordance with this Hume affirms: "The only immediate utility of all sciences, is to teach us, how to control and regulate future events by their causes" (EHU, 76). Notwithstanding all of this, in the *Dialogues* the supposedly natural character of the belief in an intelligent cause of the universe is not specifically derived from any activity which has a practical or biological significance, but from scientific enquiry, or the disinterested search for knowledge. And this puts this belief apparently at odds with the other natural beliefs and with Hume's conception of experimental reason as essentially a practical faculty. As if this were not enough, the *Natural History* profusely reveals that historical religions are not directed to satisfy a purely intellectual curiosity, and with respect to its socio-practical utility, that religion invariably has a very negative influence on morality.

The answer given to the last objection is perhaps what in the last analysis will dispose one to say that the belief in the divine is either natural or not. Concerning this point, the paradigmatical positions have been drawn up in an eloquent and detailed manner, as we have seen in chapter 4, by Stanley Tweyman, on the positive side, and J. C. A. Gaskin, on the negative.[7] I essentially agree with Tweyman's opinion that the belief in an intelligent Author is natural. But how could one then answer the objection that religious beliefs have, in the words of Gaskin, no "practical inevitability," and in addition, that they are obstacles, instead of incentives, for the formation of character and moral behavior?[8] First of all, in section 1 of chapter 9 it has been shown that there is no systematic reason which may have forced Hume not to acknowledge, even in the *Natural History*, that in the

---

[7] J. C. A. Gaskin, *Hume's Philosophy of Religion*, pp. 126–140; Stanley Tweyman, *Scepticism and Belief in Hume's Dialogues Concerning Natural Religion*, p. 133.

[8] J. C. A. Gaskin, *Hume's Philosophy of Religion*, pp. 145–149.

origin of historical religion the belief in gods also began to satisfy an incipient speculative, rational demand. On the other hand, it has just been revealed that in the *Dialogues* Hume clearly places the belief in an intelligent author of the universe on a par with the other natural beliefs. If this is true, then we should instead conclude that he indirectly recognizes here what he did not acknowledge, or only indirectly allows, in the *Natural History*; i.e., that the simple desire for knowledge for its own sake has an instinctive basis, and is also virtually present in the genesis and development of religious belief. But from this recognition it does not follow that the desire for knowledge from which science – as a cultural enterprise – springs, is not pragmatic too, or that it does have no practical usefulness; we have just seen that what Hume in fact says is that the practical is "the only *immediate* utility of all sciences" (THN, 76; italics added). But by implying that the pragmatic is not its only utility, Hume is implicitly acknowledging that we, as human beings, also experience an speculative urge which we endeavor to satisfy with the instrument that science also is.

With regard to the morally negative effects of religious beliefs, in chapter 8 it has been shown that they do not issue from their non-instinctive character, nor from their natural condition, and in addition that such a thesis is not an inevitable conclusion of Hume's scepticism. Hume's ethical depreciation of religion is based on an excessively egotistical explanation of its origins and permanent nature that even appears to clash with some chief principles of his own ethical theory, such as sympathy, general benevolence, or the feeling of humanity. Generally speaking, Hume's narrowly utilitarian view of religion prevented him from adequately recognizing in the *Natural History* and the *Dialogues* that sympathy is as prominent a feature of historical religions as self-interest unquestionably is. Yet, we have also seen that in the *History of England* Hume explicitly concedes that this aspect is present in the religious phenomenon, and fairly mitigates his negative judgment about the ethical value – both personal and social – of religious beliefs. In short, it is my opinion that we can dispose of this pragmatic objection, and hence justifiably uphold that the belief in question is natural.

Notwithstanding those objections, this general interpretation is, from my viewpoint, the least inadequate and most comprehensive of the possibilities I know of. Throughout the present work I have attempted to show, again and again, the all-important interrelatedness of *The Natural History of Religion* and the *Dialogues Concerning Natural Religion*. The point in question again makes it plain: for Hume's answers to the queries about the foundation of religion in reason and concerning its origin in human nature ultimately coincide. Religion has a rational foundation, not because reason can ever demonstrate the truth of the belief in an intelligent author of the universe, but because such a belief has its origins in the nature or ultimate constitution of human reason and in its intrinsic movement or mode of operation. That belief is an unavoidable illusion which regulates the natural movement of reason in its search for truth. In short, that belief is not only natural, but rational too.

Concerning the second point, I take issue with the conclusion reached by Stanley Tweyman.[9] Although I side with him in maintaining and arguing in favor of the naturalness of that belief, I think, however, that there are few reasons to deny its reasonableness. This is precisely why the real victory in the *Dialogues* is not of any particular character but of "true" philosophy, or reason.[10] Clearly, if – as has been asserted more than once – by 'rational' one understands either intuitively or demonstratively certain, or corroborable or verifiable by experience, then the belief in God is rational in neither of those senses. With regard to the first, because neither the ontological argument, nor any other a priori proof is valid; with respect to the second, because all the objections presented by the "I" and "Epicurus" in the *Enquiry*, and by Demea and Philo in the *Dialogues* make it overwhelmingly evident that the argument from design is in not quite comparable to a scientific hypothesis. Still, that belief is rational in a sense much more positive than that of mere absence of contradiction or of being compatible with actual experience. It is reasonable in a substantive sense, by virtue of being a constitutive condition of the rational world view, theoretical as well as practical, within which it makes sense to talk about intuitive and demonstrative certainties, and in whose absence our judgments would have no universal and enduring validity. If our experience were really and merely a succession of "internal and perishing existences," it would not be possible to distinguish between those subjects that are possible objects of experience and those other "subjects that lie entirely out of the sphere of experience" (EHU, 72). And since this is a pre-condition for being able to assert that any proposition (or belief, or opinion, or hypothesis) either rests or does not rest on experience, if we were not in possession of that distinction, then it would be senseless or impossible to verify scientific theories, for these could never be disclosures of constant relations within a common experience. One should remember that if such hypotheses are always and in principle open to corroboration by others, it is because they presume to be about, and hold for, the world in which the others and I are together, or the world of "common life," as Hume calls it.

The sense of rationality I have in mind, and which the belief in an intelligent cause makes possible, is similar to what Páll S. Árdal designates as the "virtue of reasonableness," and which Hume, when contrasting it with both demonstrative and experimental reason, denominates as "what, in an improper sense, we call reason" (THN, 536); that is, the calm passion responsible for the tendency to form the reasonable beliefs that allow us to correct our personal prejudices, take on impartial viewpoints, and form general rules of reasoning and behavior. For the same reasons that Árdal includes the rules of justice among the natural beliefs – that is, because they foster the cohesion, order and stability of the social universe of human relationships and are essential for a sensible and successful practice within it – , one would have to say that the belief in God is a natural as well as reasonable belief,

---

[9] Stanley Tweyman, *Scepticism and Belief in Hume's Dialogues Concerning Natural Religion*, pp. 121–156

[10] Maria Franco-Ferraz, "Theatre and Religious Hypothesis": 227.

since it not only has empirical support, but is also a main foundation for the constitution of the intelligibility that belongs to the manifold universe of our ordinary daily experience, of natural science, of the practical – moral and political – life, and of history. In the background of that intelligible world in which we believe we find ourselves, we examine, accept, reject, or modify our hypotheses about what is true as well as our projects for economic, political or social organization with which we strive after the well-being and improvement of our human nature.

In sum, that world of collective experience or "common life" – to which Hume repeatedly appeals in so many different contexts – is not something which is simply given beforehand; it is rather an achievement, or construction out, of the capacities and powers of the human mind. For its establishment, the belief in an intelligent author of the universe is essential. Such a belief is not merely a conclusion to which we might reason empirically, but a basic presupposition, or first "foundation of all our thoughts and actions" (THN, 225), which as such, and like the independent existence of sensible objects, "is a point which we must take for granted in all our reasonings" (THN, 187). Ultimately this is why that belief is, as Hume says in the *Natural History*, "a tenet so conformable to sound reason" (NHR, 53) that "no rational enquirer can, after serious reflection, suspend his belief a moment with regard to the primary principles of genuine Theism and Religion" (NHR, 21). And in this sense too, God is not an object of knowledge, but of "a Kind of implicit Faith." No matter how much tainted with error and terror this faith may be in positive religions, it remains still a sensible or reasonable belief. Thus Hume remarks that even the most superstitious worshipers, "'while they confine themselves to the notion of a perfect being, the creator of the world, they coincide, by chance, with the principles of reason and true philosophy" (NHR, 43).

All in all, the perceived universe is intelligible to us because we naturally, that is, tacitly and inevitably, and also sensibly, view it as the work of a supreme intelligent cause. That is not only one of the chief conclusions of Part XII of the *Dialogues*, but of the whole of Hume's many-sided, profound, and indeed "serious reflection" on religion.

BIBLIOGRAPHY

I. HUME'S WRITINGS

A Treatise of Human Nature. Ed. L. A. Selby-Bigge. 2d ed. rev., ed. P. H. Nidditch. Oxford: Clarendon Press, 1978.

An Abstract of a Treatise of Human Nature. Reprinted with an introduction by J M. Keynes and P. Sraffa. Cambridge: Cambridge University Press, 1938. Included also in A Treatise of Human Nature. Ed. L. A. Selby-Bigge. 2d ed. rev., ed. P. H. Nidditch. Oxford: Clarendon Press, 1978.

Enquiries Concerning the Human Understanding and Concerning the Principles of Morals. Ed. L. A. Selby-Bigge, 3d ed. rev., ed. P. H. Nidditch. Oxford: Clarendon Press, 1975.

The Natural History of Religion. Ed. H. E. Root. Stanford, California: Stanford University Press, 1956.

Dialogues Concerning Natural Religion. 2d ed., ed. Norman Kemp Smith. New York: The Bobbs-Merrill Co., 1947; Indianapolis, 1981.

David Hume: Essays, Moral, Political and Literary. Rev. ed., ed. Eugene F. Miller. Indianapolis: Liberty Classics, 1987.

The History of England, from the Invasion of Julius Caesar to the Revolution of 1688. 6 vols. Based on the edition of 1778. Indianapolis: Liberty Fund, Inc., 1983.

A Letter from a Gentleman to his Friend in Edinburgh. Ed. E. C. Mossner and J. V. Price. Edinburgh: Edinburgh University Press, 1967.

The Letters of David Hume. Ed. J. Y. T. Greig. 2 vols. Oxford: Clarendon Press, 1969.

New Letters of David Hume. Ed. E. C. Mossner and R. Klibansky. Oxford: Oxford University Press, 1954.

David Hume. National Library of Scotland. MSS 23151–64. Correspondence and Papers Concerning David Hume, 1727–1837, n. d. ; Manuscripts of Some of His Works, ca. 1750–1776, and Some Related Papers, 18th–19th Centuries.

II. WRITINGS OF OTHER AUTHORS

Allestree, Richard. *The Whole Duty of Man*. London: Printed for T. Garthwart at the little North Door of S. Pauls, 1659.

Alston, William P. *Religious Belief and Philosophical Thought*. New York: Harcourt, Brace & World, 1963.

309

_____ . "Religion." In *Encyclopedia of Philosophy*. Ed. Paul Edwards, VII. New York and London: Macmillan, Inc., 1967, 140–145.

Anderson, Robert F. *Hume First Principles*. University of Nebraska Press, 1966.

Annet, Peter. *The Resurrection of Jesus Examin'd by a Moral Philosopher*. London, 1740.

Anselm of Canterbury, Saint. *St. Anselm's Proslogion, with a Reply on Behalf of the Fool, and The Author's Reply to Gaunilo*. Trans. with an introduction. and philosophical comments by M. J. Charlesworth. Oxford: Clarendon Press, 1968.

Aquinas, Saint Thomas. The *Summa Contra Gentiles*. Trans. The English Dominican Fathers. 2 vols. Burns, Oates & Washbourne, 1924.

Árdal, Páll S. *Passion and Value in Hume's Treatise*. Edinburgh: Edinburgh University Press, 1966; 2nd rev. ed., 1989.

_____ . "Some Implications of the Virtue of Reasonableness in Hume's *Treatise*." In *Hume, A Re-Evaluation*. Ed. Donald Livingston and James King. New York: Fordham University Press, 1976, pp. 91–106.

Aristotle. *Aristoteles Opera*. Ex Recognitione I. Bekkeris edidit Academia Regia Borussica. 2 vols. Berlin: G. Reimer, 1831.

_____ . *Metaphysics*. Trans. Sir David Ross. In *The Basic Works of Aristotle*. Ed. Richard McKeon. New York: Random House, 1941.

Aschenbrenner, Karl. "Psychologism in Hume." *Philosophical Quarterly* 11 (1960): 28–38.

Ayer, A. J. *Hume*. New York: Hill and Wang, 1980.

Badía Cabrera, Miguel A. *David Hume's Theory of Knowledge and his Idea of God and Religion*. Doctoral Dissertation at The New School for Social Research, New York, N. Y. , 1978.

_____ . "El teísmo mitigado de los *Diálogos* de Hume." *Diálogos* 36 (1980): 7-31.

_____ . "Milagro, testimonio y verdad: El significado de la crítica de Hume." *Diálogos* 39 (1982): 37–52.

_____ . "Hume y la incurable ineficacia de la filosofía contra la superstición." *Revista Latinoamericana de Filosofía* 15, 3 (1989): 293–305.

_____ . "On Franco-Ferraz, Theism and the Theatre of the Mind." *Hume Studies* 16, no. 2 (November 1990): 131–139.

_____ . "Pasión y valor en el *Treatise* de Hume." *Diálogos* 58 (1991): 171–180.

_____ . "Hume y lo natural de la religión histórica." *La Torre* (Universidad de Puerto Rico). Número Extraordinario en Conmemoración de la Ilustración, Año V (1991), 55–69.

_____ . "La concepción de la historia en la *Historia natural de la religión* de Hume." *Diálogos* 64 (1994): 7–35.

_____ . "Hume's *Natural History of Religion*: Positive Science or Metaphysical Vision of Religion?" In *David Hume: Critical Assessments*, 6 vols. Ed. Stanley Tweyman. London and New York: Routledge, 1995. Vol. 5, *Religion*, pp. 76-83. Originally published in *Diálogos* (1985): 71–78.

_____ . "Hume's Scepticism and his Ethical Depreciation of Religion." In *Scepticism in the History of Philosophy*. Ed. Richard H. Popkin. The Netherlands: Kluwer Academic Publishers, 1996, pp. 99–114.

_____ . *La reflexión de David Hume en torno a la religión*. San Juan, Puerto Rico: Decanato de Estudios Graduados e Investigación y Editorial de la Universidad de Puerto Rico, 1996.

_____ . "Hume on Religion and History." In *Studies in Early Modern Philosophy IV*. Ed. Stanley Tweyman & David Freeman. Delmar, New York: Caravan Books, 1997, pp. 97–112.

Baier, Annette. "Hume, David (1711–1776)." In *The Encyclopedia of Ethics*. Ed. Lawrence C. Becker and Charlotte B. Becker. 2vols. New York: Garland Publishing Co., 1992, Vol. I, pp. 565–577.

Battersby, Christine. "The *Dialogues* as Original Imitation: Cicero and the Nature of Hume's Skepticism." In *McGill Hume Studies*. Ed. David Fate Norton, Nicholas Capaldi, and Wade L. Robison. San Diego, 1979, 239–252.

Beauchamp, Tom L. and Rosenberg, Alexander. *Hume and the Problem of Causation*. New York and Oxford: Oxford University Press, 1981.

Bennett, Jonathan. *Locke, Berkeley, Hume: Central Themes*. Oxford: Clarendon Press, 1971.

Box, M. A. *The Suasive Art of David Hume*. Princeton, 1990.

Brett, Nathan. "Substance and Mental Identity in Hume's *Treatise*." *Philosophical Quarterly* 22 (1972): 110–125.

Bricke, John. "On the Interpretation of Hume's *Dialogues*." *Religious Studies* 11 (1975): 1–18.

_____ . "Hume's Argument Concerning the Idea of Existence." *Hume Studies* 17, no. 2 (November 1991): 141–160.

Broad, C, D. "Hume's Theory of the Credibility of Miracles." *Proceedings of the Aristotelian Society* 17 (1916–1917): 77–94.

Brumbaugh, Robert S. *The Philosophers of Greece*. Albany: SUNY, 1981.

Bryson, Gladys. *Man and Society: the Scottish Inquiry of the Eighteenth Century*. Princeton, N. J. : Princeton University Press, 1945.

Burns, R. M. *The Great Debate on Miracles: From Joseph Glanvill to David Hume*. London and Toronto: Associated University Presses, 1981.

Butcharov, Panayot. "The Self and Perceptions." *Philosophical Quarterly* 19 (1959): 97–115.

Butler, Joseph. *The Analogy of Religion*. London: Macmillan, 1900.

Butler, Ronald J. "Natural Belief and the Enigma of Hume." *Archiv für Geschichte der Philosophie* 42 (1960): 73–100.

Calvin, John. *Institutes of the Christian Religion*. Ed. John T. McNeill, trans. and indexed Ford Lewis Battles. 2 vols. Philadelphia: The Westminster Press, 1960.

_____ . *The Cathequisme, or the Manner to Teache Children the Christian Religion. . . 1556* (New York: Da Capo Press, 1968).

Campbell, George. *A Dissertation on Miracles*. Edinburgh, 1762; rpt. New York and London: Garland Publishing, Inc., 1983.

Cantwell Smith, Wilfred. *The Meaning and End of Religion*. New York: Harper and Row, 1978.

Capaldi, Nicholas. *David Hume: The Newtonian Philosopher*. Boston: Twayne, 1975.

_____ . "Hume's Theory of the Passions." In *Hume, A Re-Evaluation*. Ed. Donald Livingston and James King. New York: Fordham University Press, 1976, pp. 172–190.

_____ . "The Dogmatic Slumber of Hume's Scholarship." *Hume Studies* 18, no. 2 (November 1992): 117-135.

Capitan, William. "Part X of Hume's *Dialogues*." In *Hume*. Ed. V. C. Chappell, 233–240.

Carlyle, Alexander. *Anecdotes and Characters of the Times*. Ed. James Kinsley. London. 1973.

Cassirer, Ernst. *The Philosophy of the Enlightenment.* Trans. Fritz C. A. Koelln and James P. Pettegrove. Boston : Beacon Press, 1955.

Cavendish, V. C. *David Hume.* New York: Dover Publications, 1968.

Chappell, V. C., ed. *Hume: A Collection of Critical Essays.* Modern Studies in Philosophy. Garden City, New York: Doubleday, 1966; London: Macmillan, 1968.

Cherbury, Herbert of. *De religione gentilium.* London: 1645.

Church, Ralph W. *Hume's Theory of the Understanding.* Ithaca, N. Y.: Cornell University Press, 1935.

Cicero. *De natura deorum. Cicero, The Nature of the Gods.* Trans. H. C. P. Mc Gregor. Middlesex, England: Penguin Books, 1972.

Clarke, Samuel. *A Discourse Concerning the Unchangeable Obligations of Natural Religion, and the Truth and Certainty of the Christian Revelation, Being Eight Sermons Preach'd at the Cathedral-Church of St. Paul, in the Year 1705, at the Lecture Founded by the Honourable Robert Boyle Esq.* London, 1706.

Clive, Geoffrey. "Hume's *Dialogues* Reconsidered." *Journal of Religion* 39 (1959): 110–119.

Coleman, Dorothy. "Hume, Miracles and Lotteries." *Hume Studies* 14, no. 2 (November 1988): 277–304.

_____. "Interpreting Hume's *Dialogues.*" *Religious Studies* 25, 2 (June 1989): 179–190.

Collingwood, R. G. *The Idea of History.* Oxford and New York: Oxford University Press, 1946.

Comte, Auguste. *Discours préliminaire sur l'esprit positif (1844).* In *Traité philosophique d'astronomie populaire.* Œuvres d'Auguste Comte, Tome XI. Paris: Éditions Anthropos, 1970.

Cornford, F. M. *From Religion to Philosophy.* Harper Torch Books. New York: Harper and Row, 1957.

Cummins, Phillip D. "Hume on the Idea of Existence." *Hume Studies* 17, no. 1 (April 1991): 61-82.

Daiches, David, Peter Jones and Jean Jones. *The Scottish Enlightenment, 1730– 1790: A Hotbed of Genius.* Edinburgh: Edinburgh University Press, 1986; 2nd. ed. Edinburgh: Saltire Society, 1996.

Davis, John W. "Going Out of the Window: A Comment on Tweyman." *Hume Studies* 13, no. 1 (April 1987): 86-97.

Descartes, René. *The Philosophical Works of Descartes.* Trans. Elizabeth Haldane and G. R. T. Ross, 2 vols. Cambridge: Cambridge University Press, 1970; *René Descartes: Oeuvres de Descartes,* Ed. Charles Adam and Paul Tannery. 13 vols.; Paris: L. Cerf, 1897–1910.

_____. *Méditations Métaphysiques.* Présentés par Florence Khodoss, Cinquième édition. Paris: Presses Universitaires de France, 1968.

Ducasse, C. J. *A Philosophical Scrutiny of Religion.* New York: Collier Books, 1965.

Duque, Félix. Estudio preliminar y notas a su edición del *Tratado de la naturaleza humana.* 2 vols. Madrid: Editora Nacional, 1977.

Dye, James. "Hume on Curing Superstition." *Hume Studies* 13, no. 2 (November 1986): 122–140.

_____. "A Word on Behalf of Demea." *Hume Studies* 15, no. 2 (November 1989): 120-140.

Ellin, Joseph. "Streminger: 'Religion a Threat to Morality'." *Hume Studies* 15, no. 2 (November 1989): 295-300.

Elliot, George F. S. *The Border Elliots and the Family of Minto.* Edinburgh: David Douglas, 1897.

Emerson, R. L. "Hume and the Bellman, Zerobabel MacGilchrist." *Hume Studies* 23, no. 1 (April 1997): 9–28.

Fergunson, Kenneth G. "An Intervention into the Flew-Fogelin Debate." *Hume Studies* 18, no. 1 (April 1992): 105-112.

Feuerbach, Ludwig. *The Essence of Christianity.* Trans. George Elliot. New York: Harper, 1957.

Findlay, J. N. "Can God's Existence Be Disproved?" In *New Essays in Philosophical Theology.* Ed. A. N. Flew and A. MacIntyre. London: SCM Press and New York: The MacMillan Co., 1955.

_____. *Ascent to the Absolute.* London: Allen & Unwin, 1970.

Flew, Antony. "Divine Omnipotence and Human Freedom." In *New Essays in Philosophical Theology.* Ed. Antony Flew and A. McIntyre. New York: Macmillan, 1959, pp. 144–169.

_____. *Hume's Philosophy of Belief.* London: Routledge and Kegan Paul, 1961.

_____. *God and Philosophy.* New York: Dell Publishing, Co., 1966.

_____. "Miracles." *Encyclopedia of Philosophy.* Ed. Paul Edwards. New York and London: Macmillan, 1967.

_____. "Fogelin on Hume on Miracles." *Hume Studies* 16, no. 1 (April 1990): 141–145.

_____. *Hume: Philosopher of Moral Science.* Oxford, 1986.

_____. "Impressions and Experiences: Public or Private." *Hume Studies* 11, no. 2 (November 1985): 183–191.

Fogelin, Robert. "What Hume Actually Said About Miracles." *Hume Studies* 16, no. 1 (April 1990): 81–86.

Force, James E. "Samuel Clarke's Four Categories of Deism, Issac Newton, and the Bible." In *Scepticism and the History of Philosophy.* Ed. Richard H. Popkin. Dordrecht: Kluwer Academic Publishers, 1996, pp. 53–74.

Franco-Ferraz, Maria. "Theatre and Religious Hypothesis." *Hume Studies* 15, no. 1 (April 1989): 220–235

Frazer, Catherine S. "Hume's Criticism and Defense of Analogical Argument." *Journal of History of Philosophy* 8 (1970): 173–179.

Furlong, E. J. "Imagination in Hume's *Treatise* and *Enquiry.*" *Philosophy* 26 (1961): 62–70.

García Roca, José. *Positivismo e Ilustración. La Filosofía de David Hume.* Valencia: Departamento de Historia de la Filosofía, Universidad de Valencia, 1981.

Gaskin, J. C. A. "God, Hume and Natural Belief." *Philosophy* 49 (1974): 281–294.

_____. *Hume's Philosophy of Religion.* London: Macmillan, 1978. 2d. ed. 1988.

Gay, Peter. *The Enlightenment: An Interpretation,* Vol. I, The Rise of Modern Paganism. 2 vols. New York: Knopf, 1966.

Gower, Barry. "David Hume and the Probability of Miracles." *Hume Studies* 16, no. 1 (April 1990): 17-32.

Gurwitsch, Aron. "On the Intentionality of Consciousness." *Philosophical Essays in Memory of Edmund Husserl.* Ed. Marvin Farber, Cambridge Mass.: Harvard University Press, 1940.

Guthrie, W. K. C. *History of Greek Philosophy.* 3 vols. Cambridge: Cambridge University Press, 1969.

Haight, David and Marjorie. "An Ontological Argument for the Devil." *The Monist* 54 (1970): 218–220.

Hall, Roland. *Fifty Years of Hume Scholarship: A Bibliographical Guide.* Edinburgh: Edinburgh University Press, 1978.

Hansen, Stacy J. "Hume's Impressions of Belief." *Hume Studies* 14, no. 2 (November 1988): 347–371.

Harris, H. S. "The 'Naturalness' of Natural Religion." *Hume Studies* 13, no. 1 (April 1987): 1-29.

Harrison, Peter. *'Religion' and the Religions in the English Enlightenment* (Cambridge: Cambridge University Press, 1990).

Hartshorne, Charles. *Man's Vision of God.* Chicago: Willet, Clark and Co., 1941.

_____. *The Logic of Perfection.* La Salle, Illinois: Open Court Publishing Co., 1962.

_____. *Anselm's Discovery: A Re-examination of the Ontological Proof for God's Existence.* La Salle, Ill., Open Court, 1965.

Harward, D. W. "Hume's *Dialogues* Revisited." *International Journal for Philosophy of Religion* 6 (1975): 137–153.

Hendel, Charles W. H. *Studies in the Philosophy of David Hume.* Princeton: Princeton University Press, 1925.

Hick, John. *Philosophy of Religion.* Englewood Cliffs, N. J.: Prentice Hall, Inc., 1963.

_____. *Evil and the God of Love.* New York: Harper & Row, 1966.

Holbach, Paul Henri Thiri, Baron d'. *Le système de la nature, ou des Lois du monde physique et du monde moral.* Paris, 1770.

Hope, V., ed. *Philosophers of the Scottish Enlightenment.* Edinburgh: University Press, 1984.

Hurbutt III, Robert H. *Hume, Newton and the Design Argument.* University of Nebraska Press, 1965.

Husserl, Edmund. *Formal and Transcendental Logic.* Trans. Dorion Cairns. The Hague: Martinus Nijhoff, 1969. *Formale und Transcendental Logik, Gesammelte Werke*, Husserliana, Band XVII. Herausgegebene von Paul Janssen. The Hague: Netherlands: Martinus Nijhoff, 1974.

_____. *Logical Investigations.* Trans. J. N. Findlay. 2 vols. New York; Humanities Press, 1970.

Jessop, T. E. "Some Misunderstandings of Hume." In *Hume.* Ed. V. C. Chappell, pp. 35–52.

_____. "Symposium: The Present-Day Relevance of Hume's *Dialogues Concerning Natural Religion.*" *Proceedings of the Aristotelian Society* 18 (1939): 218–228.

Jonas, Hans. "Spinoza and the Theory of Organism." In *Spinoza: A Collection of Critical Essays.* Ed. Marjorie Greene, Modern Studies in Philosophy. New York: Anchor Press, 1973, pp. 259–278.

Jones, Peter. *Hume Sentiments, Their Ciceronian and French Context.* Edinburgh: Edinburgh University Press, 1982.

Jordan, Jeff. "Hume, Tillotson and Dialogue XII." *Hume Studies* 17, no. 2 (November 1991): 125-140.

Kant, Immanuel. *Critique of Pure Reason.* Trans. Norman Kemp Smith. London: Macmillan, 1929.

_____. *Critique of Judgment.* Trans. J. H. Bernard. New York: Haffner Press, and London: Collier Macmillan Publishers, 1951.

Kemp Smith, Norman. *The Philosophy of David Hume.* London, 1960.

_____, ed. "Introduction." In *Dialogues Concerning Natural Religion*, by David Hume. 2d. ed. New York, 1947; Indianapolis, 1981, pp. 1–123.

Kuypers, Mary S. *Studies in the Eighteenth Century Background of Hume's Empiricism.* Oxford: Oxford University Press. 1950.

Laing, B. M. "Hume's *Dialogues.*" *Philosophy* 12 (1935): 175–190.

Laird, John. *Hume's Philosophy of Human Nature.* London: Methuen, 1932; Archon Books, 1967.

_____ . "Symposium: The Present-Day Relevance of Hume's *Dialogues Concerning Natural Religion.*" *Proceedings of the Aristotelian Society* 18 (1939): 206-217.

Langry, Bruce. "Hume, Probability, Lotteries and Miracles." *Hume Studies* 16, no. 1 (April 1990): 67-74.

Leroy, André. *La critique et la religion chez David Hume.* Paris, 1934.

Lewis, C. S. *Miracles.* London: Collins Fontana Books, 1960.

Livingston, Donald W. *Hume's Philosophy of Common Life.* Chicago: The University of Chicago Press, 1984.

_____ , and King, James T., eds. *Hume: A Re-Evaluation.* New York: Fordham University Press, 1976.

Locke, John. *An Essay Concerning Human Understanding.* Ed. A. C. Frazer, 2 vols. New York: Dover, 1959.

_____ . *The Reasonableness of Christianity, as Delivered in Scriptures.* In *The Works of John Locke*, 10 vols. London: Thomas Tegg; W. Sharppe and son; G. Offor; J Evans and Co.: also R. Griffin and Co, Glasgow; and J. Cummins, Dublin, 1823. Reprinted by Scientia Verlag Aalen, Germany, 1963

_____ . *A Discourse of Miracles*, in *The Works of John Locke*, Vol. IX.

Mackie, J. L. "Evil and Omnipotence." *Mind* 64, 254 (April 1955): 200–212.

_____ . *The Cement of the Universe.* Oxford: Clarendon Press, 1974.

MacNabb, D. G. C. *David Hume: His Theory of Knowledge and Morality.* 2nd. ed. London: Basil Blackwell, 1966.

_____ . "Hume, David." In *Encyclopedia of Philosophy.* Ed. Paul Edwards, IV, 78–79.

Maia Neto, José R. "Hume and Pascal: Pyrrhonism vs. Nature." *Hume Studies* 17, no. 1 (April 1991): 41–49.

Malcolm, Norman "Anselm's Ontological Arguments." In *Knowledge and Certainty: Essays and Lectures.* New Jersey: Prentice Hall, 1963, pp. 141–162.

Malebranche, Nicolas. *De la recherche de la vérité.* In *Œuvres Complètes de Malebranche*, Vol. III. Ed. Geneviève Rodis-Lewis. Paris: Librairie Philosophique J. Vrin, 1963.

McGrath, Alister E. *A Life of John Calvin: A Study in the Shaping of Western Culture.* Oxford and Cambridge, Mass: Basil Blackwell, 1990.

McKinnon, Alastair. "Miracle." *American Philosophical Quarterly* 4, 4 (October 1967): 309–310.

Middletton, Conyers. *Free Enquiry into the Miraculous Powers.* London, 1748.

Mill, John Stuart. *Three Essays on Religion.* London: Longmans, Green and Co., 1875.

Mossner, Ernest C. *The Life of David Hume.* London and Edinburgh: Nelson, 1954; 2d ed. Oxford: Clarendon Press, 1980.

_____ . "Hume and the Legacy of the *Dialogues.*" In *David Hume: Bicentenary Papers.* Ed. G. Morice. Austin, Texas, 1977, pp. 1–22.

_____ . "The Religion of David Hume." *Journal of the History of Ideas* 39 (1978): 653–663.

Nathan, George J. "Hume's Immanent God." In *Hume.* Ed. V. C. Chappell, pp. 396–423.

_____ . "Comment on Tweyman and Davis." *Hume Studies* 18, no. 1 (April 1987): 98-105.

Nietzsche, Friedrich. *Beyond Good and Evil.* Trans. Helen Zimmern. In *The Philosophy of Nietzsche,* The Modern Library, 1927; rpt. New York: Random House, 1954.

_____ . *The Genealogy of Morals.* Trans. Horace B. Samuel. In *The Philosophy of Nietzsche.*

Nisbet, Robert. *Social Change and History: Aspects of the Western Theory of Development.* New York and London : Oxford University Press, 1969.

Norton, David F. *David Hume: Common Sense Moralist and Sceptical Metaphysician.* Princeton, N. J.: Princeton University Press, 1982.

_____ , ed. ed. *A Companion to Hume.* New York and London: Cambridge University Press, 1993.

Noxon, James, H. "Hume's Agnosticism." *The Philosophical Review* 83 (1964): 248–261. In *Hume.* Ed V. C. Chappell, pp. 361–383.

_____ . "Hume's Concern with Religion." In *David Hume: Many-sided Genius.* Ed. Kenneth R. Merrill and Robert Shahan Norman. Oklahoma, 1976, pp. 59–82.

_____ . *Hume's Philosophical Development: A Study of his Methods.* Oxford and New York, Clarendon Press, 1973

Nuyen, A. T. "The Role of Reason in Hume's Theory of Belief." *Hume Studies* 14, no. 2 (November 1988): 372–389.

O' Higgins J. "Hume and the Deists." *The Journal of Theological Studies* 22 (1971): 479–501.

Oppy, Graham. *Ontological Arguments and Belief in God.* Cambridge: Cambridge University Press, 1995.

Ortega y Gasset, José. *Ideas y creencias.* In Vol. V of *Obras completas.* Madrid: Revista de Occidente, 1940.

Otto, Rudolf. *The Idea of the Holy.* Trans. John Harvey. Oxford: Oxford University Press, 1923.

Paluch, Stanley. "Hume and the Miraculous." *Dialogue* 5 (1966–1967): 61–65.

Parent, W. A. "An Interpretation of Hume's *Dialogues.*" *Review of Metaphysics* 30 (1976): 96–114.

Pascal, Blaise. *Pascal's Pensées.* English translation, brief notes and introduction, by H. F. Stewart. New York: Pantheon Books, 1950.

Passmore, John A. *Hume's Intentions.* Cambridge: Cambridge University Press, 1952; London: Gerald Duckworth, 1968.

Paton, J. *Kant's Metaphysic of Experience.* 2 vols. London: George Allen & Unwin and New York: The Humanities Press, 1936.

_____ . *The Modern Predicament.* London: George Allen & Unwin Ltd. and New York: The Humanities Press, 1955.

Pearl, Leon. "Hume's Criticism of the Design Argument." *The Monist* 54 (1970): 270–284.

Pears, David, ed. *David Hume: A Symposium.* London: Macmillan, 1966.

Penelhum, Terence. "Hume on Personal Identity." *Philosophical Review,* 1955; In *Hume.* Ed. V. C. Chappell, pp. 213–239.

_____ . "Divine Necessity." *Mind,* 1960.

_____ . *Hume.* London Macmillan, 1975.

_____ . "Hume's Skepticism and the *Dialogues.*" In *McGill Hume Studies*: 253-278.

_____ . "Natural Belief and Religious Belief in Hume's Philosophy." *The Philosophical Quarterly* 33, 131 (1983): 160–181.

_____ . *God and Skepticism: A Study in Skepticism and Fideism.* Dordrecht: D. Reidel Co., 1983.

Pike, Nelson, ed. "Hume on the Argument from Design." In *Dialogues Concerning Natural Religion,* by David Hume. Indianapolis and New York, 1970. Vol. V, pp. 125–238.

_____ . "Hume on Evil." In *David Hume, Critical Assessments.* Ed. Stanley Tweyman. 6 vols. London and New York: Routledge, 1995, Vol. V, pp. 300–314.

Plantinga, Alvin. ed. *The Ontological Argument.* Garden City, N. Y. : Doubleday, 1965.

_____ , *The Nature of Necessity.* Oxford: Clarendon Press, 1974.

Popkin, Richard H. "David Hume: His Pyrrhonism and his Critique of Pyrrhonism." In *Hume.* Ed. V. C. Chappell, pp. 53–98.

Popper, Karl R. *Conjectures and Refutations: The Growth of Scientific Knowledge.* 2d ed. New York: Basic Books, 1965.

Price, Henry H. *Hume's Theory of the External World.* Oxford: Oxford University Press, 1940.

Rábade Romeo, Sergio. "La noción de experiencia en el empirismo inglés: Hume." *Diálogos* 24 (1973): 33–51.

Richards, T. J. "Hume's Two Definitions of 'Cause'." In *Hume.* Ed. V. C. Chappell, pp. 148–161.

Robinson, J. A. "Hume's Two Definitions of 'Cause' Reconsidered." In *Hume.* Ed. V. C. Chappell, pp. 162–168.

Schleiermacher, Friedrich. *On Religion: Addresses in Response to its Cultured Critics.* Trans. Terence N. Tree. Richmond: John Knox Press, 1969.

_____ . *The Christian Faith,* 2 vols. Ed. H. R. Macintosh and J. S. Stewart. New York and Evanston: Harper and Row, 1963.

Sesonske, A and Fleming, N., eds. *Human Understanding. Studies in the Philosophy of David Hume.* Belmont, California: Wadsworth Publishing Co., 1965.

Sessions, William Lad. "A Dialogic Interpretation of Hume's *Dialogues.*" *Hume Studies* 17, no. 1 (April 1991): 15-40.

Sher, Richard B. *Church and University in the Scottish Enlightenment: The Moderate Literati of Edinburgh.* Edinburgh: University Press, 1985.

Smart, Ninian. "Omnipotence, Evil and Supermen." *Philosophy* 36, 137 (1961): 181–195.

_____ . *The Philosophy of Religion.* New York, Random House, 1970.

Sobel, Jordan Howard. "Gödel's Ontological Proof." In *On Being and Saying: Essays for Richard Cartwright.* Ed. Judith Jarvis Thompson. Massachussets: MIT Press, 1987.

Spinoza, Benedict de. *A Theological-Political Treatise and A Political Treatise.* New York: Dover Publications, Inc., 1951.

Stephen, Sir Leslie. *History of English Thought in the Eighteenth Century,* 2 vols., 1876, 3rd ed. 1902. New York and Burlingame: Harcourt, Brace and World, Inc., 1962.

Stewart, J. B. *The Moral and Political Philosophy of David Hume.* New York and London: Columbia University Press, 1963.

Stewart, M. A. and John. P. Wright, eds. *Hume and Hume Connexions.* Edinburgh: Edinburgh University Press, 1995. Edinburgh Studies in Intellectual History.

Stewart, M. A. "An Early Fragment on Evil." In *Hume and Hume Connexions,* pp. 160–170.

_____ . "Hume's 'Bellmen's Petition': The Original Text." *Hume Studies* 23, no. 1 (April 1997): 3–7.

Stove, D. C. *Probability and Hume's Inductive Scepticism.* Oxford: Clarendon Press, 1973.

Strawson, P. F. *Introduction to Logical Theory.* London: Methuen and Co., 1969.

Streminger, Gerhard. "Religion a Threat to Morality: An Attempt to Throw Some New Light on Hume's Philosophy of Religion." *Hume Studies* 15, no. 2 (November 1989): 295–300.

_____. "A Reply to Ellin." *Hume Studies* 15, no. 2 (November 1989): 301–306.

Stroud, Barry. *Hume.* London: Routledge and Kegan Paul, 1977.

Swinburne, Richard. *The Concept of a Miracle.* London: Macmillan, 1970.

_____, ed. *The Justification of Induction.* Oxford: Oxford University Press, 1974.

Taylor A. E. "David Hume and the Miraculous." *Philosophical Essays.* London: The Macmillan Co., 1934.

_____. "Symposium: The Present-Day Relevance of Hume's *Dialogues Concerning Natural Religion.*" *Proceedings of the Aristotelian Society* 18 (1939): 179–205.

Tertullian. *De carne Christi.* In *Opera Montanistica,* Vol. II of *Tertulliani Opera.* 2 vols. Turnholti: Typography Brepols Editores, 1954, pp. 871–896.

Thucydides. *Thucydides, History of the Peloponnesian Wars.* Trans. Benjamin Jowett. In *The Greek Historians.* Ed. R. B. Godolphin, 2 vols. New York: Random House, 1942.

Tillich, Paul. *Systematic Theology.* 3 vols. Chicago: The University of Chicago Press, 1951 and London: James Nisbet & Co. Ltd., 1953.

Tillotson, John. *The Works of the Most Reverend Dr. John Tillotson, late Lord Archbishop of Canterbury.* London, 1696.

_____. *Sermons Preach'd Upon Several Occasions.* The Second Edition Corrected. London, 1673.

_____. *The Rule of Faith.* 2nd ed. London, 1676.

_____. *A Discourse against Transubstantiation.* 3d. ed. London, 1685. First published 1684. In *Works.* Ed. T. Birch. London: R. Priestley, 1820, II.

Tindal, Mathew. *Christianity as Old as the Creation: Or, The Gospel, A Republication of the Religion of Nature.* London, 1730. Reprint of the 1st ed. New York & London: Garland Publishing Co., 1978.

Todd, William, ed. *Hume and the Enlightenment.* Edinburgh: Edinburgh University Press, 1974.

Toland, John. *Christianity not Mysterious. . .* London: 1696. Reprint of the 1st ed. New York & London: Garland Publishing Co., 1978.

Tweyman, Stanley. *Scepticism and Belief in Hume's Dialogues Concerning Natural Religion .* Dordrecht: Martinus Nijhoff, 1986.

_____. "Hume's Dialogues on Evil." *Hume Studies* 13, no. 1 (April 1987): 74-85.

_____. "Some Reflections on Hume on Existence." *Hume Studies* 18, no. 2 (November 1992): 137–149.

_____. "Hume's Dialogues on Evil." In *Dialogues Concerning Natural Religion,* by David Hume. Indianapolis and New York, 1970, Vol. V, pp. 315–322.

_____, ed. *David Hume: Critical Assessments,* 6 vols. London and New York: Routledge, 1995.

_____. *Hume on Miracles.* Bristol: Thoemmes Press, 1996.

_____. "Drama and Arguments in Hume's *Dialogues Concerning Natural Religion.*" *Diálogos* 71 (1998): 7–24.

Van der Leeuw, G. *Religion in Essence and Manifestation.* Trans. J. E. Turner. New York: Harper & Row, 1963; *Phänomenologie der Religion.* Tübingen, J. C. B. Mohr, 1933.

Wadia, P. S. "Philo Confounded." In *McGill Hume Studies*, 279–290.

_____ . "Miracles and Common Understanding." *Philosophical Quarterly* 26, 102 (1976): 69–81.

_____ . Commentary on Professor Tweyman's 'Hume on Evil'." *Hume Studies* 13, no. 1 (April 1987): 104-112.

Wallace, R. C. "Hume, Flew and the Miraculous." *Philosophical Quarterly* 20 (1970): 230–243.

Wallace, Robert. "Observations on the Account of the Miracles of the Abbé Paris." *The Laing Papers,* II. 620. 20, Special Collections, Edinburgh University Library.

Webb, Mark. "The Argument of the *Natural History*." *Hume Studies* 17, no. 2 (November 1991): 141–141–160.

Westfall, Richard S. "Isaac Newton's *Theologiae Gentilis Origines Philosophicae.*" In *The Secular Mind: Essays Presented to Franklin L. Baumer.* Ed Warren Waggar. New York: Holmes & Meier Publishers, Inc., 1982.

Whitehead, Alfred N. *Process and Reality.* New York: Macmillan, 1929.

Will, Frederick, L. "Will the Future Be like the Past." In A. Flew, ed., *Logic and Language. Second Series.* Oxford: Basil Blackwell, 1966, pp. 32–50.

Wilson, Fred. "The Logic of Probabilities in Hume's Argument against Miracles." *Hume Studies* 15, no. 2 (November 1989): 255–274.

_____ . "Hume on the Abstract Idea of Existence: Comments on Cummins"'Hume and the Idea of Existence'." *Hume Studies* 17, no. 2 (November 1991): 167–201.

Wittgenstein, Ludwig. *Wittgenstein's Notebooks 1912–1916.* Ed. G. E. M. Anscombe, R. Rhees and G, H. von Wright. Oxford: Basil Blackwell, 1961.

Wolfram, Sybil. "Hume on Personal Identity." *Mind* 83 (1974): 586–593.

Woolston, Thomas. *Free Gifts to the Clergy, Six Discourses on the Miracles.* London, 1727–1730.

Wright, John P. *The Sceptical Realism of David Hume.* Manchester: Manchester University Press, 1983.

Xenophanes. In S. G. Kirk and J. E. Raven, *The Presocratic Philosophers: A Critical History with a Selection of Texts.* Cambridge: Cambridge University Press, 1957, 1976.

Yandell, Keith E. "Hume on Religious Belief." In Hume: *A Re-Evaluation*, ed. Donald W. Livingston and James T. King. New York, 1976, pp. 109–125.

_____ . *Hume's "Inexplicable Mystery": His Views on Religion.* Philadelphia, 1990.

Zabeeh, Farhang. *Hume: Precursor of Modern Empiricism.* The Hague: Martinus Nijhoff, 1960.

INDEX

ARCHIVES INTERNATIONALES D'HISTOIRE DES IDÉES
*
INTERNATIONAL ARCHIVES OF THE HISTORY OF IDEAS

1. E. Labrousse: *Pierre Bayle.* Tome I: *Du pays de foix à la cité d'Erasme.* 1963; 2nd printing 1984   ISBN 90-247-3136-4
    For Tome II *see below under Volume 6.*
2. P. Merlan: *Monopsychism, Mysticism, Metaconsciousness.* Problems of the Soul in the Neoaristotelian and Neoplatonic Tradition. 1963; 2nd printing 1969   ISBN 90-247-0178-3
3. H.G. van Leeuwen: *The Problem of Certainty in English Thought, 1630–1690.* With a Preface by R.H. Popkin. 1963; 2nd printing 1970   ISBN 90-247-0179-1
4. P.W. Janssen: *Les origines de la réforme des Carmes en France au 17ᵉ Siècle.* 1963; 2nd printing 1969   ISBN 90-247-0180-5
5. G. Sebba: *Bibliographia Cartesiana.* A Critical Guide to the Descartes Literature (1800–1960). 1964   ISBN 90-247-0181-3
6. E. Labrousse: *Pierre Bayle.* Tome II: *Heterodoxie et rigorisme.* 1964   ISBN 90-247-0182-1
7. K.W. Swart: *The Sense of Decadence in 19th-Century France.* 1964   ISBN 90-247-0183-X
8. W. Rex: *Essays on Pierre Bayle and Religious Controversy.* 1965   ISBN 90-247-0184-8
9. E. Heier: *L.H. Nicolay (1737–1820) and His Contemporaries.* Diderot, Rousseau, Voltaire, Gluck, Metastasio, Galiani, D'Escherny, Gessner, Bodmer, Lavater, Wieland, Frederick II, Falconet, W. Robertson, Paul I, Cagliostro, Gellert, Winckelmann, Poinsinet, Lloyd, Sanchez, Masson, and Others. 1965   ISBN 90-247-0185-6
10. H.M. Bracken: *The Early Reception of Berkeley's Immaterialism, 1710–1733.* [1958] Rev. ed. 1965   ISBN 90-247-0186-4
11. R.A. Watson: *The Downfall of Cartesianism, 1673–1712.* A Study of Epistemological Issues in Late 17th-Century Cartesianism. 1966   ISBN 90-247-0187-2
12. R. Descartes: *Regulæ ad Directionem Ingenii.* Texte critique établi par Giovanni Crapulli avec la version hollandaise du 17ᵉ siècle. 1966   ISBN 90-247-0188-0
13. J. Chapelain: *Soixante-dix-sept Lettres inédites à Nicolas Heinsius (1649–1658).* Publiées d'après le manuscrit de Leyde avec une introduction et des notes par B. Bray. 1966
                                                                                ISBN 90-247-0189-9
14. C. B. Brush: *Montaigne and Bayle.* Variations on the Theme of Skepticism. 1966
                                                                                ISBN 90-247-0190-2
15. B. Neveu: *Un historien à l'Ecole de Port-Royal.* Sébastien le Nain de Tillemont (1637–1698). 1966   ISBN 90-247-0191-0
16. A. Faivre: *Kirchberger et l'Illuminisme du 18ᵉ siècle.* 1966   ISBN 90-247-0192-9
17. J.A. Clarke: *Huguenot Warrior.* The Life and Times of Henri de Rohan (1579–1638). 1966
                                                                                ISBN 90-247-0193-7
18. S. Kinser: *The Works of Jacques-Auguste de Thou.* 1966   ISBN 90-247-0194-5
19. E.F. Hirsch: *Damião de Gois.* The Life and Thought of a Portuguese Humanist (1502–1574). 1967   ISBN 90-247-0195-3
20. P.J.S. Whitemore: *The Order of Minims in 17th-Century France.* 1967   ISBN 90-247-0196-1
21. H. Hillenaar: *Fénelon et les Jésuites.* 1967   ISBN 90-247-0197-X
22. W.N. Hargreaves-Mawdsley: *The English Della Cruscans and Their Time, 1783–1828.* 1967
                                                                                ISBN 90-247-0198-8
23. C.B. Schmitt: *Gianfrancesco Pico della Mirandola (1469–1533) and his Critique of Aristotle.* 1967   ISBN 90-247-0199-6
24. H.B. White: *Peace among the Willows.* The Political Philosophy of Francis Bacon. 1968
                                                                                ISBN 90-247-0200-3

ARCHIVES INTERNATIONALES D'HISTOIRE DES IDÉES
*
INTERNATIONAL ARCHIVES OF THE HISTORY OF IDEAS

25. L. Apt: *Louis-Philippe de Ségur*. An Intellectual in a Revolutionary Age. 1969
ISBN 90-247-0201-1
26. E.H. Kadler: *Literary Figures in French Drama (1784–1834)*. 1969   ISBN 90-247-0202-X
27. G. Postel: *Le Thrésor des prophéties de l'univers*. Manuscrit publié avec une introduction et des notes par F. Secret. 1969   ISBN 90-247-0203-8
28. E.G. Boscherini: *Lexicon Spinozanum*. 2 vols., 1970   Set ISBN 90-247-0205-4
29. C.A. Bolton: *Church Reform in 18th-Century Italy*. The Synod of Pistoia (1786). 1969
ISBN 90-247-0208-9
30. D. Janicaud: *Une généalogie du spiritualisme français*. Aux sources du bergsonisme: [Félix] Ravaisson [1813–1900] et la métaphysique. 1969   ISBN 90-247-0209-7
31. J.-E. d'Angers: *L'Humanisme chrétien au 17ᵉ siècle*. St. François de Sales et Yves de Paris. 1970   ISBN 90-247-0210-0
32. H.B. White: *Copp'd Hills towards Heaven*. Shakespeare and the Classical Polity. 1970
ISBN 90-247-0250-X
33. P.J. Olscamp: *The Moral Philosophy of George Berkeley*. 1970   ISBN 90-247-0303-4
34. C.G. Noreña: *Juan Luis Vives (1492–1540)*. 1970   ISBN 90-247-5008-3
35. J. O'Higgens: *Anthony Collins (1676–1729), the Man and His World*. 1970
ISBN 90-247-5007-5
36. F.T. Brechka: *Gerard van Swieten and His World (1700–1772)*. 1970   ISBN 90-247-5009-1
37. M.H. Waddicor: *Montesquieu and the Pilosophy of Natural Law*. 1970   ISBN 90-247-5039-3
38. O.R. Bloch: *La Philosophie de Gassendi (1592–1655)*. Nominalisme, matérialisme et métaphysique. 1971   ISBN 90-247-5035-0
39. J. Hoyles: *The Waning of the Renaissance (1640–1740)*. Studies in the Thought and Poetry of Henry More, John Norris and Isaac Watts. 1971   ISBN 90-247-5077-6
For Henry More, *see also below under Volume 122 and 127.*
40. H. Bots: *Correspondance de Jacques Dupuy et de Nicolas Heinsius (1646–1656)*. 1971
ISBN 90-247-5092-X
41. W.C. Lehmann: *Henry Home, Lord Kames, and the Scottish Enlightenment*. A Study in National Character and in the History of Ideas. 1971   ISBN 90-247-5018-0
42. C. Kramer: *Emmery de Lyere et Marnix de Sainte Aldegonde*. Un admirateur de Sébastien Franck et de Montaigne aux prises avec le champion des calvinistes néerlandais.[Avec le texte d'Emmery de Lyere:] *Antidote ou contrepoison contre les conseils sanguinaires et envinemez de Philippe de Marnix Sr. de Ste. Aldegonde*. 1971   ISBN 90-247-5136-5
43. P. Dibon: *Inventaire de la correspondance (1595–1650) d'André Rivet (1572–1651)*. 1971
ISBN 90-247-5112-8
44. K.A. Kottman: *Law and Apocalypse*. The Moral Thought of Luis de Leon (1527?–1591). 1972
ISBN 90-247-1183-5
45. F.G. Nauen: *Revolution, Idealism and Human Freedom*. Schelling, Hölderlin and Hegel, and the Crisis of Early German Idealism. 1971   ISBN 90-247-5117-9
46. H. Jensen: *Motivation and the Moral Sense in Francis Hutcheson's* [1694–1746] *Ethical Theory*. 1971   ISBN 90-247-1187-8
47. A. Rosenberg: *[Simon] Tyssot de Patot and His Work (1655–1738)*. 1972
ISBN 90-247-1199-1
48. C. Walton: *De la recherche du bien*. A study of [Nicolas de] Malebranche's [1638–1715] Science of Ethics. 1972   ISBN 90-247-1205-X

ARCHIVES INTERNATIONALES D'HISTOIRE DES IDÉES
*
INTERNATIONAL ARCHIVES OF THE HISTORY OF IDEAS

49. P.J.S. Whitmore (ed.): *A 17th-Century Exposure of Superstition.* Select Text of Claude Pithoys (1587–1676). 1972   ISBN 90-247-1298-X

50. A. Sauvy: *Livres saisis à Paris entre 1678 et 1701.* D'après une étude préliminaire de Motoko Ninomiya. 1972   ISBN 90-247-1347-1

51. W.R. Redmond: *Bibliography of the Philosophy in the Iberian Colonies of America.* 1972
                                                    ISBN 90-247-1190-8

52. C.B. Schmitt: *Cicero Scepticus.* A Study of the Influence of the *Academica* in the Renaissance. 1972   ISBN 90-247-1299-8

53. J. Hoyles: *The Edges of Augustanism.* The Aesthetics of Spirituality in Thomas Ken, John Byrom and William Law. 1972   ISBN 90-247-1317-X

54. J. Bruggeman and A.J. van de Ven (éds.): *Inventaire* des pièces d'Archives françaises se rapportant à l'Abbaye de Port-Royal des Champs et son cercle et à la Résistance contre la Bulle *Unigenitus* et à l'Appel. 1972   ISBN 90-247-5122-5

55. J.W. Montgomery: *Cross and Crucible.* Johann Valentin Andreae (1586–1654), Phoenix of the Theologians. Volume I: Andreae's Life, World-View, and Relations with Rosicrucianism and Alchemy; Volume II: The *Chymische Hochzeit* with Notes and Commentary. 1973
                                                    Set ISBN 90-247-5054-7

56. O. Lutaud: *Des révolutions d'Angleterre à la Révolution française.* Le tyrannicide & *Killing No Murder* (Cromwell, *Athalie*, Bonaparte). 1973   ISBN 90-247-1509-1

57. F. Duchesneau: *L'Empirisme de Locke.* 1973   ISBN 90-247-1349-8

58. R. Simon (éd.): *Henry de Boulainviller – Œuvres Philosophiques*, Tome I. 1973
                                                    ISBN 90-247-1332-3

      For Œuvres Philosophiques, Tome II see below under Volume 70.

59. E.E. Harris: *Salvation from Despair.* A Reappraisal of Spinoza's Philosophy. 1973
                                                    ISBN 90-247-5158-6

60. J.-F. Battail: *L'Avocat philosophe Géraud de Cordemoy (1626–1684).* 1973
                                                    ISBN 90-247-1542-3

61. T. Liu: *Discord in Zion.* The Puritan Divines and the Puritan Revolution (1640–1660). 1973
                                                    ISBN 90-247-5156-X

62. A. Strugnell: *Diderot's Politics.* A Study of the Evolution of Diderot's Political Thought after the *Encyclopédie.* 1973   ISBN 90-247-1540-7

63. G. Defaux: *Pantagruel et les Sophistes.* Contribution à l'histoire de l'humanisme chrétien au 16e siècle. 1973   ISBN 90-247-1566-0

64. G. Planty-Bonjour: *Hegel et la pensée philosophique en Russie (1830–1917).* 1974
                                                    ISBN 90-247-1576-8

65. R.J. Brook: *[George] Berkeley's Philosophy of Science.* 1973   ISBN 90-247-1555-5

66. T.E. Jessop: *A Bibliography of George Berkeley.* With: *Inventory of Berkeley's Manuscript Remains* by A.A. Luce. 2nd revised and enlarged ed. 1973   ISBN 90-247-1577-6

67. E.I. Perry: *From Theology to History.* French Religious Controversy and the Revocation of the Edict of Nantes. 1973   ISBN 90-247-1578-4

68. P. Dibbon, H. Bots et E. Bots-Estourgie: *Inventaire de la correspondance (1631–1671) de Johannes Fredericus Gronovius* [1611–1671]. 1974   ISBN 90-247-1600-4

69. A.B. Collins: *The Secular is Sacred.* Platonism and Thomism in Marsilio Ficino's *Platonic Theology.* 1974   ISBN 90-247-1588-1

ARCHIVES INTERNATIONALES D'HISTOIRE DES IDÉES
*
INTERNATIONAL ARCHIVES OF THE HISTORY OF IDEAS

70. R. Simon (éd.): *Henry de Boulainviller. Œuvres Philosophiques*, Tome II. 1975
     ISBN 90-247-1633-0
     For *Œuvres Philosophiques*, Tome I *see under Volume 58.*

71. J.A.G. Tans et H. Schmitz du Moulin: *Pasquier Quesnel devant la Congrégation de l'Index.*
     Correspondance avec Francesco Barberini et mémoires sur la mise à l'Index de son édition des
     Œuvres de Saint Léon, publiés avec introduction et annotations. 1974 ISBN 90-247-1661-6

72. J.W. Carven: *Napoleon and the Lazarists (1804–1809).* 1974 ISBN 90-247-1667-5

73. G. Symcox: *The Crisis of French Sea Power (1688–1697).* From the *Guerre d'Escadre* to the
     Guerre de Course. 1974 ISBN 90-247-1645-4

74. R. MacGillivray: *Restoration Historians and the English Civil War.* 1974
     ISBN 90-247-1678-0

75. A. Soman (ed.): *The Massacre of St. Bartholomew.* Reappraisals and Documents. 1974
     ISBN 90-247-1652-7

76. R.E. Wanner: *Claude Fleury (1640–1723) as an Educational Historiographer and Thinker.*
     With an Introduction by W.W. Brickman. 1975 ISBN 90-247-1684-5

77. R.T. Carroll: *The Common-Sense Philosophy of Religion of Bishop Edward Stillingfleet (1635–
     1699).* 1975 ISBN 90-247-1647-0

78. J. Macary: *Masque et lumières au 18ᵉ [siècle].* André-François Deslandes, Citoyen et
     philosophe (1689–1757). 1975 ISBN 90-247-1698-5

79. S.M. Mason: *Montesquieu's Idea of Justice.* 1975 ISBN 90-247-1670-5

80. D.J.H. van Elden: *Esprits fins et esprits géométriques dans les portraits de Saint-Simon.*
     Contributions à l'étude du vocabulaire et du style. 1975 ISBN 90-247-1726-4

81. I. Primer (ed.): *Mandeville Studies.* New Explorations in the Art and Thought of Dr Bernard
     Mandeville (1670–1733). 1975 ISBN 90-247-1686-1

82. C.G. Noreña: *Studies in Spanish Renaissance Thought.* 1975 ISBN 90-247-1727-2

83. G. Wilson: *A Medievalist in the 18th Century.* Le Grand d'Aussy and the Fabliaux ou Contes.
     1975 ISBN 90-247-1782-5

84. J.-R. Armogathe: *Theologia Cartesiana.* L'explication physique de l'Eucharistie chez
     Descartes et Dom Robert Desgabets. 1977 ISBN 90-247-1869-4

85. Bérault Stuart, Seigneur d'Aubigny: *Traité sur l'art de la guerre.* Introduction et édition par
     Élie de Comminges. 1976 ISBN 90-247-1871-6

86. S.L. Kaplan: *Bread, Politics and Political Economy in the Reign of Louis XV.* 2 vols., 1976
     Set ISBN 90-247-1873-2

87. M. Lienhard (ed.): *The Origins and Characteristics of Anabaptism / Les débuts et les cara-
     ctéristiques de l'Anabaptisme.* With an Extensive Bibliography / Avec une bibliographie
     détaillée. 1977 ISBN 90-247-1896-1

88. R. Descartes: *Règles utiles et claires pour la direction de l'esprit en la recherche de la vérité.*
     Traduction selon le lexique cartésien, et annotation conceptuelle par J.-L. Marion. Avec des
     notes mathématiques de P. Costabel. 1977 ISBN 90-247-1907-0

89. K. Hardesty: *The 'Supplément' to the 'Encyclopédie'.* [Diderot et d'Alembert]. 1977
     ISBN 90-247-1965-8

90. H.B. White: *Antiquity Forgot.* Essays on Shakespeare, [Francis] Bacon, and Rembrandt. 1978
     ISBN 90-247-1971-2

91. P.B.M. Blaas: *Continuity and Anachronism.* Parliamentary and Constitutional Development in
     Whig Historiography and in the Anti-Whig Reaction between 1890 and 1930. 1978
     ISBN 90-247-2063-X

ARCHIVES INTERNATIONALES D'HISTOIRE DES IDÉES
*
INTERNATIONAL ARCHIVES OF THE HISTORY OF IDEAS

92. S.L. Kaplan (ed.): *La Bagarre*. Ferdinando Galiani's (1728–1787) 'Lost' Parody. With an Introduction by the Editor. 1979   ISBN 90-247-2125-3
93. E. McNiven Hine: *A Critical Study of [Étienne Bonnot de] Condillac's [1714–1780] 'Traité des Systèmes'*. 1979   ISBN 90-247-2120-2
94. M.R.G. Spiller: *Concerning Natural Experimental Philosphy*. Meric Casaubon [1599–1671] and the Royal Society. 1980   ISBN 90-247-2414-7
95. F. Duchesneau: *La physiologie des Lumières*. Empirisme, modèles et théories. 1982
ISBN 90-247-2500-3
96. M. Heyd: *Between Orthodoxy and the Enlightenment*. Jean-Robert Chouet [1642–1731] and the Introduction of Cartesian Science in the Academy of Geneva. 1982
ISBN 90-247-2508-9
97. James O'Higgins: *Yves de Vallone* [1666/7–1705]: *The Making of an Esprit Fort*. 1982
ISBN 90-247-2520-8
98. M.L. Kuntz: *Guillaume Postel* [1510–1581]. Prophet of the Restitution of All Things. His Life and Thought. 1981   ISBN 90-247-2523-2
99. A. Rosenberg: *Nicolas Gueudeville and His Work (1652–172?)*. 1982   ISBN 90-247-2533-X
100. S.L. Jaki: *Uneasy Genius: The Life and Work of Pierre Duhem* [1861-1916]. 1984
ISBN 90-247-2897-5; Pb (1987) 90-247-3532-7
101. Anne Conway [1631–1679]: *The Principles of the Most Ancient Modern Philosophy*. Edited and with an Introduction by P. Loptson. 1982   ISBN 90-247-2671-9
102. E.C. Patterson: *[Mrs.] Mary [Fairfax Greig] Sommerville* [1780–1872] *and the Cultivation of Science (1815–1840)*. 1983   ISBN 90-247-2823-1
103. C.J. Berry: *Hume, Hegel and Human Nature*. 1982   ISBN 90-247-2682-4
104. C.J. Betts: *Early Deism in France*. From the so-called 'déistes' of Lyon (1564) to Voltaire's 'Lettres philosophiques' (1734). 1984   ISBN 90-247-2923-8
105. R. Gascoigne: *Religion, Rationality and Community*. Sacred and Secular in the Thought of Hegel and His Critics. 1985   ISBN 90-247-2992-0
106. S. Tweyman: *Scepticism and Belief in Hume's 'Dialogues Concerning Natural Religion'*. 1986
ISBN 90-247-3090-2
107. G. Cerny: *Theology, Politics and Letters at the Crossroads of European Civilization*. Jacques Basnage [1653–1723] and the Baylean Huguenot Refugees in the Dutch Republic. 1987
ISBN 90-247-3150-X
108. Spinoza's *Algebraic Calculation of the Rainbow & Calculation of Changes*. Edited and Translated from Dutch, with an Introduction, Explanatory Notes and an Appendix by M.J. Petry. 1985   ISBN 90-247-3149-6
109. R.G. McRae: *Philosophy and the Absolute*. The Modes of Hegel's Speculation. 1985
ISBN 90-247-3151-8
110. J.D. North and J.J. Roche (eds.): *The Light of Nature*. Essays in the History and Philosophy of Science presented to A.C. Crombie. 1985   ISBN 90-247-3165-8
111. C. Walton and P.J. Johnson (eds.): *[Thomas] Hobbes's 'Science of Natural Justice'*. 1987
ISBN 90-247-3226-3
112. B.W. Head: *Ideology and Social Science*. Destutt de Tracy and French Liberalism. 1985
ISBN 90-247-3228-X
113. A.Th. Peperzak: *Philosophy and Politics*. A Commentary on the Preface to Hegel's *Philosophy of Right*. 1987   ISBN Hb 90-247-3337-5; Pb ISBN 90-247-3338-3

ARCHIVES INTERNATIONALES D'HISTOIRE DES IDÉES
*
INTERNATIONAL ARCHIVES OF THE HISTORY OF IDEAS

114. S. Pines and Y. Yovel (eds.): *Maimonides* [1135-1204] *and Philosophy.* Papers Presented at the 6th Jerusalem Philosophical Encounter (May 1985). 1986   ISBN 90-247-3439-8

115. T.J. Saxby: *The Quest for the New Jerusalem, Jean de Labadie* [1610–1674] *and the Labadists (1610–1744).* 1987   ISBN 90-247-3485-1

116. C.E. Harline: *Pamphlets, Printing, and Political Culture in the Early Dutch Republic.* 1987   ISBN 90-247-3511-4

117. R.A. Watson and J.E. Force (eds.): *The Sceptical Mode in Modern Philosophy.* Essays in Honor of Richard H. Popkin. 1988   ISBN 90-247-3584-X

118. R.T. Bienvenu and M. Feingold (eds.): *In the Presence of the Past.* Essays in Honor of Frank Manuel. 1991   ISBN 0-7923-1008-X

119. J. van den Berg and E.G.E. van der Wall (eds.): *Jewish-Christian Relations in the 17th Century.* Studies and Documents. 1988   ISBN 90-247-3617-X

120. N. Waszek: *The Scottish Enlightenment and Hegel's Account of 'Civil Society'.* 1988   ISBN 90-247-3596-3

121. J. Walker (ed.): *Thought and Faith in the Philosophy of Hegel.* 1991   ISBN 0-7923-1234-1

122. Henry More [1614–1687]: *The Immortality of the Soul.* Edited with Introduction and Notes by A. Jacob. 1987   ISBN 90-247-3512-2

123. P.B. Scheurer and G. Debrock (eds.): *Newton's Scientific and Philosophical Legacy.* 1988   ISBN 90-247-3723-0

124. D.R. Kelley and R.H. Popkin (eds.): *The Shapes of Knowledge from the Renaissance to the Enlightenment.* 1991   ISBN 0-7923-1259-7

125. R.M. Golden (ed.): *The Huguenot Connection.* The Edict of Nantes, Its Revocation, and Early French Migration to South Carolina. 1988   ISBN 90-247-3645-5

126. S. Lindroth: *Les chemins du savoir en Suède.* De la fondation de l'Université d'Upsal à Jacob Berzelius. Études et Portraits. Traduit du suédois, présenté et annoté par J.-F. Battail. Avec une introduction sur Sten Lindroth par G. Eriksson. 1988   ISBN 90-247-3579-3

127. S. Hutton (ed.): *Henry More (1614–1687). Tercentenary Studies.* With a Biography and Bibliography by R. Crocker. 1989   ISBN 0-7923-0095-5

128. Y. Yovel (ed.): *Kant's Practical Philosophy Reconsidered.* Papers Presented at the 7th Jerusalem Philosophical Encounter (December 1986). 1989   ISBN 0-7923-0405-5

129. J.E. Force and R.H. Popkin: *Essays on the Context, Nature, and Influence of Isaac Newton's Theology.* 1990   ISBN 0-7923-0583-3

130. N. Capaldi and D.W. Livingston (eds.): *Liberty in Hume's 'History of England'.* 1990   ISBN 0-7923-0650-3

131. W. Brand: *Hume's Theory of Moral Judgment.* A Study in the Unity of *A Treatise of Human Nature.* 1992   ISBN 0-7923-1415-8

132. C.E. Harline (ed.): *The Rhyme and Reason of Politics in Early Modern Europe.* Collected Essays of Herbert H. Rowen. 1992   ISBN 0-7923-1527-8

133. N. Malebranche: *Treatise on Ethics* (1684). Translated and edited by C. Walton. 1993   ISBN 0-7923-1763-7

134. B.C. Southgate: *'Covetous of Truth'.* The Life and Work of Thomas White (1593–1676). 1993   ISBN 0-7923-1926-5

135. G. Santinello, C.W.T. Blackwell and Ph. Weller (eds.): *Models of the History of Philosophy.* Vol. 1: From its Origins in the Renaissance to the 'Historia Philosophica'. 1993   ISBN 0-7923-2200-2

136. M.J. Petry (ed.): *Hegel and Newtonianism.* 1993   ISBN 0-7923-2202-9

ARCHIVES INTERNATIONALES D'HISTOIRE DES IDÉES
*
INTERNATIONAL ARCHIVES OF THE HISTORY OF IDEAS

ARCHIVES INTERNATIONALES D'HISTOIRE DES IDÉES
*
INTERNATIONAL ARCHIVES OF THE HISTORY OF IDEAS

KLUWER ACADEMIC PUBLISHERS – DORDRECHT / BOSTON / LONDON